MATERIAL REMAINS

INTERVENTIONS: NEW STUDIES IN MEDIEVAL CULTURE
Ethan Knapp, Series Editor

MATERIAL REMAINS

READING THE PAST IN MEDIEVAL AND EARLY MODERN BRITISH LITERATURE

Edited by Jan-Peer Hartmann
and Andrew James Johnston

THE OHIO STATE UNIVERSITY PRESS
COLUMBUS

Copyright © 2021 by The Ohio State University.
All rights reserved.

Library of Congress Cataloging-in-Publication Data

Names: Hartmann, Jan-Peer, editor. | Johnston, Andrew James, editor.
Title: Material remains : reading the past in medieval and early modern British literature / edited by Jan-Peer Hartmann and Andrew James Johnston.
Other titles: Interventions: new studies in medieval culture.
Description: Columbus : The Ohio State University Press, [2021] | Series: Interventions: new studies in medieval culture | Includes bibliographical references and index. | Summary: "Examines the understanding and experience of temporality as registered through the representation of found objects in medieval and early modern accounts, such as *Beowulf*, King Arthur, and Richard III. These essays re-evaluate how the Middle Ages is periodized"—Provided by publisher.
Identifiers: LCCN 2021008942 | ISBN 9780814214749 (cloth) | ISBN 0814214746 (cloth) | ISBN 9780814281376 (ebook) | ISBN 0814281370 (ebook)
Subjects: LCSH: English literature—Middle English, 1100–1500—History and criticism. | English literature—Early modern, 1500–1700—History and criticism. | Material culture in literature. | Archaeology in literature.
Classification: LCC PR255 .M38 2021 | DDC 820.9/3583010

Other identifiers: ISBN 9780814257999 (paper) | ISBN 0814257992 (paper)

Cover design by Jordan Wannemacher
Text design by Juliet Williams
Type set in Minion Pro

CONTENTS

List of Illustrations vii

Acknowledgments ix

INTRODUCTION Reading the Past through Archaeological Objects
ANDREW JAMES JOHNSTON AND JAN-PEER HARTMANN 1

PART I • TRACES

CHAPTER 1 Found Bodies: The Living, the Dead, and the Undead in the Broad Medieval Present
SARAH SALIH 21

CHAPTER 2 The Beaker in the Barrow, the Flagon with the Dragon: Accessorizing *Beowulf*
ROBERTA FRANK 38

CHAPTER 3 Evidence of the Past in the Legend of the Seven Sleepers
NEIL CARTLIDGE 57

CHAPTER 4 The Return of the King: Exhuming King Arthur and Richard III
PHILIP SCHWYZER 78

PART II • ENTANGLEMENTS

CHAPTER 5	Global *Beowulf* and the Poetics of Entanglement ANDREW JAMES JOHNSTON	103
CHAPTER 6	Weapons of Healing: Materiality and Oral Poetics in Old English Remedies and Medicinal Charms LORI ANN GARNER	120
CHAPTER 7	Saracens at St. Albans: The Heart-Case of Roger de Norton NAOMI HOWELL	145
CHAPTER 8	The Ruthwell Cross and the Riddle of Time JAN-PEER HARTMANN	172

PART III • SPECTACLE AND PERFORMANCE

CHAPTER 9	Archaeo-Theatrics JONATHAN GIL HARRIS	193
CHAPTER 10	11 Ways of Looking at Renaissance Ruins ANDREW HUI	210
CHAPTER 11	But men seyn, "What may ever laste?": Chaucer's House of Fame as a Medieval Museum JOHN HINES	240

Bibliography — 259

List of Contributors — 283

Index — 285

ILLUSTRATIONS

FIGURE 6.1	*Herbarium*, entry for woodruff, *astula regia*	125
FIGURE 6.2	Leaf-shaped spearhead, early medieval England	125
FIGURE 7.1	Charles William James Praetorius RA, depiction of the heart-case of Roger de Norton	146
FIGURE 7.2	Cross fragment of the Mourning Virgin	152
FIGURE 7.3	Resurrection of the Dead	153
FIGURE 7.4	Ground plan of St. Albans Abbey, 1910	158
FIGURE 7.5	Matthew Paris, drawing of the "Kaadmau" cameo	165
FIGURE 8.1	W. Penny, engraving of Ruthwell monument fragments	177
FIGURE 9.1	Pillar of Ashoka	204
FIGURE 10.1	Sebastiano Serlio, frontispiece of *Quinto libro d'architettura di Sebastiano Serlio Bolognese*, 1584	212
FIGURE 10.2	Charles Estienne, *De dissectione partium corporis humani*, 1545	217
FIGURE 10.3	Andrea Mantegna, *Martyrdom of St. Sebastian*, 1480	218

FIGURE 10.4	Vittore Carpaccio, *Meditation on the Passion*, 1510	219
FIGURE 10.5	Vittore Carpaccio, *The Dead Christ*, 1520	220
FIGURE 10.6	Unknown, *Ideal City*, ca. 1480–84	221
FIGURE 10.7	Sandro Botticelli, *The Punishment of Korah*, ca. 1480	222
FIGURE 10.8	Antoine Caron, *Massacres of the Triumvirate*, 1566	222
FIGURE 10.9	Francesco di Giorgio Martini, *Nativity*, 1490s	224
FIGURE 10.10	Leonardo, *Adoration of the Magi*, unfinished, 1481	226
FIGURE 10.11	Leonardo, sketch for *Adoration of the Magi*, unfinished, 1481	226
FIGURE 10.12	François de Nomé, *Ruins with Augustine and the Child*, 1623	230
FIGURE 10.13	Giulio Romano, *Sala dei giganti*, 1524–34	230
FIGURE 10.14	Jean Cousin, *Enfants nus jouant dans des ruines*, 16th century	232–33
FIGURE 10.15	Lorenz Stoer, *Geometria et perspectiva*, 1567	234
FIGURE 10.16	Nicolas Poussin, *Landscape with St. John of Patmos*, 1640	236
FIGURE 10.17	Henri Fuseli, *The Artist Moved by the Grandeur of Antique Fragments*, ca. 1778	237
FIGURE 11.1	From the monumental brass of Bishop Robert de Wyvill, ca. 1375	250

ACKNOWLEDGMENTS

The editors of this collection have been extremely fortunate in the support and encouragement they have received from so many quarters. In particular, we thank the German Research Foundation ("Deutsche Forschungsgemeinschaft") for funding the project that generated this book, i.e., the Collaborative Research Center "Episteme in Motion: Transfer of Knowledge from the Ancient World to the Early Modern Period" (SFB 980 "Episteme in Bewegung: Wissenstransfer von der Alten Welt bis in die Frühe Neuzeit"—project number 191249397). We would also like to express our gratitude to our colleagues, both present and former, who have in some way or other contributed to the successful completion of this book: Martin Bleisteiner, Sarah-Jane Briest, Sven Duncan Durie, Wolfram Keller, Lea von der Linde, Peter Löffelbein, Margitta Rouse, Regina Scheibe, and Kai Wiegandt. Special thanks go to our student research assistants Elisabeth Korn, Mats Siekmann, and Elena Radwan, who spent many hours of work on the formatting of the manuscript. We are also indebted to Ana Maria Jimenez-Moreno, Kristen Elias Rowley, and Eugene O'Connor at The Ohio State University Press who, at various stages of the publishing process, took care of this project.

And finally, we wish to thank all those friends who have been joining us for our discussions at our Collaborative Research Center and in various other contexts since 2012, and whose intellectual input helped to shape the ideas that eventually led to our editing this volume. Apart from those scholars who contributed a chapter to this book, special thanks go to Anke Bernau, Josh Davies, Carolyn Dinshaw, Irina Dumitrescu, Joshua Easterling, Ananya Jahanara Kabir, Ethan Knapp, Clare Lees, David Matthews, Marijane Osborn, and James Simpson.

INTRODUCTION

Reading the Past through Archaeological Objects

ANDREW JAMES JOHNSTON AND JAN-PEER HARTMANN

Medieval and early modern literature was fascinated with archaeology. Indeed, narrative and fictional depictions of archaeological objects—ruins, fragments, buried artifacts or treasures—occur with such frequency in the surviving literature of medieval and early modern Britain that one might be tempted to speak of a *topos*. Scenes involving the discovery, description, circulation, or contemplation of objects from the past can be found in texts ranging from hagiography—the *topos* of the *inventio*—to elegiac poetry, from historiography to romance. Such scenes are by no means restricted to any one region or period. Through the story of the Roman legions burying immense treasure hoards immediately before abandoning the British Isles in 407, as mentioned in the A and F recensions of the *Anglo-Saxon Chronicle*, we find that the very origins of medieval English history are conceived of in archaeological terms,[1] while William Caxton's preface to his edition of Malory's *Morte Darthur*

---

1. The story is not found in Bede's *Historia ecclesiastica gentis anglorum*, which the *Chronicle* texts follow closely up to this point. Bede, too, invokes an archaeological landscape, however, when he refers to cities, lighthouses, bridges, and roads as evidence of the former Roman occupation of Britain (*Historia ecclesiastica* 1.21). The *Historia ecclesiastica* includes a number of further episodes involving material remains, including *spolia* and a Roman sarcophagus reused for the burial of the Anglo-Saxon saint Æthelthryth (4.19). An overview of such "archaeological" encounters in early Anglo-Saxon texts can be found in Michael Hunter, "Germanic and Roman Antiquity and the Sense of the Past in Anglo-Saxon England," *Anglo-Saxon England* 3 (1974): 29–50.

defends the historical authenticity of his Arthurian material by referring to various examples of material remains still surviving from Arthur's days:

> First in the Abbey of Westminster, at Saint Edward's shrine, remaineth the print of his seal in red wax closed in beryl, in which is written 'Patricius Arthurus, Britannie, Gallie, Germanie, Dacie, Imperator.' Item in the castle of Dover ye may see Gawain's skull and Craddock's mantle; at Winchester, the Round Table; in other places, Lancelot's sword and many other things.[2]

In "the print of his seal in red wax closed in beryl," especially, we encounter both the trace-like character of much archaeological evidence as well as those typical human attempts, be they simple or elaborate, to fix and preserve historical artifacts. In the case of Arthur's seal, it is not the material object itself that has come down to us, but what remains is rather the seal's form imprinted on a type of matter quite distinct from the seal itself. And while, in purely technical terms, this is just the way in which a seal ought to operate, the notion of the seal's imprint surviving in the medium of wax itself encapsulates a fundamental aspect of archaeological experience: the sense of an elusive materiality always on the brink of vanishing; a materiality, moreover, that points to an absence, to the absence of a culture long lost. Thus, material remnants of the past prove always to be under threat in the manner that Gayatri Chakravorty Spivak, paraphrasing Jacques Derrida, has described as the "mark of the absence of a presence, an always already absent present."[3] At the same time, the beryl casing that protects the imprint of King Arthur's seal belongs to that particular culture of preservation and conspicuous display that medieval civilization had developed for a very specific kind of historical materiality: the relic, with its promise of establishing, through a physical presence, a form of contiguity with the past. Relics were frequently displayed in monstrances where they could be seen through screens made from crystal or gemstones.[4] Here, the notion of presence involved is defined not by a paradoxical absence, but by the mark of the sacred.

---

2. William Caxton, "Appendix: Caxton's Prefix," in *Le Morte Darthur: The Winchester Manuscript*, by Sir Thomas Malory, ed. Helen Cooper (Oxford: Oxford University Press, 1998), 528–30.

3. Gayatri Chakravorty Spivak, "Translator's Preface," in *Of Grammatology*, by Jacques Derrida, trans. Gayatri Chakravorty Spivak (Baltimore: Johns Hopkins University Press, 1998), xvii.

4. Seeta Chaganti, *The Medieval Poetics of the Reliquary: Enshrinement, Inscription, Performance*, The New Middle Ages (New York: Palgrave Macmillan, 2008); for the aesthetic strategies and epistemological implications of the style of display involved in the medieval culture of the reliquary, see especially pages 1–45.

When we speak of medieval and even early modern archaeology, the term *archaeology* must obviously not be understood in the sense of a modern academic discipline endowed both with a complex hermeneutic methodology and with a highly sophisticated scientific and technological toolkit.[5] Rather, archaeology here must be seen as a set of approaches that privilege material remains and physical objects as a site and/or occasion for critically engaging with the issue of history.[6] The approach of the present volume thus differs from what John Hines has pithily referred to as the '*Beowulf* and Sutton Hoo' syndrome, that is, attempts to illumine literary passages by pointing out archaeological parallels and vice versa.[7] Rather, the contributions found in this volume examine medieval and early modern engagements—fictional or actual—with material objects that are regarded as ancient, as stemming from a past that in some way differs from the present. Such encounters with the material past, we argue, inevitably raise questions of historical continuities, alterity or change, whether they do so explicitly or implicitly. Our purpose in "reading the past through archaeological objects," then, is not to reconstruct a historical past by means of its archaeological and literary remnants; rather, we are interested in what Philip Schwyzer terms the "archaeological imagination" of literature, that is, the ways in which literary engagements with objects from

---

5. Arguably, the beginnings of archaeology as a discipline can be traced to early modern antiquarian engagements with the material remains of antiquity and the Middle Ages, as discussed, for instance, in the papers by Jonathan Gil Harris and Andrew Hui in this volume. However, the systematic excavation of archaeological remains only began in the eighteenth century. For a short overview of the development of modern archaeology, see John Hines, *Voices in the Past: English Literature and Archaeology* (Cambridge: D. S. Brewer, 2004), 15–18.

6. Several of the present volume's contributors have been instrumental in establishing the kind of approach favored here; see, for instance, Hines, *Voices in the Past*; Philip Schwyzer, *Archaeologies of English Renaissance Literature* (Oxford: Oxford University Press, 2007); Andrew James Johnston, "*Beowulf* and the Remains of Imperial Rome: Archaeology, Legendary History and the Problems of Periodisation," in *Anglistentag 2008 Tübingen: Proceedings*, ed. Lars Eckstein and Christoph Reinfandt, Proceedings of the Conference of the German Association of University Teachers of English 30 (Trier: Wissenschaftlicher Verlag Trier, 2009), 127–36. For a similar approach, from an archaeological perspective, see Sarah Semple, *Perceptions of the Prehistoric in Anglo-Saxon England: Religion, Ritual, and Rulership in the Landscape* (Oxford: Oxford University Press, 2013).

7. "The striking and extensive coincidences between the material world in which the action of the Old English epic *Beowulf* is set and the material-cultural phase brought emphatically to the forefront of Anglo-Saxon archaeology by the excavation of the Sutton Hoo Mound 1 ship burial in 1939 have given rise to a number of authoritative, descriptive accounts of the parallels, that only draw ever greater attention to the absence of any real idea of what one might actually make of them" (Hines, *Voices in the Past*, 28–29). See also Roberta Frank, "*Beowulf* and Sutton Hoo: The Odd Couple," in *Voyage to the Other World: The Legacy of Sutton Hoo*, ed. Calvin B. Kendall and Peter S. Wells (Minneapolis: University of Minnesota Press, 1992), 47–64 and her essay in this volume.

the past can open up, complicate, or question certain historical or temporal perspectives.⁸ Such forms of historical understanding either deriving from or associated with medieval and early modern archaeology should not, therefore, be reduced to a straightforward instance of what is often seen as the standard narratives of medieval historiographical tradition—many of which remained influential far into the early modern age—with their supposedly triumphalist Christian supersessionism. On the contrary, as several of the contributions to this volume argue, the literary discussion of material remains often appears to provide an alternative perspective on history, one that may well contrast with simplistic modern notions of Christian teleology.

Precisely because archaeology focuses on the materiality of historical experience, does an archaeological experience of history possess the potential to extend links beyond the established boundaries of region and period that have governed medieval accounts of history as well as modern reconstructions of the Middle Ages as a period. As objects move through trade, exchange, or plunder, they enter into new cultural, political, and economic networks and entanglements and survive into differently delineated time periods. The medieval use of *spolia* is a case in point. As Denis Ferhatović has recently shown, the creative appropriations of *spolia* throughout the Middle Ages open up all manner of perspectives on medieval notions of history, notions that often involve complex layerings and therefore defy a single point of view.⁹ Besides, materiality exerts its own pull on historical experience since it raises the question of the social and cultural status of the objects concerned, the question of their use and continued usefulness, of their beauty and aesthetic value, and of the ways in which the material object itself is subject to interpretation and appropriation and, therefore, can be inserted into new cultural contexts. As Arjun Appadurai points out, even though things may not possess any meanings apart from those imputed to them by human actors, their social and cultural significance or value lies in their "life-histories" or "careers" that often transcend individual human lives or uses.¹⁰

Because material objects have the uncanny ability to survive their makers and since matter seems to invite manifold varieties of creativity, objects from the past—as they are recontextualized culturally and historically—are also often physically recast, restructured, or integrated into larger assemblages. As

---

8. Schwyzer, *Archaeologies*, 2.

9. Denis Ferhatović, *Borrowed Objects and the Art of Poetry: Spolia in Old English Verse* (Manchester: Manchester University Press, 2019), 1–21.

10. Arjun Appadurai, "Introduction: Commodities and the Politics of Value," in *The Social Life of Things: Commodities in Cultural Perspective* (Cambridge: Cambridge University Press, 1986), 5.

Bruno Latour points out in his critique of periodization, the entangled temporalities of objects "[do] not invite us to use the labels 'archaic' or 'advanced,' since every cohort of contemporary elements may bring together elements from all times."[11] Latour is primarily thinking of object categories rather than of individual things—the electric drill that was invented in the twentieth century, the hammer that is hundreds of thousands of years old—but his words apply equally well to specific objects that "move through different hands, contexts, and uses,"[12] thereby becoming part of temporal, cultural, and material entanglements.[13] In medieval and early modern literature, the archaeological object does not primarily serve as a museum piece almost clinically divorced from its origins and contexts, but rather as a bearer of symbolic and aesthetic meaning that unfolds in what Jonathan Gil Harris refers to as the notion of the palimpsest, a concept that denotes "a complex, polychronic assemblage of material agents."[14] Due to their very materiality, objects from the past hold the potential for becoming involved in multitemporal structures that may seek to deny or flatten the degree to which they draw on or engage with a complex range of different historical contexts. Frequently, literary depictions of such objects strategically exploit and highlight that multitemporal quality, a quality that easily exceeds the purposes that may have occasioned the (fictional) creation of the multitemporal object in the first place. As those "material agents" Harris refers to enter into such an "assemblage," they can either be transformed and culturally reappropriated or else visibly resist such transformation and reappropriation, dramatically insisting on their cultural Otherness, as the ancient sword hilt seems to do that Beowulf brings back from the grendelkin's underwater cave. In the much-debated scene when Hrothgar appears to be contemplating the sword hilt Beowulf has presented to him, the object in question seems to maintain a force of unintelligibility to the characters of the poem, whereas the readers are informed of the hilt's nature and history by the narrator.[15] This creates a stark opposition between the presence of an obviously

---

11. Bruno Latour, *We Have Never Been Modern*, trans. Catherine Porter (Cambridge, MA: Harvard University Press, 1993), 75.

12. Appadurai, "Introduction," 34.

13. See Ian Hodder, *Entangled: An Archaeology of the Relationships between Humans and Things* (Chichester: Wiley-Blackwell, 2012).

14. Jonathan Gil Harris, *Untimely Matter in the Time of Shakespeare* (Philadelphia: University of Pennsylvania Press, 2008), 17. While Harris's principal focus is on early modern literature, his notion of the palimpsest can just as fruitfully be employed in the context of medieval literary engagements with objects from the past.

15. Andrew James Johnston, "Medialität in *Beowulf*," *Germanisch-Romanische Monatsschrift* 59, no. 1 (2009): 129–47; Andrew James Johnston, "*Beowulf* as Anti-Virgilian World Literature: Archaeology, Ekphrasis, and Epic," in *The Shapes of Early English Poetry: Style, Form,*

costly object and the protagonists' failure to make sense of it; an instance of what Patricia Clare Ingham, in a different context, has called "an experience of epistemological poverty as such, of the difficulty (altogether common) of knowing what to make of something never before seen or experienced."[16]

Here we also witness the problem that Lorraine Daston highlights as one of the more paradoxical aspects of human artifacts, namely "that things are simultaneously material and meaningful."[17] This is an issue that affects the modern historian or archaeologist just as much as the characters in medieval fiction:

> On the one side there are the brute intransigence of matter, everywhere and always the same, and the positivist historiography of facts that goes with it; on the other side, there are the plasticity of meaning, bound to specific times and places, and the corresponding hermeneutic historiography of culture.[18]

It is from this dual nature of the object—both physical matter and product of human culture, and hence enmeshed in the ineluctable signifying processes that this entails—that the archaeological artifact's simultaneous availability for and resistance to cultural appropriation stems. And these two perspectives do not necessarily exclude each other. Indeed, as new materialist thinkers such as Karen Barad have pointed out, it is impossible to clearly delineate between the material and the social, between matter and meaning, since nonhuman elements are always part of human practices: "Practices of knowing and being are not isolable; they are mutually implicated."[19] Or, in the words of Ian Hodder, "things and society co-produce each other."[20] Composite archaeological objects, especially, may actually betray different degrees of cultural readability at the same time, and so may be capable of participating in different temporalities simultaneously, amongst other things through being linked to different historical materialities, with each of these materialities evoking one or more different relations to temporality. It is cases such as these that exemplify

---

History, ed. Irina Dumitrescu and Eric Weiskott (Kalamazoo, MI: Medieval Institute Publications, Western Michigan University, 2019), 48–50.

16. Patricia Clare Ingham, "Little Nothings: *The Squire's Tale* and the Ambition of Gadgets," *Studies in the Age of Chaucer* 31 (2009): 76.

17. Lorraine Daston, *Things That Talk* (New York: Zone Books, 2008), 17.

18. Daston, *Things That Talk*, 16.

19. Karen Barad, *Meeting the Universe Halfway: Quantum Physics and the Entanglement of Matter and Meaning* (Durham, NC: Duke University Press, 2007), 185.

20. Hodder, *Entangled*, 1.

what Carolyn Dinshaw has called "multiple temporalities."[21] An example can be found, for instance, in the dragon's lair in *Beowulf*. Here, as Howard Williams has suggested, the building's very structure integrates features belonging to a broad variety of historical and architectural traditions. While some clearly evoke prehistoric associations—a megalithic funerary monument—others resemble the sophisticated products of Roman engineering or may even remind us of early medieval ecclesiastical architecture. This combination of different yet nevertheless simultaneously present temporal and cultural associations powerfully conveys a palimpsestic sense of the structure described.[22] It is by no means surprising that an Anglo-Saxon epic set in migration period Scandinavia should be capable of envisaging a palimpsestic archaeological space of a kind that implies a multiple repurposing of a historical site. On the contrary, *Beowulf*'s fictional depictions of archaeological sites and ancient artifacts resonate powerfully with Sarah Semple's observations on the intensity and creativity that the leaders of Anglo-Saxon political society betrayed in adapting the archaeological traces of older cultures to their own propagandistic uses. Semple remarks on "the sheer scale, in temporal and selective terms, at which the ancient past was recognized and harnessed to the purposes of tradition-making by communities and elite families and individuals in Anglo-Saxon England."[23] But an awareness of such forms of cultural reappropriation of archaeological sites or artifacts was certainly not restricted to the Anglo-Saxon age. As Gale R. Owen-Crocker points out, the Green Chapel in *Sir Gawain and the Green Knight* seems to betray the typical characteristics of this kind of multilayered archaeological material space, one that is endowed, moreover, with a particularly otherworldly atmosphere, not least because it shares many traits with the kind of megalithic burial mound that was repeatedly reused in later periods.[24] And practices of cultural or political reappropriation do not stop here: as Andrew Hui shows in his contribution to this volume, during the early modern period, ancient sites in ruin could also form the backdrop of Christian appropriations of classical antiquity, and mod-

---

21. Carolyn Dinshaw, "Temporalities," in *Middle English*, ed. Paul Strohm, Oxford Twenty-First Century Approaches to Literature (Oxford: Oxford University Press, 2007), 120.

22. Howard Williams, "*Beowulf* and Archaeology: Megaliths Imagined and Encountered in Early Medieval Europe," in *The Lives of Prehistoric Monuments in Iron Age, Roman, and Medieval Europe*, ed. Marta Díaz-Guardamino, Leonardo García Sanjuán, and David Wheatley (Oxford: Oxford University Press, 2015), 77–97.

23. Semple, *Perceptions*, 224.

24. Gale R. Owen-Crocker, *The Four Funerals in "Beowulf" and the Structure of the Poem* (Manchester: Manchester University Press, 2009 [first published 2000]), 63–64. The connection between the Green Chapel and megalith tombs was first made by Bertram Colgrave, "Sir Gawayne's Green Chapel," *Antiquity* 12, no. 47 (1938), 351–53.

ern archaeological endeavors are frequently implicated in powerful political or institutional claims, too, as Philip Schwyzer makes clear in his discussion of the 2012 excavation of the remains of Richard III.[25]

Within such palimpsestic assemblages, one may, therefore, encounter a complex set of entangled temporalities, and it is on the basis of these entangled temporalities that a given object can be perceived not simply as a passive thing to be transmitted in time, but as a veritable agent of temporality—one that is capable of actually transmitting time itself, capable of making temporality available for future cultural and political appropriation. It goes without saying that this type of temporal capability can be put on display with varying degrees of self-consciousness and self-reflexivity. Hence, both in extra-literary reality and in its textual and fictional representations, we find the material object from the past located at a nexus of entangled temporalities where it may possess something approaching a historical agency of its own. This is what the art historians Alexander Nagel and Christopher S. Wood have described as the historical artifact's "anachronic" character: the object from the past is capable of cutting through levels of time even as it binds them together. Nagel and Wood use the term *anachronic* to describe a given work of art's capacity not merely for creating temporalities of its own but for staging a dialogue between different approaches to time and the past as the historical object "hold[s] incompatible models in suspension." Such an artwork may possess the potential to "'fetch' a past, create a past, perhaps even fetch the future."[26]

As Nagel and Wood explain:

> No device more effectively generates the effect of a doubling or bending back of time than the work of art, a strange kind of event whose relation to time is plural. The artwork is made or designed by an individual or by a group of individuals at some moment, but it also points away from that moment, backward to a remote ancestral origin, perhaps, or to a prior artifact, or to an origin outside of time, in divinity. At the same time it points forward to

---

25. Like philology, the development of modern archaeology is in many respects intertwined with nationalist projects of the nineteenth and early twentieth centuries that sought to trace the origins of the respective nation states to an imagined common past. See, for instance, Michael Dietler, "A Tale of Three Sites: The Monumentalization of Celtic Oppida and the Politics of Collective Memory and Identity," *World Archaeology* 30, no. 1 (1998): 72–89; and Bettina Arnold and Henning Hassmann, "Archaeology in Nazi Germany: The Legacy of the Faustian Bargain," in *Nationalism, Politics, and the Practice of Archaeology*, ed. Philip L. Kohl and Clare Fawcett (Cambridge: Cambridge University Press, 1996), 70–81.

26. Alexander Nagel and Christopher S. Wood, *Anachronic Renaissance* (New York: Zone Books, 2010), 18.

all its future recipients who will activate and reactivate it as a future event. The work of art is a message whose sender and destination are constantly shifting.[27]

This special capacity Nagel and Wood here ascribe to the work of art in a very particular, potentially even an ahistorically aesthetic sense, is one, we argue, that can easily be extended to the textual and fictional representations of ancient artifacts and historical objects as they are found, unearthed, stolen, exchanged, refashioned, put on display, and creatively reappropriated in medieval and early modern literature. These objects, too, are frequently involved in complex processes of temporal entanglement. This is what John M. Hill seems to have been thinking of when he suggested that *Beowulf* conceives of "objects and of social relationships as having identity through time, essentially as being what they are only in virtue of their entire history or, if applicable, of their cycle."[28] But while Hill was thinking in terms of this relation to temporality as "a basic continuity with that past,"[29] we prefer an approach emphasizing the multiplicity and plurality both of the pasts our texts look back to and of the temporalities they construct. This multiplicity and plurality both of the pasts represented and of the temporalities constructed in medieval texts is something that easily gets lost in the binaries of modern periodization and their concomitant cultural binaries. Our approach to the temporalities of fictional medieval and early modern artifacts therefore shares James Simpson's concern with the way in which the New Historicist dynamic of subversion and containment easily obscures the problem of alterity because it lacks the sensibility for imagining "the historical possibility of a complex set of jurisdictions competing for discursive participation."[30] Without wishing to claim that all the archaeological objects in medieval and early modern literature always display a potential for negotiating such competing jurisdictions—and here we would emphasize temporal jurisdictions, i.e., the ways in which different histories demand to be understood—we do think that this is something they are very much prone to do.

The papers in this volume collectively seek to explore ways in which medieval and early modern British texts employ descriptions of archaeological objects or material artifacts from the past in order to produce specifically

---

27. Nagel and Wood, *Anachronic Renaissance*, 9.
28. John M. Hill, *The Cultural World in "Beowulf"* (Toronto: University of Toronto Press, 1995), 41.
29. Hill, *Cultural World*, 40.
30. James Simpson, *Reform and Cultural Revolution*, Oxford English Literary History 2, 1350–1547 (Oxford: Oxford University Press, 2002), 219.

aesthetic and literary responses to questions of historicity as well as the epistemological conditions of historical knowledge and notions of temporality.

The contributions are divided into three sections, following thematical considerations rather than the chronological order of the texts discussed (as far as such a chronology can be ascertained—a notoriously difficult task with regard to much Old English literature). The papers in the first section deal with archaeological remains primarily as traces of the past. Traces, we have seen, can be perceived as presences of something that is itself absent, like the footprint indicating a foot no longer there. Archaeological remains, as the remnants of things that are gone themselves, point toward the past, but, like the imprint of the seal that draws attention to the absence of the seal itself, they are always fragmentary, always under threat of obliteration. As such they also represent the elusiveness of a past that only ever allows partial access. The Middle English alliterative poem *St. Erkenwald* is a case in point. As Sarah Salih points out in her discussion of the tomb found in the poem during construction work on St. Paul's Cathedral, archaeological remains "are regular vehicles for messages to the future, though the passage of time often interferes with their reception."[31] As the writing on the tomb remains illegible, the past would have stayed opaque to the Londoners of the poem's present without the information provided by the corpse itself, allowed, as it is, to speak only through a miracle. Even more strikingly, the corpse dissolves once the miraculous baptism, brought about by accident rather than intention, has been performed, leaving behind nothing but the illegible tomb. As with the giant sword Beowulf recovers from Grendel's underwater cave, the archaeological act itself further fragments and endangers the trace from the past, thereby increasing the artifact's precariousness. Yet in spite of this precariousness, archaeological objects can display a striking degree of agency when brought into contact with the present, inviting a variety of ways in which to handle, perceive, or construct them. This is especially obvious in the case of saintly relics, which in many hagiographical narratives "demand" to be found, initiating a search conducted with the help of dreams and visions. But the object's desire for discovery is present also in cases of seemingly less "undead" matter. As Salih points out, the continued existence of the material traces of the past—not always perceived as such—can construct a number of different temporal relations with the present, which the present may in turn seek to exploit or resist.

Arguably, such an ambiguous material agency can also be detected in the chapter that concludes the first section of the volume, in which Philip Schwyzer discusses narratives concerning medieval, early modern, and pres-

---

31. See p. 22, this volume.

ent-day encounters with dead bodies. Schwyzer examines Gerald of Wales's account of the alleged excavation of King Arthur at Glastonbury in 1191 and the 2012 discovery of Richard III under a supermarket car park in Leicester. Both events were exploited politically, yet, as Schwyzer demonstrates, by their very nature they also contributed to shaping the excavators' responses to the remains as traces of the past. Although both excavations concern nonsaintly kings, they conform remarkably well to the pattern of medieval *inventio*, arguably the archetypal medieval archaeological narrative, but one that is usually reserved for the rediscovery of a saint's relics.[32] Indeed, Schwyzer argues, the similarities between the two events—including forensic details that cannot be attributed to literary *topoi* alone—are so close and so extensive that one event could be described as a "reiteration" or "reenactment" of the other, even though a direct connection between the two cannot be established and is indeed unlikely. Archaeological traces thus have a capacity for constructing temporal connections that elude simplistic claims to historical continuity or supersession. Nevertheless, Schwyzer maintains, although the excavation of Richard III can be seen as a genuinely medieval event, the public response it elicited ironically recalls the "radical anachronic imaginings of post-Reformation historical thought" associated with the Tudor England from which modern actors involved in the excavation sought to salvage the king.[33] As the case of Richard III shows, the interplay of social and material actors can bring forth different and potentially conflicting temporalities simultaneously, temporalities in no way anticipated by the original intentions of the human actors involved.

Both Salih and Schwyzer focus on events and narratives that can be associated with the motif of *inventio*. Yet the archaeological practice foregrounded in these *inventio*-narratives also conforms to the practice most commonly associated with archaeology in the modern popular imagination: the excavation, or simply, the dig. Wiglaf's descent into the dragon's lair to unearth the hoard that had been deposited there centuries earlier can be seen as part of the same paradigm. Roberta Frank discusses a number of different objects in *Beowulf*, arguing that the Old English words employed for these items—for the most part belonging to a special poetic lexicon not used in prose—possessed a differing degree of archaic flavor recognizable to the Anglo-Saxon audience but usually lost on the modern reader. By employing archaic terms

---

32. Monika Otter discusses the *inventio* in her seminal *Inventiones: Fiction and Referentiality in Twelfth-Century English Historical Writing* (Chapel Hill: University of North Carolina Press, 1996). Although Otter is mainly concerned with twelfth-century Latin historiography, her discussion is highly relevant to the genre in general.

33. See p. 100, this volume.

that invoke differently aged objects, Frank argues, the text performs linguistically what Wiglaf does manually—digging down with words to expose "a trove of long-forgotten objects," thereby achieving a "layering of 'things'" to "measure the pastness of a past that itself had depth."[34]

The legend of the Seven Sleepers, too, is concerned with traces of the past: seven young Christians, persecuted by the third-century Roman emperor Decius, hide in a cave that is subsequently sealed. When, by chance, the cave is reopened two centuries later, the youths, who by now have turned into traces of the past themselves, awake from a miraculous sleep. One of the men enters the city of Ephesus, which has by now become a Christian city. Not only is he surprised at the city's transformation, but also, and more intriguingly, the city's inhabitants are puzzled when he attempts to buy bread with the outdated coins he carries with him. The inhabitants not only recognize the coins as traces from the past, they immediately imagine that they must stem from a hidden treasure trove the youth has found but failed to report. For the Ephesians, the coins thus automatically become associated with a specific kind of archaeological activity—even though that activity has not, in fact, taken place. The cave contains yet another trace of the past, this time in written form: a lead plaque that commemorates the story of the sleepers, a message from the past that the city's bishop, in the role of proto-archaeologist, interprets. Neil Cartlidge discusses three versions of the legend, the anonymous Old English prose narrative, the thirteenth-century Anglo-French version by Chardri, and the "vulgate" Latin text that is probably their common source. As Cartlidge demonstrates, these texts show a relatively sophisticated awareness of the historicity of numismatics, which they in turn attribute to the past communities they describe: not only do we witness a complex sense of history, but that sense of history is projected onto the very past that it contributes to evoking.

The contributions in the second section deal with objects that function as nodes in social, cultural, and temporal structures that can be described as "entanglements." Through the traces of past usages that are inscribed upon them, these artifacts can be seen as constructing a potentially infinite set of spatial, temporal, and material relations. Both Andrew James Johnston's and Naomi Howell's papers make reference to the Anglo-Saxon "dinar" displayed on the cover of this volume, an eighth-century gold coin minted in the Anglo-Saxon kingdom of Mercia during the reign of King Offa, bearing Offa's name as well as Arabic inscriptions in Kufic script, including a shortened version of the *Shahada*, the Islamic Creed. Produced in England, but faithfully reproducing the design of dinars minted during the reign of the Abbasid Caliph

---

34. See pp. 56, 48, this volume.

al-Mansur, the coin was brought to Rome via an unknown route and at some unknown date.[35] It invokes, in Johnston's words, "an intricate network of relationships in which economic, political, cultural, and religious factors are tightly interwoven" across time and space.[36] Johnston finds a comparable interwovenness in the cultural world of *Beowulf*, whose objects similarly reference not only different times, as Frank's contribution demonstrates, but also different cultural, political, and religious spheres, thus belying the seemingly self-enclosed insularity of its exclusively Germanic setting. This inextricable entanglement of different points of reference becomes visually manifest in the hilt of the giant sword, whose characterization as "wreoþenhilt ond wyrmfah" (*Beowulf*, line 1698a) recalls the intricate interlace designs of interwoven animal bodies found in early Irish and Anglo-Saxon art, both on artifacts, such as weapons and jewelry, and in manuscript illuminations.[37] As an ekphrastically visualized metaphor of entanglement, Johnston argues, the hilt emblematizes the capacity of *Beowulf*'s archaeological artifacts for interweaving points of cultural reference as different as migration age Scandinavia, Roman antiquity, pagan Germanic legend, and biblical history.

---

35. See "Gold imitation dinar of Offa," British Museum (registration number: 1913,1213.1), accessed August 26, 2020, https://www.bmimages.com/preview.asp?image=00031108001. According to our colleague at the Freie Universität Berlin, Andreas Ismail Mohr, the coin's main Arabic inscriptions can be translated as "no God except God alone, He has no partner" (obverse) and "Muhammad [is] the messenger of God" (reverse). These two inscriptions make up a shortened version of the *Shahada*, frequently found in this form on Arabic coins. Around the margins, the "dinar" is inscribed with additional text in Arabic. On the obverse, this can be translated as "Muhammad is the messenger of God; He [God] sent him with the Instruction in the Law and the True Religion, so that He may give it victory over all religion." On the reverse, the text records the (original) coin's minting date: "In the name of God. This dinar was minted in the year seven and fifty and one-hundred." The date, 157 AH (773–774 CE) suggests the reign of the second Abbasid caliph Abu Ja'far Abdallah ibn Muhammad al-Mansur (95–158 AH or 714–775 CE), although al-Mansur's name is not mentioned on the coin. The date was probably copied unwittingly from the coin's model, though it is in accord with the span of Offa's own reign (757–796 CE). The British Museum's note that "it is unlikely that any Christian king would have sent the pope a coin with and [sic] inscription stating that 'there is no God but Allah alone'" is misleading; even if Offa or his minters had been able to read the Arabic inscription, the first part of the *Shahada* (translated more correctly as "no God but God alone") would have been less controversial to Christians than the second part, "Muhammad is the messenger of God." Even so, Kufic inscriptions were valued in Christian contexts even if they included unequivocal allusions to the Islamic religion; see Isabelle Dolezalek, *Arabic Script on Christian Kings: Textile Inscriptions on Royal Garments from Norman Sicily*, Das Mittelalter, Perspektiven mediävistischer Forschung, Beihefte 5 (Berlin: de Gruyter, 2017). We are grateful to Andreas Ismail Mohr for his expert advice on this matter.

36. See p. 104, this volume.

37. *Beowulf* is quoted from R. D. Fulk, Robert E. Bjork, and John D. Niles, eds., *Klaeber's "Beowulf" and "The Fight at Finnsburg*," 4th ed. (Toronto: University of Toronto Press, 2008).

Lori Ann Garner pursues the entanglement of medicinal and martial discourses in Old English traditional remedies by examining how the very materiality of weapons and martial practices mentioned in the texts creates meaning and can thus be expected to have shaped both the respective texts' reception and the medical practices in which they were involved. The mention of particular weapons and martial practices—each carrying specific social connotations—points to a variety of different uses, from metaphors describing the "battle" between healer and illness or descriptive markers for plants, such as *sperewyrt* [spear-plant] or *strælwyrt* [arrow-wort], whose leaves recall the very form of arrowheads, to actual uses as practical tools or ritual props. Looking at the weapon imagery of Old English remedies from a material perspective reveals how the physical details and material properties of the weapons mentioned shape aesthetic responses and reveal complex networks of signification that help us appreciate how health and healing were understood in early medieval England.

Howell's contribution focuses on an object that in many respects resembles the Anglo-Saxon "dinar" discussed above: the heart-case of St. Albans abbot Roger de Norton (d. 1290). Probably produced in twelfth-century Afghanistan, the wooden box, delicately painted and adorned with Kufic lettering, was used as a container for the abbot's heart, separated from his body before burial. This at first sight surprising connection of what may appear as spatially and culturally distant spheres draws attention to a number of different intersecting narratives and traditions concerning the foundation and refoundations of St. Albans, which reprise the motif of the *inventio* also discussed in Salih's and Schwyzer's contributions. Drawing attention to the allegedly Saracen origins of the account of St. Alban's martyrdom, propagated by the influential twelfth-century St. Albans historian Matthew Paris in his *Vie de St. Auban*, Howell argues that the Christian reuse of a "Saracen" box should not—or not only—be read as an act of appropriation highlighting Christian supersession, but also as an act of reparation or reciprocity in which the combination of Christian and "Saracen" elements not only points to the institution's alleged origins but also looks forward to future moments of "discovery, reconnection, and refoundation" when it may, again, be taken as a prophetic message from an insufficiently understood past.[38]

Taking Erich Auerbach's essay *Figura* as point of departure, Jan-Peer Hartmann discusses the Ruthwell monument as a node connecting different materialities, temporalities, and medialities. Figural interpretation—the basis of exegetical practice—posits a spiritual accord or identity between different

---

38. See p. 171, this volume.

entities that are nevertheless historically and materially separate. The monument thereby establishes a temporal model according to which a later event is prefigured in an earlier one, while both also point to an eschatological future that presents the ultimate fulfillment of salvation history. The runic poem inscribed into the monument, Hartmann argues, uses a specifically literary approach—the medium of fiction—to draw attention to the particular tension between the monument's figural and historical aspects: by setting up a fictitious speaker who claims identity both with the monument—through the specific material context of the inscription—and with the original wooden cross—through the details of the narration—the poem reveals the ultimate incommensurability of the two aspects contained in the concept of *figura*. The poem's speaker, as the voice of the "true" cross, does not share in the historical experience or "knowledge" of the monument as its representation. What is more, the fictitious nature of the account—in reality, neither the original cross nor the stone monument are capable of feeling and speaking—reveals a third perspective, one that moves beyond a purely figural view of the monument.

Hartmann's paper is positioned at the intersection between the second and third parts of the collection because it emphasizes a participatory aspect of material culture frequently highlighted in medieval and early modern archaeological practices. As Jonathan Gil Harris points out in his essay, while "we often imagine archaeology through the template of the 'dig,'" medieval and early modern archaeological practices often produce spectacles, staging rather than unearthing the past and thereby revealing its "theatrical constructedness."[39] Such an archaeological performativity, for which Harris coins the term *archaeo-theatrics*, characterizes the Ruthwell monument, whose potential use in liturgical practices presupposes an observer who performatively participates in the temporal negotiations required by the monument's figural interpretation. This kind of archaeo-theatrics also characterizes practices involving relics, which were not merely unearthed and placed in shrines but also displayed and handled, touched and kissed. Harris himself discusses James I's coronation procession, designed to discover London's past as a prologue to the present; the second edition of John Stow's *Survey of London* (1603), which presents a fictionalized walk through a city staged both in its present state and as it allegedly was in antiquity; and the famous graveyard scene in *Hamlet*, which exposes the past as an always already performed act. He is particularly interested in the extreme case of Thomas Coryate, an eccentric Englishman who staged his journey to India as a voyage of discovery, ostensibly directed at finding the grave of Marlowe's Tamburlaine

---

39. See pp. 193, 194, this volume.

the Great. En route, Coryate theatrically emulated legendary and/or historical personages such as Ulysses and Alexander the Great, performing such acts as, amongst other things, dubbing his companions with a borrowed sword in the ruins of Troy. Coryate's identification of a 42-foot inscribed pillar from the fourth century BCE as a trace of Alexander the Great recalls the latter's march through most of what was then known of Asia, a march that Coryate's own journey was supposed to imitate. Coryate's antics, Harris argues, draw attention to the central role of narrative in making sense of the past's material remains, demonstrating that the past itself is never complete but "constantly being refashioned in the stories we tell about it and its objects."[40]

The capacity of material remains for eliciting different and sometimes conflicting responses and perspectives is highlighted also in Andrew Hui's discussion of the status of ruins in early modern visual culture. Early modern culture—like medieval or modern cultures, one might add—had no single way of looking at ruins; rather, Hui argues, the ruin constituted an open site onto which humanists could project very different ideas and perspectives. Hui discusses eleven different perspectives on ruins that were, if not in all cases ubiquitous, then at least widespread in early modern thought. As Hui demonstrates, ruins were both "material and metaphoric, architectural and allegorical," and always responsive to "architectural needs, fashions, and exigencies of the moment."[41] In keeping with Sebastiano Serlio's assertion that "perspective would be nothing without architecture and the architect nothing without perspective,"[42] Hui argues that Renaissance architecture and perspective were both informed by the perception and visualization of ruins.

As in the examples discussed by Harris, there is thus a pronounced performative and even theatrical aspect to Hui's ruins in that they are staged spectacles onto which a variety of philosophical, ethical, theological, and political practices and discourses could be projected. John Hines, too, stresses the interactive nature of premodern (fictional) encounters with material remains. Indeed, he observes that traces of the material past are so pervasive that no society can escape some form of engagement with it; nevertheless, he maintains, the later Middle Ages witnessed a fundamental change in the cognitive status of the material world that "proved essential to the transition from the medieval world to the early modern."[43] Discussing Chaucer's *House of Fame* as a literary archetype of a museum, Hines argues that the poem remained

---

40. See p. 209, this volume.
41. See p. 210, this volume.
42. Sebastiano Serlio, *Sebastiano Serlio on Architecture*, trans. Vaughan Hart and Peter Hicks (New Haven, CT: Yale University Press, 1996), 37.
43. See p. 241, this volume.

incomplete because the reconceptualization of the classical heritage and its material remains in the present had not reached a point that allowed Chaucer to bring the poem to a satisfactory ending. Hines's observation that Chaucer's museum embodies interactive and participatory ideals also favored by present-day museum pedagogy draws attention to the often discontinuous and nonteleological nature of historical responses to material remains over time. Whatever their manifold differences, the medieval viewpoint that material objects possess a substantial discursive capacity of their own can be brought into meaningful dialogue with new materialist approaches that stress the agential status of matter within cultural practices.

The urge to stage the material traces of the past in ways that creatively engage with or enact that past may be especially strong in late medieval and early modern texts and practices. Yet a playful engagement with material remains can be detected throughout the time span under discussion in this volume, as well as before and beyond. Material remains may elicit different aesthetic and performative responses in different cultural environs, and they are subject to trends or fashions that are never, however, absolute. Literary practices always provide the possibility of a counter-discourse, the potential to conceptualize aesthetically what is not or cannot be theorized explicitly. It is the collective aim of the papers gathered in this volume to demonstrate that the literary depiction of archaeological objects generates new forms of historical understanding that can provide alternative ways of reflecting on historical processes, ways of thinking that may even move beyond both the established master narratives of medieval and early modern historiography as well as the kind of master narratives that undergird modern forms of periodizing the Middle Ages and the early modern period.

PART I

TRACES

CHAPTER 1

Found Bodies

*The Living, the Dead, and the Undead
in the Broad Medieval Present*

SARAH SALIH

Archaeology permits the past to emerge into the present as a temporal disruption carried in a material object. Finding the object, making sense of the object, and making a narrative about the object are interdependent activities; current archaeological practice has "developed approaches that problematize suggestions of a 'great divide' between . . . scholar and object" as it retreats from the apparent certainties of positivism and acknowledges the contribution of the interpreter.[1] The archaeological process is a network as described by Bruno Latour, a circulation and exchange of energies between people and things: between the object, its finder, the place and time from where it came, the place and time of its emergence. Latour writes that "action is not done under the full control of consciousness; action should rather be felt as a node, a knot, and a conglomerate of many surprising sets of agencies that have to be slowly disentangled."[2] Such agencies are enacted by inanimate things as well as humans: "*Any thing* that does modify a state of affairs by making a difference is an actor . . . things might authorize, allow, afford, encourage, permit,

---

1. Dan Hicks and Mary C. Beaudry, "Introduction: The Place of Historical Archaeology," in *The Cambridge Companion to Historical Archaeology* (Cambridge: Cambridge University Press, 2006), 4.
2. Bruno Latour, *Reassembling the Social: An Introduction to Actor-Network Theory* (Oxford: Oxford University Press, 2005), 44.

suggest, influence, block, render possible, forbid, and so on."[3] In this instance, actors might include what is found as well as those who find it, and they might carry out a wide range of activities. Material things, often being longer-lived than humans, are regular vehicles for messages to the future, though the passage of time often interferes with their reception.

Current popular narratives of archaeology begin with human action: Howard Carter's discovery of the "wonderful things" in the tomb of Tutankhamun, perhaps, or the adventures of his fictional counterpart, Indiana Jones. Stories of human agency and adventure lead to the discovery of inert, if wonderful, things. Archaeology lends itself to narration in the heroic mode:

> The archaeologist is a passionate and totally devoted adventurer and explorer who conquers ancient sites and artifacts, thereby pushing forward the frontiers of our knowledge about the past. The associated narratives resemble those of the stereotypical hero who embarks on a quest to which he is fully devoted, is tested in the field, makes a spectacular discovery, and finally emerges as the virtuous man (or, exceptionally, woman) when the quest is fulfilled.[4]

Such narratives, that is, systematically overestimate the importance of human activity and minimize that of nonhuman actors. The stories of discoveries then bifurcate: more sober accounts go on to chronicle identification, scholarship, the construction of museums and visitor centers to display and interpret the finds, with control and agency remaining firmly with the human. But more sensationalist stories of archaeology then very often turn to the limitations of human agency, to tell of things that, once found, showed themselves not to be passive objects, but lively and indeed dangerous ones: the cursed diamond, the revenant mummy, or the Ark of the Covenant. Roger Luckhurst argues that such vengeful loot takes an "uncanny revenge on colonial power," that these tales are a vernacular version of Thing Theory, a recognition that agency may not be limited to the human, and that material objects have the capacity to operate upon us.[5] These are stories that tell popular and memorable versions of Latour's theoretical account of how humans pour energies into material things, things that then act as agents upon other humans, and often do so in unpredictable ways, exceeding the intentions of their makers.

---

3. Latour, *Reassembling the Social*, 71–72.

4. Cornelius Holtorf, *From Stonehenge to Las Vegas: Archaeology as Popular Culture* (Lanham, MD: AltaMira, 2005), 55.

5. Roger Luckhurst, *The Mummy's Curse: The True History of a Dark Fantasy* (Oxford: Oxford University Press, 2012), 236–37.

Medieval popular narratives were also intrigued by the vivacity of the excavated thing and the kinds of intervention it might make into their present. In the medieval world, things of the past were recognized, marked, and treasured as such; they were used to verify and carry narratives. Roberta Gilchrist identifies heirlooms, such as a ninth-century whalebone sword pommel found in a twelfth-century deposit in Coppergate, York, which she argues was likely to have spoken to its owners of ancestry and masculine prowess; in Coppergate, mercantile and artisanal households curated antique warrior bling for which they had not much practical use, but which spoke of a militant and seafaring past.[6] The London Stone, probably once part of a Roman building, was a landmark and some kind of actant in the city, and though the legend that identifies it as Brutus's stone of foundation cannot be securely attested for the Middle Ages, it is likely to have been one of the stories told about it.[7] An antique intaglio of Bacchus was repurposed into a seal in the fourteenth century, with the legend "Iesus est amor meus" [Jesus is my love], packing a very complex narrative of continuity across cultures.[8] The stone certainly and the jewel probably are things that were never lost and never needed to be found, but which are framed in such a way as to suggest that their antiquity carries power. The stone may have been accorded powers to protect the city or to witness oaths; a seal is always a significant object as the extension of a persona, and this one surely makes a point of containing and channeling the ancient power of the intaglio with the Christian frame. The presence of such objects thickens and complicates their present, ensuring that it is never fully synchronic.

But one has a different kind of relationship with a thing that has been there all the time from that with a thing that has just been excavated; the newly discovered thing constitutes an encounter that must be processed, understood, and told. And encounters by excavation must have been very common. Narratives of finding elaborate and mystify encounters with the things of the past. The Luck of Edenhall, a Middle Eastern glass cup now in the Victoria and

---

6. Roberta Gilchrist, "The Materiality of Medieval Heirlooms: From Sacred to Biographical Objects," in *Mobility, Meaning and the Transformations of Things: Shifting Contexts of Material Culture through Time and Space*, ed. Hans Peter Hahn and Hadas Weiss (Oxford: Oxbow, 2013), 170–82.

7. John Clark, "London Stone: Stone of Brutus or Fetish Stone—Making the Myth," *Folklore* 121, no. 1 (2010): 38–60.

8. British Museum 1923, 0508.1; see Martin Henig, "The Re-use and Copying of Ancient Intaglios Set in Medieval Personal Seals Mainly Found in England: An Aspect of the Renaissance of the 12th Century," in *Good Impressions: Image and Authority in Medieval Seals*, ed. Noel Adams, John Cherry, and James Robinson, British Museum Research Publication 168 (London: British Museum, 2008), 25–34.

Albert Museum, generated a narrative of its origin.[9] At some point between the thirteenth and the seventeenth century its exotic but mundane history as a luxury import was forgotten in favor of a local but supernatural origin as a fairy cup.[10] Fairy cup narratives, claiming that a found item was given or abandoned by the fairies, euphemize the process of excavating objects from barrows, substituting the transgressive encounter with nonhumans for the transgressive encounter with the dead. They minimize human agency in order to gloss over the pillaging of burial sites and in doing so produce objects that have the ability to make their own way into human social life, carrying their fairy power with them.

Medieval England was a visibly preoccupied landscape, its inhabitants' awareness of their mysterious forebears evident in legends such as Merlin's translation of Stonehenge from Ireland.[11] As the continued presence of the London Stone exemplifies, many late medieval settlements were on the sites of earlier settlements, Roman or early medieval. So medieval England was built on the foundation of a past that was not quite dead. The co-presence of the dead and the living, a practice characteristic of Christianity from its earliest days, was known to produce temporal heterogeneity.[12] Osbern Bokenham reports that England was notable for the presence of incorrupt saints:

> No-wheere of no peple in oo prouynce be foundyne so many seyntis bodies liynge hool aftur hur dethe, incorupt & hauynge þe similitude & þe examplary of finalle incorupcioun, as byne in Yngelond; and he exemplifiethe by seynt Edward and seynt Edmund kyngis, seynt Alphege & seynt Cutberde bishops. Item at Wecestre in þe Cathedralle-churche besides þe highe-awtere one þe sowthe side þer liethe a bischoppe, called John Constaunce, þe body vncorupte, þe vestimentis in like wise as holle & as soote as my be; and seynt Andree wife twyes queen & maydoun & y dar boldly by auctoryte of experience addyne her-to kynge Edwardis doughtre þe furst aftir þe conquest.[13]

---

9. "The Luck of Edenhall," V&A Museum, accessed June 2, 2020, https://collections.vam.ac.uk/item/ O33111/the-luck-of-edenhall-beaker-and-case-unknown/.

10. Glyn Davies, "New Light on the Luck of Edenhall," *Burlington Magazine* 152 (2010): 4–7.

11. Geoffrey of Monmouth, *The History of the Kings of Britain*, trans. Lewis Thorpe (London: Penguin, 1966), 196–98.

12. Robert Bartlett, *Why Can the Dead Do Such Great Things: Saints and Worshippers from the Martyrs to the Reformation* (Princeton, NJ: Princeton University Press, 2013), 622.

13. Carl Horstmann, "Mappula Angliae, von Osbern Bokenham," *Englische Studien* 10 (1886): 11. Thanks to Mami Kanno for introducing me to this passage.

England, then, is permanently temporally complicated by the presence of incorrupt saints who both extend the early medieval past into Bokenham's own present day and look forward to the moment of the resurrection. More broadly, beyond the specific claims about England and incorrupt bodies, the passage claims that invention narratives explore what happens when such time-traveling entities come face to face with the present. Medieval archaeological narratives typically begin not with the heroic archaeologist, but with the thing that demands to be found. Medieval people building and repairing must have found things of the past very often: there was no particular incentive to go looking for them, so their experience must have been, indeed, that these things turned up of their own volition.

Finding the not-quite-dead bodies of saints is both a paradigm of encounter with the local past and a special case, as saints are not confined by temporality. Stories about finding things, or being found by them, rehearse different conceptions about how we might relate to the past, how it acts upon us and we upon it. Pierre Nora's distinction between memory and history articulates what is at stake:

> Memory and history, far from being synonymous, are thus in many respects opposed. Memory is life, always embodied in living societies and as such in permanent evolution, subject to the dialectic of remembering and forgetting, unconscious of the distortions to which it is subject, vulnerable in various ways to appropriation and manipulation, and capable of lying dormant for long periods only to be suddenly reawakened. History, on the other hand, is the reconstruction, always problematic and incomplete, of what is no longer. Memory is always a phenomenon of the present, a bond tying us to the eternal present; history is a representation of the past.[14]

Saints, clearly, belong to the eternal present and thus to memory. Complementarily, Hans Ulrich Gumbrecht in *Our Broad Present* distinguishes "presence culture" from "meaning culture"; meaning culture is associated with a kind of historical thought in which, "as mankind moves along in time, it thinks it has left the past behind," an assumption that aligns with Nora's articulation of history as that which is no longer.[15] In our own present day, however, Gumbrecht argues, "we no longer live in historical time," and "*pasts* flood our

---

14. Pierre Nora, "General Introduction: Between Memory and History," in *Realms of Memory: Rethinking the French Past*, trans. Arthur Goldhammer, ed. Lawrence D. Kritzman (New York: Columbia University Press, 1996–98), 1:3.

15. Hans Ulrich Gumbrecht, *Our Broad Present: Time and Contemporary Culture* (New York: Columbia University Press, 2014), xii, 1.

present," participating in our social networks.¹⁶ Though Gumbrecht is not particularly concerned with medieval history, he cites medieval Christianity as paradigmatic of presence culture in which "humans consider themselves to be part of the world of objects instead of ontologically separated from it."¹⁷ His characterization of late medieval culture's openness to multiple temporality is congruent with studies such as James Simpson's characterization of "reformist culture," or Alexander Nagel and Christopher Wood's characterization of the "anachronic."¹⁸ The alarm bell, for a medievalist, is that both Nora's and Gumbrecht's analyses are embedded in long chronologies that place the medieval, as a period dominated by memory or by presence culture, on the far side of a rupture. This chronology is potentially a more sophisticated rearticulation of the now discredited idea that the medieval lacked a sense of history and might thus revive some clichés that medievalists might reasonably have thought we had seen off by now, such as the nostalgia for the supposed lost organic unity of medieval "quiet hierarchies."¹⁹

However, these analyses can be pried loose from chronology: no period is monolithic in its articulation of its relation to the past, and different uses of the past coexist. Specifically, the variations in late medieval body-finding narratives play out differentiated responses to the past. At stake in excavation stories is the question of whether what is found can participate in the present, or whether it speaks only of a past that is no longer. To ask this question is also to ask whether a body is dead or alive, whether we found it, or whether it found us. Alexandra Walsham tells of an ancient statue found in Buxton, Derbyshire, in the mid-fifteenth century, which was identified as an image of St. Anne and sparked a revival of pilgrimage to St. Ann's Well.²⁰ Modern archaeology and art history would classify this as a misidentification: the statue cannot have been originally intended to represent St. Anne, who was culted in the British Isles only from the twelfth century, and is more likely, as Walsham suggests, once to have been the pagan goddess of the spring.²¹ But though this is, in its

---

16. Gumbrecht, *Our Broad Present*, xiii.
17. Gumbrecht, *Our Broad Present*, 3.
18. James Simpson, *Reform and Cultural Revolution*, Oxford English Literary History 2, 1350–1547 (Oxford: Oxford University Press, 2002), 62; Alexander Nagel and Christopher S. Wood, *Anachronic Renaissance* (New York: Zone Books, 2010).
19. D. W. Robertson's account of the "quiet hierarchies" of the innocent medieval world is routinely decried (*A Preface to Chaucer: Studies in Medieval Perspectives* [Princeton, NJ: Princeton University Press, 1963], 51).
20. Alexandra Walsham, *The Reformation of the Landscape: Religion, Identity and Memory in Early Modern Britain and Ireland* (Oxford: Oxford University Press, 2011), 62.
21. Gail McMurray Gibson, *Theater of Devotion: East Anglian Drama and Society in the Late Middle Ages* (Chicago: University of Chicago Press, 1989), 82.

own terms, a perfectly valid interpretation, it privileges the moment of origin and dismisses the later utilization of the statue as a misreading. Those who identified the statue as Anne thus made it so and incorporated it into their own present, insisting that it was not an ancient thing but an anachronic one. Their use of it exemplifies Rita Felski's argument that the "busy life of the literary [or, in this case, material] artefact refutes our efforts to box it into a moment of origin, to lock it up in a temporal container."²² In contrast, the iconic story of Renaissance archaeology is of the finding of the antique statue of Laocoön and his sons in Rome in 1506, which was immediately identified and canonized as a thing of the past, "the Laocoön mentioned by Pliny."²³ It was incorporated into a historicist effort to understand ancient art. The difference between the two stories is not just about medieval and early modern sensibilities but also of a kind of use that requires chronology, and a kind of use that requires a broad present. The aestheticizing and historicizing response to Laocoön, at the inception of period-based art history, is interested in its precise moment of origin: the devotional response to St. Anne is interested in what the statue can do in the present, to which its origin is irrelevant.

Human remains are a special class of found object. As Thomas Laqueur argues, caring for the bodies of the dead is culturally universal: "As far back as people have discussed the subject, care of the dead has been regarded as foundational—of religion, of the polity, of the clan, of the tribe, of the capacity to mourn, of an understanding of the finitude of life, of civilization itself."²⁴ When a body is found many years later, it lacks the sense of continuity with the living person that informs mortuary rituals. Later excavators can see at a glance what such a body is; the natural next question is to wonder who it is and to seek supplemental information—grave goods, inscriptions, historical records, direct visionary inspiration—to answer that question and restore the anonymous body to its name. Confronting the dead, excavators confront an image of their own mortality, seeing future as well as past.

> Thenkes ye no ferlé, • bot frayns at me fere:
> Thagh ye be never so fayre, • thus schul ye fare!²⁵

---

22. Rita Felski, "Context Stinks!" *New Literary History* 42, no. 4 (2011): 580.

23. Quoted in Richard Brilliant, *My Laocoön: Alternative Claims in the Interpretation of Artworks* (Berkeley: University of California Press, 2000), 37.

24. Thomas W. Laqueur, *The Work of the Dead: A Cultural History of Mortal Remains* (Princeton, NJ: Princeton University Press, 2015), 9.

25. John Audelay, "Three Dead Kings," in *Poems and Carols (Oxford, Bodleian Library MS Douce 302)*, ed. Susanna Fein, TEAMS Middle English Texts Series (Kalamazoo, MI: Medieval Institute Publications, 2009), online edition, accessed June 2, 2020, http://d.lib.rochester.edu/teams/text/fein-audelay-poems-and-carols-meditative-close#3dk, lines 109–10.

This is the message of the three dead to their living counterparts, and nonambulant corpses say the same.

The paradigmatic found body is a saintly body, and a saintly body is anachronic. Saint-cult is an exercise in memory, insisting on the presentness of the past and keeping the saintly body in the present, where it is visible, accessible, and agential, rather than, say, reburying it. Monika Otter summarizes the narrative conventions of such *inventiones*:

> The relics are found either by coincidence, usually in connection with some construction or renovation project, or by divine guidance, through dreams or visions. The search for the right place and the digging itself are usually much emphasized; it is stressed that the community "earned" the relic through its intense desire and hard work. There must be an audience present, minimally represented by the bishop or other high clerics in charge, but often described as a large crowd of clergy and laity. There will be some confirmation that the relic is genuine: the body may be incorrupt, or at least emit a pleasing fragrance; sometimes there is an inscription or some identifying artifact. The *inventio* is followed by a *translatio*, that is, the body is brought to a more worthy shrine, and its authenticity is further confirmed by miracles.[26]

Whether relics are found by accident or under visionary instruction, humans are necessary instruments but not the originators of the finds. Narratives of invention and translation more often understand the saint to be the agent of this activity. Relics are regularly conceptualized as having agency as to their location and their interaction with devotees; hence, relic-theft may be justified on the grounds that a relic that allows itself to be relocated has exercised a preference for its new location.[27]

Typically, a saint communicates with a devotee, instructing them to begin the process of exhumation. Osbern Bokenham's fifteenth-century life of St. Margaret of Antioch, a legendary late antique virgin martyr, includes a detailed account of her multiple inventions and translations. Initially, when Antioch is threatened by political instability, the abbot Austin excavates the hidden relics of Margaret, "in a syluerene vessel, wyth gemmys freshly / Arayed" (lines 1056–57), and those of another virgin, St. Eupepria, from their original cult

---

26. Monika Otter, *Inventiones: Fiction and Referentiality in Twelfth-Century English Historical Writing* (Chapel Hill: University of North Carolina Press, 1996), 28–29.

27. Patrick Geary, *Furta Sacra: Thefts of Relics in the Central Middle Ages*, rev. ed. (Princeton, NJ: Princeton University Press, 1990), 109.

sites, for their own safekeeping, and takes them to Italy, his homeland.[28] He falls ill and dies, leaving the relics in a Benedictine monastery in the "vale Palantes" (line 1109), where they are enshrined and formally translated; but in due course, this place, too, falls victim to political instability and has to be abandoned. At this point, the neighboring "Ruuyllyans" (line 1194) opportunistically swipe the relics and carry them off in procession to their own church to be enshrined with St. Felicity. This shrine, too, is eventually destroyed and the site abandoned.

Margaret then forces her way into the near-present, the year 1405, when Bokenham himself was twelve or thirteen years old, and not greatly distant even from the perspective of 1443, when he wrote this legend.[29] The saint finally loses patience with these repeated failures to ensure her a permanent cult center and takes matters into her own bony hands. Tired of being left in a deserted site, she appears to a hermit to tell him in no uncertain terms to do something about it:

> Ion hyht the toon, to whom dede appere
> Seynt Margrete, seyng on this manere:
>
> "Ion, goddys seruaunt, as fast as thou kan,
> On myn erand mounth Flask go to,
> And vn-to the pryour of seynt Flauyan,
> Wych is ther clepyd Burgundio,
> And sey hym, god wil that he his deuer do,
> That neythyr I ner seynt Felycyte
> In solytarye place lengere lefth be."
> (*Legendys,* lines 1231–39)

There follows a lengthy story of archaeological investigation under the distinctly authoritarian direction of Margaret. John the hermit duly heads off to Mount Flask, where he is initially unable to persuade the prior of the local monastery to start the dig, forcing Margaret to return to order him to go back to the prior and try again. Their initial attempts are unsuccessful; they dig under the pavement of the abandoned church, where "they founde nowt—that dede hem greue" (line 1309). John then tries another nearby site

---

28. Osbern Bokenham, *Legendys of Hooly Wummen,* ed. Mary S. Serjeantson, EETS o.s. 206 (London: Oxford University Press, 1938), quoted by line in the text.
29. Douglas Gray, "Bokenham, Osbern," *Dictionary of National Biography.*

"where growe brymblys & many a thorn.
Here shal I hope no labour be lorn."
Wher they dede delue, & wyth-inne a stounde,
More than they sowten ther they founde.

For wyth the bodyes of the virgyns two,
Felycyte an eek Seynt Margarete,
Thre rybbys ther they foundyn also
Of Cosme & Damyan, smelling ful swete;
And an epitaphye of marbyl was wrete
On this wyse: "lo! her in this chest
Margretys body & felicites doth rest."
(*Legendys*, lines 1320–30)

St. Margaret is very much the driver of the final excavation, both the start and the goal of the process, although she was apparently content to let the human agents take the lead earlier; when it is not active, her body is latent, waiting for the appropriate moment to use its power. An invention of a saint is necessarily led by the saint themselves, in order to demonstrate that they have the energy to operate in the material world and thus can support a viable cult site. St. Margaret's agency generates further human agencies. She acts through other bodies, using John the hermit, who uses the monks to get to her burial place; but they are not particularly reliable instruments, often ineffectual or resistant, and have to be continually harried. From the point of view of John and the monks, the excavation is a frustrating, laborious, and unpredictable process. The material world resists their energies, forcing them through thorns and briars, and although they think they know what they are looking for, the narrative leads to the surprise of finding more than they sought.

But saintly agency, too, has limitations and is unevenly distributed amongst the group. Although the monks find two whole bodies and fragments of two others, Margaret is the spokeswoman for the whole bag of bones. Perhaps a whole-body relic exercises personhood more easily than a fragment; certainly the spare ribs, Cosmas and Damian, sweet though they may smell, have nothing to say for themselves. Or Margaret is perhaps empowered by her relative celebrity, as one of the most popular virgin martyr saints: certainly, she seems to expect John the hermit to have heard of her and to show due deference. Margaret is able to introduce her relics into the fifteenth century because she was already there: she had a long-established cult centered on her patronage of women in labor.[30]

---

30. Carole Hill, "'Leave my Virginity Alone!': The Cult of St Margaret of Antioch in Norwich; In Pursuit of a Pragmatic Piety," in *Medieval East Anglia*, ed. Christopher Harper-Bill

Archaeology, argues Cornelius Holtorf, is a process carried out for the benefit of the present, a proposition borne out in the account of Margaret's inventions and translations.[31] James Simpson comments that in this story, "There can be no direct access to the past. . . . Finding it involves both digging and visions, and moving it involves loss."[32] Finding the body does not constitute new knowledge about the past in which Margaret lived and died; her legend remains stable while her relics embark on new life and activity in the present. The final translation is marked by intense activity, procession, church-building, cult-forming: the relics make something happen and change the world that they have emerged into. They announce their chosen cult site by becoming too heavy to move and force the owner of this house to relinquish it by bringing on storms. Bokenham indeed introduces this narrative of translation by describing how a ring that had been held against a fragmentary relic of the saint—a part of her foot, which must have a translation history quite different from that told in the main narrative—had rescued him from persecution. He is interested in the invention and translation of the relics because he thinks of Margaret not as belonging to the past but as an active participant in his own world; not history, but memory.

Saint-cult gives the normative account of how to deal with finding bodies: such bodies are brought into the present day, put to work as sites of memory and centers of cultic activity; agency is multiplied and widely distributed through the network, with the saints themselves making a significant contribution. Two other narratives of finding bodies resemble such *inventiones,* but then take unexpected turns. Perhaps the most famous archaeological find of medieval England was the discovery of the graves of King Arthur and Queen Guinevere at Glastonbury Abbey in 1191, and perhaps the richest narrative of an archaeological find in medieval England is the anonymous alliterative poem *St. Erkenwald,* which in the late fourteenth century recounts the chance discovery in the late seventh century of the tomb of a virtuous pagan judge in St. Paul's Cathedral, London. In both, an already holy site is further sanctified and dignified by the presence of traces of the glorious past as recounted in the historical tradition derived from Geoffrey of Monmouth. The excavated material bodies generate narrative, enriching the present time and place of their discovery by making the past present. Both are also, of course, at some level, fake or fictive discoveries, though they are presented in truth-claiming narratives. *St. Erkenwald*'s tale of the Trojan past imagines a pagan temple underlying the present St. Paul's; the discovery of Arthur and Guinevere was an even more ambitious fiction, enacted with material bodies in real time. The

---

(Woodbridge, UK: Boydell Press, 2005), 225–45.

31. Holtorf, *From Stonehenge to Las Vegas,* 15.
32. Simpson, *Reform and Cultural Revolution,* 398.

finds are thus the products of, as well as the triggers for, narrative: they are narratives made material. They are examples of what Latour names "factish," artifacts that are all the more real precisely because they are constructed as repositories of human energies, attention, and desires. And in contrast with relic *inventiones*, which celebrate the contemporary energy of old bones, these two narratives demonstrate some disquiet with a broad present and seek to limit or contain the agency of the intrusive thing of the past.

To begin with King Arthur, in a near-contemporary account by Gerald of Wales:

> Furthermore, in our times, while Henry II was ruling England, the tomb of the renowned Arthur was searched for meticulously in Glastonbury Abbey; this was done at the instruction of the king and under the supervision of the abbot of that place, Henry, who was later transferred to Worcester Cathedral. With much effort the tomb was excavated in the holy burial-ground that had been dedicated by Saint Dunstan; it was found between two tall, emblazoned pyramids, erected long ago in memory of Arthur. Though his body and bones had been reduced to dust, they were conveyed from below into the air, and to a more dignified place.[33]

This is more like heroic archaeology than Margaret's story. It is directed by the wishes of great men, secular and religious authorities, whose agendas happen to coincide in thinking that finding Arthur's body would be beneficial. Everything goes to plan: the king has been informed (mundanely, by an ancient poet rather than a vision) that the body will be found extra deep, in a hollowed oak bole, and so it is.[34] The power of expectation is such that the body is already known before it is found, and its material presence is only a confirmation of that knowledge: it is not so much taken out of the ground as put into it. Human agency, ingenuity, and labor make the find: the body itself is inert, fully dead, and/or disintegrated. Gerald draws some historical conclusions about the "industry and exquisite prudence" of those who buried Arthur, concealing his grave from raiders but also marking it for posterity with an inscribed cross: he sees the finding as a successful completion of the

---

33. Gerald of Wales, *Speculum Ecclesiae*, cited from "The Tomb of King Arthur," trans. John William Sutton, The Camelot Project (Rochester, NY: Robbins Library, University of Rochester, 2001), accessed June 2, 2020, http://d.lib.rochester.edu/camelot/text/gerald-of-wales-arthurs-tomb.

34. Gerald of Wales, *Liber de Principis Instructione*, cited from "The Tomb of King Arthur," trans. John William Sutton, The Camelot Project (Rochester, NY: Robbins Library, University of Rochester, 2001), accessed June 2, 2020, http://d.lib.rochester.edu/camelot/text/gerald-of-wales-arthurs-tomb.

intentions of the long-gone people who buried Arthur.[35] The past successfully communicates with the present through the body, but Arthur himself does nothing.

The early reports are remarkably inconsistent in their accounts of what actually was found at Glastonbury. Were "the body and bones ... reduced to dust," leaving only one lock of fair hair, as Gerald writes in the *Speculum,* or were they so substantial as to reveal Arthur's monstrously large size and his death-wound, as Gerald also writes in the *Liber de Principis Instructione*?[36] Was it the body of Arthur alone (in Camden's engraving of the cross marking the grave); of Arthur and Guinevere (Gerald); or Arthur, Guinevere, and Mordred (Margam chronicle)?[37] The bodies are ruthlessly shifted and edited to suit the specific needs of present actors. These interests are not hard to discern: modern commentators take it for granted that the discovery was faked for financial and political purposes, and contemporaries were probably able to draw the same conclusion. Glastonbury Abbey had a rebuilding campaign to finance and crafted the find to catch the attention of the new king, Richard I.[38] Gerald spells out the usefulness of the find to the Anglo-Norman monarchy: proving Arthur historical and proving him dead, it thus disproved Welsh legends that hope for Arthur's return.[39] Finding his grave thus has the twofold advantage for King Richard of discouraging Welsh resistance to Anglo-Norman rule and making him the custodian of this prestigious forebear.[40] This political function was so useful that Edward I, in the following century, revived Arthur's death in a translation ceremony that demonstrated that the "supposedly sleeping king was now no more than ancient bones."[41]

The find was still confirming Arthur's historicity three centuries later in Caxton's preface to Malory, but its anomalous details did not prompt a reexamination of the textual tradition, which felt no need to make revisionist narratives that accounted for Arthur's extraordinary size or his mysterious first wife: once again, archaeology has a function in the present that does

---

35. Gerald of Wales, *Speculum Ecclesiae.*
36. Gerald of Wales, *Liber de Principis Instructione.*
37. Richard Barber, "Was Mordred Buried at Glastonbury?," in *Glastonbury Abbey and the Arthurian Tradition,* ed. James P. Carley (Cambridge: D. S. Brewer, 2001), 145–59.
38. Charles T. Wood, "Guenevere at Glastonbury? A Problem in Translation(s)," in *Glastonbury Abbey,* ed. Carley, 83–100, 88.
39. Gerald of Wales, *Speculum Ecclesiae.*
40. Philip Schwyzer, "Exhumation and Ethnic Conflict: From *St. Erkenwald* to Spenser in Ireland," *Representations* 95, no. 1 (2006): 14; Robert Allen Rouse and Cory James Rushton, "Arthurian Geography," in *The Cambridge Companion to the Arthurian Legend,* ed. Elizabeth Archibald and Ad Putter (Cambridge: Cambridge University Press, 2010), 228.
41. Wood, "Guenevere at Glastonbury?," 92.

not require reexamination of the past.[42] The excavated Arthur has work to do in the present day, enhancing the authority of the Angevin monarchy and attracting visitors to Glastonbury Abbey, but this work depends on him being dead and staying that way. The archaeological activity of finding, displaying, and memorializing his body contains it and constrains its agency; his relics have no animacy. While the external process of reburying him in a fine marble tomb that then attracts visitors is identical to that of the translation of a saint, the impact is the opposite, for the crucial difference is that Arthur is absent and inaccessible. Saints' tombs are media through which the *virtus* of the body may be accessed; Arthur's tomb is more like a museum vitrine, hygienically isolating this thing of the past from the present. This is a process of memory construction, in its shaping of a past that speaks to the needs of the present, but it is also one that depends upon the idea of history: that what is past is past, and no longer operative. It is very much to the point of the exercise that Arthur be not memory, as he is in the Welsh legends that constitute him a potential contemporary political actor, but only history.

The excavated pagan in *St. Erkenwald* offers another, differently nuanced, account of the relation of past and present, and the distribution of agency. Criticism recognizes *St. Erkenwald* as a poem particularly concerned, in John Scattergood's phrase, with "the custody of the past."[43] The opening narrative of the poem, telling the Bedan history of the conversion of London's pagan sites, sets up a model of historical memorialization in which the past is remembered even as it is superseded. As Cynthia Turner Camp writes of the poem's temple-to-church transformations, "These tangible pieces of civic architecture function as the primary technology of urban memory, retaining reminders of past use amidst their new uses and meanings."[44] Yet the main narrative is more troubled by the material traces of the past. A magnificent tomb containing an incorrupt body, crowned and robed, is found by accident as masons dig a new foundation for St. Paul's cathedral. A tomb once more acts as a frame that establishes a temporal relation; this one is "a time capsule that so long as it remains unopened preserves its contents in temporal stasis," and which upon opening enters the seventh-century present.[45] Whereas Arthur was deliber-

---

42. Thomas Malory, *Works*, ed. Eugène Vinaver (Oxford: Oxford University Press, 1971), xiv.

43. John Scattergood, *The Lost Tradition: Essays on Middle English Alliterative Poetry* (Dublin: Four Courts Press, 2000), 179.

44. Cynthia Turner Camp, "Spatial Memory, Historiographic Fantasy and the Place of the Past in *St. Erkenwald*," *New Literary History* 44, no. 3 (2013): 476.

45. Jeffrey Jerome Cohen, *Stone: An Ecology of the Inhuman* (Minneapolis: University of Minnesota Press, 2015), 109.

ately sought, the Body[46] is apparently found by mere chance, though given the poem's opening account of the successive layers of Trojan, British, and Saxon settlement in London, it is not surprising that a trace of it might show up. Indeed, Roman sepulchers must occasionally have been found in medieval England; such a chance find is marked as miraculous in the legend of St. Æthelthryth and might have been one trigger of this narrative.[47] The find, like that of a saintly relic, is apparently an accidental byproduct of the renovation work; the Body, however, lacks a saint's ability to get himself found and is able to do no more than hope that something might happen to end the unfortunate stasis he was placed in.

St. Erkenwald stages in more detail than either of the other accounts the possibility that an excavation may constitute an encounter with alterity: as Scattergood argues, it foregrounds the difficulty of making sense of the past and privileges clerical explanations of history.[48] While the legends identifying Margaret and Arthur were easily and conveniently legible, allowing transparent and untroubled communication between the past and the present, the description of the judge's tomb emphasizes incomprehension and bafflement: the tomb is "ferly" (line 47), a marvel, the incorrupt body, suspended between life and death, is horribly uncanny, and the tomb's inscription is runish and obscure, baffling even the learned clerics of the cathedral.[49]

> The sperle of þe spelunke þat sparde hit o-lofte
> Was metely made of þe marbre and menskefully planede,
> And þe bordure enbelicit wyt bryȝt golde lettres,
> Bot roynyshe were þe resones þat þer on row stoden.
> (*St. Erkenwald,* lines 49–52)

The tomb looks, to the eyes of a linear art history, like a multitemporal or repurposed object, a Roman sarcophagus inscribed with early medieval runes. It is an agent, with a voice, but not a very effective one. The "problematic and incomplete reconstruction" of historical enquiry, to return to Nora's terms, is emphasized: no records identify the man, and neither Erkenwald, nor the reader, ever actually find out what the mysterious runish letters said or what

---

46. I take the term "the Body" from an MA essay by Catherine Chang.
47. Bede, *The Ecclesiastical History of the English People, The Greater Chronicle, Bede's Letter to Egbert,* ed. Judith McClure and Roger Collins (Oxford: Oxford University Press, 1994), 204.
48. Scattergood, *Lost Tradition,* 190.
49. Malcolm Andrew, Ronald Waldron, and Clifford Peterson, eds., *Saint Erkenwald* in *The Complete Works of the Pearl Poet,* trans. and intr. Casey Finch (Berkeley: University of California Press, 1993), quoted by line in the text.

the Body's name was. Agency in this tale is weak but widely distributed: a lot of things happen, but none of the actors really know what they are doing. Everything happens by Providence, or, as it appears to the participants in the events, by accident. The Body is found by accident, by Londoners who do not know what to do with it; Bishop Erkenwald baptizes it by accident, when his tears fall on it. The long-ago mourners who buried the Body with royal honors succeed in attracting the attention of posterity, but their communication gets through imperfectly, muffled by the effects of time, even though the material object emerges unscathed. The energies they have poured into the construction of a tomb carrying a legible message have been frustrated over time and, in any case, have nothing to do with the actual miracle, the preservation of the Body, for that is carried out by God.

The climax of the narrative is in sharp contrast to the hagiographic resonances of the tale. A hagiographic tale of finding an incorrupt corpse would be about the continuing agency and present existence of the saint and would culminate in a translation to a finer tomb, which would continue to be the cult center. But at the end of *St. Erkenwald*, nothing is left. Once the Body has been baptized, it dissolves:

> Bot sodenly his swete chere swyndid and faylide
> And alle the blee of his body wos blakke as þe moldes,
> As roten as þe rottok þat rises in powdere.
> For as sone as þe soule was sesyd in blisse
> Corrupt was þat oþir crafte þat couert þe bones.
> (*St. Erkenwald*, lines 342–46)

The only one of my three examples to confirm Bokenham's claim that England is characterized by the presence of incorrupt bodies (Margaret is found in Italy, Arthur and Guinevere are skeletal) ends up disproving it instead: almost as soon as the Body's presence is known, it is over. And the marvelous tomb is apparently forgotten about; certainly, there is no indication that, for example, it was displayed in St Paul's to memorialize the miracle. The poem's narrative depends, as Cohen argues, on "the persistence of stone," and yet the stone tomb fades away once its work is done.[50] The miracle itself is not recorded in the collection of St. Erkenwald's miracles, nor, as far as anyone knows, was it recorded at the cult site.[51] Camp argues that the disappearance of the Body allows it to enter "the collective memory of the citizenry," but it is not clear in the poem that it does so: its work is "to dramatize the bishop's

---

50. Cohen, *Stone*, 109.
51. See E. Gordon Whatley, trans. and ed., *The Saint of London: The Life and Miracles of St. Erkenwald* (Binghamton, NY: Medieval and Renaissance Texts and Studies, 1989).

place in the scheme of salvation, as the consecrated vessel, 'blessyd and sacryd' (line 3), through which divine grace is channeled from God to sinful, benighted humanity"; this being done, Erkenwald is remembered instead.[52] While Erkenwald's own relics existed and were active in the poem's present, visited, for example, by Richard II as part of his ritual reconciliation with London, the Body remained absent.[53] The disquieting encounter with a past that is at once thoroughly known—Trojan, masculine, bureaucratic, hierarchical—and yet, when the Londoners try to make sense of it, completely baffling, is resolved by the disintegration of the anomalous pagan trace. *St. Erkenwald* breaks the pattern of archaeological discoveries being primarily active in the present. The discovery of the Body does bring new information about New Trojan society and culture, yet while he has some work to do in the present, his activity is severely curtailed, and he retreats, materially, to a distant and inaccessible past as he crumbles to dust. Temporal uniformity is restored: the past is excavated, makes its contribution to the present by affirming the sanctity of Bishop Erkenwald, and then, its job done, goes away again. The temporal wound is healed; London "has left the past behind," securing itself as, in Gumbrecht's terms, a historical culture.[54] The poem ends with a dissolve into the immaterial, with the sound of bells. This poem, then, resists a broad present; it rehearses the difficulty and dissatisfactions of history.

Body-finding narratives all center on managing relations with the past and its material traces. There is no single late medieval relation to the past any more than there is a single modern relation. The same procedures and objects, such as tombs and their excavations, might construct quite different temporal relations with the continued life of the past, as manifested in the bodies of the dead and undead. The medieval world, like the modern world, was full of the active things of the past and had a number of ways of handling them. Some were invisible, some anachronic, some repurposed, some marked off as temporally alien. Some waited silent and inert until awakened by some chance incident. Pasts might be invited, or might intrude themselves, into the present; sometimes the present fought back to expel these importunate pasts. The variations in these narratives testify that the late medieval people recognized the temporal heterogeneity of their moment and made decisions as to whether to exploit or resist such emergent pasts.

---

52. Camp, "Spatial Memory," 486; E. Gordon Whatley, "Heathens and Saints: *St. Erkenwald* in Its Legendary Context," *Speculum* 61 (1986): 352.

53. Richard Maidstone, *Concordia: The Reconciliation of Richard II with London*, trans. A. G. Rigg, ed. David R. Carlson, TEAMS Middle English Texts Series (Kalamazoo, MI: Medieval Institute Publications, 2003), online edition, accessed June 2, 2020, http://d.lib.rochester.edu/teams/text/rigg-and-carlson-maidstone-concordia, line 348.

54. Gumbrecht, *Our Broad Present*, xii.

CHAPTER 2

The Beaker in the Barrow, the Flagon with the Dragon

Accessorizing Beowulf

ROBERTA FRANK

Material Relics

Beowulf is studded with fragments of stories, tales almost but not quite told. The fabric of the poem is thick with metal accessories, portable objects, encrusted, hoary, and glinting, traumatized by the horrors they have witnessed and will witness still. Wordsworth meditated about peering into the life of things.[1] The *Beowulf* poet attests to their self-regard: a hero arms himself for an underwater dive; his mailcoat, helmet, and sword get ready for their close-ups.[2] A stone barrow conceals the paraphernalia of ancient days, treasures tarnished and corroding, a hint of golden moss under a sleeping dragon. A swirl of ornate metal emerges from the depths of the earth, from a past that, "too dead now to be articulated in memorial language, a past with no names left, one just beyond our recovery, glitters and glows in the exquisite objects of the hoard, objects that force on us, as always, images of those hands and

---

1. William Wordsworth, *Lines Composed a Few Miles Above Tintern Abbey* (1798), line 46.
2. The term *poet* and its accompanying possessive pronoun are here used as shorthand for the unidentified author(s) of the poem. Citations of *Beowulf* in this essay are from R. D. Fulk, Robert E. Bjork, and John D. Niles, eds., *Klaeber's "Beowulf" and "The Fight at Finnsburg,"* 4th ed. (Toronto: University of Toronto Press, 2008) (Identified hereafter as *Klaeber* 4).

fingers (now dust and bones) that once crafted and cherished the artifacts."[3] The king of the Danes gazes upon an antediluvian gold sword-hilt, the work of giants whose molars and bones had attracted attention in Virgil's Italy, Augustine's Utica, and Procopius's Beneventum.[4] The *Beowulf* poet grounds his stories repetitively, relentlessly in artifacts, dispatching them, like spies, to track the stratified residue of a history in retreat.

In *Gulliver's Travels*, Swift famously satirized the Royal Academy's various schemes for universal nonphonetic communication: "Since Words are only names for *Things*, it would be more convenient for all Men to carry about them such *Things* as were necessary to express the particular Business they are to discourse on."[5] Swift touted the health benefits of this object language: speech, as everyone knows, corrodes the lungs; and a display of goods and utensils, much the same in all lands, would reduce misunderstandings among ambassadors, resulting in fewer deaths on the battlefield. Augustine proposed an underlying similarity between the animate and inanimate: "We, accordingly, who enjoy and use other things, are things ourselves."[6] The "it-" or "object-novels" of eighteenth-century England had personified objects, such as coins, inkwells, and wooden legs, tell of their adventures as they circulated from hand to hand.[7] In Gabriel García Márquez's *One Hundred Years of Solitude*, the town of Macondo, troubled by amnesia, labels every object with a descrip-

---

3. Edward B. Irving Jr., *Rereading "Beowulf"* (Philadelphia: University of Pennsylvania Press, 1989), 114. On the shifting temporalities of *Beowulf*, see Gillian R. Overing, "*Beowulf*: A Poem in Our Time," in *The Cambridge History of Early Medieval English Literature*, ed. Clare A. Lees (Cambridge: Cambridge University Press, 2013), 309–31; also Roy M. Liuzza, "*Beowulf*: Monuments, Memory, History," in *Readings in Medieval Texts: Interpreting Old and Middle English Literature*, ed. David F. Johnson and Elaine Treharne (Oxford: Oxford University Press, 2005), 91–108.

4. On ancient discoveries of giant bones and Augustus's fossil collections, see Adrienne Mayor, *The First Fossil Hunters: Paleontology in Greek and Roman Times* (Princeton, NJ: Princeton University Press, 2000), especially 104–56. Virgil, *Georgics* 1.494–97, famously noted that Italian farmers often turned up giant bones (also empty helmets and rusty javelins) in their plowed fields; Augustine, *The City of God* 15.9, reported that he had seen with his own eyes an immense human molar that he believed "belonged to some giant"; Procopius, *De Bello Gothico* 5.15.8, averred that the giant tusks of the Calydonian Boar at Beneventum were "well worth seeing."

5. Jonathan Swift, *Gulliver's Travels*, ed. Colin McKelvie (Belfast: Appletree Press Limited, 1976), part 3, chapter 5, 163.

6. "Nos itaque qui fruimur et utimur aliis rebus, res aliquae sumus" (Augustine, *De doctrina christiana* 1.22).

7. See Mark Blackwell, *The Secret Life of Things: Animals, Objects, and It-Narratives in Eighteenth-Century England* (Lewisburg, PA: Bucknell University Press, 2007). See also Julie Park, *The Self and It: Novel Objects and Mimetic Subjects in Eighteenth-Century England* (Stanford, CA: Stanford University Press, 2009); and Jennifer van Horn, *The Power of Objects in Eighteenth-Century British America* (Chapel Hill: University of North Carolina Press, 2017).

tion of its purpose: "This is the cow. She must be milked every morning."[8] The *Beowulf* poet gives his artifacts, his restless and "unruly engines of memory,"[9] a function too. The humans they attach themselves to rarely fare well.

The call of things is loud these days. Publishers advertise materiality in book titles, such as *Proust's Overcoat* and *Napoleon's Buttons*[10] and in bestsellers (spawned by *Cod: A Biography of the Fish That Changed the World*) that serially proclaim the hegemony of the potato, cotton, coffee, sugar, the pencil, the zipper, paper, the toilet, and more—a tumbling, numbing torrent of objects. Realia-hunger generates titles such as *Tangible Things: Making History through Objects, Cleopatra's Nose: 39 Varieties of Desire, 100 Diagrams that Changed the World, The History of the World in 1,000 Objects, 99 Disobedient Objects, Tutenkhamen's Tracksuit: The History of Sport in 100 Objects, The History of America in 101 Objects, A History of New York in 101 Objects*, and *A History of Birdwatching in 100 Objects*.[11] At least three recent books promise *The First World War in 100 Objects*. *Beowulf* studies were "thing-oriented" long before the appearance of *A History of the World in 100 Objects*, the British Library *succès fou* of 2010.[12] The title page of J. R. Clark Hall's collected edition of Knut Martin Stjerna's essays on *Beowulf*, published in 1912, advertised and included 128 illustrations.[13] John D. Niles's beautifully illustrated edition of Seamus Heaney's translation of the poem contains more than one hundred images of "things,"[14] while Marijane Osborn's *Beowulf: A Verse Translation with Treasures of the Ancient North*, a pioneer 1983 publication, depicts no fewer

---

8. Gabriel García Márquez, *One Hundred Years of Solitude*, trans. Gregory Rabassa (London: Penguin Books, 2014), 48.

9. Liuzza, "Monuments, Memory, History," 98.

10. *Hamlet's BlackBerry, Einstein's Mirror, Foucault's Pendulum, Wittgenstein's Poker, Heidegger's Hut, Turing's Cathedral, Balzac's Omelette, Cezanne's Carrot, Vermeer's Hat, Flaubert's Parrot, Flaubert's Barometer, Rousseau's Dog, Michelet's Little Door, Galileo's Telescope, Galileo's Middle Finger, The Duchess of Malfi's Apricots.*

11. For sports fans, *A History of Football in 100 Objects*; for other conditions of readers, Shakespeare, The Future, The Navy, Sports, Cricket, Ireland, Finland, The Beatles, The Universe, My Life, History, Public Health, Design, Stirling, St Albans, Norfolk, Cheltenham, Derry, Kent, Fermanagh, Oneonta, *A History of Children's Books*, and scores more, all in one hundred objects. Recent, more restrained additions to this list-based literary genre include *Fifty Early Medieval Things* and *A History of Intellectual Property in 50 Objects*.

12. This "100 Objects" book has been reprinted in at least ten languages. Downloads of its companion podcasts early topped 35 million viewers. Its author, Neil MacGregor, was appointed foundational artistic director of the Humboldt Forum in Berlin in 2015, shortly before the conference that gave rise to this volume.

13. Knut Stjerna, *Essays on Questions Connected with the Old English Poem of "Beowulf,"* trans. and ed. John R. Clark Hall (Coventry: Curtis & Beamish, 1912).

14. John D. Niles, ed., *Beowulf: Translated by Seamus Heaney; An Illustrated Edition* (New York: Norton, 2008).

than ninety-one artifacts and manuscript drawings.[15] (The first printed edition of *Beowulf* in 1815 contained no images whatsoever.)[16] Archaeologists report that enterprising Anglo-Saxons were active at Bronze Age burial mounds and Neolithic long barrows as well as at the graves of their own contemporaries.[17] It's the news that has stayed news. Thanks to the Treasure Act of 1996 and an army of metal detectorists, fresh finds from Anglo-Saxon sites are being unearthed at a healthy clip.[18] The 2009 discovery of the Staffordshire hoard with its 3,500-plus gold and silver fragments, including parts from over a hundred swords, has energized *Beowulf* studies, much as Sutton Hoo Mound 1 did seventy years earlier.[19] The mud has things for medievalists still.[20]

---

15. Marijane Osborn, *Beowulf: A Verse Translation with Treasures of the Ancient North* (Berkeley: University of California Press, 1983). See also Randolph Swearer, Raymond Oliver, and Marijane Osborn, *"Beowulf": A Likeness* (New Haven, CT: Yale University Press, 1990); and Marijane Osborn, "Translations, Versions, Illustrations," in *A "Beowulf" Handbook*, ed. Robert E. Bjork and John D. Niles (Lincoln: University of Nebraska Press, 1997), 341–72.

16. Grímur Jónsson Thorkelin, ed., *De Danorum rebus gestis secul[i] III & IV. Poëma danicum dialecto anglosaxonica* (Copenhagen: T. E. Rangel, 1815).

17. Leslie Webster, "Archaeology and *Beowulf*," in *"Beowulf": An Edition*, ed. Bruce Mitchell and Fred C. Robinson (Oxford: Blackwell, 1998), 183–94, at 194; Sarah Semple, *Perceptions of the Prehistoric in Anglo-Saxon England: Religion, Ritual, and Rulership in the Landscape* (Oxford: Oxford University Press, 2013), 13–16 and bibliography therein. For an early account of Anglo-Saxon interest in barrow-opening, see Thomas Wright, "On Antiquarian Excavations and Researches in the Middle Ages," *Archaeologia* 30 (1844): 438–48.

18. On the implications of the Treasure Act, see Leslie Webster, "Ideal and Reality: Versions of Treasure in the Early Anglo-Saxon World," in *Treasure in the Medieval West*, ed. Elizabeth M. Tyler (York: York University Press, 2000), 49.

19. The cover of Craig Williamson, trans. and ed., *"Beowulf" and Other Old English Poems* (Philadelphia: University of Pennsylvania Press, 2011) shows a detail from the replica of the Sutton Hoo helmet; six years later, the cover of Williamson, trans., *The Complete Old English Poems* (Philadelphia: University of Pennsylvania Press, 2017) features a gold filigree mount from the Staffordshire hoard. See Kevin Leahy and Roger Bland, *The Staffordshire Hoard*, 2nd ed. (London: British Museum, 2014). Papers from the Staffordshire Hoard Symposium, March 2010, are available at http://finds.org.uk/staffshoardsymposium. See also Leslie Webster, "Imagining Identities: The Case of the Staffordshire Hoard," in *Anglo-Saxon England and the Visual Imagination*, ed. John D. Niles, Stacy S. Klein, and Jonathan Wilcox (Tempe: Arizona Center for Medieval and Renaissance Studies, 2016), 25–48.

20. Basic articles on *Beowulf* and archaeology include Rosemary Cramp, "*Beowulf* and Archaeology," *Medieval Archaeology* 1 (1957): 57–77; Webster, "Archaeology and *Beowulf*"; Catherine M. Hills, "*Beowulf* and Archaeology," in *A "Beowulf" Handbook*, ed. Bjork and Niles, 291–310; John Hines, "*Beowulf* and Archaeology—Revisited," in *Aedificia Nova: Studies in Honor of Rosemary Cramp*, ed. Catherine E. Karkov and Helen Damico (Kalamazoo, MI: Medieval Institute Publications, 2008), 89–105. Brief surveys of current object-oriented ontologies relevant to medieval studies include Jeffrey Jerome Cohen, "Stories of Stone," *Postmedieval: A Journal of Medieval Cultural Studies* 1 (2010): 56–63; Graham Harman, "The Well-Wrought Broken Hammer: Object-Oriented Literary Criticism," *New Literary History* 43 (2012): 183–203; and Christopher Abram, "Kennings and Things: Towards an Object-Oriented Skaldic Poetics," in

The visual culture of the Anglo-Saxons with its complex ornamentation, elaborate frames, and formulaic motifs mirrors similar tendencies in their poetic art.[21] But Old English verse has its own rules, and its words for things obdurately refuse to be slotted into the archaeological record. Any number of pots, containers, storage jars, cups, pans, cauldrons, buckets, beakers, and bowls have been dug up from different Anglo-Saxon centuries and sites; Sutton Hoo Mound 1 alone provides twenty-eight vessels; the Taplow old churchyard barrow, nineteen; but none of these objects is certifiable as a *ful, wæge, orc, bune, fæt,* or any other cup in *Beowulf*.

The poet's images of swords and helmets, mailcoats and neck-rings are equally vague and blurred, a visual equivalent of the indeterminate schwa, a portrait produced by combining features from photographs taken at different times and places. Beowulf's precious necklace may have looked somewhat like the gold neck-rings from Olst, Netherlands, ca. 400,[22] or the very different great gold collar from Färjestaden, Öland, ca. 500, pictured in Klaeber's first edition.[23] Did the antediluvian sword-hilt gazed at by Hrothgar resemble the eighth-century silver-gilt grip and pommel from Fetter Lane, London, the intricate sword-hilt from Snartemo, Vest-Agder, Norway, ca. 500 (featured on the cover of *Klaeber 4*),[24] or the Chessel Down, Isle of Wight, composite sword-handle (ca. 500), an artifact connected to *Beowulf* as early as 1856, shortly after its discovery?[25] Matchmaking—inviting words and things to date

---

The Shape of Early English Poetry: Style, Form, History, ed. Irina Dumitrescu and Eric Weiskott (Kalamazoo, MI: Medieval Institute Publications, 2019), 161–88.

21. See Leslie Webster, "Encrypted Visions: Style and Sense in the Anglo-Saxon Minor Arts, A. D. 400–900," in *Anglo-Saxon Styles,* ed. Catherine E. Karkov and George Hardin Brown (Albany: State University of New York Press, 2003), 11–30; Leslie Webster, "Style: Influences, Chronology and Meaning," in *The Oxford Handbook of Anglo-Saxon Archaeology,* ed. Helena Hamerow, David A. Hinton, and Sally Crawford (Oxford: Oxford University Press, 2011), 460–500.

22. Pictured in Webster, "Archaeology and *Beowulf,*" fig. 19.

23. Frederick Klaeber, ed., *"Beowulf" and "The Fight at Finnsburg"* (Boston: D. C. Heath and Co., 1922), fig. 4.

24. On the ability of illustrations to both cut off and enact emotional responses to *Beowulf,* see Siân Echard, "Boom: Seeing *Beowulf* in Pictures and Print," in *Anglo-Saxon Culture and the Modern Imagination,* ed. David Clark and Nicholas Perkins (Cambridge: D. S. Brewer, 2010), 129–45.

25. John Hewitt briefly notes the find and its relevance to the poem in "Proceedings of the Meeting of the Archaeological Institute," *Archaeological Journal* 13 (1856): 188. On the practice in the mid-nineteenth century of coupling objects mentioned in *Beowulf* with those excavated from Anglo-Saxon cemeteries and fields, see Roberta Frank, "*Beowulf* and Sutton Hoo: The Odd Couple," in *Voyage to the Other World: The Legacy of Sutton Hoo,* ed. Calvin B. Kendall and Peter S. Wells (Minneapolis: University of Minnesota Press, 1992), 47–64, at 49–50. See, too, S. C. Hawkes and R. I. Page, "Swords and Runes in South-East England," *Antiquaries Journal* 47 (1967): 12.

one another—is fun but rarely ends in marriage. For poetry perpetuates: the aurochs or wild ox, long disappeared from Anglo-Saxon England, is still the name for the second rune of the futhorc in the late Old English *Runic Poem*.[26] The man who stole the dragon's *fæted wæge* [gold-plated vessel] got something precious and rare, a jar like nothing else in sixth-century Geatland, even though we have no idea what it looked like. The artifacts of *Beowulf* are virtual treasure, objects with a mission.

Mind the Gap

Nineteenth-century German scholars complained about *Beowulf*'s disconcerting *Sprünge* [leaps], its *Sprunghaftigkeit* [erratic jumps], its pitiless channel shifting.[27] Lewis Carroll's Alice commented on how oddly an Anglo-Saxon messenger progressed along a path, observing his strange contortions and "attitudes," his stop-and-go manner.[28] Objects migrating from person to person in *Beowulf* engage in similar vertigo-inducing jumps and spins. "Follow the money," a directive popularized by the 1976 film *All the President's Men,* is probably good advice for audiences of *Beowulf* too. Hrothgar rewards Beowulf with eight horses, one bearing a gem-studded royal Danish saddle (lines 1020–42), the most distinguished of trappings and confirmation of the recipient's high social worth. A thousand lines later, on his return home, Beowulf presents the horses to his king and queen: four to Hygelac (line 2163) and three to Hygd (line 2174). What has become of the eighth steed, the one with the regal trappings? The poet artfully forgets to say. By filling in the gap ourselves, we confirm the import of what is missing.

Beowulf has one big backstory, almost none of which is told in the poem. It is present as mysterious dark matter, sensed in part by the shadows cast by individual artifacts. The poet does the narrative equivalent of a striptease, alluding to an object in a way that hides or represses something important,

---

26. R. I. Page, *An Introduction to English Runes* (London: Methuen, 1973), 76.

27. Franz Joseph Mone, "Zur Kritik des Gedichts vom Beowulf," in *Untersuchungen zur Geschichte der teutschen Heldensage*, 2nd series of the Bibliothek der gesammten deutschen National-Literatur (Quedlinburg, 1836), 1:130; Alois Brandl, "Die angelsächsische Literatur," in *Grundriss der germanischen Philologie*, ed. Hermann Paul, 2nd ed. (Strassburg: Karl J. Trübner, 1901–9), pt. A, 2:1005. Issued separately with the same pagination under the title *Geschichte der angelsächsischen Literatur* (Strassburg: Karl J. Trübner, 1908). Klaeber famously used "Lack of Steady Advance" as a subtitle (3rd ed., Boston: D. C. Heath and Co., 1950), lvii. *Klaeber 4*, xcv, discusses the poet's convoluted storytelling under the heading "Non-Linear Narration."

28. Lewis Carroll, *Through the Looking-Glass, and What Alice Found There* (London: Macmillan, 1871), ch. 7.

while simultaneously drawing attention to it. Back in Geatland, Beowulf hands over to Hygelac the other precious artifacts he received from Hrothgar (lines 2152–54), in the order in which they were originally given (lines 1020–24). Before presenting the mailcoat, he pauses, announcing that the Danish king wanted him to say a few words about it. Beowulf then recites its genealogy in a *gid* [song, formal statement] a passage rich in alliteration and half-rhymes:

> Me ðis hildesceorp   Hroðgar sealde,
> snotra fengel;   sume worde het
> þæt ic his ærest ðe   est gesægde:
> cwæð þæt hyt hæfde   Hiorogar cyning,
> leod Scyldunga   lange hwile;
> no ðy ær suna sinum   syllan wolde,
> hwatum Heorowearde,   þeah he him hold wære,
> breostgewædu.   Bruc ealles well!
> (lines 2155–62)

Hrothgar, the wise prince, gave me this battle-shirt. He commanded that I should first tell you in certain words his good-will. He said that King Heorogar owned it, man of the Scyldings, for a long time. Not at all the sooner did he wish to give the breast-garment to his son, bold Heoroweard, although he was loyal to him. Enjoy all well.

The mailcoat, a Danish heirloom, had once belonged to Hrothgar's older brother and predecessor on the throne. The latter for some unstated reason did not give the armor to his own (and loyal) son Heoroweard. The history of the mailcoat stops here. Why is this family drama rehearsed? Why mention Heoroweard at all?[29] Is it because this prince's resentment at being skipped over, first by his father and now by Hrothgar, will bring the glory of Heorot to an end? (In Norse tradition, Heoroweard gets his own back, asserting his claim to the kingdom and attacking and killing his cousin Hrothulf, whose heroic last stand at Heorot/Lejre was widely celebrated in Saxo's Denmark.) Causal connections are never made. A key moment in the fall of the Scyldings is hinted at—and then repressed.[30] But the poet's partial allusion with its

---

29. Heoroweard is apparently forgettable still: he is the only cousin omitted from the genealogical chart in *Klaeber* 4, lii.

30. The standard early discussion of Scylding analogues is Axel Olrik, *Danmarks heltedigtning: En oldtidsstudie*. Vol. 1, *Rolf Krake og den ældre Skjoldungrække* (Copenhagen: G. E. C. Gad, 1903–19), translated and revised in collaboration with the author by Lee M. Hollander, *The Heroic Legends of Denmark* (New York: American-Scandinavian Foundation, 1919). Convenient

aching incompleteness (who is Heoroweard and why should we care?) draws the viewer, willy-nilly, into the memory game. Mail-coats, whether inherited or won as plunder, survive to stir up trouble. "Enjoy all well," says Beowulf to Hygelac, as he hands over the battle-gear. The imperative singular of OE *brucan* [to enjoy, make use of] carries ominous overtones in *Beowulf* (the only poem in which the form occurs). OE *bruc* [enjoy] is otherwise invoked only by Wealhtheow, first when she hints to her husband that it was time to do some estate planning (line 1177) and again when she gives Beowulf a neck-torque whose downward trajectory is quickly mapped (line 1216). When a character in *Beowulf* says "enjoy" in connection with an artifact, the wish seems seriously time-limited, and the health benefits of the object minimal. If the value of an object is measured in terms of its helpfulness to its owner, the "things" of *Beowulf* are underachievers.

The motive of revenge, of unending tribal conflict, controls the movements of other objects over two or more generations. Hrothgar will not achieve peace by marrying off his daughter to Ingeld (lines 2024–69). A plundered ancestral sword will see to that. When an old Heathobard with a long memory spots the heirloom in a Danish retainer's possession, all bets are off.[31] Five hundred lines later, it will be Wiglaf's own sword, stripped by his father from the Swedish prince he slew, that signals trouble down the line. The battle with the dragon has begun: Beowulf's blade has just failed; Wiglaf rushes to his side, wielding his sword for the first time. Suddenly all action stops. The narrator takes time out to discuss that heirloom's lineage (lines 2611–25). After stripping his opponent's corpse, Wiglaf's father brought the sword to the king of the Swedes, the slain prince's estranged uncle, who "did not speak of the feud" but promptly gave him the weapon as a reward. Years later, ownership descends to Wiglaf. The narrative insert now stops; the contest with the dragon resumes. But this fourteen-line interlude has opened a vista onto a grim past and grimmer future. Possession of the sword implicates Wiglaf: he

---

translations of the Scylding material can be found in *Klaeber* 4, 291–315, and in John D. Niles, ed., *"Beowulf" and Lejre* (Tempe: Arizona Center for Medieval and Renaissance Studies, 2007), 297–387. Marijane Osborn notes that three different occasions for the burning of Hrothulf's hall are available in the traditions, each taking place in a different generation ("Legends of Lejre, Home of Kings," in *"Beowulf" and Lejre*, ed. Niles, 252).

31. This is the same Ingeld (Hinieldus) named in the "pagan song" to which the Anglo-Saxon poet and scholar Alcuin objected in his much-cited letter of December 796 (Alcuin, "Epistola 81," in *Monumenta Alcuiniana*, ed. W. Wattenbach and Ernst Dümmler, Bibliotheca rerum Germanicarum 6 [Berlin: Weidmann, 1873], 357). See Mary Garrison, "Quid Hinieldus cum Christo?," in *Latin Learning and English Lore: Studies in Anglo-Saxon Literature for Michael Lapidge*, ed. Katherine O'Brien O'Keeffe and Andy Orchard (Toronto: University of Toronto Press, 2005), 2:237–59. On the Old Norse side, see Russell Poole, "Some Southern Perspectives on Starcatherus," *Viking and Medieval Scandinavia* 2 (2006): 141–66.

has inherited his father's guilt along with his weapon. After Beowulf's death, the trajectory of vengeance will touch Wiglaf. Each slaying, each atrocity generates the next. In *Beowulf*, the automaticity of revenge (called by W. H. Auden the earth's only perpetual motion machine) is figured by an artifact moving from hand to hand, a wrought object that can bring down a kingdom. Wiglaf's heirloom, an iron conduit of memory, will be a *damnosa hereditas*.

In an earlier passage, the *Beowulf* poet presents the adventures of a necklace in discreet mosaic-like pieces, nonchronologically, using flashbacks and flash-forwards that resemble the untidy, tangled workings of human memory. An object that outlives its owners is a useful poetic shorthand for time's passage, for the tenacity of the inhuman:

> Him wæs ful boren, ond freondlaþu
> wordum bewægned, ond wunden gold
> estum geeawed, earmreade twa,
> hrægl ond hringas, healsbeaga mæst   1195
> þara þe ic on foldan gefrægen hæbbe.
> Nænigne ic under swegle selran hyrde
> hordmaððum hæleþa syþðan Hama ætwæg
> to þære byrhtan byrig Brosinga mene,
> sigle ond sincfæt— searoniðas fleah   1200
> Eormenrices, geceas ecne ræd.
> Þone hring hæfde Higelac Geata,
> nefa Swertinges nyhstan siðe,
> siðþan he under segne sinc ealgode,
> wælreaf werede; hyne wyrd fornam   1205
> syþðan he for wlenco wean ahsode,
> fæhðe to Frysum. He þa frætwe wæg,
> eorclanstanas ofer yða ful,
> rice þeoden; he under rande gecranc.
> Gehwearf þa in Francna fæþm feorh cyninges,   1210
> breostgewædu, ond se beah somod.
> Wyrsan wigfrecan wæl reafeden
> æfter guðsceare; Geata leode
> hreawic heoldon.
> (lines 1192–1214a)

A flagon was brought to him and friendship extended in words, and wound gold presented with good will, two armlets, a mail-shirt, and rings, and the greatest of neck-collars that I have heard of on earth. I know under the heavens of no better hoard-gift of warriors, since Hama carried off to that bright fortress the necklace of the Brosings, gems and ornamental setting—he fled the treacheries of Eormenric, chose eternal counsel. Hygelac of the Geats, Swerting's nephew, had that ring on his last journey when he defended his booty under a banner, guarded the battle-spoils; fate took him after he for pride went looking for woe, a feud with Frisians. He wore that ornament, those gem-stones, over the cup of the waves, that powerful lord; he fell under his shield. The life of the king, then, his mail-coat, and that collar too, fell into the grasp of the Franks. Lowlier warriors looted the corpses after the war-mowing; the men of the Geats occupied a corpse-camp.

Beowulf gets a neck-ring, and at once the poet directs our gaze back, far back, to another necklace, that of Freyja in the Norse pantheon, a treasure out of the mythic past later stolen by Hama from Ermanaric, king of the Goths (d. 375). Then fast-forward to the future, to Beowulf's own lord, Hygelac, who will be wearing the gifted Danish torque when slain on a Frisian battlefield. All is lost, life and jewel together. But not so quick. A thousand lines later, we learn that Beowulf on his return to Geatland bestowed the famed gold necklace on Hygelac's queen (line 2172). Perhaps she subsequently gave this adornment to her husband, accessorizing him as he set off to raid the Frisian territory of the Franks. Two hundred lines later, a corrective spin: after Hygelac's fall in Frisia, Beowulf killed his slayer, retrieved the loot, necklace included, and headed home (lines 2354–62, 2503–6). Five hundred lines later, dying near his dragon, he unclasps a golden torque from his neck and gives it to Wiglaf, his relative and heir-apparent (line 2809). Is it the same necklace? "Enjoy," the Danish queen had said, some sixty years and 1,600 lines earlier (line 1216). After getting the best treasure he'd ever seen, young Beowulf must have felt that this was the beginning of the rest of his life, not, as things turned out, a premonition of the end.

Words and Things

The fifth- and sixth-century Scandinavian present of *Beowulf* intersects over a period of four centuries with the later Anglo-Saxon world that preserved the poem. Students of the poem are regularly assured that the objects in the dragon's collection provide "an image of Anglo-Saxon not prehistoric riches";[32] these artifacts "differ little from those of the possessions of Beowulf and his

---

32. Webster, "Archaeology and *Beowulf*," 194.

contemporaries in the surviving text, which would themselves have been archaic in the late tenth century when it was written down. So for Anglo-Saxons the past was, in a sense, the present."[33] "[The poet] makes no distinction between the antique artifacts unearthed from the dragon's hoard—the poem's most ancient event—and the trappings of warriors like Beowulf himself."[34] Helmet, byrnie, sword, armbands, and cups reflect the latest earthbound trends: "The poets were not dreaming up gilded visions but delineating the tastes of the world around [them]."[35] In Old English poetic descriptions, there is little attempt to draw a specific material context: "No local peculiarities can be distinguished in the way men fought their battles or drank their mead or in any of the practices which the poem depicts."[36] To some degree all such statements are just. Even in works deeply concerned with history, by poets who studiously avoid obvious anachronisms, a strong shade of "now-ness," of shared visual experience, is inevitable. Think pillow, bed, hearth, or glove in Elizabethan times. Old English poetic diction itself scorns visual specificity: it prizes vagueness and the metaphorical, refusing to treat size, altitude, material, weight, dampness, or hue as distinct entities.[37] In *Beowulf*, the external appearance of Hrunting and Naegling is irrelevant: what matters is that named swords failed at need. The poet uses the word *beag* to designate a circular ornament, whether finger-ring, arm-ring, neck-ring, collar, torque, or crown. Its essence, all that glinting and shimmering, is what counts, not its size or location or designer. Still, as the narrative of *Beowulf* progresses, history seems increasingly not just its backdrop but its subject;[38] the poet deploys material objects, one by one, to measure the pastness of a past that itself had depth. His sense of historic succession is so strong, the internal chronology of the poem so carefully worked out, that it would be odd if these artifacts

---

33. Webster, "Archaeology and *Beowulf*," 184.

34. Roy M. Liuzza, trans. and ed., *Beowulf: Second Edition* (Peterborough, ON: Broadview Press, 2013), Preface, 23; Roy M. Liuzza, *Beowulf: A New Verse Translation* (Peterborough, ON: Broadview Press, 2000), 26.

35. Charles R. Dodwell, *Anglo-Saxon Art: A New Perspective* (Manchester: Manchester University Press, 1982), 30.

36. Dorothy Whitelock, *The Audience of "Beowulf"* (Oxford: Clarendon Press, 1951), reprinted in Whitelock, *From Bede to Alfred: Studies in Early Anglo-Saxon Literature and History* (London: Variorum Reprints, 1980), 93.

37. For important insights into the lexis of Old English poetry, see Mark Griffith, "Old English Poetic Diction Not in Old English Verse or Prose—and the Curious Case of Aldhelm's Five Athletes," *Anglo-Saxon England* 43 (2014): 99–132, and the bibliographical references therein.

38. See Janet Thormann, "Enjoyment of Violence and Desire for History in *Beowulf*," in *The Postmodern "Beowulf": A Critical Casebook*, ed. Eileen A. Joy and Mary K. Ramsey (Morgantown: West Virginia University Press, 2006), 299–301.

themselves were not differentially aged, that he did not ask them to register a discontinuity, a rupture, between the poem's present—the material culture of fifth-century Scandinavia—and a many-storied long-ago. The notion that changing referents demand changing terms was not invented by the philologists of the Italian Renaissance.[39]

The poet's chronological tidiness is visible at gift-giving scenes in Heorot. Among the objects Beowulf receives from the Danish king are two *earmreade* [arm-ornaments] (line 1194); this compound occurs only here.[40] The skald Arnórr Þórðarson reporting Cnut's generosity to his hall companions uses the same term, *armhrauð* [arm-ornament]; this Old Norse compound never occurs again.[41] Gold arm-rings, preferably in pairs, were the archetypal reward for service in a royal court. Anything less (as numerous saga-anecdotes confirm) suggested that the marriage of skald/warrior and king was on the rocks. Did the *Beowulf* poet's term for arm-ring lend Danish coloration to Danish bracelets in a fifth-century Danish hall? Or did a later Icelandic skald choose the same word to showcase Cnut's multilingual empire? The use of a recondite compound for the arm-ornaments of Heorot suggests the patina of age, along with a touch of Danish modern. The poet may have been equally determined to distinguish his prehistoric artifacts—a goddess's necklace, an antediluvian hilt, a thousand-year-old cup—from those circulating in a fifth-century Danish hall. Whenever we look back at *Beowulf*, we find the poet looking back too, through a series of increasingly powerful long-distance glasses.

Prehistory required strong lenses and exotic vocabulary. The *Beowulf* poet highlights the ancient, mythical neck-ring of the Brosings (*Brosinga mene*) by using a recherché term: *mene* (line 1199) [necklace], a word that occurs in Old English poetry only in *Beowulf*, and elsewhere in the corpus mainly in

---

39. See Thomas M. Greene, "Anti-Hermeneutics: The Case of Shakespeare's Sonnet 129," in *Poetic Traditions of the English Renaissance*, ed. Maynard Mack and George de Forest Lord (New Haven, CT: Yale University Press, 1982), 151.

40. The compound *beahwriða* (line 2018), probably "bracelet," occurring (like *healsbeag*) only in *Beowulf*, refers similarly to circlets distributed in Heorot; *earmbeag* [arm-ring], in poetry restricted to *Beowulf* and identifying hoard-bracelets, occurs five more times in the corpus, as a gloss to Latin *armilla, armillum dextrale, dextrocherium,* and *bracchiale*. See *The Dictionary of Old English: A-H Online*, ed. Angus Cameron et al. (Toronto: Dictionary of Old English Project, 2016) (*DOE*); and *The Dictionary of Old English Corpus on the World Wide Web* (Toronto: Dictionary of Old English Project, 2009). Isidore of Seville, *The Etymologies* 19.31.15, notes that an armband (*armilla*) is to be worn by men.

41. The skaldic stanza in question has been edited by Diana Whaley in Kari Ellen Gade and Edith Marold, eds., *Poetry from Treatises on Poetics*, Skaldic Poetry of the Scandinavian Middle Ages 3 (Turnhout: Brepols, 2017), 4.

glosses to Latin *monile* [necklace] and *lunula* [little moon, ornament].[42] In Old Norse, the word *men* [necklace, torque] occurs widely in both eddic (10 times) and skaldic verse (ca. 45 times). One eddic poem names Freyja's *men Brísinga* three times; an early ekphrastic poem by the skald Þjóðólfr ór Hvini (ca. 900) refers to Loki as *girðiþjófr Brísings* [thief of Brísing's girdle] (perhaps referring to a neck-band, perhaps to some other cincture).[43] In addition to *mene* [necklace], the *Beowulf* poet calls this mysterious, prehistoric necklace a *sigle* (line 1200) [neck-ring, jewel], a simplex that in Old English poetry occurs only here (cf. Old Norse poetic *sigli*).[44] The foreignness and rarity of both terms combine to paint the goddess's ornament darker and more mysterious than the great Danish necklace bestowed on Beowulf.

Both *sigle* and *sincfæt* alliterate across the caesura with *searo-*, the "artful" or "crafty" hostilities that Hama flees. The same two words, *sigle* and *searo*, were linked a few lines earlier, when ancient Frisian plunder was described as *sigle searogimma* (line 1157) [neck-rings, artful jewels].[45] The compound *sincfæt*, normally "precious cup" in *Beowulf* and elsewhere, seems to be given another, more restricted sense in line 1200: "concave setting, precious container," allowing images of gem and vessel to begin to blend and fuse. The passage ends with Hygelac's fall in Frisia—the poem's keynote historical disaster—narrated in terms evoking a bejewelled vessel, a sea change into something rich and strange. The king

> ... þa frætwe wæg,
> eorclanstanas ofer yða ful,
> rice þeoden; he under rande gecranc.
> (lines 1207b–1209)

---

42. *Mene* (< Germanic **manjan*) has cognates in Old Saxon, Old High German, and Langobardic—as well as Greek, Celtic, Slavic, and Sanskrit. See Ferdinand Holthausen, *Altenglisches etymologisches Wörterbuch* (Heidelberg: Carl Winter Universitätsverlag, 1934); Jan de Vries, *Altnordisches etymologisches Wörterbuch*, 2nd rev. ed. (Leiden: Brill, 1962); Vladimir Orel, *Handbook of Germanic Etymology* (Leiden: Brill, 2003); Julius Pokorny, *Indogermanisches etymologisches Wörterbuch*, 2 vols. (Bern: Francke, 1948–69). Isidore of Seville, *Etymologies* 19.31.12, notes that the *monile* is a gift (*munus*) for a woman, if on occasion worn by boys and horses.

43. Margaret Clunies Ross, ed., "Haustlöng 9," in *Poetry*, ed. Gade and Marold, 3:444–45.

44. *Sigle* (like Old High German *sigilla* glossing Latin *lunula*) may be a borrowing from Latin *sigillum* [little images]; the etymology is uncertain. Lunulae, like *monilia*, are primarily female ornaments (Isidore, *Etymologies* 19.31.17).

45. The Old Norse cognate of Old English *searo-* is poetic *sörvi* [(stone) neck-ring]; *sörva-Gefn* [Freyja of the stone-necklace] is a skaldic woman-kenning. See Roberta Frank, "Onomastic Play in Kormákr's Verse: The Name Steingerðr," *Mediaeval Scandinavia* 3 (1970): 7–30.

... bore those ornaments, precious stones, over the cup of the waves, that powerful lord; he fell under the shield (-rim or -boss).

An unexpected metaphor for sea—"cup of the waves"—is prefaced by the gemstones of a fifth-century necklace and embraced by a circular shield.[46] The *Beowulf* poet leaves the external appearance of his objects vague; what matters is their interiority. Round, hollow things—a shimmering necklace, cup, and shield-rim or -boss; later a walled barrow—transmute the sorrow of history into the lineaments of aesthetic pleasure.

Digging Deep

Our world has many old living things: ancient lichens in Greenland, a seagrass meadow in the Balearic Islands, Antarctic mosses, a Palmer's oak in Riverside, California, and—oldest of all—Siberian actinobacteria buried in the permafrost of the Kolyma lowlands.[47] It contains remarkably ancient objects too: a stunning 40,000-year-old stone arm-ring newly unearthed from the Altai mountains of Siberia, deep in the Denisova Cave; a million-year-old Tanzanian hand-axe; a pair of 15,000-year-old sagebrush sandals from a cave in Oregon; a pair of 5,500-year-old leather shoes from a cave in Armenia; here, a 4,000-year-old dental bridge; there, a 4,000-year-old golden cup from Rillaton, Cornwall, sometimes used to illustrate the stolen hoard cup in *Beowulf*.[48]

George Eliot observed of poor Mr. Casaubon that "we all of us, grave or light, get our thoughts entangled in metaphors, and act fatally on the strength of them."[49] A ladder (the image sometimes used to "explain" evolution) misleadingly puts *homo sapiens* on the top rung.[50] Such orientation metaphors are not universal: Chinese and Japanese poets talk of ascending to the past, while British archaeologists still place—as on a chronicle page—the oldest period at

---

46. Skaldic sea-kennings include "necklace of the land" and "shield-rim of the land."

47. See Rachel Sussman, *The Oldest Living Things in the World* (Chicago: University of Chicago Press, 2014).

48. See *Beowulf: Translated*, ed. Niles, 150. (Swearer, Oliver, Osborn, *"Beowulf": A Likeness*, 83, illustrates the same line with the Jelling Cup from ca. 950, central Jutland, Denmark.) *Beowulf: Translated*, ed. Niles, 183, evokes the remaining barrow-cups of the poem with a gathering of chased and embossed Bronze Age gold bowls from Midskov, Funen, Denmark.

49. George Eliot, *Middlemarch: A Story of Provincial Life* (London: Blackwood & Sons, 1871), pt. 1, ch. 10, 32.

50. Cf. "We continually make errors inspired by unconscious allegiance to the ladder of progress, even when we explicitly deny such a superannuated view of life" (Stephen Jay Gould, *Wonderful Life: The Burgess Shale and the Nature of History* [New York: W. W. Norton, 1989], 35).

the top of time charts with more recent periods below: geological time envisaged as a river flowing to the sea of the present.[51] The direction "down" in the West is equated with going back in time; underground space is identified as the past, the storage basement of history. *Deopnes* [deepness] in the Old English lexicon refers to depth of meaning, the hidden profundity of a work (*DOE*, s.v.). In the works of medieval English historians such as William of Newburgh and Matthew Paris, a descent, as in *Beowulf*, will uncover the past, extracting accumulated knowledge and memory.[52]

In *Beowulf*, the most ancient artifacts come from the lowest strata, a reflex of the poet's archaeological imagination. Virgil (*Aeneid* 8.190) roots the monster Cacus, associated with primordial evils, deep in an underground cave. The golden sword-hilt that Beowulf retrieves from Grendel's subterranean mere has the longest memory of all the relics in the poem. For this wrought object displays a cryptic story of beginnings (fratricide, miscegenation) and endings (death by deluge);[53] it also records, probably in runic letters, the person for whom the sword was made. The hilt, fragmented and baleful, is brought up to the surface so as to expose history. It is *wreoþenhilt* [(perhaps) a hilt with twisted ornamentation] and *wyrmfah* (line 1699) [(perhaps) with serpentine adornments], compounds found nowhere else in the corpus. Its inscription is a protest against forgetting, a message scratched onto the wall of a condemned prisoner's cell. The pace of the poem slows to "reader-time" as Hrothgar studies and contemplates the artifact, as in a museum today visitors stare in wonder at a 4,000-year-old cuneiform fragment on which the story of the Flood has been incised. Gareth Hinds's graphic novel *Beowulf* depicts the hero's emergence from the mere. The sword-hilt is massive and, in a close-up, inscribed with cuneiform characters. Hinds has stripped away the expected insular/Viking decorative elements and presented instead what he later described as "extreme age, even primitivism."[54] Even in translation, some things in the poem just seem more ancient than others.

---

51. George Lakoff and Mark Johnson, *Metaphors We Live By*, 2nd ed. (Chicago: University of Chicago Press, 2003), ch. 4. See also Eve Sweetser, *From Etymology to Pragmatics: Metaphorical and Cultural Aspects of Semantic Structure* (Cambridge: Cambridge University Press, 1990), 7; Mary Thomas Crane, "Surface, Depth, and the Spatial Imaginary: A Cognitive Reading of *The Political Unconscious*," *Representations* 108 (2009): 76–97.

52. See Monika Otter, *Inventiones: Fiction and Referentiality in Twelfth-Century English Historical Writing* (Chapel Hill: University of North Carolina Press, 1996), especially ch. 3 "Underground Treasures," 93–128.

53. The passage has given explicators some difficulty: it may allude to the misbehavior of the giants before the deluge or to Cain's primal crime: see Dennis Cronan, "The Origin of Ancient Strife in *Beowulf*," *North-Western European Language Evolution* 31–32 (1997): 57–68.

54. Gareth Hinds, *Beowulf* (Cambridge, MA: Candlewick Press, 1999). Quoted from his e-mail (9 June 2009) to Siân Echard, "Boom," 143.

The final downward movement of *Beowulf* begins when the last survivor plants his nation's treasure in a deep barrow. This speaker's words for specific objects—for example, the sequence *fæt* (line 2256) [gold plate], *beadugrima* (line 2257) [war mask, helmet], *herepad* (line 2258) [battle-shirt, mailcoat]— are not found elsewhere in poetry or prose. In his grief, he pauses momentarily to single out a *fæted wæge* (line 2253) [plated cup], a *dryncfæt deore* (line 2254) [precious drinking vessel], an emblem of past conviviality. There is something about this flagon that, like Auden's cracked cup, "opens a lane to the land of the dead" (*As I Walked Out One Evening*, line 44). For it is the theft of this *fæted wæge* thirty lines later (line 2282) that sets the dragon guarding the hoard off on his killing spree. Old English *wæge* is a poetic word, archaic diction that we struggle to hear.[55] The past participle *fæted* [ornamented with (gold) plate] is cognate with Gothic *(ga)fetjan* [to adorn] and belongs to the poetic register. The plated cup itself, disinterred from a barrow in Geatland, is thus doubly backward-looking, evoking bedrock beginnings in a windswept northern landscape. The stoniness and depth of this megalithic barrow is emphasized by the poet and by recent *Beowulf* spin-offs, including Neil Gaiman's *The Graveyard Book*: "It's steps down," he said, "made of stone. And there's stone all above us."[56] Beowulf's dragon is at the coalface of things.

Precious cups are prominent among the barrow's treasures. When Wiglaf first enters its cavernous interior, he sees *fyrnmanna fatu* (line 2761) [vessels of ancient men], their ornaments tarnished and corroded. The extreme age of the vessels (deposited by the last survivor, protected by a curse, and then brooded over by a dragon for 300 years) is later emphasized; their adornments are completely eaten through by rust, as if they had lain in the earth a thousand years (line 3050). These cups, called *orcas* (lines 2760, 3047) and *bunan* (lines 2775, 3047), are present neither in fifth-/sixth-century Heorot nor in tenth-century Anglo-Saxon wills or inventories. Old English *orc* [cup] was an early loanword from Latin and Greek (*orca* [large earthenware vessel]), but it developed a darker cast in Old English: three different Latin words referring to heathen sacrificial bowls are glossed *orc* by three different early eleventh-century Anglo-Saxons. (Tolkien, who had a feel for such things, put his Orcs deep underground.)[57] The etymology of Old English *bune* [cup] is

---

55. *Wæge*, cognate with Old Saxon *wegi* [cup] and probably Old Norse *veig* [strong drink] occurs, compounded, four more times in *Beowulf*, referring on each occasion to a mead-filled goblet or bowl making the rounds in a late fifth- or early sixth-century Scandinavian hall. On *wæge* [flagon], see Roberta Frank, "Three 'Cups' and a Funeral in *Beowulf*," in *Latin Learning and English Lore*, ed. O'Brien O'Keefe and Orchard, 1:418.

56. Neil Gaiman, *The Graveyard Book* (HarperCollins e-books, 2008), ch. 2.

57. See Roberta Frank, "Old English *Orc* 'Cup, Goblet': A Latin Loanword with Attitude," in *Alfred the Wise: Studies in Honour of Janet Bately*, ed. Jane Roberts and Janet L. Nelson (Woodbridge, UK: Boydell & Brewer, 1997), 15–24.

uncertain. Its three gloss occurrences render Greek and Latin *carchesium*, originally a "drinking cup, libation vessel," but then, beginning with Virgil, a kind of ancient "sacrificial vessel."[58] The barrow's vessels are retrieved from the deepest level of the poet's many-storied long-ago. Wiglaf, by gathering into his arms a wealth of glittering *bunan* [goblets] and *orcas* [beakers], is embracing a prestigious past, an antiquity beyond and behind that of the poem's North.[59] After Beowulf's death, his people stare amazed at these cups, ancient receptacles brought up from the bowels of the earth only to be interred again. They remain and endure, despite the mutability to which they are subject.

One of the major surprises in store for the reader of *Beowulf* is the reinterment of the dragon's hoard in the final moments of the poem. Beowulf had asked only for a barrow on the headland, high, so that it might be visible to passing ships (lines 2802–8). An in-gathering of unpolished, old, and rusty objects was not on his wish list.[60] Much has been written about this "material" turn in the poem, the mourners' deposition of ancient gold with their leader's ashes, the metal of the treasure not melted on the pyre but surviving, entombed, into the living present. Depositing in the ground what had been wrested from it is emblematic of human mortality; just so, the lifeless Golden Bough brought as passport by Aeneas to the shades is not so much given to Proserpina as returned to her (*Aeneid* 6.136–48; 200–11). The poet consigns an outworn past to the earth, where it belongs and still lives, perhaps never to resurface.[61] A little earlier in the poem, Beowulf's approaching death was figured as the plundering of his soul's hoard (line 2402), life carried out of his body and then hidden from sight again. The Farrar, Straus, and Giroux cover for Heaney's translation offers a faceless mailed head, seen from the back and against a black background, signaling uncertainty, unknowability.[62] The burial

---

58. For details, see Frank, "Three 'Cups,'" 1:410–11.

59. Old English *ful(l)* [(filled) goblet, beaker], cognate with Old Norse *full* [toasting cup], is restricted in *Beowulf* to the ritual drinking vessels circulating in late fifth-century Heorot, an intimate part of aristocratic Danish court life; this cup-name disappears after the first third of the poem. It is associated in the poem with a specific setting, a mark of affiliation, like an institutional medallion or signet ring.

60. Cf. "Gold once out of the earth is no more due unto it" (Sir Thomas Browne, *Hydrotaphia, Urne-buriall, or, a Discourse of the Sepulchral Urnes Lately Found in Norfolk* [London: Brome, 1658], ch. 3). Theodoric, as recorded by Cassiodorus, *Variae* 4.34 (ca. 507/11), gave permission to remove gold from sepulchers that no longer had an owner: "It is not greedy to take away what its owner can never mourn the loss of."

61. "Perhaps" is inserted here because grave-robbing is still alive—and a livelihood—in many parts of the world. The *New York Times*, July 16, 2007, had as headline: "Tomb Robbing Makes Comeback in China." Since the 1980s, this practice has become an epidemic—and a pop culture phenomenon.

62. Seamus Heaney, trans., *Beowulf: A New Verse Translation* (New York: Farrar, Straus and Giroux, 2000).

mound itself, the final artifact glimpsed in the poem, inserts the memory of a vanished past into later times. The wall surrounding the barrow, "as worthy as the finest workmanship could devise" (lines 3161–62), is an image of loss fixed in art, to be gazed upon as one would view a beautifully wrought vase. Nicolai Grundtvig (1783–1872), the only prominent poet ever to edit *Beowulf,* gave the poem the title "Beowulf's Barrow," seeing the textual artifact as analogous to the hero's monumental tomb, both memorials built by human hand to traverse the sea of centuries.[63] In his last interview, Jacques Derrida, too, spoke of *survivance,* the poet's work that survives his death and exceeds him.[64]

•

Medieval Europeans had no sense of history, or so we're repeatedly told; they lived in a kind of cyclical agricultural present, lacking curiosity about old objects and their former users. The most recent history of archaeology is brisk when it reaches our period: "During the Middle Ages, interest in the material remains of the past was even more limited and transient than it had been in classical times, apart from the collection and preservation of holy relics."[65] Mary Carruthers, writing largely about post-Anglo-Saxon centuries, observes:

> Few features of medieval scholarship are so distinctive as an utter indifference to the pastness of the past, to its uniqueness and its integrity "on its own terms." . . . Ordinarily, medieval scholars show no apparent interest in archaeology or historical philology. . . . The sole relic of the ancients with which medieval scholars vigorously concerned themselves was written texts; this choice itself is interesting, for there were other artifacts of antiquity still readily visible.[66]

The poet of *Beowulf* focused his gaze on just such old objects, looking back at them with a lover's eye. His reconstruction of a northern heroic age in *gearda-*

---

63. For an English translation of Grundtvig's poem justifying the title, see Fred C. Robinson, "The Afterlife of Old English: A Brief History of Composition in Old English after the Close of the Anglo-Saxon Period," in *The Tomb of Beowulf and Other Essays on Old English* (Oxford: Blackwell, 1993), 301–3.

64. Jacques Derrida, *Apprendre à vivre enfin: Entretien avec Jean Birnbaum* (Paris: Galilée / Le monde, 2005), 26.

65. Bruce G. Trigger, *A History of Archaeological Thought,* 2nd ed. (Cambridge: Cambridge University Press, 2006), 52.

66. Mary J. Carruthers, *The Book of Memory: A Study of Memory in Medieval Culture* (Cambridge: Cambridge University Press, 1990), 193–94.

geās (line 1) [days of yore] puts onstage a series of glinting artifacts that strut about, rant, and fret over the past that they have been asked to perform, before running off, unbowed, behind the curtain. His characters "speak here and now with an authority that derives from having been . . . there and then."[67] The material past in *Beowulf* is not over and done, but a "down below" come to light.

Freud's private collection of over 2,000 antiquities was likely larger than the dragon's hoard. The painstaking work of the archaeologist's spade, the unpeeling of layer after layer of the past in order to reveal a deep, more primitive core, was for him akin to the nature of psychoanalysis. The *Beowulf* poet, digging down with carefully chosen words, achieved an analogous layering of "things," exposing a trove of long-forgotten objects and making them precious again.

---

67. Carlo Ginzburg, *Ecstasies: Deciphering the Witches' Sabbath*, trans. Raymond Rosenthal (London: Penguin, 1991), 307.

CHAPTER 3

Evidence of the Past in the Legend of the Seven Sleepers

NEIL CARTLIDGE

Medieval saints' legends typically locate themselves in an imagined past remote from the world of their intended consumers. The rhetorical force of such narratives generally derives from a contrast between an exemplary Then and the ordinary and unheroic Now: contrast between those ancient days in which Christians regularly went unflinchingly to martyrdom, and these latter days in which such spiritual excellence seems scarcely achievable. In the stark light of this contrast, history tends to be flattened out.[1] Although hagiography might be defined as a series of attempts at understanding the particular dispensations of Christianity within history as a whole—and so as a genre that is historically aware almost by definition—the more fiercely it insists on the urgency of finding a way of understanding Christianity's particular dispensations in the present moment, the more it would seem to insist on the essential Otherness or remoteness of the past itself. In this respect, it often seems to deny the past even the capacity for a temporal consciousness of its own, thus leaving relatively little space for any differentiating or relativizing perspectives on the locatedness of particular moments within the flow of time.

---

1. Cf. Alison Goddard Elliott, *Roads to Paradise: Reading the Lives of the Early Saints* (Hanover, NH: Brown University Press / University Press of New England, 1987), 2–6.

However, the legend of the Seven Sleepers apparently offers a significant departure from this pattern.[2] In this story, the representation of time is necessarily much more complex, because the miracle that gives it its distinctive shape essentially consists of a miraculous distortion of time. This tale concerns seven young Christians from the city of Ephesus (in Asia Minor) who attempt to escape religious persecution at the hands of the third-century Roman emperor Decius. Seeking refuge in a cave under a nearby mountain, they are effectively buried alive when Decius discovers their hiding place and orders that the entrance to the cave be walled up. Miraculously, though, God places them into a gentle sleep, and they remain asleep until the reign of the fifth-century emperor Theodosius II. By this time, Ephesus has long been a Christian city. Then by chance the cave is reopened, and soon afterward the Seven Sleepers wake up, each of them believing that only a single night has passed. They decide to send one of their number into Ephesus to buy provisions, where he is, of course, flabbergasted by what seems to him the sudden transformation of the city. When he tries to buy bread at a bakery, the bakers are puzzled by the archaic coins with which he tries to pay, and they accuse him of having found (and failed to report) a treasure trove. This in turn leads to his arrest and arraignment before the city authorities. Under interrogation, he eventually confesses his true identity. The citizens are initially incredulous—not surprisingly—but they allow the young man to prove his story by leading them into the cave, where they find unambiguous evidence that the seven young men have indeed slept since the reign of Decius. The emperor travels from Constantinople to Ephesus in order to meet them, but shortly after this, the Seven Sleepers suddenly and simultaneously expire.

---

2. On the legend of the Seven Sleepers generally, see John Koch, *Die Siebenschläferlegende, ihr Ursprung und ihre Verbreitung: Eine mythologisch-literaturgeschichtliche Studie* (Leipzig: Reissner, 1883); Michael Huber, *Die Wanderlegende von den Siebenschläfern: Eine literaturgeschichtliche Untersuchung* (Leipzig: Harrassowitz, 1910); Arthur Allgeier, "Untersuchungen zur syrischen Überlieferung der Siebenschläferlegende," *Oriens Christianus* n.s. 4–8 (1915–18); Paul Peeters, "Le texte original de la Passion des Sept Dormants," *Analecta Bollandiana* 41 (1923): 369–85; Ernest Honigmann, "Stephen of Ephesus (April 15, 448–Oct. 29, 451) and the Legend of the Seven Sleepers," in *Patristic Studies*, Studi e testi 173 (Vatican City: Biblioteca Apostolica Vaticana, 1953), 125–68; Louis Massignon, "Le culte liturgique et populaire des VII dormants martyrs d'Ephèse (Ahl Al-Kahf): Trait d'union Orient-Occident entre l'Islam et la Chrétienté," in *Opera Minora*, ed. Y. Moubarac (Beirut: Dar Al-Maaref, 1963), 3:119–80; Pieter W. van der Horst, "Pious Long-Sleepers in Greek, Jewish, and Christian Antiquity," in *Tradition, Transmission, and Transformation from Second Temple Literature through Judaism and Christianity in Late Antiquity: Proceedings of the Thirteenth International Symposium of the Orion Center for the Study of the Dead Sea Scrolls and Associated Literature, Jointly Sponsored by the Hebrew University Center for the Study of Christianity, 22–24 February, 2011*, ed. Menahem Kister, Hillel Newman, Michael Segal, and Ruth Clements (Leiden: Brill, 2015), 93–111.

The Sleepers are rescued from the hands of their persecutors in third-century Ephesus, in effect, only so that they can travel in time. What the legend essentially celebrates is this amazing journey in time—not their escape from the emperor Decius. Indeed, in a sense, they do not escape at all, for they still die young as a result of his persecution. From their own perspective, their lives are only a little longer, if at all, than they would have been had God not intervened. The effect of the miracle is not to bring about their rescue from martyrdom but to alter the terms in which their deaths might be understood—to make it possible to read the ideal of martyrdom in new ways. In particular, the miraculous reawakening of the Seven Sleepers was interpreted from at least the sixth century onward—and possibly right from the very beginning of their cult—as a demonstration of the truth of the doctrine of resurrection in the body on Judgment Day. Even in dying for their Christian beliefs, the seven young men are witness to the validity of Christian belief in eternal life. Indeed, in several versions of the story it is explicitly stated that God intended the miracle to be interpreted as an emphatic refutation of the heretical doubts about this doctrine that were expressed in various ways during the fifth century, particularly in the context of the so-called Origenist controversy.[3] The fact that God chooses to restore these seven young men to life just as they were in their own, true, original bodies is presented as confirmation of the doctrine that when God comes "to judge the quick and the dead . . . all men shall rise again with their bodies"[4] and that each of these bodies will be intact and continuous with its original substance. At the same time, the enduringly wide appeal of the legend clearly has much less to do with its perceived relevance to this one theological controversy than with its scope to support a much broader exemplarity. At the most basic level, the miracle of the Seven Sleepers is a compellingly dramatic demonstration of the absoluteness of God's power, which is here shown to extend even to those aspects of the structure of the universe that generally seem most fixed, such as time itself. The Seven Sleepers' experience shows that God can—if he chooses—make the past suddenly obtrude into the present and, conversely, make the present suddenly seem very contingent on the past, in such a way as to blur

---

3. On the Origenist controversy and its context, see Elizabeth A. Clark, *The Origenist Controversy: The Cultural Construction of an Early Christian Debate* (Princeton, NJ: Princeton University Press, 1992); Caroline Walker Bynum, *The Resurrection of the Body in Western Christianity, 200–1336* (New York: Columbia University Press, 1995), 86–94.

4. I am here citing the Athanasian Creed, according to its translation in the Anglican *Book of Common Prayer*, accessed June 2, 2020, https://www.churchofengland.org/prayer-and-worship/worship-texts-and-resources/book-common-prayer.

the very difference between past and present, and to reduce temporality itself to an apparently arbitrary construct entirely subject to his will.

Moreover, this is a story that gains extra impact from the way in which it seems to dramatize the very workings of hagiography—in effect, to develop what might be called a meta-hagiographical perspective. So, for example, it paradoxically casts the Seven Sleepers as witnesses to their own martyrdom. We see the strangeness and wonder of God's treatment of them to some extent through their own eyes, and they themselves become involved in the explanation and interpretation of the miracle they embody. Meanwhile, the fifth-century Ephesian community to which they travel through time is implicitly presented as a prototype of the medieval Christian communities whose only physical contact with martyr-saints was normally via relics of their dead bodies—only in this case the community is placed in the oddly privileged position of encountering some *bona fide* Christian martyrs, not just through their relics but as living, breathing human beings. In a very literal sense, the legend of the Seven Sleepers imagines a reanimation of history, by which the past is allowed to communicate directly with the present. At one level, this imagined reanimation seems to bypass the objects and symbols that generally passed in the Middle Ages as evidence for the historical existence of the ancient martyrs (in the sense that the Seven Sleepers communicate directly with the community of believers without any mediation by relics or any other kind of token): but at another level, it offers an explanation of precisely what it is—and how it is—that the physical evidence of the past is spiritually significant. The narrative itself becomes a conscious imitation or reenactment of the different kinds of authenticating processes that are an integral part of the construction of most hagiographical legends. In other words, it becomes an *inventio* in all the complex suggestiveness of this word as described by Monika Otter. As she points out, *inventio* is "a liturgical term [that] refers to the discovery of a saint's relics and to the feast commemorating that event," but also, "*inventiones* are brief narratives about such findings of relics."[5] Indeed, the legend of the Seven Sleepers seems to offer a particularly clear support for Otter's argument that *inventio* narratives are very revealing about medieval attitudes to narrative and to the past, in general:

> When they tell foundation stories that involve digging up a saint's relics, the dig—the search and descent to a "deeper level," the "opening up" of what lay "hidden"—says as much about the intellectual process of projecting a past,

---

5. Monika Otter, *Inventiones: Fiction and Referentiality in Twelfth-Century English Historical Writing* (Chapel Hill: University of North Carolina Press, 1996), 21.

a historical origin, as it does about the physical origin of the physical relics kept in the monastery.[6]

In this sense, the legend readily expresses what could be described as an "archaeological" mentality. At the same time, the story of the Seven Sleepers seems to lay bare some of the fundamental assumptions underlying the construction of hagiographical narratives only in order to problematize them in what seems like an unusually determined way. Much of the action of this particular narrative consists of a celebration of the incongruities created by God's upsetting of the usual temporal order—emphasizing the power implicit in such miracles, but also at least hinting at the absurdity of such divine capriciousness. Indeed, most versions of the legend of the Seven Sleepers seem to encourage the enjoyment of a certain amount of situation comedy—despite the apparent risk to the dignity of their saintly protagonists, or even to the very idea of miracle.

Variants of the legend of the Seven Sleepers are very widely current in medieval Christianity (and they also have an important place in Islamic tradition as well). There are versions in Greek, Syriac, Coptic, Armenian, Persian, and Arabic, as well as Latin; and the Latin versions in turn gave rise to an extensive tradition in the vernacular languages, including French, German, Italian, Spanish, Swedish, Irish, and English. One of the liveliest of these vernacular versions is a poem in thirteenth-century Anglo-French by a writer who refers to himself only as *Chardri*—which is presumably to be read as a creative inversion of the name *Richard*, although unfortunately we know nothing else about him.[7] Whoever he was, Chardri is one of the most self-possessed and accomplished of all thirteenth-century English writers, the author of another saint's life besides the Seven Sleepers (that is, the *Life of St. Josaphaz*, which is a thinly Christianized version of the Life of the Buddha) and also of a debate-poem called *The Little Debate* (*Le Petit Plet*), which is (despite its name) quite a substantial text, at nearly 1,800 lines long. However, Chardri continues to be relatively little known even among specialists in the literary culture of medieval England, despite the fact that all three of the poems ascribed to him survive in the same manuscripts as two of the most

---

6. Otter, *Inventiones*, 4.

7. John Koch, ed., *Chardry's Josaphaz, Set Dormanz und Petit Plet: Dichtungen in der Anglo-Normannischen Mundart des XIII. Jahrhunderts* (Heilbronn: Henninger, 1879); Brian S. Merrilees, ed., *La vie des set dormanz by Chardri*, Anglo-Norman Text Society 35 (London: Westfield College / Anglo-Norman Text Society, 1977); Neil Cartlidge, trans. and ed., *The Works of Chardri: Three Poems in the French of Thirteenth-Century England; "The Little Debate," "The Life of the Seven Sleepers," and "The Life of St Josaphaz"* (Tempe: Arizona Center for Medieval and Renaissance Studies, 2015).

significant and substantial literary works written in English during the thirteenth century: *The Owl and the Nightingale* and Laʒamon's *Brut*.[8] Chardri's treatment of the Seven Sleepers is relatively free, and, although it is generally assumed that he based his poem on one of the so-called "vulgate" Latin versions of the legend, a text known to scholarship as L_1,[9] he nevertheless adds so much to this text that, as Brian Merrilees put it, "at no point, except perhaps for individual lines, can [Chardri's version] be considered a translation."[10] L_1 is also the basis for the "longer" of the two Old English versions of the Legend found among Ælfric's *Lives of the Saints*—although this text is now generally thought to be by someone other than Ælfric;[11] and it too is a relatively unconstrained treatment of the text—"a free elaboration of [the] source material," as its editor Hugh Magennis puts it, "carried out with skill and confidence" in such a way as to produce "one of the most attractive and impressive of all Old English saints' lives."[12]

In this essay, I am going to focus on these two particular versions of the legend of the Seven Sleepers and on their common source in L_1. Specifically, I will argue that this legend accommodates an "archaeological" consciousness in several specific ways: first, in the depiction of attitudes to, and knowledge of, ancient coinage; second, in the treatment of the theme of treasure trove and of treasure, more generally; and third, in its use of (rather museum-like) notices and inscriptions in order to label the Sleepers' cave and authenticate the passage of time.

---

8. Chardri's works are found in both of the extant manuscripts of *The Owl and the Nightingale*, Jesus College, Oxford, MS 29 (part 2) and London, British Library MS Cotton Caligula A.9. The Cotton Caligula MS also contains one of the only two extant copies of Laʒamon's *Brut* (the other being the fire-damaged BL MS Otho C.13). Chardri's work survives elsewhere only in Rome, Vatican Library MS Reg. lat. 1659 (part 2), which contains only the *Little Debate* (not the saints' lives).

9. L_1 = Michael Huber, ed., "Passio Septem Dormientium," in *Beitrag zur Visionsliteratur und Siebenschläferlegende des Mittelalters: Eine literargeschichtliche Untersuchung; I. Teil: Texte*, Beilage zum Jahresbericht des humanistischen Gymnasiums Metten (1902–3): 39–78; this is based on a Munich MS. For a text based on two MSS closer to the Old English, see Hugh Magennis, ed., *The Anonymous Old English Legend of the Seven Sleepers*, Durham Medieval Texts 7 (Durham: Department of English Studies, 1994), 74–91.

10. Merrilees, *Set Dormanz*, 5.

11. Ælfric of Eynsham, *Catholic Homilies* II, XXVII, vv. 222–23, in *Ælfric's Catholic Homilies: The Second Series, Text*, ed. Malcolm Godden, EETS s.s. 5 (London: Oxford University Press, 1979), 247–48 (summary version). The longer version (of unknown authorship) is in W. W. Skeat, ed., *Ælfric's Lives of Saints*. 1881 (Reprint, London: Oxford University Press, 1966): 1:488–541, originally published in EETS 76, 82, 94, 114 (London: Trübner & Co., 1881–1900). It has been more recently edited in Magennis, *Seven Sleepers*. Magennis does not provide a translation of the Old English text, so the translations printed below are my own.

12. Hugh Magennis, "Style and Method in the Old English Version of the Legend of the Seven Sleepers," *English Studies* 66 (1985): 287.

Coinage becomes an issue in the story when one of the Seven Sleepers attempts to buy some bread in the morning after their long sleep. In all three of the versions I have mentioned, this particular Sleeper is called "Malchus." According to Chardri, the silver coins that Malchus takes with him into the city are "blancs" [white]—so new, that is, that they are still bright and untarnished.[13] But, of course, they are only new from Malchus's own perspective: from the point of view of the bakers they are incontrovertibly old—minted long ago and stamped accordingly. The very "whiteness" of these "old" silver coins is itself a kind of archaeological anomaly, which in turn points to the disruption of time created by the miracle that Malchus now inhabits. Chardri also emphasizes that such anomalies are readily evident to the fifth-century citizens of Ephesus because they are numismatically literate—capable, that is, of an informed and inquisitive approach to the origins of coinage. When Malchus throws his money onto the counter at the baker's shop, we see the baker picking them up and carefully examining them:

"E Deu," fet il, "quel argent ci a?
Mut est ore de autre pris
Ke nus n'usum en cest païs."
Cil le mustra a sun veisin
Ke mut s'esmervilla sanz fin,
Car unkes itel munee
Ne fu veu en lur cuntree.
Mut i musent de tutes parz
E les sages e les musarz
E dient ben: "Por verité,
Cist vaslet ad tresor truvé."
(*Set Dormanz*, lines 1146–56)

"God," he said, "what kind of money is this? It's money of a very different stamp from what we use in this country." The baker showed it to his neighbor, who marveled at it endlessly, since they had never seen money like that in their land. On every side people were discussing it, both the clever and the slow-witted, and they all agreed, "The truth is that this lad has found a treasure-trove."

In the Old English text, the scene is also vividly realized:

---

13. Merrilees, *Set Dormanz*, line 990.

And hi þa cypemen swiþe georne þa penegas sceawodon, and hi swilces feos fregnðearle wundredon; and hi þa penegas þær to wæfersyne beheoldon, and fram bence to bence heom betweonan ræhton, and to sceawigenne eowodon, and heom betweonan cwædon, "Butan tweon hit is soð þæt we ealle her geseoð, þæt þæs uncuþa geonga cniht swiðe ealdne goldhord wel gefyrn funde, and hine nu manega gear dearnunga beyhdde."[14]

Then the traders eagerly looked at the coins and were absolutely amazed at such money, gazing at the coins there as if they were some kind of spectacle; and they passed them between them from bench to bench, running up to look at them; and they said among themselves, "Doubtless it's true what we all see here, that this young man, this stranger, found an ancient treasure long ago and has secretly concealed it for many years."

Although these two vernacular versions of the legend both add substantially to the Latin, what they add is very much in the spirit of the source, where the treatment of the bakers' reaction to seeing this money is already markedly dramatic:

Ipsi uero considerauerunt argenteos et mirati sunt, et unus ad alterum in sedilibus uendentium panes argenteos ostendebant alterutris, et dicebant ad seipsos, "Iste iuuenis thesaurum inuenit occultatum plurimis annis."

They examined the money and were astonished, and one showed the money to another at the benches of the bread sellers, and they said among themselves, "This young man has found a treasure hidden for many years."[15]

The rather nonsensical suggestion in the Old English text that "the young man" has been hiding the treasure for many years is probably the result of a mistranslation of the Latin (the Old English apparently taking the suggestion in the Latin that the treasure had been hidden for many years to mean that it had been hidden for many years by the "young man"), but in general, both of the vernacular texts follow the Latin closely in their emphasis on the amazement that is created by the coins themselves. This might seem like a strangely limited or mundane way of illustrating the miracle of the Seven Sleepers' travel through time, but then again it ought not to be in any way surprising that money should function here as a means of marking the passing of time—

---

14. Magennis, *Seven Sleepers*, 49–50.
15. Magennis, *Seven Sleepers*, 84–86.

between the third century, that is, when Malchus's money was new, and the fifth century when it turned into items of curiosity—if only because coins can be seen not just as functional artifacts but also as historical documents on a small scale.

In all three of these versions of the legend, the extent of Malchus's dislocation from his own time is revealed, made measurable, and in effect calibrated by the inscriptions on the coins. In the Latin, it is simply said that the Ephesians notice that the superscription of the coins is more than 372 years old.[16] In the French, this observation is made much more explicit—and much more dramatic:

> E nus truvum en l'escrit
> De l'enprente ke ben nus dit
> K'el tens Decie l'emperur,
> Quant il primes fu seinnur,
> Fist forger icest dener.
> Mauveis truant pautener,
> Treis cenz anz sunt ja passez
> E seissante dous e plus assez
> Pus cel tens ke ceo esteit,
> Ceo dit chescun ke le dener veit.
> (*Set Dormanz*, lines 1377–86)

We've noticed that the stamped inscription clearly says this coin was minted in the time of the Emperor Decius, at the beginning of his reign. You wicked, good-for-nothing rogue, more than 362 years[17] have passed since those days—that's the opinion of everyone who's looked at the coin.[18]

In the Old English, meanwhile, the attention given to Malchus's coins gives rise to an elaborate and not entirely coherent account of the different issues of coinage in the emperor Decius's reign. This has been of particular interest to Anglo-Saxonists because of the relative richness and precision of its numis-

---

16. "Ecce enim superscriptio argenteorum plus quam CCCLXX duos annos habet" (Magennis, *Seven Sleepers*, 88–89).

17. On the different figures (362 in Chardri, vs. 372 in L_1), see Merrilees, *Set Dormanz*, 4.

18. Cf. "Her mæg geseon ælc man þe telcræftas ænig gescead can, and þisra peninga ofergewrit her eallum mannum openlice þæt swutelað, þæt hit mare is for an þonne þreo hund geara and twa and hundseofontig wintra syððan ðyllic feoh wæs farende on eorðan" (Magennis, *Seven Sleepers*, 53) [Here can anyone who has any understanding of arithmetic see what the inscription on these pennies openly reveals, that it is more than 372 years since this money was current on earth].

matic vocabulary.[19] However, what clearly comes across in each case is the assumption that everybody in the community, and not just its merchants and record-keepers, is prepared to take what seems like an almost connoisseurial interest in coins as informative objects, and not just as pieces of bullion. This is by no means implausible—after all, it is the information stamped on the coins that provides the most obvious guarantee of their bullion value, and medieval people had to be numismatically aware, if only because the relationship between different types of coinage tended to be much less standardized than they are today. As Joel Kaye points out, "We live in a world of single, relatively stable, national currencies. When these and similar standardizations are not present, the task of simply staying on top of accounts requires intense concentration."[20] In effect, what all three texts invoke at this point is precisely this "intense concentration"—the critical rigor, that is, that medieval people might have expected to be brought to the handling of different kinds of coinage. In the context of the tale, this curiosity about coinage becomes a kind of metonym for the very idea of a scientific attitude to the past. In effect, coinage becomes a standard of measurement that enables the fifth-century inhabitants of Ephesus to quantify the distance in time that Malchus has traveled to get to them. Just as modern archaeologists often use coins as a relatively precise means of dating the objects with which they are found, so too the Ephesian community is shown to use coins as a means of dating Malchus himself.

Another distinctly "archaeological" dimension to the legend of the Seven Sleepers is to be found in its reference to the laws on treasure trove. Before the fifth-century Ephesians reach the point of recognizing that the coins actually belong to Malchus, they naturally assume that the ancient coins are much older than he is, and they jump to the logical conclusion that Malchus has discovered an ancient hoard. As the bakers tell Malchus in Chardri's version:

"Car vus avez tresor truvé
E si serrez leres pruvé,

---

19. On the Old English text's suggestion that Decius released several different coinages, and the significance of its vocabulary to the history of the language, see Dorothy Whitelock, "The Numismatic Interest of the Old English Version of the Legend of the Seven Sleepers," in *Anglo-Saxon Coins: Studies Presented to F. M. Stenton*, ed. R. H. M. Dolley (London: Methuen, 1961), 188–94, reprinted in Whitelock, *History, Law and Literature in 10th–11th Century England* (London: Variorum, 1981), 188–94. See also Catherine R. E. Cubitt, "'As the Lawbook Teaches': Reeves, Lawbooks and Urban Life in the Anonymous Old English Legend of the Seven Sleepers," *English Historical Review* 124 (2009): 1025–27.

20. Joel Kaye, "Monetary and Market Consciousness in Thirteenth and Fourteenth Century Europe," in *Ancient and Medieval Economic Ideas and Concepts of Social Justice*, ed. S. Todd Lowry and Barry Gordan (Leiden: Brill, 1998), 374.

Si vus ne fetes ceo ke dirrum.
L'aver od vus cuncelerum,
Si vus nus dites en priveté
U vus avez cest tresor truvé.
Car ceo est ancienne munee
Ke vus nus avez ici dunee.
Le tresor nus mustrez par tens;
De ceo frez vus," funt il, "granz sens."
(*Set Dormanz*, lines 1199–1208)

"You've found some treasure, and you'll be exposed as a thief if you don't do what we say. We'll cooperate with you in hiding the hoard, as long as you tell us, in secret, where you found it—for these are antique coins that you've just given us. Show us the treasure straightaway," they said, "if you know what's good for you!"

When Malchus continues to deny all knowledge of this "tresor truvé," they haul him before the city's viscount ("viscunte"), who readily accepts the bakers' interpretation of the situation:

"Vaslet," fet il, "ben est prove
Ke tu as grant tresor truvé,
Car en tun poin fu l'argent pris,
E de ceo as tu mut espris
Ke ne venistes avant a mei
Pur mustrer le tresor le rei. . . .
Jeo te frai malement descumfire:
Ne dormiras pas en plume mole,
Mes girras enz mut orde geole
Deske recunussez la verur
Del tresor Decie l'emperur."
(*Set Dormanz*, lines 1305–10, 1403–8)

"Young man," [the viscount] said, "it's clearly proven that you've found some great treasure by the fact that you were caught with this money in your hands; and, in this, you've committed a serious fault: you didn't come to me before in order to report the treasure to the king. . . . If you don't tell me about the treasure, I'll make sure you're cruelly discomfited. You won't be sleeping on soft feathers: you'll be lying in a filthy gaol until you admit the truth about the emperor Decius's treasure."

In the Old English, the traders likewise offer to cooperate with Malchus in concealing the hoard,[21] and then take him to the city's "portgerefa" [port-reeve], who, like Chardri's viscount, insists on his legal authority to investigate cases of undeclared treasure trove:

> Ic gedo þæt man sceall þe wel fæste gewriðan, ægðer ge hande ge fet, and þe, eall swa seo domboc be swilcum mannum tæcð, oft and gelome swingan and to ealre sorge tucigan: þonne scealt þu þines unþances þone hord ameldian þe þu sylfwilles ær noldast cyðan.[22]

> I will command you to be bound very tightly, both hand and foot, and—just as the law-book teaches in relation to such men—to be whipped frequently and tormented with every kind of pain: then, like it or not, you will reveal the hoard, even though you would not do so of your own will.[23]

As far as I know, Chardri's treatment of the treasure trove motif has attracted no scholarly comment: by contrast, interpreters of the Old English text have suggested that it provides valuable evidence for the particular nature of Anglo-Saxon attitudes to the law. Dorothy Whitelock, for example, suggests that the text's references to Malchus's treasure trove should be taken as an indication that even as early as the tenth century "the secret possession of ancient treasure" was recognized as an offence under English law. She regretfully admits that

> since the account of the accusation brought against the possessor of ancient coins is taken over from the Latin source, it cannot be regarded as safe evidence for the attitude in Anglo-Saxon England to the finding of buried

---

21. [The Bakers:] "þu þe þus eald feoh gemettest and þus ealde penegas hider brohtest, þe on gefyrndagum geslægene wæron on yldrena timan. Sege us nu þæt soð buton ælcon lease, and we beoð þine geholan and ealne wæg þine midsprecan. Ne we nellað þe ameldian, ac hit eall stille lætan, þæt hit nan man ne þearf geaxian buton us sylfum" (Magennis, *Seven Sleepers*, 50) [You have come across some old money and brought the old coins here, which were struck long ago in the time of our ancestors. Admit this to us, truly without any lies, and we will be your accomplices and speak wholly on your behalf. We don't want to report you: we'd rather keep quiet about it, so that nobody needs to find out about it apart from us]. Cf. L_1: "Nuntia nobis, et erimus communes tecum et cooperiemus te" (Magennis, *Seven Sleepers*, 86–87) [Tell us, and we will be in league with you and will conceal you].

22. Magennis, *Seven Sleepers*, 54.

23. Cf. L_1 (where the official is identified as a "proconsul"): "Pro hoc te abrenuntio nunc, et uinctum manibus et pedibus tradam te legibus, usquequo confitearis inuentum quod inuenisti" (Magennis, *Seven Sleepers*, 88–89) [Therefore I denounce you now and will bring you bound hand and foot to the courts, until you confess the find which you have made].

treasures. Yet one would have expected the translator to have offered some comment or words of explanation to his readers if this attitude had not seemed to him perfectly natural.[24]

More recently, Catherine Cubitt and Hugh Magennis have argued that the rather legalistic language used by the city officials in the course of their attempts to browbeat Malchus into admitting the source of his coins can be read as evidence for "pragmatic literacy among town officials in Anglo-Saxon England."[25] This whole approach seems to me too narrowly focused. The fact is that the treasure trove theme is a constant feature of the legend, right from the earliest versions, including Jacob of Sarug and Gregory of Tours, right through to Chardri, *The Golden Legend,* and beyond. It is no more (or less) indicative of Anglo-Saxon attitudes to law or legality than of late-antique or late-medieval ones. Indeed, the principle that finders of hidden treasure should expect to share the proceeds of the find with the owner of the land was firmly established in Roman law. In the second-century *Institutes of Gaius,* it is stated:

> Thesauros, quos quis in suo loco invenerit, divus Hadrianus naturalem aequitatem secutus ei concessit qui invenerit. idemque statuit, si quis in sacro aut in religioso loco fortuito casu invenerit. at si quis in alieno loco non data ad hoc opera, sed fortuitu invenerit, dimidium domino soli concessit. et convenienter, si quis in Caesaris loco invenerit, dimidium inventoris, dimidium Caesaris esse statuit. cui conveniens est, ut, si quis in publico loco vel fiscali invenerit, dimidium ipsius esse, dimidium fisci vel civitatis.

> Divine Hadrian, in accordance with natural justice, granted to the finder any treasure trove discovered on his own property; and he decreed that the same should apply in the case of anyone fortuitously discovering treasure in a holy or religious place. But if anyone finds something on land he does not own, half of it should be granted to the owner of the land (so long as the discovery was by chance rather than by deliberately searching). And correspondingly, if anyone finds something on imperial property, then Hadrian granted half of it to the finder, and half to the emperor. Correspondingly also, if anyone finds something on land owned by the community or by the state-treasury,

---

24. Whitelock, "Numismatic Interest," 188.
25. Cubitt, "As the Lawbook Teaches," especially 1028–34; Hugh Magennis, "Crowd Control? Depictions of the Many in Anglo-Saxon Literature, with Particular Reference to the Old English Legend of the Seven Sleepers," *English Studies* 93 (2012): 125.

then half goes to the finder, and the other half to the community or to the state-treasury.[26]

The principle expressed here was further refined in the *Digest* of the Emperor Justinian,[27] which in fact postdates the earliest versions of the legend, but which emerges from much the same cultural world, the Eastern Roman Empire of the fifth/sixth centuries. The *Institutes* and the *Digest* probably follow quite closely the legal assumptions that would have been made in Ephesus at this period—and it is in Ephesus that the story is set, not in England, as both Chardri and the author of the Old English version are clearly well aware. From this point of view, it is hardly necessary to assume that either of them would have felt obliged to mark any difference between their understanding of the law and that of the ancient Ephesians, even if any such difference existed.

In any case, the argument that the treasure should be shared is clearly one that suits the people making it. That Malchus is accused of taking a treasure trove only shows that this was a tactic people might have employed, not that they necessarily had a solid legal case, or that they would have been supported by anything they could have found in any English lawbook. It certainly seems very likely that the Roman law interpretation of treasure trove had already percolated into English popular consciousness by the time that the Old English text was written, and in the course of the twelfth century, it was explicitly incorporated into English written law,[28] but it was perhaps to some extent *because* of the influence of the legend of the Seven Sleepers that such ideas had become familiar in the first place. In other words, it makes much more sense to see the legend's representation of treasure trove more as a potential influence *on* English law than as a reflection of any distinctively Anglo-Saxon concern with the legal issues raised by the discovery of buried treasure.

In all the versions of the legend, such treasure is implicitly a symbol of the saints themselves—saints being both precious to God but also typically embodied in medieval culture in the form of shrines resplendent with gold and jewels. However, this is a symbolism that Chardri seems to exploit partic-

---

26. *Institutiones*, 2.1.39. Quoted from *Institutiones*, ed. Paulus Krueger, in *Corpus Iuris Civilis: Editio stereotypa*, 13th ed. (Berlin: Weidmann, 1920), 1:12 (my translation).

27. *Digesta*, 41.1.63. See *Digesta*, ed. Theodorus Mommsen, rev. Paulus Krueger, in *Corpus Iuris Civilis*, 1:696–97, and Alan Watson, trans., *The Digest of Justinian*, rev. ed. (Philadelphia: University of Pennsylvania Press, 1988), 4:14–15.

28. See Cecil S. Emden, "The Law of Treasure-Trove, Past and Present," *Numismatic Chronicle and Journal of the Royal Numismatic Society* 9 (1929): 85–105; George Francis Hill, *Treasure Trove in Law and Practice, from the Earliest Time to the Present Day* (Oxford: Clarendon, 1936); Joel Roache, "Treasure Trove in *The Pardoner's Tale*," *Journal of English and Germanic Philology* 64 (1965): 1–6.

ularly determinedly, and indeed "treasure" could be seen as one of the themes that distinctively recur in his work. For example, in his other extant saint's life (*La vie de seint Josaphaz*), Christianity itself is at one point explicitly figured as "treasure so valuable that it's worth more than silver or gold,"[29] and in both of his saints' lives, he gives extended consideration to the idea of idol worship, which he represents as a kind of foolish misunderstanding of the very meaning of treasure in the context of religion. He has one of the Seven Sleepers defiantly explain to their persecutor Decius that it is because of their bullion value that pagan idols are transient things, whereas the intangible "treasure" of Christianity will last forever:

> L'or ki ore i est cloufiché
> De tenailles ert araché,
> De marteaus le frunt depecerunt
> De tun deu ke l'or aurunt;
> E ceo serra mut grant hunte,
> Car de lui ne tendrunt plus cunte.
> Nostre tresor ne poet embler
> Nul ki sache tant enginner,
> Car en teu cel l'avum ja mis
> U nul ne poet estre mendis.
> (*Set Dormanz*, lines 405–14)

Those who want to take the gold of your gods will smash their faces with hammers. And that will be a very great shame, for people won't care about them anymore. No one can take away our treasure, no matter what they might contrive, for we've placed it in heaven, where no one can be a beggar.

At the end of his poem, Chardri shows us the Christian emperor Theodosius collecting up all of his treasure in order to do honor to the relics of the seven saints, but they then appear to him in a dream, demanding to be returned to the cave, but also warning him against trying to honor them in this way (*Set Dormanz*, lines 1761–80). This develops a suggestion made in the Latin,[30] but it

---

29. "Si riche tresor / Ki meuz vaut k'argent u or! / C'est une pere mervilluse / Unc mes n'oi si preciuse," Chardri, *Vie de seint Josaphaz* in Koch, *Dichtungen*, lines 759–62.
30. Cf. L_1: "Et in ipsa nocte apparuerunt sancti imperatori, et dixerunt ei, 'Ex terra surreximus, neque ex auro neque ex argento. Et nunc dimitte nos unde surreximus'" (Magennis, *Seven Sleepers*, 90–91) [Then on the same night the saints appeared to the emperor and said to him, "We have risen from the earth, not from (*better*: not on account of) gold or silver. Now release us to the place from which we arose."]

also seems to be consonant with Chardri's characteristic interest in the meaning and proper use of treasure. As requested, the emperor does return the bodies of the saints to their cave, but Chardri (and only Chardri) adds that he nevertheless decorates it in considerable splendor, "fu trestut envirun doree" (line 1792) [(gilding) it all over] and enclosing it "pas clos de fust en bois, / Mes fu de marbre e de liois" (lines 1793–94) [not with beams of wood, but with marble and limestone]—which seems like a rather obvious contradiction of the saints' expressed indifference to material wealth. But this is typical of the pervasive tension within Chardri's work between a rather austere unworldliness that denies value to material things, on the one hand, and, on the other, a rather refined sensitivity to beautiful and valuable objects for their own sake. It is not a tension that Chardri ever resolves explicitly himself, but it is perhaps implicit that the objects in the world are only beautiful or valuable to the extent that God's grace makes them meaningful.[31]

There is a third respect in which the legend's "archaeological consciousness" manifests itself. When the Seven Sleepers are walled into their cave, the cave is provided with a kind of notice or inscription labeling it as the site of Decius's attempt at murdering the seven young men, because it so happened that there were two Christians present when Decius ordered the cave to be walled in—and these two decided to make a record of events for future generations. As Chardri explains:

> Cil unt escrit en plum lur vie,
> L'utrage e la desverie
> Ke l'emperur lur aveit fet.
> Tut sanz noise e tut sanz plet
> Cucherent le plum el mur,
> Si k'il furent mut asseur
> Ke jamés ne porrireit,
> Tant cum il ilokes girreit.
> Mut le firent cointement
> Ke nul ne l'aperçut de la gent.
> Custume esteit as anciens
> Ke vesquirent en icel tens
> D'escrivre enz en plum l'estoire;
> Kar plum ja ne porrira
> Tant cum en en sec liu girra.
> (*Set Dormanz*, lines 783–98)

---

31. On these points, see further Cartlidge, *Works of Chardri*, 14–18.

Using lead, these men wrote down the lives of the seven: the cruelty and fury directed against them by the emperor. Without any noise or fuss they set the lead in the wall in such a way as to be sure that, as long as it stood there, it would never wear away. They did it so cleverly that none of the people saw it. It was customary among the ancients who lived in that time to write the history of anything that they wished to remember on lead, for lead will never decay, as long as it lies in a dry place.[32]

It is this notice/inscription that later provides validation of the story that Malchus tells the fifth-century Ephesians; and it could be argued that the activity of these two Christians is in itself consciously "archaeological" in the sense that they are consciously creating a monument out of the cave, explicitly labeling it as a place of archaeological interest. From a modern perspective, the leaden object sounds almost like a "blue plaque," one of the metal tablets erected by organizations like English Heritage in order to commemorate the association between a particular place and a particular historical figure or event. Certainly, when the fifth-century bishop of Ephesus discovers this inscription in the cave, he becomes almost literally an archaeologist, someone who takes on the responsibility to interpret the material evidence of the past to the public at large:

Tant k'il esgarda sur destre,
Si vit le plum desuz une pere,
Dunt nus parlames ça arere,
U lur vie fu tute escrite
De chef en chef, cum ele est dite . . .
L'eveske prist le plum en main,
De ceo ne fist il pas ke vilein,
Le seel ne brisa ne ne l'uvri
Deske tut le pople fu auni.

---

32. Cf. L₁: "cogitarent scribere martirium sanctorum in paginis plumbeis et cum reliquiis sanctorum deponere illud in medio lapidum constitutorum in ore speluncae . . . scribentes litteras, et sigillantes deposuerunt secrete" (Magennis, *Seven Sleepers*, 80–81) [they planned to write the saints' martyrdom on tablets of lead and to set this with the remains of the saints in the midst of the stones placed in the mouth of the cave . . . they wrote the document and sealed it and deposited it secretly]; and the Old English: "And hi ða twegen . . . þas halgan martyrrace eall swa heo gewearð on anum leadenum tabulan ealle mid stafon agrofon, and hi ðæt gewrit mid twan sylfrenan inseglum on anre teage geinsegledon and wið þa halgan þærinne swiðe digollice ledon" (Magennis, *Seven Sleepers*, 43) [And these two . . . inscribed the story of this holy martydom, just as it happened, in writing on a leaden tablet, and they sealed this document in a box with two silver seals, and then with great secrecy laid it in (the cave) with the saints].

Quant assemblee fu la presse
De la gent ki fu engresse,
Le viscunte cummande eraument
Ke se teisent tute la gent
Por oir ke l'eveske dirra
De ceo ke enz el plum lirra.
L'eveske icel seel depece
E si esgarda une grant pece
En cel plum k'i fu escrit.
(*Set Dormanz,* lines 1482-86, 1493-1505)

As soon as [the bishop] looked to his right, he saw the lead on the wall: the lead of which we spoke earlier, on which the story of the seven was completely written out, from beginning to end, just as it has been told.... The bishop took hold of the lead. He did not do with it what an uncourtly person would have done: he did not break the seal or open it until all the people were assembled. When the crowd had gathered, all of them agog, the viscount promptly commanded them all to be silent, in order to hear the bishop tell them what he could read on the lead. The bishop broke the seal and studied for a long while what was written in the lead.[33]

Yet what exactly is the nature of this leaden object? How do the authors of the different versions of the legend seem to have understood it? The Latin refers to an "inscribed leaden tablet" and an inscription on "leaden sheets," but also (at the point when it is rediscovered by the bishop) to a "chest sealed with two silver seals" ("loculum sigillatum duobus sigillis argenteis"). The Old English likewise mentions an inscription on a leaden tablet ("on anum leadenum tabulan"), and it too talks about a chest sealed with two silver seals. In

---

33. Cf. **L₁**: "Et cum uenirent in initio introitus speluncae, inuenerunt in dextera loculum sigillatum duobus sigillis argenteis.... Postquam uero collecti sunt, ante eos proconsul resigillauit eum. Inuenit tabulam plumbeam scriptam" (Magennis, *Seven Sleepers,* 88-89) [And when they came to the opening of the entrance to the cave they found on the right hand side a box sealed with two silver seals.... After they were assembled, the proconsul unsealed it before them, and when he opened it he found a written tablet of lead]. Huber's text has a "nihinum loculum" [an onyx box]. Cf. also the Old English: "And mid þy þe hi in becomen, þa gemetton hi on þa swiðran hand ane teage, seo wæs geinsæglod mid twam sylfrenan insæglan.... Syððan hi ealle þær ætforan þam bisceope gegaderode wæron, þa feng se portgerefa to þære tege, and he on gewitnysse ealles folces hi uninsæglode, and hi sona unhlidode, and þærinne funde ane leadene tabulan eall awritene" (Magennis, *Seven Sleepers,* 55) [And when they went in, they found on the right a box, which was sealed with two silver seals.... As soon as they were all gathered in front of the bishop, the port-reeve took the box, and unsealed it in the presence of all the people, immediately opened it, and found inside it a leaden tablet with writing on it].

other words, both the Latin and the English agree that the story of the sleepers is both inscribed on lead and then placed in some kind of little box, while Chardri makes no mention of any kind of box and moreover seems to suggest that the lead is somehow set into or onto the wall. The observation that lead is used for inscriptions because it does not decay is unique to Chardri, which suggests that he has thought about the matter (and is prepared to take his own line in relation to it), but his description of the object is nevertheless especially confusing—perhaps even more so than in the Latin or the Old English. Chardri takes over from his source the detail of the bishop breaking the seal before reading the writing, but since he has not explained what kind of seal this is, he rather invites the assumption that the seal belongs to something like a letter.[34] At the same time, he makes it very clear that the two Christians placed the lead on a wall, in such a way as to suggest that it has something of the qualities of a monumental inscription (even if it is at the same time covered or enclosed in such a way that the bishop needs to open it up in order to read it). On the face of it, these two aspects of his description of the leaden object are hard to reconcile.

Indeed, none of these three representations of this informative piece of lead is entirely easy to interpret, but I would suggest that all of them seem to have been affected to some extent by an awareness of the way in which objects sometimes known as *tabulae* were frequently located in medieval churches and other formal architectural settings. According to Michael van Dussen, a *tabula* in this sense is

> a surface made of alloy, stone or wood that was affixed to a wall, pillar or monument; its purpose was typically to display text that provided information about a structure or institution, propaganda, indulgences, or a commemorative message. In the case of stone or metal tabulae, the text was engraved, whereas wooden tables had parchment leaves pasted to them on which text was inscribed with ink.[35]

He goes on to argue that the *tabula* in this sense was "a familiar textual form in Chaucer's England" and indeed that "it was in Chaucer's time, and continuing into the following century, that the tabula first *became* a widespread

---

34. Perhaps at this point Chardri was influenced by some of those saints' lives in which the saint *is* identified by a letter: see, e.g., Maurizio Perugi, ed., *La vie de Saint Alexis* (Geneva: Droz, 2000), lines 371–85.

35. Michael van Dussen, "Tourists and *Tabulae* in Late-Medieval England," in *Truth and Tales: Cultural Mobility and Medieval Media*, ed. Fiona Somerset and Nicholas Watson (Columbus: The Ohio State University Press, 2015), 238.

textual form."[36] It is certainly true that the extant and recorded examples of such *tabulae* tend to date from this period or later, but this does not mean that such items could not have been relatively common much earlier than this, and indeed I would suggest that Chardri's particular interpretation of his source's reference to a "tabula" is perhaps an indication that even in the thirteenth century the term already connoted something like the objects that van Dussen describes. Indeed, it is striking how closely the role played by the leaden tablets in the legend of the Seven Sleepers matches van Dussen's description of the functions of *tabulae* in late-medieval England. "Tablets [he says] could serve as concise chronicles, distillation, as it were, of more expansive legendary histories," and they were sometimes used specifically to "advertise the fame and virtues of a pilgrimage shrine."[37] In effect, what the two Christians in the legend of the Seven Sleepers provide at this point is exactly what medieval people expected to see when they visited a place made holy by its association with the martyrdom of a saint—that is: a metal label telling the story of what happened there, and "advertising" its significance as a target of pilgrimage. Precisely because such *tabulae* were both physically fixed in a particular place, and at the same time composed of text that could be framed or contained in a range of different ways—in diptych or triptych form, or sometimes with multiple leaves—they tend to have something of the same ambiguity that characterizes descriptions of the leaden item in the legend of the Seven Sleepers, an object that seems to be simultaneously both box-like, monument-like, and letter-like. Medieval *tabulae* could even take the form of a chest (as the writing in the cave is said to do in the Latin and the Old English, though not in Chardri). One of the most striking surviving examples of a medieval *tabula* of this kind, the Glastonbury Magna Tabula, is described by its editor, Jeanne Krochalis, as "a large, hollow wooden box, about 3 feet by 1½ feet, with two hinged wooden leaves inside"; and onto these leaves are pasted parchment-sheets bearing some 600 lines of text commemorating the history of Glastonbury Abbey.[38] In the end, it is difficult to be entirely sure quite how Chardri, the author of the Old English version of the legend, or the author of their Latin source imagined the objects that are said to enclose the writing discovered in the cave of the Seven Sleepers—and perhaps they were not entirely clear about the matter themselves. But it is at least possible that the very complexity and (apparent) contradictoriness of their descriptions reflects

---

36. Van Dussen, "Tourists and *Tabulae*," 242.
37. Van Dussen, "Tourists and *Tabulae*," 238.
38. Jeanne Krochalis, "*Magna Tabula*: The Glastonbury Tablets," Pts. 1 and 2, *Arthurian Literature* 15 (1997): 93–183; 16 (1998): 41–82; reprinted together in *Glastonbury Abbey and the Arthurian Tradition*, ed. James P. Carley (Cambridge: D. S. Brewer, 2001), 435–568.

a complexity of practice that had already developed in relation to the labeling of shrines and other spiritually significant places—and which was perhaps already substantially established long before it became "the widespread textual form" that Chaucer knew.

The legend of the Seven Sleepers is a story that naturally foregrounds what can be described as "archaeological" ways of thinking, if only because successfully explaining the full implications of this legend's miraculousness necessarily means finding ways of calibrating two different and distinct points in the past: both the third-century perspective of the Seven Sleepers themselves, and the fifth-century perspective of the Christian community in which they so strangely reawake. In the legend, both third-century people and fifth-century people engage in certain quite specific kinds of archaeological practice, making use of particular cultural artifacts not just as a means of measuring historical distance but also as a means of interpreting and consciously conserving what they view as historically significant evidence. It is only as a direct result of these communities' willingness to engage in such "archaeological" activities that the full extent of God's disruption to the temporal order is made clear within the story itself, for this is a miracle that can only be substantiated by depicting people using artifacts to construct history even in the context of a relatively remote past. At the same time, the very fact that the legend of the Seven Sleepers depicts "archaeological" practices as a means of exploring, interpreting, and testing sanctity might be taken to suggest that such practices could be seen as symbolic of hagiography itself—in the sense that the effort of identifying and validating saintliness (which is the essential business of hagiography) is repeatedly represented in the different versions of this particular legend as an exercise rooted in the critical assessment of material remains.

CHAPTER 4

The Return of the King

Exhuming King Arthur and Richard III

PHILIP SCHWYZER

"Not since the Middle Ages . . ."—the phrase is heard from time to time, usually with reference to some particularly brutal or inhumane practice. To be charged with replicating medieval behaviors is to be shunted beyond the pale of enlightened civilization; more often than not, the accusation betrays a shallow grasp of medieval and post-medieval history alike.[1] How would it be, though, if something that had not occurred since the Middle Ages really were to happen again in the modern world? What would be the terms and consequences of a direct link between a medieval and a modern moment, one that simply bypassed the Renaissance and the Enlightenment? This chapter explores the case of a recent event that had genuinely not occurred since the Middle Ages—namely, the discovery and exhumation of a long-lost British king. A close comparison of accounts of the late-twelfth-century exhumation of King Arthur at Glastonbury and the twenty-first-century discovery of Richard III in Leicester indicates that medieval narratives still have the power

---

1. "We have seen a campaign of ISIS and genocide against Christians, where they cut off heads. Not since the Middle Ages have we seen that. We haven't seen that, the cutting off of heads" (Donald J. Trump, Remarks at the National Prayer Breakfast: February 2, 2017. Archived by The American Presidency Project, accessed June 2, 2020, http://www.presidency.ucsb.edu/ws/index.php?pid=123068). The comments occurred in the course of justifying the recently imposed ban on travel to the United States from seven majority-Muslim countries. On the wider phenomenon, see James L. Smith, "Medievalisms of Moral Panic: Borrowing the Past to Frame Fear in the Present," *Studies in Medievalism* 25 (2016): 157–72.

of shaping our responses to events—perhaps even the power to shape events themselves. Yet the comparison also serves to mark the gulf that lies between us and our medieval predecessors, not least in regards to the perceived shape and trajectory of time.

The medieval narrative under discussion here is a species of *inventio*—that is, an account of the marvelous discovery of long-lost bones or bodily remains. Such narratives, of course, typically involve the remains of Christian saints. The origins of the *inventio* genre lie in late antiquity, in the fifth-century *Revelatio Sancti Stephani*, which describes the discovery of the remains of St. Stephen and other early Christians, and the *Inventio Crucis*, which recounts the recovery of the True Cross.[2] As Gordon Whatley has argued, these and other early *inventiones* reveal

> an array of shared narrative motifs, including visions or other divine promptings initiating the search for long-buried relics; episodes of obstruction, delay, and resistance; inscriptions and documents; prayers and miracles (including expulsion of demons) that facilitate the discovery, or help authenticate the relics; and the enshrinement and/or distribution of the precious remains.[3]

Writing of *inventio* narratives in twelfth-century England, Monika Otter offers a comparable catalogue:

> The relics are found either by coincidence, usually in connection with some construction or renovation project, or by divine guidance, through dreams or visions. The search for the right place and the digging itself are usually much emphasized; it is stressed that the community "earned" the relic through its intense desire and hard work. There must be an audience present, minimally represented by the bishop or other high clerics in charge, but often described as a large crowd of clergy and laity. There will be some confirmation that the relic is genuine: the body may be incorrupt, or at least emit a pleasing fragrance; sometimes there is an inscription or some identifying artifact. The *inventio* is followed by a *translatio*, that is, the body is

---

2. Monika Otter, *Inventiones: Fiction and Referentiality in Twelfth-Century English Historical Writing* (Chapel Hill: University of North Carolina Press, 1996), 26–29; Martin Heinzelmann, *Translationsberichte und andere Quellen des Reliquienkultes* (Turnhout: Brepols, 1979), 77–80.

3. E. Gordon Whatley, "Constantine the Great, the Empress Helena, and the Relics of the True Cross," in *Medieval Hagiography: An Anthology*, ed. Thomas F. Head (New York: Routledge, 2001), 77.

brought to a more worthy shrine, and its authenticity is further confirmed by miracles.[4]

Where Whatley identifies an array of shared motifs or family resemblances in the early texts, Otter summarizes a definite narrative structure and sequence. Their accounts are not identical, but both involve the core narrative of (1) signs; (2) discovery; (3) authentication; (4) enshrinement. Both also note the means whereby a fairly simple story may be dilated into a longer, suspenseful tale, be it through obstructions that must be overcome, or detailed attention to the process of digging. If each of the motifs or steps in the sequence serves as partial confirmation that the relics are genuine, then the story's adherence to the *inventio* genre through the accumulation of familiar motifs provides a further degree of confirmation. Rather than weakening the reader's faith (because the narrative is obviously based on previous *inventiones*), the establishment of generic conformity strengthens the case.

The two narratives with which this chapter is centrally concerned share many features with conventional *inventiones*, but they depart from the genre in two crucial respects, namely, that the bodies in question are not those of saints and that they are instead those of British kings.[5] Together, these narratives comprise a secular-royal spin-off or subgenre of the hagiographical *inventio*. Paradoxically, we can speak in this case of a medieval subgenre that has only recently emerged, now that the discovery of Richard III in a car park in Leicester in 2012 can be read alongside the exhumation of Arthur at Glastonbury in 1191. There are, of course, a number of further examples of medieval and modern *inventiones* that bear a partial resemblance to the cases in question (involving, for instance, the bodies of saints who were also British kings; or of kings who were neither saintly nor British; or of the tombs of British kings from which the body was absent), but they do not conform in all respects to this specific subgenre.[6] There are also two intriguing examples

---

4. Otter, *Inventiones*, 28–29.

5. On resemblances between the discovery of Richard III and conventional *inventiones*, see Ann E. Bailey, "Anthropology, the Medievalist . . . and Richard III," *Reading Medieval Studies* 41 (2015): 33–34.

6. A number of Anglo-Saxon saints were also kings, though only occasionally does the posthumous disappearance of the body allow for an *inventio* narrative. The head of Saint Edmund the Martyr was briefly lost in the woods but made itself known to searchers by calling out *hic, hic, hic*. The remains of Edward the Martyr, lost after the Reformation, were discovered in excavations at Shaftesbury Abbey in 1931. Examples of royal secular *inventiones* from beyond Britain include the famous discovery of the tomb of the Merovingian king Childeric at Tournai in 1653; in that case, attention was largely absorbed by the array of rich grave goods, whilst "little attention went to the human remains" (Bonnie Effros, *Merovingian Mortuary Archaeology and the Making of the Early Middle Ages* [Berkeley: University of California Press, 2003],

from the sixteenth century, neither of them a complete *inventio* yet nonetheless intriguing for the purposes of this discussion, to which I will turn in conclusion.

The discovery of the remains of King Arthur and his queen at Glastonbury in the last decade of the twelfth century is the subject of two near-contemporary accounts by Gerald of Wales, contained in his *Liber de Principis Instructione* (begun ca. 1192) and *Speculum Ecclesiae* (ca. 1217).[7] Later accounts by Adam of Damerham and others are substantially based on Gerald's testimony.[8] Gerald may well have been an eyewitness to the event, and even been in some sense its designated chronicler, though he does not explicitly make this claim.[9] The discovery, identification, and subsequent reburial of Richard III (2012–15), widely reported in the international media, have been dealt with in a number of scholarly articles and several books, including *The Bones of a King: Richard III Rediscovered* (2015), by members of the University of Leicester's Greyfriars Research Team, and *Finding Richard III: The Official Account of Research by the Retrieval and Reburial Project* (2015), which recounts the same events from the perspective of members of the Richard III Society involved in funding and initiating the search.[10] As I shall argue here, the *inventiones* of King Arthur

---

32). The Anglo-Saxon tomb discovered at Prittlewell in 2003 may have belonged to Sæberht of Essex (d. 616), who was not a saint, but human remains were not found within the tomb.

7. *Liber de Principis Instructione* (*PI*) and *Speculum Ecclesiae* (*SE*) will be cited in the text; the English translation by Lewis Thorpe is in Gerald of Wales, *The Journey Through Wales / The Description of Wales*, trans. Lewis Thorpe, ed. Betty Radice (London: Penguin, 1978). For the Latin texts, see Richard Barber, "Was Mordred Buried at Glastonbury?," in *Glastonbury Abbey and the Arthurian Tradition*, ed. James P. Carley (Cambridge: D. S. Brewer, 2001), 620–24. John Prise's sixteenth-century transcription of the Arthurian material in *SE* (John Prise, *Historiae Britannicae Defensio / A Defence of the British History*, ed. Ceri Davies [Toronto: PIMS, 2015]) includes passages lacking in the surviving manuscript, BL MS Cotton Tiberius B XIII.

8. Antonia Gransden, "The Growth of Glastonbury Traditions and Legends in the Twelfth Century," in *Glastonbury Abbey*, ed. Carley, 44–45. Gransden posits that Gerald's two surviving accounts of the exhumation, as well as Adam of Damerham's thirteenth-century report, are based on a lost text, probably also by Gerald. Adam adds one key detail not found in Gerald's account (though possibly derived from the lost source), that the site of the excavation was surrounded by curtains. Like other aspects of the Glastonbury exhumation, this feature was replicated in the exhumation of Richard III (The Greyfriars Research Team, *The Bones of a King: Richard III Rediscovered*, with Maev Kennedy and Lin Foxhall [Chichester: John Wiley & Sons, 2015], 183).

9. Opinions differ as to whether Gerald was actually present at the exhumation, or arrived slightly later, in time to see the relics before they were reinterred; in either case it seems the monks of Glastonbury relied on Gerald to provide the authorized report of the event. See Gransden, "Glastonbury Traditions and Legends," 45, 49–50; Barber, "Mordred Buried at Glastonbury," 155.

10. A. J. Carson, ed., *Finding Richard III: The Official Account of Research by the Retrieval and Reburial Project* (Horstead, UK: Imprimis Imprimatur, 2015).

and Richard III share a number of distinctive motifs and a strikingly similar sequence of events. Conforming in many respects to the conventional *inventio* narrative outlined by Whatley and Otter, they also share features that are not typical of hagiographical *inventiones*.

Glastonbury and Greyfriars: The Common Narrative

The exhumation narratives of King Arthur and Richard III are both structured around a sequence of nine episodes, as enumerated here. (The numbering refers to the chronological sequence of events, not necessarily to the narrative sequence of any given account.)

1. Many deny that the King's grave can be found.
2. Yet the true location of the body is revealed by old records . . .
3. . . . and also in dreams or visions, which prompt the excavation.
4. The search for the right place and the digging itself are much emphasized.
5. The unusual shape of the bones provides immediate confirmation that the remains are genuine.
6. The body is found to have been hastily buried.
7. It bears traces of many wounds; a gaping hole in the skull gives evidence of the death blow.
8. The excavation is hailed as a triumph of archaeological truth over poetic deception.
9. The *inventio* is followed by a *translatio*, and the royal body receives reburial close by in a newly remodeled church.

In the pages that follow, I will demonstrate how the two exhumations conform to this structure, and then consider how we might begin to interpret or account for their surprising similarities.

1. Many deny that the King's grave can be found

Prior to the excavation at Glastonbury, the location of King Arthur's remains was not only unknown but widely regarded as unascertainable, since even his death was not an established fact. The Welsh *Englynion y Beddau*, or Stanzas of the Graves, referred to Arthur's unknown resting place as a mystery or wonder to baffle the world ("anoeth bid, bet y Arthur"), and William of

Malmesbury (ca. 1125) blamed the fact that "Arthur's grave is nowhere to be seen" ("Arturis sepulcrum nusquam visitur") for the persistence of fables that he might return.[11] In the twelfth and early thirteenth centuries, Geoffrey of Monmouth, Wace, and Laȝamon all affirmed that Arthur was borne away to Avalon to be healed of the grievous wounds received at the battle of Camlann; all acknowledged, with varying degrees of enthusiasm, the possibility that he might not be gone for good. As Gerald remarks in *De Principis Instructione*, "legends had always encouraged us to believe that there was something otherworldly about his ending, that he had resisted death, and had been spirited away to some far-distant spot" (*PI*, 281).

For centuries, similar mystery surrounded the burial place of Richard III. Although he was known to have been interred in the church of the Greyfriars in Leicester in 1485, the dissolution and subsequent demolition of the priory in the 1530s left the whereabouts of his remains a matter of mystery. In 1611, the historian John Speed recorded that the remains had been torn from their resting place at the dissolution and disposed of in the nearby river Soar: "His body also (as tradition hath delivered) was borne out of the City, and contemptuously bestowed under the end of *Bow-Bridge*, which giveth passage over a branch of *Stowre* upon the west side of the Towne."[12] This tradition was widely disseminated and repeated down to the early twenty-first century. A Victorian plaque near the east end of Bow Bridge claims, "Near this spot lie the remains of Richard III, last of the Plantagenets 1485." (The plaque survives, though supplemented since 2005 by a smaller plaque disputing the account.) Prior to their exhumations, then, Arthur and Richard III were both believed by many to lie over (or under) the water, their resting places not only unknown but by definition unlocatable.

2. Yet the true location of the body is revealed by old records . . .

In spite of the popularity of Speed's tale about the River Soar, the location of Richard's original interment was well known, having been recorded by historians, including John Rous, Polydore Vergil, and Robert Fabyan in the late

---

11. Patrick Sims-Williams, "The Early Welsh Arthurian Poems," in *The Arthur of the Welsh*, ed. Rachel Bromwich, A. O. H. Jarman, and Brynley F. Roberts (Cardiff: University of Wales Press, 1991), 49–50; O. J. Padel, *Arthur in Medieval Welsh Literature* (Cardiff: University of Wales Press, 2013), 37–38; William of Malmesbury, *De gestis regum anglorum libri quinque & Historiae novellae libri tres*, ed. William Stubbs (Cambridge: Cambridge University Press, 2012), 3.287, 1:342.

12. John Speed, *The History of Great Britaine* (London, 1611), 725. See Philip Schwyzer, *Shakespeare and the Remains of Richard III* (Oxford: Oxford University Press, 2013), 30–35.

fifteenth and early sixteenth centuries.[13] The location of Arthur's body was likewise, according to Gerald, indicated in the abbey's own records, as well as in the inscriptions on two pyramids standing in the Glastonbury burial ground "although they had been almost obliterated long ago by the passing of many years" (*SE*, 286). These records and inscriptions do not survive, if indeed they ever existed, and Gerald is quick to add, in both of his accounts of the matter, that their evidence was not as valuable as that provided by King Henry II, on the basis of bardic lore: "The king had told the Abbot on a number of occasions that he had learnt from the historical accounts of the Britons and from their bards that Arthur had been buried in the churchyard there between two pyramids" (*SE*, 286–87). Like the documents and inscriptions they are called upon to supplement, these Welsh oral traditions are entirely unattested.

3. ... and also in dreams or visions, which prompt the excavation

Dreams and visions play a prominent role in many *inventio* narratives, reflecting the influence of the seminal *Revelatio Sancti Stephani*, in which the priest Lucianus receives a series of dream visitations instructing him to search for the bodies of Stephen and his companions. Gerald duly reports that at Glastonbury "holy monks and other religious had seen visions and revelations" (*PI*, 282). The content of the visions is not recorded, and this brief and formulaic mention seems mainly prompted by a desire to conform to the conventions of the genre. A rather more interesting tale of the paranormal has become part of the narrative of the discovery of the "King in the Car Park." The Ricardian enthusiast Philippa Langley, who played a central role in prompting the excavation project, reported,

> My passion for the search was based on personal intuition, which only became stronger and stronger. The moment I walked into that car park in Leicester the hairs on the back of my neck stood up, and something told me this was where we must look. A year later I revisited the same place, not

---

13. "The body of king Rycherd nakyd of all clothing, and layd uppon an horse bake with the armes and legges hanginge downe on both sydes, was browght to thabbay of monks Franciscanes at Leycester, a myserable spectacle in good sooth, but not unworthy for the mans lyfe, and ther was buryed two days after without any pompe or solemne funeral" (Polydore Vergil, *Three Books of Polydore Vergil's English History, Comprising the Reigns of Henry VI, Edward IV, and Richard III*, ed. Sir Henry Ellis [London: Camden Society, 1844], 226). Robert Fabyan (*The New Chronicles of England and France* [London, 1516]) reports the same (fol. ccxxx^r).

believing what I had first felt. And this time I saw a roughly painted letter "R" on the ground (for "reserved parking space," obviously!). Believe it or not, it was almost directly under that "R" that King Richard was found.[14]

In press interviews, Langley has further heightened the hints of supernatural intervention, reporting that "it was a warm day but I suddenly felt cold" after first entering the car park in response to an inexplicable "overwhelming urge."[15] Her account conforms remarkably well to the motif commonly found in *inventiones*, including the delivery of a second, more explicit vision to the dreamer who has been reluctant or unable to take action after the first revelation.

4. The search for the right place and the digging itself are much emphasized

Gerald's account of the exhumation of Arthur in *De Principis Instructione* recounts how the search was initiated and describes what was found (with particular attention to Arthur's bones and an inscribed cross), but pays scant attention to the actual process of excavation. The passage in *Speculum Ecclesiae*, later and slightly longer, redresses this omission, describing how the monks first encountered a broad stone, about seven feet deep, with the inscribed cross on the underside, and only after continuing to a depth of sixteen feet came upon the remains of Arthur himself within a hollowed oak. A troubling incident in which a monk seized upon a bright lock of hair, apparently belonging to Arthur's wife, only to have it crumble to dust in his hands, provides matter for a moralizing set piece. In *Speculum Ecclesiae*, the process of excavation not only leads to significant results but is itself a significant and signifying performance.

The excavation in the Leicester car park features prominently in book-length accounts of the discovery of Richard III (Chapter 2 in *The Bones of the King*, and the penultimate chapter in *Finding Richard III*). The remains of

---

14. Philippa Langley, "A Personal Message from Philippa Langley," The Richard III Society: Looking for Richard, accessed June 2, 2020, http://www.richardiii.net/leicester_dig.php.

15. Michael Holden, "One Woman's Quest to Redeem the King under the Car Park," *Reuters World News* (February 2013), accessed June 2, 2020, https://www.reuters.com/article/us-britain-richard/one-womans-quest-to-redeem-the-king-under-the-car-park-idUSBRE91705I20130208; Elizabeth Day, "Philippa Langley: 'I Just Felt I Was Walking on Richard III's Grave. I Can't Explain It,'" *Observer* (December 2013), accessed June 2, 2020, https://www.theguardian.com/uk-news/2013/dec/08/philippa-langley-richard-third-car-park. See also Bailey, "Anthropology, the Medievalist," 33.

the king were in fact partially revealed in the first archaeological trench on the first day of the dig (August 25, 2012); further investigation on September 5 revealed the skeleton's dramatically curved spine, which first led the archaeologists to believe that this might be the body of Richard III; a week later, the discovery was announced to the public, though the identity of the body would not be confirmed through DNA and other evidence for another five months. In the two and a half weeks between the commencement of the excavation and the revelation of the discovery, the progress of the dig was followed in surprising detail by the news media, with tantalizing suggestions that a find might be imminent.[16]

5. The unusual shape of the bones provides immediate confirmation that the remains are genuine

In all accounts of the Leicester excavation, the moment on September 5 when Dr. Jo Appleby exposed the skeleton's spinal column, revealing an "S" shaped curvature, provides the climax. For the University of Leicester archaeologists, who had never considered it likely that they would find the King's body, and had undertaken the search primarily as an opportunity to excavate the medieval priory, it was an extraordinary moment: "Morris rushed over to Buckley and whispered to him, 'You have to come see this.'"[17] Philippa Langley of the Richard III Society recalls drastically mixed emotions. "The spinal column has a really abnormal curvature. This skeleton has a hunchback. The word hits me like a sucker-punch. No, I can't take it in. Are they saying this is Richard?"[18] The paradox of the discovery, for Langley and like-minded Ricardians, was that no other evidence could have demonstrated so immediately and powerfully that the bones were indeed those of Richard III; yet the tradition of Richard's curved spine, which Ricardians had long argued was the invention of Tudor propagandists from Thomas More to Shakespeare, was precisely what they had expected to disprove through the exhumation of his remains. For Langley, the curvature testifies at once that this cannot be Richard, and that it can only be Richard. "Are they saying this is Richard?"

---

16. See, for instance, Greig Watson, "Richard III Dig: How Search Reached Leicester Car Park," *BBC News* (September 2012), accessed June 2, 2020, http://www.bbc.co.uk/news/uk-england-leicestershire-19474848. The report quotes Buckley saying, "We are getting quite near it, if it's there. It is quite a tingle." The remains had been uncovered and tentatively identified three days before.

17. Greyfriars Research Team, *Bones of a King*, 19–20.

18. Philippa Langley and Michael Jones, *The King's Grave: The Search for Richard III* (London: John Murray, 2013).

At Glastonbury, too, according to Gerald's report, the shape of the king's skeleton provoked astonishment:

> The bones of Arthur's body which were discovered there were so big that in them the poet's words seem to be fulfilled: "All men will exclaim at the size of the bones they've exhumed." ["Grandiaque effossis mirabitur ossa sepulchris"; Virgil, *Georgics* 1.497] The abbot showed me one of the shin-bones. He held it upright on the ground against the foot of the tallest man he could find, and it stretched a good three inches above the man's knee. The skull was so large and capacious that it seemed a veritable prodigy of nature [prodigium vel ostentum], for the space between the eyebrows and the eye-sockets was as broad as the palm of a man's hand. (*PI*, 283–84)

In the passage cited from Virgil's *Georgics*, the poet imagines future farmers—smaller denizens of a more peaceable age—discovering the bones of the warriors of his own time and reckoning them to have been giants. Yet this is not quite what Gerald has in mind, for he clearly considers Arthur to have been prodigious in stature by the standards of his age, not just those of the twelfth century. His description of grotesquely large royal bones has an interesting precedent in the Anglo-Latin *Liber Monstrorum*, which speaks of the Geatish king Hygelac, numbered among the "monstra mirae magnitudinis" [monsters of great size], whose gigantic bones were preserved on an island in the Rhine and "pro miraculo ostendentur" [exhibited as a wonder].[19] Arthur and Hygelac were great men in every sense, but also in some sense monsters. The description of Arthur as *prodigium* hints that the fabled king not only cannot but by all means should not return in the present. For Gerald at Glastonbury, as for some observers at Leicester, the unusual form of the bones provokes a degree of unease or dismay, even as it authenticates their royal identity.

6. The body is found to have been hastily buried

Like the size of Arthur's bones, the shape of his grave gave rise to wonder mixed with anxiety: "Arthur's body was discovered, not in a stone sarcophagus, carved out of rock or of Parian marble, as would have been seemly for so famous a king, but in wood, in an oak-bole hollowed out for this purpose and buried deep in the earth, sixteen feet or more down." This unusual

---

19. See Andy Orchard, *Pride and Prodigies: Studies in the Monsters of the "Beowulf"-Manuscript* (Toronto: University of Toronto Press, 2003), 109–10.

and comparatively undignified mode of interment seems to cause Gerald a moment of worry, prompting him to add that the obsequies were "hurried no doubt [*nimirum*] rather than performed with due pomp and ceremony, as this period of pressing disturbance made only too necessary" (*SE*, 287). The hypothesis of hasty burial is hard to tally with the extreme depth of the interment and the labor it must have involved, but it provides an alternative to what would otherwise indicate a disturbing lack of due ceremony and respect.

Richard III's grave at Leicester, which was too short for the body so that the royal head was left jutting up against one side, posed a similar conundrum for observers: mere haste or intentional disrespect? In their initial report in the journal *Antiquity*, the archaeologists left the question open:

> Only a little extra effort by the grave-diggers to tidy the grave ends would have made this grave long enough to receive the body conventionally. That they did not, instead placing the body on one side of the grave, its torso crammed against the northern side, may suggest haste or little respect for the deceased.[20]

In *The Bones of a King*, these remarks are softened somewhat to emphasize haste rather than definite disrespect:

> As the grave was in consecrated ground within the church, and in a relatively prestigious spot, whoever was buried there would certainly have had a proper Christian funeral, however minimal that might have been. He was almost certainly buried in haste, from the evidence of the grave itself, but the archaeological evidence cannot tell us the degree of respect with which he was (or was not) committed to the earth.[21]

The repetition of "certainly," echoing Gerald's *nimirum*, betrays a hint of anxiety on the question; both authors, perhaps, are protesting too much.

7. The body bears traces of many wounds; a gaping hole in the skull gives evidence of the death blow . . .

On Arthur's gigantic skull, Gerald reports, "ten or more wounds could clearly be seen, but they had all mended except one. This was larger than the others

---

20. Richard Buckley et al., "'The King in the Car Park': New Light on the Death and Burial of Richard III in the Grey Friars Church, Leicester, in 1485," *Antiquity* 87 (2013): 531.

21. Greyfriars Research Team, *Bones of a King*, 21.

and it had made an immense gash [*hiatum*]. Apparently it was this wound which had caused Arthur's death" (*PI*, 284). In the case of Richard, osteological analysis led to remarkably similar conclusions. "Ten peri-mortem wounds have been identified on the remains, eight on the skull and two on the post-cranial skeleton. Two large wounds underneath the back of the skull, consistent with a halberd and a sword blow, are likely to have been fatal."[22] The close similarity between these passages, in terms of their detail and even to some extent their syntax, is remarkable, and will be discussed further below.

8. The excavation is hailed as a triumph of archaeological truth over poetic deception

As noted previously, multiple retellings of Arthur's history in the twelfth century held open the possibility that he was still alive. Although the legend was current in texts written in Latin, French, and English, Gerald singles out the poets of Wales as responsible for propagating these falsehoods and of employing them to political purposes as a means of resisting English rule.[23]

> The credulous Britons and their bards invented the legend that a fantastic sorceress called Morgan had removed Arthur's body to the Isle of Avalon so that she might cure his wounds there. According to them, once he has recovered from his wounds this strong and all-powerful king will return to rule over the Britons in the normal way. The result of all this is that they really expect him to come back, just as the Jews, led astray by even greater stupidity, misfortune and misplaced faith, really expect their Messiah to return. (*SE*, 286)

At long last, Gerald asserts, "the fairy tales have been snuffed out, and the true and indubitable facts are made known" (*SE*, 285). Indeed, although the monks of Glastonbury undoubtedly undertook the excavation primarily for the benefit of their own house, the interest of figures such as Henry II must have been prompted at least in part by the opportunity it afforded to refute troublesome Welsh traditions.

---

22. Buckley et al., "King in the Car Park," 536.
23. Although English, Latin, and Anglo-French authors typically associate belief in Arthur's return with the Welsh, references to the tradition in medieval Welsh literature are surprisingly rare; see Padel, *Arthur*, 38; Philip Schwyzer, "British History and 'The British History': The Same Old Story?," in *British Identities and English Renaissance Literature*, ed. David J. Baker and Willy Maley (Cambridge: Cambridge University Press, 2002), 11–23.

Commentary in the wake of the discovery of Richard III's remains closely echoed Gerald's claim that false legends had at last given way to "true and indubitable facts." The legends, in this case, were laid at the door of one fabulist in particular: William Shakespeare. Countless commentators drew the contrast between Shakespeare's grotesque stage villain and the "real" king in the car park; the blunt material fact of the Greyfriars skeleton was heralded as trumping Shakespeare's beguiling, immaterial fiction. This was, after all, the aim of those members of the Richard III Society who pressed for and funded the dig—and regardless of the revelation that the king's spine was indeed curved, they were remarkably successful in spinning the discovery to the media and the general public as proof that Shakespeare was wrong about Richard. Thus, a study of the skeleton's spinal curvature in *The Lancet* was breathlessly reported by *Bloomberg* as proof that "the slings and arrows of literary insults aimed at King Richard III grossly embellish the deformities of the supposed hunchback whose villainy endures thanks to William Shakespeare."[24] The new Richard III Visitor Centre in Leicester features an area devoted to Shakespeare's influence, provocatively headlined "Portrayal or Betrayal." As an excerpt from Philippa Langley's diary—featured in the exhibition—declares hopefully, "With the extraordinary story of the search generating new interest in learning about Richard, I am encouraged to see that people are now talking about him as a medieval king and that Shakespeare's anti-hero is no longer a realistic portrayal." It was, as Richard Toon and Laurie Stone have observed, as if the skeleton were capable of its own auto-rehabilitation, "as if the bones should remake the man."[25]

9. The *inventio* is followed by a *translatio,* and the royal body receives reburial close by in a newly remodeled church

In both of his accounts, Gerald affirms that the remains of King Arthur were reburied within the abbey church in a marble tomb; *Speculum Ecclesiae* adds that the tomb was *egregium* (excellent) and that the reinterment was accompa-

---

24. Makiko Kitamura, "Shakespeare's Deformed Richard III Disputed by Scientists," *Bloomberg* (May 2014), accessed June 2, 2020, https://www.bloomberg.com/news/articles/2014-05-29/shakespeare-s-deformed-richard-iii-disputed-by-scientists; cf. Jo Appleby et al., "The Scoliosis of Richard III, Last Plantagenet King of England: Diagnosis and Clinical Significance," *The Lancet* 383, no. 9932 (2014): 1944.

25. Richard Toon and Laurie Stone, "Game of Thrones: Richard III and the Creation of Cultural Heritage," in *Studies in Forensic Biohistory: Anthropological Perspectives,* ed. Christopher M. Stojanowski and William N. Duncan (Cambridge: Cambridge University Press, 2016), 47.

nied by fitting solemnities. Neither text notes that the church was being rebuilt at this time, following a disastrous fire at Glastonbury in 1184. Indeed, the discovery of the legendary king has been seen as a bid to generate financial support for the renovations; Arthur's exhumation was more an effect than a cause of the rebuilding program. In the case of Richard III, however, the discovery of the skeleton did lead directly to an extensive and expensive renovation and reordering of the interior of Leicester Cathedral. Following protracted public controversies over both the location of the burial and the design of the tomb, the king's remains were laid to rest on March 26, 2015, in an elaborate ceremony attended by celebrities, members of the royal family, and enthusiasts from many countries. Neither Arthur nor Richard had traveled more than a few dozen meters from their first resting place to their second.[26]

Coincidence or Copy?

From the initial portents to the final translation of the remains, the sequence of events outlined above overlaps closely with the mainstream medieval *inventio* tradition. Yet both of these narratives involving nonsaintly British kings diverge from or supplement that tradition in similar ways. The stress on the unusual form of the royal bones, for instance, does not seem to have an obvious parallel in hagiography. Saints' remains are identified by their sweet smell, but do not tend to be remarkable in shape; even the skull of St. Christopher, part of which belonged to Glastonbury Abbey, seems to have been normal in appearance, although Christopher was reputed to have been a giant with, in some traditions, the head of a dog.[27] That kings should leave behind gigantic bones, on the other hand, was not unheard of, as seen in the case of Hygelac. Equally distinctive is the emphasis placed in these royal *inventiones* on the refutation of false poetic traditions, and on the interpretive problems posed by what might be deemed either disrespectful or hasty burial. Although composed more than 800 years apart, the accounts of the exhumations of King Arthur and Richard III bear more resemblance to one another than either does to the standard hagiographical *inventio*.

---

26. Richard III's resting place in Leicester may well be his last, but Arthur was translated at least once more, in 1278, when he and his queen were laid in a new black marble coffin before the high altar in a ceremony attended by Edward I and Queen Eleanor.

27. James P. Carley, ed., *The Chronicle of Glastonbury Abbey: An Edition, Translation and Study of John of Glastonbury's "Cronica sive antiquitates Glastoniensis ecclesie"* (Woodbridge, UK: Boydell Press, 1978), 202–3.

In adjudicating the question of where Richard III should be granted reburial, the High Court observed that "the archaeological discovery of the mortal remains of a King of England after five hundred years may fairly be described as '*unprecedented.*'"[28] In fact, the exhumation at Glastonbury provides a remarkably close precedent (albeit, arguably, a partially fictive one). The parallels are so numerous that a clear case can be made that the exhumation of Richard III not only resembled but was *based on* the discovery of King Arthur at Glastonbury, in much the same way that so many medieval *inventio* narratives were based on the *Revelatio Sancti Stephani*. Greyfriars 2012 was a close rewriting of Glastonbury 1191. This point applies to the literary selection and narrative ordering of events in texts, such as *The Bones of a King* and *Richard III Rediscovered*, but also, and with no less force, to the facts and events themselves. Like many medieval excavations in search of saints' remains, which were undertaken on the model of earlier successful *inventiones*, the Greyfriars dig can be regarded as a material reenactment of the exhumation of Arthur. In a real way, the archaeology itself is a citation.

There are, to be sure, some very powerful commonsense objections to this line of argument. The Greyfriars dig really did take place, and the shape of the grave and the skeleton it contained are matters of public, peer-reviewed record. There is no reason to suggest that any aspect of the excavation or the subsequent forensic analysis was faked or misrepresented in order to conform to the Glastonbury model. Richard's skull really did have an appalling hole in it, and the immediate cause of that injury was a fifteenth-century halberd, not the writings of a twelfth-century cleric. Yet while the materials unearthed at Greyfriars bear the marks of real events that took place with little or no reference to *inventio* narratives, they have also, in and after their unearthing, been made subject to the production of archaeological knowledge.[29] Their status as facts depends not only on their fifteenth-century origins but on an array of disciplinary and cultural discourses, involving both explicit and implicit instances of citation.

---

28. Judgment in the Case of Plantagenet Alliance Ltd -v- The Secretary of State for Justice & Others, Case No: CO/5313/2013, 23 May 2014, paragraph 155; italics in original. The claimant (Plantagenet Alliance) had argued that due to the unprecedented nature of the discovery there was a duty to consult with Richard III's surviving relatives as to his final resting place. The court concurred that the discovery was unprecedented but found no duty to consult.

29. On the production of knowledge in the interaction of material evidence and archaeological authority, see Nadia Abu El-Haj, *Facts on the Ground: Archaeological Practice and Territorial Self-Fashioning in Israeli Society* (Chicago: University of Chicago Press, 2001); Robert Chapman and Alison Wylie, *Evidential Reasoning in Archaeology* (London: Bloomsbury, 2016); Maria Theresia Starzmann, "Der 'Orient' als Grenzraum: Die koloniale Dimension wissenschaftlicher Narrative zum Nahen Osten," *Forum Kritische Archäologie* 7 (2018): 1–17.

The comparably cloven skulls of Richard III and King Arthur provide a case in point. When Gerald of Wales described the great cleft in Arthur's skull, he was already working in an established hagiographical and osteological tradition. Twenty-one years before the Glastonbury excavation, Thomas Becket had famously been subjected to a series of perimortem wounds to the skull, including the fatal sword blow that cut away the crown or *corona*. At Canterbury, subsequently, both the detached corona and the skull from which it came were regarded as relics of unparalleled worth. The example of Becket's broken skull undoubtedly provided Gerald with a model for his description of Arthur's cranial wounds.[30] More than this, it established the status of a skull damaged in this manner as a very particular, very powerful kind of fact. Unlike abrasions on the ribs or vertebrae, which for the trained osteologist may testify to equally lethal violence, the spectacle of a broken skull requires no specialist training for the observer to understand that it represents the moment and the manner of death. As spectacular fact, the broken skull not only testifies to a historical event, but contains and perpetuates that event, almost inevitably eliciting from the observer a mental reenactment of the moment of death. This capacity was widely evident in the reporting of the discovery and analysis of Richard III's injuries, and in the images of the skull released by the Greyfriars project.[31] Thus, while the mere fact of Richard's broken skull may not depend on literary and hagiographical traditions, its peculiar facticity is deeply embedded in them. And just as Canterbury and Glastonbury in the twelfth century set out to rebuild a church on the foundation of a cloven skull, so in the twenty-first century did Leicester Cathedral.

Many essential elements of the Greyfriars narrative—from the motives and expectations of those who organized it, to the archaeological findings themselves, to the skillful packaging of the outcome by the University of Leicester and its reception in the media—follow the lineaments of medieval *inventio* narratives generally and the Glastonbury story more specifically. This

---

30. I am grateful to Naomi Howell for the observation that Arthur's skull, as described by Gerald, is a citation of Becket's. For further discussion of the role of relics in ecclesiastical rebuilding and refoundations, see her chapter in this volume.

31. See, for instance, https://le.ac.uk/richard-iii/identification/osteology/injuries/skull-4-6. A poster-style display of the various injuries to the Leicester skeleton produced by *MailOnline* commences in the top right corner with an image of the base of the skull, beneath the large heading "The Fatal Blows," and with the blade of a halberd poised in immediate proximity to the wound: Nick McDermott, "500 Years on, the Grisly Secrets of Richard III's Lost Grave Are Revealed," *MailOnline* (February 2013), accessed June 2, 2020, http://www.dailymail.co.uk/news/article-2273535/500-years-grisly-secrets-Richard-IIIs-lost-grave-revealed-King-discovered-car-park-stripped-tied-suffered-humiliation-wounds-death.html. Notably, reference to "the fatal blows" invites the viewer to witness not only the evidence of violence, but the moment of violence itself.

does not necessarily suggest that any of the central participants were familiar with the writings of Gerald of Wales, much less that they consciously set out to reproduce a twelfth-century event. Nor is it entirely satisfactory to speak in terms of a more diffused and indirect influence, as if the sequence of Gerald's narrative comprised a set of cultural materials somehow still available in the twenty-first century. Although some motifs characteristic of *inventiones* are likely to have filtered down through subsequent cultural epochs (the dreams and visions presaging the discovery of a corpse finding a line through the Gothic, for example), the full structure of the narrative is specifically medieval, and has no obvious route of transmission through the early modern and modern periods. Thus, although I have proposed that the Greyfriars excavation was "based on" the exhumation of King Arthur, this basis cannot be located in the intentions of the main actors, nor even in cultural memories of the narrative. How, then, can the close similarity be explained?

The conclusion seems unavoidable that the Greyfriars excavation arrived independently at a number of the same events and steps in the narrative sequence as those recorded by Gerald of Wales. This is by no means to say that the resemblance between the two narratives is a matter of mere coincidence. Rather, when faced with similar problems, the participants in the Greyfriars dig drew on a similar set of interpretive and institutional resources as had been available to Gerald of Wales, arriving, unremarkably, at similar conclusions. Where the problems they encountered were "medieval," in the sense that they had not presented themselves since the Middle Ages, it is no surprise that the resources drawn upon were also apt to be medieval. Thus, the Greyfriars archaeologists could rely on their understanding, roughly overlapping with that of Gerald of Wales, of the norms of medieval elite burial. The manner in which events unfolded in 2012–15 was also heavily shaped by surviving "medieval" institutions (or institutions with their origins in the Middle Ages), including the Church of England and the English monarchy, both of which tend to be strongly guided by precedent, however remote. Questions such as where to bury a rediscovered monarch were answered with reference to tools and protocols developed in the medieval period.[32]

The correspondence between the two events can thus be traced to a set of interlocking factors:

a. Cultural memory, in the form of motifs from medieval *inventiones* transmitted through the literature of later periods;

---

32. See Ann E. Bailey, "Richard III: A Medieval Relic?," *History Today* 65, no. 8 (2015): 11–17.

b. The involvement of abiding cultural and institutional structures that steered the two projects toward similar outcomes;

c. Sheer coincidence (but mediated, in every case, by either "a" or "b").

To the extent that "a" applies, that is, to the extent that the authors of the Greyfriars narrative consciously or unconsciously adopted medieval motifs in order to produce a modern reenactment of a medieval event, the exhumation and reinterment of Richard III can be seen as instances of medievalism. To the extent that "b" holds true, they can be seen rather as authentically medieval events, notwithstanding their temporal situation in the second decade of the twenty-first century. As the unfolding of the Greyfriars story demonstrates, the Middle Ages still inhabit a corner of modern time.

The Shape of Time

For all its similarities with its twelfth-century predecessor, there remains a sense in which the discovery of Richard III must be seen as anything but medieval, indeed antimedieval. The starkest difference between these two archaeological narratives lies in the perceived effect of the exhumation on the shape of historical time. The difference is not that which we might expect when juxtaposing a twelfth-century narrative with one from the present day. In harmony with modern understandings of the arrow of time, Gerald's linear vision of history emphasizes the pastness of the past. Once King Arthur was alive, but now, demonstrably, he is not. Time will not run backward; the Britons would do well to abandon their hopes. In both *De Principis Instructione* and *Speculum Ecclesiae*, Gerald incorporates an instructive anecdote involving a monk who seized hold of a miraculously preserved lock of Guinevere's hair, only to see it crumble to dust in his hands; such is the reward of those who imagine the past can be revived in the present. Archaeology as Gerald understands it does not make the dead live again, but only offers confirmation and closure.[33]

The exhumation of Richard III, on the other hand, has been widely hailed as an opportunity to redeem the wrongs of history. As Langley declared on the day the identity of the bones was confirmed: "The discovery of King Richard is an historic moment when the history books will be rewritten. A wind of

---

33. Philip Schwyzer, *Archaeologies of English Renaissance Literature* (Oxford: Oxford University Press, 2007), 57–58.

change is blowing, one that will now seek out the truth about the real Richard III. And as regards our mandate from those around the world: We have searched for Richard, and we have found him—it is now time to honor him."[34] A year later, speaking in the run-up to Richard's reburial, Langley took a suitably quieter tone, but made the same point. The purpose of the reinterment ceremony was "to give Richard what he didn't get in 1485 . . . to recognize what went on in the past, but not repeat it, to make peace with the past."[35] Nor is Langley alone in seeing in the emergence of Richard's remains the chance to set right historical wrongs—as well as the chance to recognize that history has, all along, been in some way false. This impulse seemed particularly strong among those who fought for Richard to be reburied in York Minster rather than Leicester, in the case that came before the High Court in 2014. Burial in York would not only accord with what they took to be the king's wish, it would be bringing the king home to his northern capital. As Sam Knight observed in a perceptive article in *Prospect Magazine*: "For many Ricardians, rescuing the King from the place where he was killed and humiliated . . . is also about rescuing him from history."[36]

It's not only that historical wind blowing in Langley's remarks, but the idea of rescuing someone, or a whole country, from history, of going back and fixing something that went wrong in the past, that calls to mind the longing Walter Benjamin ascribes to the Angel of History, whose wings are caught in the storm blowing from Paradise. "The angel would like to stay, awaken the dead, and make whole what has been smashed."[37] This is, arguably, the deep mission of the Richard III Society. The widely publicized reconstruction of the king's face even gestures at physical resurrection. As Phil Stone, chairman of the Society, commented when the face was unveiled: "When I looked him in the eye, 'Good King Richard' seemed alive and about to speak."[38] Other observers, unaffiliated with the Society, bore witness to the temporal distortions provoked by Richard III's eruption into the modern world. On the day of his reinterment in Leicester Cathedral, the historical novelist Philippa Gregory

---

34. Philippa Langley, "4th February 2013: The *Looking for Richard Project*—Philippa Langley's Speech," The Richard III Society: Looking for Richard, accessed June 2, 2020, http://www.richardiii.net/leicester_dig.php.

35. Bryony Jones, "Richard III: Farewell to a King," *CNN* (March 2015), accessed June 2, 2020, https://edition.cnn.com/2015/03/22/europe/richard-iii-farewell/index.html.

36. Sam Knight, "Where should Richard III Lie?," *Prospect Magazine* (December 2013), accessed June 2, 2020, https://www.prospectmagazine.co.uk/magazine/battle-over-the-burial-richard-iii-become-savage.

37. Walter Benjamin, "Theses on the Philosophy of History," in *Illuminations*, trans. Harry Zorn, ed. Hannah Arendt (London: Pimlico, 1999), 249.

38. Quoted and discussed in Toon and Stone, "Creation of Cultural Heritage," 56.

spoke of the "veil of time . . . almost disappearing"; the historian Helen Castor spoke of "the fifteenth century bursting into the twenty-first."[39] As Toon and Stone comment, "Contemplating the bones, we are operating simultaneously in several times and places: the history of England, the history of Leicester, the present day, historical time, and mythic time, where fantasy-fiction and history aren't clearly delineated."[40]

The multitemporality of the modern Ricardian moment bears some echoes of medieval discourses: the Eucharistic fusion of disparate times, the openness to posthumous miracles, the dead saint who opens his mouth and speaks.[41] Yet the perceived disruption of linear time marks a total departure from the temporal order implicit in Gerald of Wales's account of the exhumation of King Arthur. Whereas so many other aspects of the Leicester narrative find a parallel in twelfth-century Glastonbury, the focus on historical redemption is, I would argue, more characteristic of English Renaissance and specifically post-Reformation thought. In temporal terms, this medieval king has had an early modern *inventio*.

The English Reformation of the sixteenth century has been described as the most historically minded of all European Reformations.[42] Protestant historians like John Bale, John Leland, and John Foxe propounded an idealized vision of the early British church, which had been pure and practically apostolic before Augustine of Canterbury introduced the Roman contagion. For some, the Reformation was specifically a return to the spirit of Glastonbury—not so much the Glastonbury of King Arthur as that of Joseph of Arimathea, who had brought the Christian religion to Britain within a few years of Christ's death and resurrection. For Reformation historians, this idealized past was lost only in the sense of having been lost from view. Thus Leland promised that his historical research would "open [a] window," letting in the light that had been "by the space of a whole thousand yeares stopped up," whilst Foxe argued that the uncorrupted Christianity of early centuries had persisted across time, though "scarse visible or knowne to worldly eyes."[43] Like Richard in the soil of Leicester, the true church had been long concealed but never really gone, always awaiting discovery and revivification.

Yet this most historical of Reformations was also, in a deep way, antihistorical, especially in regard to medieval history. For if, as reformed historians

---

39. Quoted in Bailey, "Richard III"; Bailey, "Anthropology, the Medievalist," 37.
40. Toon and Stone, "Creation of Cultural Heritage," 57.
41. See Bailey, "Anthropology, the Medievalist," 38.
42. F. J. Levy, *Tudor Historical Thought* (San Marino, CA: Huntington Library, 1967), 79.
43. John Leland and John Bale, *The Laboryouse Journey and Serche of Johan Leylande* (1549), sig. D7ᵛ; John Foxe, *Actes and Monuments* (London, 1583), fol. *iiiiʳ.

argued, the Catholic Church had drawn a veil over the truth, then all the chronicles authored by medieval monks must be treated with caution if not dismissed entirely, contaminated as they were with popish propaganda. At best, medieval chronicles were guilty of "partiall dealing and corrupt handling of Historyes"; at worst, they were not true history at all.[44] The task of the Protestant historian was to sift the grains of truth from this mass of falsehood and make what had been hidden visible once more. Bale was particularly active in his efforts to rehabilitate the reputation of the infamous King John, whom he hailed as a virtuous proto-Protestant slandered by monkish chroniclers; in addition to authoring a play with John as its protagonist, Bale claimed to have witnessed the opening of John's tomb at Worcester in 1529, where the king was revealed in all his regalia, refuting rumors spread by the "hissing throng" that the body was not there.[45] Much like twenty-first-century Ricardians, Bale saw the revelation of the intact royal body as constituting effective proof of the king's virtue, giving the lie to centuries of malicious propaganda. His poetic account of the opening of John's tomb corresponds in interesting ways with the *inventio* narratives centering on King Arthur and Richard III; Bale was certainly familiar with the writings of Gerald of Wales, and may have borrowed from him the idea of the exhumation disproving (otherwise unreported) claims that the royal body could not be found.

Nor was this the only variant on the secular-royal *inventio* narrative to which the fertile atmosphere of the English Reformation would give rise. The Anglo-Welsh writer Arthur Kelton's *Commendacyon of Welshmen* (1546) recalled the prophecy made by an angel to the last British king, Cadwaladr, according to Geoffrey of Monmouth. Told that the reign of the Britons was over, Cadwaladr had retired to Rome, where he had been buried in a forgotten grave. Yet Kelton cites the belief that when Cadwaladr's bones returned to Britain, the Britons would rule themselves again:

In the prophesy
Whiche did specifye
The holy translacion
Of Cadwaladre
Frome Rome hidre
By Santificacion

---

44. Leland and Bale, *Laboryouse Journey*, fol. *iii^v.

45. Thea Tomaini, *The Corpse as Text: Disinterment and Antiquarian Enquiry, 1700–1900* (Woodbridge, UK: Boydell Press, 2017), 25, 34–36.

That when his bones
Were translated ones
In to this region
Then shulde the Brutes
Receave ther frutes
And fyrst possession.[46]

The location of Cadwaladr's tomb in Rome was unknown in Kelton's time, and there is no record of an attempt in this period to locate the king's remains and return them to Britain.[47] Yet Kelton concludes that the prophesied translation has already come about, because his successor, Henry VIII, has separated himself from Rome:

For this is he
Ye maye well se
Whose bones are translated
By sentence devyne
Frome Rome this tyme
Newly separated

Accordingly
As the prophesy
Afore had expressed
When Cadwalader's bones
Translated were ones
All thinges shulde be redressed.[48]

A marginal note attempts to clarify the slightly mystifying argument of these verses: "Cadwalader bones translated by seperacion by twene Rome & vs." Playing cleverly (or desperately) on the doctrine of the king's two bodies, Kelton argues that Henry VIII's royal body is also Cadwaladr's body, and that by separating himself from Rome he has effectively brought Cadwaladr home. Like the Ricardian reading of the exhumation of Richard III, Kelton's narra-

---

46. Arthur Kelton, *A Commendacyon of Welshmen* (London, 1546), sig. fol. 1^{r-v}.

47. Thirty years later, Welsh Catholic exiles in Rome argued strenuously that a mysterious ancient tomb in the Vatican belonged to Cadwaladr. They were opposed by English Catholics who ascribed the tomb rather to the seventh-century King of Wessex, Cædwalla (Jason Nice, *Sacred History and National Identity: Comparisons Between Early Modern Wales and Brittany* [Abingdon: Routledge, 2016], 144–49).

48. Kelton, *Commendacyon of Welshmen*, sig. f6^v.

tive associates the recovery of royal remains with the redemption of history. The main difference is that in Richard III's case the discovery of the dead king prompts the exposure of falsehoods and the recovery of a lost link with the past. In Cadwaladr's case, the order is reversed: the exposure of the lies and recovery of the genuine past prompts, indeed *is*, the rediscovery of the king.

Neither the exhumation of King John nor the translation of Cadwaladr constitutes a full example of a royal *inventio*. John's body was never really lost; Cadwaladr's was never really found. Taken together, however, they suggest a narrative precursor to the exhumation of Richard III, sharing with that later example a temporal vision that is simply not to be found in Gerald of Wales's account of the Glastonbury excavation. For Bale and Kelton, as for Langley and others in the twenty-first century, the recovery of a royal body catalyzes or coincides with the restoration of historical truths and the reparation of historical wrongs. The desire to intervene in the past and set history on a different course was certainly not unknown in the Middle Ages (when it was often expressed in acts of forgery). It is in the Reformation era, however, that the dream of recovering lost historical worlds attaches itself repeatedly to the project of exhuming lost British kings. That sixteenth-century project would find its delayed fruition in Leicester in 2012.

As I argued in the first part of this chapter, the similarities between the exhumations of King Arthur and Richard III are so close and so extensive that the latter can fairly be described as a reiteration or reenactment of the former. To a certain extent, the Greyfriars excavation can be characterized as a genuinely medieval event, one which happened to coincide with the launch of the iPhone 5 and the global success of Psy's "Gangnam Style." Yet this medieval event was not granted a medieval reception. Rather, the discovery of Richard III was celebrated in terms that closely recall the radical anachronic imaginings of post-Reformation historical thought. There is an abundance of irony here. In seeking to rescue a medieval king from the calumnies of Tudor propagandists, Richard's admirers have re-embedded him in a quintessentially Tudor temporal discourse whose explicit aim was to bypass or overwrite the history of the later Middle Ages. The response to Richard's reemergence has not been overly medieval, as some commentators have claimed. Arguably, it has not been medieval enough.

PART II

ENTANGLEMENTS

CHAPTER 5

Global *Beowulf* and the Poetics of Entanglement

ANDREW JAMES JOHNSTON

One of the exhibits on display in the British Museum's Department of Coins and Medals is a gold coin minted in the Anglo-Saxon Kingdom of Mercia in the eighth century. It dates from between 773 and 796, the period when Mercia reached its cultural and political zenith under the rulership of King Offa and assumed a position of hegemony among the Anglo-Saxon kingdoms. Mercian ascendancy was not to last, however: before long, the Kingdom of Wessex further to the south took over as the dominant regional power.

Offa's reign is memorable among other things for his tension-ridden diplomatic relations with the Carolingian Empire; and the Mercian coin, too, testifies to the breadth of Offa's political and economic horizons. Apart from the king's name, it bears inscriptions in Arabic, including a shortened version of the *Shahada*, the Islamic Creed. Both the inscription and the coin's overall design imitate the appearance of a dinar minted in 773 or 774 during the reign of the Abbasid Caliph al-Mansur.[1] While, all in all, the Mercian coin is

---

1. The coin bears the inscription, in Arabic, "This dinar was minted in the year 157." There is no mention of the caliph's name on the coin itself, but the date falls within al-Mansur's reign (754–75 CE). In light of Mercia's tension-ridden relations with the Carolingian Empire, it is noteworthy that copies of Arabic dinars were minted under Charlemagne, too; for images of a Carolingian coin bearing the same date in Arabic, but probably minted between 780 and 793, see "Dinar/Solidus mancusus 157 AH" at Künker Münzauktionen und Goldhandel, accessed June 2, 2020, https://www.kuenker.de/en/archiv/stueck/124043. I thank Andreas Ismail Mohr for bringing this coin to my attention and for advice on the inscriptions.

a remarkably faithful copy of the Arab original, a number of small but easily recognizable inaccuracies leave little doubt that its Anglo-Saxon creators had no actual knowledge of Arabic and were quite possibly unaware of the inscription's meaning. The British Museum acquired this particular object in 1913. Because this numismatic treasure was discovered in Rome, it was suggested that it had originally formed part of a special tribute to the Pope. This once widespread theory is now no longer accepted, not least because of the Mercian coin's specific inscription. The explanation currently offered in the British Museum's electronic catalogue is that it was intended for the cosmopolitan markets of Southern France, where Arabic coinage was a widely recognized and highly esteemed means of payment.[2]

The Anglo-Saxon "dinar" is thus squarely placed at the center of an intricate network of relationships in which economic, political, cultural, and religious factors are tightly interwoven. Displaying an impressive degree of technological competence, Offa's moneyers supplied their king with a piece of currency that allowed the English economy to tap into international trade. This international trade extended over long distances and across several political boundaries, including the relatively recent but nonetheless highly significant cultural and ideological dividing line between Christianity and the Muslim world. What we are dealing with here is thus a product of material culture—the product of sophisticated craftsmanship—that operates as both object and medium within processes of exchange; processes through which a complex and far-ranging network of relationships is constituted.

To the modern scholar, the coin's embeddedness in a complex network of transnational relations may seem hardly surprising—after all, the lively cultural and economic exchange between the Christian and the Islamicate sphere has become, by now, a well-tilled field of scholarly inquiry.[3] The persistence of elements of a monetary economy even after the Roman Empire's demise is a long-established fact. Just as well-known are the existence of far-flung

---

2. The coin (shown on the cover of this volume) is in the British Museum (registration number: 1913,1213.1). For a description, see "Gold imitation dinar of Offa," in Google Arts & Culture, accessed June 2, 2020, https://artsandculture.google.com/asset/gold-imitation-dinar-of-offa/CwH2MNp-VHT9lA. See also the chapter by Naomi Howell in this volume for further references to objects with Kufic or pseudo-Kufic inscriptions.

3. See, for instance, John Tolan, Henry Laurens, and Gilles Veinstein, *Europe and the Islamic World: A History* (Princeton, NJ: Princeton University Press, 2013); Brian A. Catlos, *Muslims of Medieval Latin Christendom, c. 1050–1614* (Cambridge: Cambridge University Press, 2014); Sharon Kinoshita, *Medieval Boundaries: Rethinking Difference in Old French Literature* (Philadelphia: University of Pennsylvania Press, 2006); Isabelle Dolezalek, *Arabic Script on Christian Kings: Textile Inscriptions on Royal Garments from Norman Sicily*, Das Mittelalter, Perspektiven mediävistischer Forschung, Beihefte 5 (Berlin: de Gruyter, 2017); and Howell's chapter in this volume.

trade routes in the eighth century and the premodern penchant for pressing a wide variety of political and cultural claims via artistic imitation in the field of coinage. On the face of it, an Anglo-Saxon coin that quite literally bears an Arabic imprint—or from an aesthetic point of view: an Arabic coin with an Anglo-Saxon inscription—no longer appears to be anything very much out of the ordinary.

Yet a closer look at the coin's theoretical and methodological implications and their specific contexts does seem worthwhile. Were we to examine the precious object from the vantage point of current historiographical methodology, the most promising approach that springs to mind would be what is commonly referred to as "global history"—an approach whose historical focus is not, as one might assume, directed toward the spatial totality of our planet, but rather at the manifold interconnections and relationships that link local phenomena to units much larger in scale, especially to seemingly remote cultural, economic, and political contexts. What is at stake is thus a history of entanglements that investigates the diversity and complexity of relationships across the boundaries of what, in a spirit of cavalier Eurocentrism, previous generations of scholarship would simply have taken for granted as separate "cultural spheres" or "periods."[4]

Even if, as they imitated an Abbasid coin, Mercia's ruler and his moneyers were predominantly concerned with trade relations to Southern France, they nonetheless entered into a cultural, economic, and political network that stretched from Wales all the way to India, throwing into sharp relief, from a transcultural point of view, the problematic status both of established cultural spheres and of received period boundaries. After all, as the German Arabist Thomas Bauer has only recently reminded us, the notion of an "Islamic Middle Ages" does not really make any sense.[5]

What I wish to examine in this paper is the nexus between the theoretical and methodological questions raised by artifacts such as this English-Arabic coin and the poem that has, since the nineteenth century, been considered the most canonical of Old English texts: the poem known today as *Beowulf*— a poem in which, as Peter S. Baker notes, coins are conspicuously absent, as though the text were imagining its fictional heroic world as a moneyless economy.[6] If we reflect for a moment on the Mercian "dinar" with its Arabic

---

4. Sebastian Conrad, *What Is Global History?* (Princeton, NJ: Princeton University Press, 2016), 4–5.

5. Thomas Bauer, *Warum es kein islamisches Mittelalter gab: Das Erbe der Antike und der Orient* (Munich: C. H. Beck, 2018), 11–31.

6. Peter S. Baker, *Honour, Exchange and Violence in "Beowulf,"* Anglo-Saxon Studies 20 (Cambridge: D. S. Brewer, 2013), 37–38.

and Anglo-Saxon/Latin ("Offa Rex") inscriptions, and if we then examine the literary text that is *Beowulf* against the backdrop of tangible historical artifacts like this coin, embedded as it is in a tangle of wide-reaching cultural threads, the result may at first appear to be a little disappointing. By comparison, the fictional world in which the epic is set proves to be oddly limited in scope, confining itself exclusively to the Germanic cultural area around the Baltic and the North Seas, a geographical space inhabited by Geats, Swedes, Danes, Franks, and Frisians where representatives of other cultural, political, or linguistic entities are conspicuous for their absence. Given that early scholarship on *Beowulf* placed the epic firmly in a very specific—that is, Germanic—historical and cultural context, almost automatically assuming not only an early date of composition but also a relatively close relationship between the narrative and the actual historical reality of migration-period Scandinavia, this problem did not become especially virulent for a long time.

Roberta Frank was the first scholar to point out the peculiar, highly artificial insularity of this fictional world, the literary landscape belonging to the heroic-elegiac mode of Anglo-Saxon poetry. This is an imaginary cultural sphere where we do, indeed, encounter the abovementioned Geats, Swedes, Danes, and Frisians, along with the occasional Franks. Yet of all the other Germanic tribes that were involved in the upheavals of the migration period, only the Goths tend to feature prominently in Anglo-Saxon heroic and elegiac literature. Neither the Vandals nor the Burgundians make a prominent appearance, nor do any other Germanic peoples play a truly important role, let alone the non-Germanic ones: in the particular case of *Beowulf*, there is no reference whatsoever to Arabs or to Constantinople.[7] This curious absence is not specific to the poem. Generally speaking, the Germanic peoples form a remarkably exclusive circle in Anglo-Saxon poetry.[8] What is more, from the vantage point of literary history, this circle's exclusivity constitutes a comparatively late development. In this, I again follow Roberta Frank, who has demonstrated that Anglo-Saxon poetry dealing with Germanic subject matter pertaining to the migration period did not really emerge before the tenth century.[9] According to Frank, this type of poetry is the product of a very particular stage of Anglo-Saxon literary history, a time when Germanic—and especially Gothic—themes were *en vogue*. Frank goes on to argue that this literary trend deliberately emphasized a very specific part of the Germanic liter-

---

7. Roberta Frank, "Germanic Legend in Old English Literature," in *The Cambridge Companion to Old English Literature*, ed. Malcolm Godden and Michael Lapidge, 2nd ed. (Cambridge: Cambridge University Press, 2013), 89.

8. The poem "Widsith" can be seen as a remarkable exception.

9. Frank, "Germanic Legend," 87–89.

ary tradition. For her, the traditional interpretation of Anglo-Saxon poetry as a straightforward manifestation of a stable inventory of traditional stories and motifs shared by all Germanic peoples can no longer be sustained.

In this highly selective choice of themes and subject matter, the emphatically literary and self-consciously sophisticated character of Anglo-Saxon poetry becomes evident. This holds true especially for poems such as *Deor*, a text usually categorized as an "elegy." There is compelling evidence that *Deor* reflects—and indeed even showcases—its own artificiality—cultivating, as it were, a sophisticated Germanic, and especially Gothic, *chic*.[10]

As far as *Beowulf* is concerned, however, this is only half the truth: as I have pointed out elsewhere, the epic repeatedly and systematically punctures and calls into question the supposedly self-enclosed insularity of its Germanic world. Most conspicuously, this sense of puncturing is achieved on an archaeological level, that is, on the level of the material remains left behind by historical cultures that have long since perished, remnants with which the characters find themselves confronted time and again.[11] Two kinds of archaeological artifact intrude upon the world of the protagonists: on the one hand, we are presented with what appear to be Roman remains; on the other, the text describes an object with a biblical context. In addition, we encounter several artifacts from within the Germanic protagonists' own cultural sphere which, without expressly being singled out as archaeological in the sense outlined above, are assigned a specific historical status even as they remain in active use or circulation.

The objects linked to Roman antiquity are archaeological in that they are embedded in the landscape or described as parts of buildings: there is the paved road that the newly arrived Geats follow as they approach the royal hall of Heorot—paved, and thus unmistakably Roman in origin: "stræt wæs stanfah" (line 320a) [the road was paved with stones].[12] There is also the *fagne flor* (line 725) within the hall itself, the shiny, colorful, and hence probably tes-

---

10. For the connections between *Deor*'s ingenious approach to Germanic legend and history, on the one hand, and its self-conscious exploration of its own literariness, on the other, see Andrew James Johnston, "The Riddle of *Deor* and the Performance of Fiction," in *Language and Text: Current Perspectives on English and Germanic Historical Linguistics and Philology*, ed. Andrew James Johnston, Ferdinand von Mengden, and Stefan Thim (Heidelberg: Carl Winter Universitätsverlag, 2006), 133–50.

11. Andrew James Johnston, "*Beowulf* as Anti-Virgilian World Literature: Archaeology, Ekphrasis, and Epic," in *The Shapes of Early English Poetry: Style, Form, History*, ed. Irina Dumitrescu and Eric Weiskott (Kalamazoo, MI: Medieval Institute Publications, Western Michigan University, 2019), 37–58.

12. All quotations from *Beowulf* are taken from R. D. Fulk, Robert E. Bjork, and John D. Niles, eds., *Klaeber's "Beowulf" and "The Fight at Finnsburg,"* 4th ed. (Toronto: University of Toronto Press, 2008).

sellated floor that provides the surface on which Beowulf's dramatic fight with Grendel takes place. The Old English term *fag* has a wide range of meanings—"colorful," "mottled," "stained," "shiny," "glittering," "polymorphous"—making it difficult to pinpoint the surface's exact appearance: continuing a line of thought suggesting that Heorot's floor may have been inspired by the Roman ruins in Bath, Seth Lerer has even gone so far as to suggest that the poem may here be envisaging a Roman mosaic depicting Orpheus.[13] What does seem to be fairly clear in light of the overall context is that the floor of Heorot consists of a hard material, such as stone or tiles, that is either multicolored and/or reflective of light, and hence probably of Roman origin. Finally, there are also the stone arches in the Dragon's lair—the *stanbogan* (line 2545)—which, from an Anglo-Saxon perspective, would likewise be identifiable as the remains of Roman architecture, as Emily V. Thornbury has pointed out.[14]

It could, of course, be argued that the presence of Roman ruins in Denmark is first and foremost the result of the epic's naive ignorance in regard to historical difference, or, in other words, simply another example of the lack of historical consciousness so frequently attributed to the Middle Ages by modern historiography. However, given the fact that the historical Denmark of the migration period was situated far beyond the borders of the Roman Empire, I would prefer to interpret the presence of these ruins in the text as instances of deliberate anachronism. Or to put it differently: if the epic deals with Roman ruins almost obsessively, it does so precisely because learned Anglo-Saxons of the tenth century would have been well aware of the fact that the Romans had never actually set foot in Denmark, enabling them to grasp the text's conspicuously anachronistic thrust.

The biblical archaeological artifact intruding upon the space of the poem's imagined cultural homogeneity is the giant sword Beowulf discovers during

---

13. Seth Lerer, "'On fagne flor': The Postcolonial *Beowulf*," in *Postcolonial Approaches to the European Middle Ages*, ed. Ananya Jahanara Kabir and Deanne Williams (Cambridge: Cambridge University Press, 2005), 77–102.

14. Emily V. Thornbury contends that the stone arches in the Dragon's lair—twice referred to as *enta geweorc* (line 2717 and line 2774)—deliberately allude to a specifically Roman past, since they are reinforced by a further reference to Roman culture, the *segn eallgylden* (line 2767) that has been taken to describe a Roman standard. The latter's Romanness can be argued on etymological grounds (Emily V. Thornbury, "*Eald enta geweorc* and the Relics of Empire: Revisiting the Dragon's Lair in *Beowulf*," *Quaestio* 1 [2000]: 82–92). For an in-depth analysis of the different ways in which Anglo-Saxon poetry deployed the metaphor *enta geweorc*, see Lori Ann Garner, *Structuring Spaces: Oral Poetics and Architecture in Early Medieval England* (Notre Dame, IN: University of Notre Dame Press, 2011), 112–68. An interesting reading of the *stanbogan*—one that does not necessarily exclude their Roman connections—is offered by Gale Owen-Crocker, who suggests that the word may refer to a crypt (*The Four Funerals in "Beowulf" and the Structure of the Poem* [Manchester: Manchester University Press, 2009], 62).

his fight with Grendel's mother: the "ealdsweord eotenisc" (line 1558) [ancient giant sword]. After coming into contact with the blood of the grendelkin, all that remains of the weapon that saved Beowulf's life is its hilt. This object, too, constitutes a striking anachronism. And in that capacity, the hilt raises a question that keeps recurring throughout the text: what is the nature of the relationship between the Germanic heathens of the migration period and the text's overarching framework of salvation history, a framework into which the epic inserts itself in spite of—or, according to J. R. R. Tolkien, precisely *because of*—its pagan setting?[15] The giant sword is literally referred to as *eotena geweorc* [work of giants], a term which Anglo-Saxon poetry ordinarily, but not exclusively, deploys in reference to Roman ruins. At the same time, the sword is neatly integrated into a biblical narrative, namely the apocryphal Book of Enoch, which describes the destruction of the giants in the great Flood and credits them with having, among other things, instructed humankind in the art of metalwork.[16] This, according to the text, is what the inscription on the hilt is about. At this juncture, a literal understanding of the term *giant sword* creates something of a problem as far as the epic's sense of historical logic is concerned—after all, the giants who forged the sword would hardly have had been given the time and opportunity to eternalize the story of their own extinction on an elaborately crafted artifact. However, given that Grendel and his mother could well be interpreted as descendants of the biblical giants, it is quite possible to read the two characters as historical remnants. If, by killing them, Beowulf does, indeed, wipe out the last members of the race of giants, this would necessarily turn him into a useful, if unwitting, agent of the divine plan of salvation.[17] The presence of the giant sword would thereby expose the poem's culturally secluded sphere of early Germanic history as a kind of pagan

---

15. J. R. R. Tolkien, "The Monsters and the Critics," in *The Monsters and the Critics and Other Essays*, ed. Christopher Tolkien (London: Harper Collins, 1997), 26–27.

16. The apocryphal *Book of Enoch* (8:1) relates how the fallen angels taught humans both metalwork and writing. They procreated with women descended from Cain and thus engendered the race of Giants, who were later destroyed by the Flood (see, for example, Johann Köberl, "The Magic Sword in *Beowulf*," *Neophilologus* 71 [1987]: 124; and Richard J. Schrader, "The Language on the Giant's Sword Hilt in *Beowulf*," *Neuphilologische Mitteilungen* 94 [1993]: 141–47).

17. Allen J. Frantzen has questioned Beowulf's easy integration into a teleological Christian narrative. Instead of seeing Beowulf as the hero who fulfills God's purpose with respect to Cain's descendants, Frantzen suggests that the very existence of the sword may actually imply that the Flood never achieved its goal in the first place. His reading conceives of Beowulf's destruction of Grendel and his mother not as evidence of the relentless progress of Christian history, but as the beginning of a fresh cycle of violence (Allen J. Frantzen, *The Desire for Origins: New Language, Old English, and Teaching the Tradition* [New Brunswick: Rutgers University Press, 1990], 188).

illusion—an illusion that, ironically, *Beowulf*'s archaic characters are themselves unable to fathom precisely because they are heathens.

If we follow the assumption that the text portrays the pagan Geats and Danes as illiterate, this could thus be interpreted as a metaphor for their being cut off from the Christian hope of salvation. And the text leaves no doubt whatsoever that the ornamentation on the hilt is, indeed, a form of writing:

> Swa wæs on ðæm scennum   sciran goldes
> þurh runstafas   rihte gemearcod,
> geseted ond gesæd,   hwam þæt sweord geworht,
> irena cyst   ærest wære,
> wreoþenhilt ond wyrmfah.
> (lines 1694–98a)

> On the sword-guard of bright gold there was also rightly marked through rune-staves, set down and told, for whom that sword, best of irons, had first been made, its hilt twisted and ornamented with snakes.[18]

I would like to focus on the two adjectives at the conclusion of the description of the sword hilt: *wreoþenhilt ond wyrmfah*. The second term, *wyrmfah*, does not present us with any serious difficulties: it means "decorated with snake/serpent- or dragon-like ornaments." *Wyrmfah* clearly refers to the type of ornamentation familiar from early medieval Irish and Anglo-Saxon art, where it is omnipresent on objects such as weapons and jewelry, but also in manuscript illuminations: interwoven bodies of animals—for the most part modeled on serpents or dragons—entangled in complex geometrical patterns.

In comparison, the word *wreoþenhilt* constitutes something close to a minor crux—at least, if we are to believe the glossary provided by the editors of the standard edition of *Beowulf*. They offer two different ways of paraphrasing *wreoþenhilt*, namely as "HILT wrapped with a grip or with twisted ornamentation."[19] Though these two explanations are not *absolutely* mutually exclusive, they do, if taken seriously, point in two very different directions, and critics have tended to opt for either one or the other.

If we accept *wreoþenhilt* to mean "(wrapped) with twisted ornamentation" then the term has a meaning fairly close, though not exactly identical,

---

18. E. Talbot Donaldson, *Beowulf: A Prose Translation*, ed. Nicholas Howe, Norton Critical Edition, 2nd ed. (New York: W. W. Norton and Company, 2002), 29.

19. Fulk et al., eds., *Klaeber's "Beowulf,"* 460.

to that of *wyrmfah*.²⁰ The first adjective would be just a little less specific in its depiction of the actual iconographic scheme than the second. The combination of *wreoþenhilt ond wyrmfah* would thus constitute a comparatively straightforward hendiadys where two words express more or less the same idea or, at least, very similar ideas. The other interpretation would imply, however, that the hilt is wrapped with a special material, probably metal wire, a design for sword hilts that occurs elsewhere in the text. In this case, the phrase *wreoþenhilt ond wyrmfah* would be conjoining two very different terms and epistemic perspectives, with the first describing the hilt's material structure and technical makeup and the second its artistic design and iconographical scheme. This is exactly how James Paz understands the words: "spiral-hilted and serpent-stained."²¹

The first interpretation, the one positing the presence of a hendiadys, would be reinforced by the alliteration. Both in Modern English and Modern High German, this kind of alliterative hendiadys has survived in particular formulaic expressions consisting in the pairing of similar, related, or complementary concepts that often combine to produce the sense of a larger totality, as in "kith and kin," "bits and bytes," "Haus und Hof," "Kind und Kegel," or "Tür und Tor." In the second case, the alliteration would actually accentuate the difference between the two perspectives invoked by the two adjectives.

Yet, in the light of the specific structure of *wreoþenhilt ond wyrmfah* and, especially, in the light of its particular placement within a larger narrative unit, I would argue that *Beowulf* does not so much invite its audience to choose between these two interpretations, but rather seems to imply both options at the same time: first, an interpretation that sees in the two elements of the phrase a juxtaposition of the technical with the aesthetic; and second, a reading that interprets the second element of the phrase, *wyrmfah*, in terms of a more precise and concrete rendering of the aesthetic implications already contained in the first element, *wreoþenhilt*.

It is the relative semantic vagueness of *wreoþenhilt* that allows for both interpretations simultaneously, the technical and the aesthetic. And because in the pairing of *wreoþenhilt* and *wyrmfah* the more ambiguous term precedes the one that is more concrete and hence more precise, readers and listeners

---

20. Hilda Ellis Davidson's discussion of *wreoþenhilt* conflates the two possible interpretations, the technical one with the iconographic/artistic, though with a very heavy emphasis on the latter: "This hilt is called *wreoþenhilt*, and such a term is not difficult to explain from what we know of hilt decoration. It might be used of any of the hilts with interlacing ornament dating from the sixth century and later" (Hilda Roderick Ellis Davidson, *The Sword in Anglo-Saxon England* [Oxford: Clarendon Press, 1962], 136).

21. James Paz, *Nonhuman Voices in Anglo-Saxon Literature and Culture* (Manchester: Manchester University Press, 2017), 52.

are put into a position where it becomes possible, as the reading or listening experience progresses, to reinterpret the first term in the semantic light of the second. At first encounter, the reader or listener may well conclude that *wreoþenhilt* refers to the sword hilt's wire-wrapped construction. But on the introduction of the word *wyrmfah*, the possibility is raised that what has been presented here has, in fact, been an aesthetic-cum-iconographic description all along, that is, that *wreoþenhilt* might be just as much about artistic design as *wyrmfah*. This notion of a deliberate ambiguity that unfolds as the reading progresses is all the more plausible since, immediately prior to the lines in question, the text has already been moving back and forth between the different aspects of the hilt's construction and ornamentation as well as signification, that is, between the different areas of knowledge involved in the hilt's fashioning: first, the letters are explicitly characterized with an eye to their materiality, namely as an engraving (*gemearcod*); second, the description proceeds to what one might call the inscription's typographical layout (*geseted*); finally, the letters are conceptualized as semantic, syntactic, and morphological units (*gesæd*). In every step, the properties of the concept next to be introduced have already been semantically prepared for by the preceding one. Yet exactly at the point where the description of the sword hilt reaches the most explicitly semantic level of meaning, that of an actual linguistic message—"gesæd, hwam þæt sweord geworht" (line 1696)—the text immediately returns to the issue of the sword's most basic and concrete materiality by referring to the *irena cyst* from which it is made: the best, or literally, the "choicest" iron. Thus, even before we come to *wreoþenhilt ond wyrmfah*, we have already seen the text oscillating between the principles of material construction, on the one hand, and aesthetic presentation and semantic signification, on the other. In the poem's description of the sword hilt, both the archaeological artifact itself and its description prove, therefore, to be multifaceted and pervaded by a sense of fundamental ambiguity. Ultimately, the element that appears to be the least ambiguous is the one with which the extended descriptive passage ends: the adjective *wyrmfah*, referring, as we have seen, to the complex and intricate networks of geometrically entangled serpent bodies typical of Anglo-Saxon art.[22]

---

22. Victoria Symons argues for a cultural tradition to be found in both Old English and Old Norse literature and iconography of associating dragons' twisted bodies with writing, especially with runes, as well as treasure. She posits that this combination of motifs produces a tension between the dragons' tendency to conceal treasure and the runes' capacity for revealing secrets (Victoria Symons, "*Wreoþenhilt ond wyrmfah*: Confronting Serpents in *Beowulf* and Beyond," in *Representing Beasts in Early Medieval England and Scandinavia*, ed. Michael D. J. Bintley and Thomas J. T. Williams [Woodbridge, UK: Boydell Press, 2015], 73–93).

Before taking a closer look at the interwoven patterns that this archaeological artifact so prominently displays and that appear to constitute the climax of the sword's ekphrastic description, a brief excursus into a relevant chapter in the history of *Beowulf* scholarship is called for.

In 1967, the American medievalist John Leyerle published what could be called a narratological paper on *Beowulf*, a heavily illustrated essay in which he rather boldly asserted a number of direct parallels between Anglo-Saxon visual art, especially its interlaced dragon ornaments, and the epic's overarching narrative structure. According to Leyerle, the entangled bands of overlapping dragon bodies are nothing short of a visual metaphor for *Beowulf*'s narrative structure itself, a feature he considers to be typical of medieval literature as a whole: instead of being told in a linear and straightforward fashion, the narrative exhibits a constant back and forth between recurrent motifs and motif clusters that are conjoined not unlike woven braids.[23]

Leyerle's position was provocative and remains so: even today, there is a widespread tendency to assume that the poem is characterized by a series of digressions embedded in the main plot, although there is disagreement as to which, and thus how many, passages ought to be classified as digressive. For Leyerle, the so-called "digressions" in *Beowulf* are actually no such thing—the passages in question merely represent the different narrative threads as they intermittently appear on the surface of the textual fabric. His argument culminated in the audacious statement that "there are no digressions in *Beowulf*."[24]

Despite the fact that Leyerle's essay is included as a classic of the discipline in R. D. Fulk's influential anthology of groundbreaking research on *Beowulf*, his ideas do not seem to command very much attention anymore.[25] Today, it is Leyerle's "fatal contradiction thesis" that is considered his most important critical legacy, a thesis according to which the epic takes a critical view of the concept of heroism embodied by Beowulf and thus sets its protagonist up to fail.[26] In John D. Niles's excellent recent overview of the criticism on Anglo-Saxon literature, Leyerle is mentioned only with respect to the question of

---

23. John Leyerle, "The Interlace Structure of *Beowulf*," in *Interpretations of "Beowulf": A Critical Anthology*, ed. R. D. Fulk (Bloomington: Indiana University Press, 1991), 146–58.

24. Leyerle, "Interlace Structure of *Beowulf*," 156.

25. By contrast, during the 1970s and much of the 1980s the ways in which the concept of interlace might bring into dialogue the visual aesthetics of early medieval British art and *Beowulf*'s poetic and narrative structures was a much-discussed subject among critics. For an overview, see Gillian Overing, *Language, Sign, and Gender in "Beowulf"* (Carbondale and Edwardsville: Southern Illinois University Press, 1990), 35–37 and 118n2.

26. See for example the treatment of Leyerle in Jodi-Anne George's comprehensive overview of *Beowulf* criticism (*"Beowulf": A Reader's Guide to Essential Criticism* [Houndmills, UK: Palgrave Macmillan, 2010], 69).

epic heroism's moral value.[27] To a certain extent, this may be the case because Leyerle and his work are strongly associated with the New Criticism, a critical method that has fallen out of favor in Anglo-Saxon Studies and in English Studies as a whole, albeit for completely different reasons.[28] Tom Shippey sums up the central critique leveled at Leyerle, when, drawing on Morton Bloomfield, he states: "'Interlace' . . . is only a metaphor, misleading if one thinks that verbal art, inevitably linear, can approach the effect of visual art seen as a simultaneous whole."[29] But given that visual culture theorists have long since dismantled Gotthold Ephraim Lessing's time-honored dichotomy of verbal art as *Zeitkunst* vs. visual art as *Raumkunst*, with the first inevitably unfolding in time and the second in spatial simultaneity,[30] Leyerle's interest in the links between verbal and visual structures in Anglo-Saxon cultural experience might one day be reassessed.

The reason why I have dedicated so much space to a discussion of Leyerle's notion of the epic's structure is not because I plan on following in his narratological footsteps—although this might well prove to be a profitable undertaking. Rather, I feel that Leyerle's argument developed out of a remarkable intuition concerning the significance of the interlaced ornamentation for *Beowulf* as a whole. I will, however, pursue an angle that is slightly different from Leyerle's own: the interlace patterns, I argue, are of such eminent relevance to the poem because they are deployed as a central, if not as *the* central, historical and metapoetic metaphor in precisely the passage examined above—a passage to which, as we shall see, the term *central* applies in more than one sense.

Let us recall that the description of the sword is provided at the very pinnacle of Beowulf's heroic career, immediately after he has, by slaying the grendelkin, unwittingly aligned pagan history with Christian *Heilsgeschichte*. What is more, the significance of the passage is further underscored by the presence

---

27. John D. Niles, *Old English Literature: A Guide to Criticism with Selected Readings* (Chichester: Wiley-Blackwell, 2016), 156, 167.

28. Take this fascinating example of an all-out attack on the New Critical perspectives that had dominated *Beowulf* scholarship in the 1950s, 1960s, and to a large extent also in the 1970s: in 1982, Joseph Harris complained that "our preoccupation with interpretation since Tolkien's famous lecture—coupled perhaps with resignation over the impossibility of establishing facts—has drawn energies away from the healthy traditional approach that seeks an order of works: that is, from literary history" (Joseph Harris, "*Beowulf* in Literary History," *Pacific Coast Philology* 17 [1982]: 16).

29. Tom Shippey, "Structure and Unity," in *A "Beowulf" Handbook*, ed. Robert E. Bjork and John D. Niles (Lincoln: University of Nebraska Press, 1997), 166.

30. See for instance W. J. T. Mitchell's critique of "the impulse to purify media" as one "of the central utopian gestures of modernity" (*Picture Theory: Essays on Verbal and Visual Representation* [Chicago: University of Chicago Press, 1994], 5).

of an archaeological artifact the biblical origin of which casts the poem's main protagonist as an auxiliary of God's plan of salvation in a very tangible, material sense. In describing this object, the poem draws our attention to the exact same interlaced ornamentation that remains emblematic of Celtic and Anglo-Saxon culture even today.

Zooming in on the one archaeological object in which the interconnectedness—or to be more precise, the inextricable interwovenness—of pagan history and salvation history in *Beowulf* becomes most visually manifest, the passage culminates in the use of *wyrmfah*, a word that like no other in the epic encapsulates the aesthetic principle of interlacement. Not only does the scene represent the apex of Beowulf's heroic exploits—but, occurring in line 1698 out of a total of 3182, the word *wyrmfah* is also located almost exactly in the middle of the poem. Clearly, this metaphor is central by any account.

The metaphor's impact is heightened even more by the fact that the epic's characters are by no means aware of this interwovenness and indeed *cannot* be aware of it. If history is here revealed as a history of (potentially multiple) entanglement(s) where different forms of cultural experience and different notions of temporality enter into a complicated relationship, the dramatic irony employed by the text confers an ineluctable epistemological advantage on the epic's audience as compared to its characters. Even if the interest in salvation history is dominant here and claims superiority over pagan culture, the epic's historical scope is not exclusively confined to a biblically inspired narrative. After all, with its specifically archaeological perspective, *Beowulf* also accommodates Roman antiquity, a form of antiquity that always maintains its presence as a further temporal layer potentially in tension with biblical history.

Admittedly, it would undoubtedly be anachronistic to claim the Anglo-Saxons of the tenth century as the precursors of modern global history merely on the strength of observations concerning the significance of an ekphrastically visualized metaphor of entanglement in *Beowulf*.[31] After all, the epic's Christian perspective is beyond question. For the time being, we shall have to proceed on the assumption that there is a hierarchical relationship between the narrator's global Christian vantage point and the culture of Germanic paganism described in the text. By contrast, global history as practiced today deploys the concept of entanglement with the express goal of overcoming Eurocentrism, and consequently of rejecting any kind of hierarchy between different cultural perspectives. And yet we should not take this issue too

---

31. For an interpretation of the letters on the sword within a specifically ekphrastic literary discourse, see Haiko Wandhoff, *Ekphrasis: Kunstbeschreibungen und virtuelle Räume in der Literatur des Mittelalters*, Trends in Medieval Philology 3 (Berlin: de Gruyter, 2003), 18.

lightly: similar to the archaeological remains of past cultures that continue to subvert the epic's supposed historical and cultural homogeneity by allowing a glimpse of different historical circumstances and alternative cultural spaces, the notion of the interwovenness of distinct cultural and historical traditions that is embodied in the *wyrmfah* decorations on an archaeological object from another culture seems to be associated with a certain sense of unease. After all, the metaphor of entanglement as such does not imply an unproblematic, much less an absolute, hierarchy between the historical experiences and cultural traditions that *Beowulf* invokes; nor do the epic's ruins and historical artifacts lend themselves to easy integration into a narrative of Christian triumphalism. As Denis Ferhatović has recently pointed out in his study of material artifacts in Old English poetry, the presence of *spolia* and borrowed objects in Anglo-Saxon poems enables these texts to "display a wider range of attitudes towards the pagan and Jewish past, not exhausted by Christian supersessionism."[32]

In fact, from a specifically Anglo-Saxon perspective, the ubiquitous Roman ruins in *Beowulf* point toward a historical period when the Gospel had already been established in the British Isles, only to be eradicated again by the Anglo-Saxons' own ancestors. And the objects, too, prove to be something of a vexed issue: the giant sword adorned with interlaced dragon ornaments on its hilt can be retrieved from the underwater cave only at the cost of its partial destruction. It looks as though parts of the object were trying to resist the Christian triumph executed by an unwitting Beowulf—an object that, in James Paz's words, exerts the troubling power of its thingness when it "does not behave how it is meant to behave."[33]

At this point, it becomes inevitable to ask if and in how far the historical and metapoetic metaphors attached to the sword are actually compatible. *Prima facie,* in its capacity as the instrument of the giants' destruction that integrates the Germanic hero into Christian salvation history, the sword's function seems fairly unequivocal and ideologically successful. Yet if we see the sword as a work of art, its multiple meanings are more difficult to pinpoint. And it is, after all, precisely as a work of art that the text describes the sword in the greatest of possible detail: its specific ekphrastic status—the image of an inscription evoked by language, the contents of which the listeners or readers in turn visualize in their own imagination—places it squarely in the tradi-

---

32. Denis Ferhatović, *Borrowed Objects and the Art of Poetry:* Spolia *in Old English Verse* (Manchester: Manchester University Press, 2019), 168.

33. Paz, *Nonhuman Voices,* 45.

tion of the *paragone* with its manifold potential for aesthetic self-reflexivity.[34] Whereas the aesthetic fascination radiating from this artifact is both clearly spelled out in the text and keenly felt by the epic's pagan Germanic characters, the object's meaning nonetheless eludes them because they appear to be illiterate. At the same time, the victory over the last giants—Beowulf's contribution to salvation history, or in other words, his belated completion of the Flood—proves to be the source of material loss: the sword survives as a fragment only.

An interesting ambiguity becomes apparent here: despite the damage the historical object sustains in Beowulf's fight against Grendel's mother, in purely aesthetic terms, the fragment loses none of its fascination. This holds true on the level of the plot, where Hrothgar is clearly transfixed by it, but also, owing to the object's complex ekphrastic representation, on the level of the narration, and thus also in regard to the epic's audience. The sword's fragmentary status opens up multiple perspectives, both historical and aesthetic, with potential metapoetic implications. In the end, we are faced with an aporia that even Tolkien was unable to resolve completely: what is the relationship between the epic's unequivocally Christian message and the text's no less unequivocal aesthetic fascination with both the accursed race of giants and the pagan Germanic warriors with their culture of heroism?

Once again, the word *wyrmfah* provides one, if not *the* answer: as interwoven as the Christian Gospel and *Beowulf*'s pagan history may well be, a certain residue of incommensurability remains. The giant sword's continuing beauty and Beowulf's heroism cannot, in the final analysis, fully be contained within a Christian interpretative framework. The visual metaphor of entanglement and interwovenness as embodied in the sword hilt's *wyrmfah* ornamentation establishes a link between different historical perspectives and cultural traditions. But as this visual metaphor of entanglement connects and juxtaposes these different perspectives, it does not merge them to the point of their becoming indistinguishable. Even as the serpents' bodies in the aforementioned depictions of medieval Irish and Anglo-Saxon art become entangled to a degree where we might feel it impossible ever to disentangle them, these bodies do remain separate as different strands, though it may be difficult or

---

34. In classical rhetorical theory, ekphrasis denotes a specific type of verbal representation that emphasizes vividness. As Ruth Webb observes: "So, not only was ekphrasis not understood as a term for 'description of a work of art,' it was not even understood in the same terms as our 'description'" (*Ekphrasis, Imagination and Persuasion in Ancient Rhetorical Theory and Practice* [Farnham, UK: Ashgate, 2009], 70). Here, the term *ekphrasis* is not used in this original sense, but in its more recent meaning of a detailed description of an imaginary work of visual art—or, in James A. W. Heffernan's definition, "a verbal representation of a visual representation"—a convention Virgil inherits from Homer (*Museum of Words: The Poetics of Ekphrasis from Homer to Ashbery* [Chicago: University of Chicago Press, 1993], 3).

potentially impossible to say which body ultimately belongs to which serpent's head.

What is the meaning of all this in the context of global history that I discussed at the beginning of this paper by drawing on the example of the Anglo-Saxon coin with an Arabic inscription? If recent global history highlights processes of social, cultural, and political entanglement in order to overcome historiographical Eurocentrism, *Beowulf* follows a similar approach in staging entanglement as a metaphor for the connectedness of culturally and historically heterogenous kinds of experience. This type of connectedness not only makes visible the differences between the epic's various cultures—the pagan Germanic culture of the characters, the Old Testament culture of the sword hilt, the Christian culture of the narrator, and, different yet again, the Roman culture of the ruins and archaeological remains—it simultaneously opens up multiple perspectives on the objects and events described, and keeps these perspectives in a state of precarious balance.

While Christian *Heilsgeschichte* does prevail over the giants, their cultural heritage continues to be present in the form of an artifact that is fragmented, yet possibly all the more aesthetically fascinating for that. This is the root of the residual incommensurability described above: it comes into being via the object's preserving of a remainder of intrinsic aesthetic value that cannot be erased by the ideological triumph of Christianity. Ultimately, the consequences of this incommensurability are not only metapoetic in the sense that it points toward a concept of art as the particular domain of the aesthetic; as I would argue, it also has an impact on the way that the poem conceives of history. The sword's intrinsic aesthetic value springs from an Otherness that can never fully be brought under control—an Otherness to which we are always already connected via multiple forms of entanglement and interwovenness, but with which we never completely merge.

In a paradoxical role reversal, the pagan hero is turned into the agent of God; and while the biblical object's origin as *eotena geweorc* does link it to salvation history, the artifact simultaneously represents the non-Christian Other. What the complex cosmopolitanism of King Offa's Arabic coin—or more precisely, the Anglo-Saxon imitation of an Arabic dinar—highlights in this context is the fact that the cultural insularity of the epic's fictional world is marked from the outset as a highly artificial state that invites deconstruction. The epic achieves this deconstruction by systematically dismantling every semblance of Germanic purity via the intrusion of archaeological artifacts from other cultural spheres. At the same time as *Beowulf* draws on the metaphor of entanglement and interwovenness, the poem makes use of its deconstruction of Germanic purity in order to develop out of the tension-ridden encounter of different cultural spaces a concept of the aesthetic as a distinct sphere. While this sphere obviously cannot be conceptualized in terms of a modern notion of the autonomy of art, it does seem to engender a remarkably precise notion of the aesthetic as a value in and of itself, because, instead of being reducible to any one cultural sphere, that sense of the aesthetic emanates from the very interstices of cultural entanglement.[35]

---

35. Some of the research on which this paper is based was funded by the Deutsche Forschungsgemeinschaft (DFG, German Research Foundation) under Germany's Excellence Strategy (Cluster of Excellence "Temporal Communities," EXC 2020, project number 390608380).

CHAPTER 6

Weapons of Healing

Materiality and Oral Poetics in Old English Remedies and Medicinal Charms

LORI ANN GARNER

For a volume such as *Material Remains*, seeking to generate new understandings of history through literary depictions of archaeological objects, the genre of medieval medical texts might seem at first like an outlier. Freely mixing seemingly atemporal cultural and linguistic traditions, surviving Old English medical texts defy simple periodization and staunchly resist any straightforward interpretation of medicinal or literary history. And analysis of the small number of those remedies incorporating poetic incantations—enigmatic verse frequently dismissed as mere superstition—might seem even less likely to yield meaningful historical or archaeological insights. Yet it is precisely through such practically oriented poetry (a primary focus in the present study) that we are able to witness some of the most candid images of archaeological objects and thus best understand how and what these objects signified.

Simultaneously literary and pragmatic, verse incantations embedded within medical texts operate on a metaphorical level, frequently drawing on what has been termed *sympathetic magic* in evoking narrative contexts that parallel desired healing, and an unquestionably literal level, whereby very specific rituals and herbal preparations effect healing, thus allowing us powerful insights into practical use and associative meanings attached to particular physical objects. Among the most obvious such images are those involving weaponry. As is often the case even today,[1] warfare and battle permeate metaphors and practices of healing, ailment, and disease, precipitating high stakes battle and warfare. Weaponry as depicted in early medieval medical texts serves as a powerful mode of understanding health and healing as conceived in early medieval England.

On a larger cultural level, the epic *Beowulf*, the historical *Battle of Maldon*, and even Old English renderings of biblical narratives such as *Judith* or *Exodus* contain numerous obvious images of battle, and, accordingly, the descriptions of weapons and warfare found in these and many other such narrative contexts have been studied extensively.[2] However, equally compelling images of warriors and weaponry do occasionally appear in less conspicuous places, including manuscripts devoted to health and herbal healing. The Old English medical texts show us a world where plants are named for spears and arrows, where healing rituals employ swords and knives, and where healers can recite poems depicting fully armed warriors or even a full-scale battle. The oral traditional nature of these remedies has of course long been noted,[3]

---

1. As but one of many examples, see the documentary "Cancer Warrior," directed by Nancy Linde (*Nova*, aired February 27, 2001, on PBS), on Judah Folkman's innovative research toward inhibiting the growth and spread of cancer tumors, or the widespread "Fight for the Cure" campaign against breast cancer, which frequently involves images of boxing gloves (e.g., "Fight for the Cure Pink Ribbon T-Shirt," The Breast Cancer Site Store, accessed June 2, 2020, https://store.thebreastcancersite.greatergood.com/collections/all/products/70368-fighting-for-the-cure-pink-ribbon-tank-top). Such depictions are far from unproblematic, however. On the damaging ableism inherent in portrayals of nonnormative bodies as enemies at odds with a normative ideal, see, for instance, Eli Clare, *Brilliant Imperfection: Grappling with Cure* (Durham, NC: Duke University Press, 2017).

2. See especially N. P. Brooks's thorough examination of weapons and armor in "Weapons and Armour," in *The Battle of Maldon, A. D. 991*, ed. Donald Scragg (Oxford: Blackwell, 1991), 208–19; Erin Mullally's study of weaponry in "The Cross-Gendered Gift: Weaponry in the Old English *Judith*," *Exemplaria* 17 (2013): 255–84; and any of the many explorations of weapons and warfare in *Beowulf*, such as David C. van Meter, "The Ritualized Presentation of Weapons and the Ideology of Nobility in *Beowulf*," *Journal of English and Germanic Philology* 95 (1996): 175–89.

3. See, e.g., Lea Olsan, "The Inscriptions of Charms in Anglo-Saxon Manuscripts," *Oral Tradition* 24 (1999): 401–19; Lea Olsan, "Latin Charms of Medieval England: Verbal Healing in a Christian Oral Tradition," *Oral Tradition* 7 (1992): 116–42; Lori Ann Garner, "Anglo-Saxon Charms in Performance," *Oral Tradition* 19 (2004): 20–42; Leslie K. Arnovick, *Written Reliquaries: The Resonance of Orality in Medieval English Texts* (Amsterdam: John Benjamins Publishing, 2006), especially 104–8; and John D. Niles, "Orality," in *The Cambridge Companion to Textual Scholarship*, ed. Neil Fraistat and Julia Flanders (Cambridge: Cambridge University Press, 2013), 209–11. The use of the term "oral traditional" here does not deny the manuscript context and influence of writing on these complex texts but rather draws attention to the "fundamental expressive strategy" described by Foley whereby traditional elements continue to have force and meaning in the context of written texts (John Miles Foley, "How Genres Leak

and, as John Miles Foley observed, the type of overlap we see here between genres as seemingly far removed as epic poetry and medical manuals affords "a built-in opportunity to deepen the resonance" of oral-connected texts.[4] What the approach of *Material Remains* provides, then, is a clearer path to understanding precisely how depictions of material objects, such as weapons and war gear, items more typical of heroic poetry, can still create meaning in medical texts.

Reading the spears, knives, swords, and armor of the healing remedies as "material artifacts" situated at the intersection of oral tradition and literate culture reveals complex networks of signification. Each weapon, each piece of armor, and each battle strategy carries specific social connotations and evokes particular situations of use. Far more than simple metaphors and superstition-inspired abstractions, the physical details of weaponry in the medical texts work to guide our interpretations and aesthetic responses, leading us to a deeper and richer understanding of how health and healing were understood in early medieval England.

To this end, we will first examine general signification patterns of war gear across the major Old English medical texts, exploring the diverse functions of weapons as medical tools, as ritual objects, and as descriptive markers in plant names (such as *spere-wyrt*). Next, we will turn our attention to a text commonly known as the *Journey Charm*, which employs an elaborate military metaphor equating each of the four Gospel authors with specific items of war gear. Last, this material artifacts approach will be applied to an incantation depicting a full-scale battle in *Wið færstice*, a remedy that includes an inset poem so seemingly disconnected from the rest of this otherwise unremarkable preparation of an herbal salve that some have argued for it to be analyzed in complete separation from the remedy as a whole.[5] I, however, argue here that the incantation and herbal preparation instead actually work in tandem to convey a full-fledged battle between healer and ailment and that neither the ritual nor the incantation is complete without the other. As we will see, this

---

in Traditional Verse," in *Unlocking the Wordhord: Anglo-Saxon Studies in Memory of Edward B. Irving, Jr.*, ed. Mark C. Amodio and Katherine O'Brien O'Keeffe [Toronto: University of Toronto Press, 2003], 77). On the complex matrix of oral tradition and literate culture in medieval England, see Mark C. Amodio, *Writing the Oral Tradition: Oral Poetics and Literate Culture in Medieval England* (Notre Dame, IN: University of Notre Dame Press, 2004).

4. Foley, "How Genres Leak," 79.

5. Howell Chickering's (highly influential) analysis, for instance, recommends separating the incantation, which he considers "a masterpiece," from the remainder of the remedy on the grounds that "as modern readers we bring only an aesthetic appreciation to the charm, not a real belief" and thus "can only perceive the literary force of its verbal magic" (Howell Chickering, "The Literary Magic of *Wið Færstice*," *Viator* 2 [1972]: 95, 104).

approach reveals a concept of healing more logical and more consistent than has sometimes been assumed, and the implications for the editing, translation, and interpretation of these often enigmatic texts are therefore quite significant and wide-reaching.

Healing as Warfare in Old English Medical Texts

Even a cursory exploration of Old English remedies reveals how prominent images of battle were within the healing tradition. The so-called *Nine Herbs Charm* explicitly praises the herb mugwort for its "miht wiþ þa[m] laþan ðe geond lond færð" (line 6) [power against the enemy who travels over the earth].[6] A metrical charm against a swarm of bees, which involves a direct address to "sigewif" (line 9) [victory women],[7] begins with the same "hwæt" (line 4) that activates the heroic register in the famous prologue to *Beowulf*.[8] Even those remedies that do not explicitly invoke images of warfare nonetheless present illness and disease as enemies to be conquered, the vast majority of the remedies in surviving manuscripts establishing an agonistic relationship between healer and ailment with the word *wið* [against].[9] The healer thus becomes a hero, and the numerous weapons that appear in the medical texts serve to "arm" the practitioner in battle against ailments.

In this context, plants named for weapons—a phenomenon we see across all the major medical texts—serve the dual function of being both aid to identification and a healer's weapon against disease. For instance, *garclife* [(literally) spear-burr or spear-burdock], a flowering plant whose nomenclature "refers to the towering pointed and spear-like florescence of the plant and

---

6. MS Harley 585, entry 79. Metrical Charm 2 in Elliott Van Kirk Dobbie, ed., *The Anglo-Saxon Minor Poems*, Anglo-Saxon Poetic Records 6 (New York: Columbia University Press, 1942). Except where otherwise noted, citations from Harley 585, also known as *Lacnunga*, are from Edward Pettit's excellent edition *Anglo-Saxon Remedies, Charms, and Prayers from British Library MS Harley 585: The Lacnunga*, 2 vols. (Lewiston: Edwin Mellen Press, 2001).

7. *Sigewif* could also be understood as singular, possibly referring to the queen. For discussion of this line in relation to beekeeping, see Lori Ann Garner and Kayla M. Miller, "'A Swarm in July': Beekeeping Perspectives on the Old English *Wið Ymbe* Charm," *Oral Tradition* 26, no. 2 (2011): 367–69.

8. On the "*hwæt* paradigm" as a traditional marker, see John Miles Foley, *Immanent Art: From Structure to Meaning in Traditional Oral Epic* (Bloomington: Indiana University Press, 1991), 214–23.

9. The *Lacnunga*, *Herbarium*, and *Leechbooks* all follow this pattern, as the opening remedies of these manuscripts show: "wið heafodwræce" [against a headache] (*Lacnunga*); "wið unhyrum nihtgengum" [against the terrible night-goers] (*Herbarium*); "wið heafodece" [against a headache] (*Leechbook III*).

its burr-like fruit,"[10] appears in the *Lacnunga* (entry cvxvi) as part of a lung-salve; in the *Herbarium* (xxxii) with remedies for such ailments as sore eyes, warts, or snakebite; and in *Leechbook II* (viii and li)[11] within recipes for digestive issues and ailing lungs. Our own familiar garlic, *garleac* [(literally) spear-leek], is also referenced in various manuscripts, such as *Leechbook II* (xxxii, lvi, and xli) and *Leechbook III* (lxi and lx).[12] Likewise, *sperewyrt* [spear-plant] is included in the *Lacnunga* (cxxxv) in a remedy for pustules and in the *Herbarium* (xcvii) for bladder pain, toothache, and intestinal worms.[13] *Strælwyrt* [arrow-wort] appears in *Leechbook I* (vi.4) as part of a remedy for tooth pain, so named presumably because "the forked alignment" of this plant, today known more commonly as club moss, bears "a great similarity to small arrows sticking in the soil."[14]

An especially interesting case involves *Herbarium* entry xxxiii for a plant with the native name *woodruff*, the juice of which was to be used in an ointment for leg or foot pain, and the roots in a drink for liver problems (figure 6.1). While the Old English *Herbarium* usually offers fairly close translations of Latin remedies dating back to Late Antiquity, and while there are Latin exemplars for most if not all of the *Herbarium*'s entries, it is important to keep in mind that the translation process was not one of slavish copying but rather one of "merging and adaptation."[15] For example, the Latin medical text for this particular entry[16] employs *asfodulus* as the primary name for this herbaceous plant, with *astula regia* [king's spear] appearing only as a secondary

---

10. *Dictionary of Old English Plant Names*, s.v. "garclife." http://oldenglish-plantnames.org/. See also Hans Sauer and Elisabeth Kubaschewski, *Planting the Seeds of Knowledge: An Inventory of Old English Plant Names* (Munich: Herbert Utz Verlag, 2018), 107.

11. Except where otherwise noted, citations from the *Leechbooks* are from Oswald Cockayne, ed., *Leechdoms, Wortcunning, and Starcraft of Early English*, 3 vols., 1857 (Reprint, Wiesbaden: Kraus, 1965), and citations from the *Herbarium* are from Hubert Jan De Vriend, ed., *The Old English Herbarium and Medicina de quadrupedibus* (Oxford: Oxford University Press, 1984), MS Cotton Vitellius c iii.

12. For a complete list of references, see *Dictionary of Old English Plant Names*, s.v. "garleac." The editors clarify that the name refers to the shape of the leaves rather than the garlic root. See Sauer and Kubaschewski, *Seeds of Knowledge*, 107.

13. See *Dictionary of Old English Plant Names*, s.v. "spere-wyrt." See Sauer and Kubaschewski, *Seeds of Knowledge*, 220.

14. *Dictionary of Old English Plant Names*, s.v. "strælwyrt." See Sauer and Kubaschewski, *Seeds of Knowledge*, 227.

15. Maria Amalia D'Aronco, "Anglo-Saxon Plant Pharmacy and the Latin Medical Tradition," in *From Earth to Art: The Many Aspects of the Plant World in Anglo-Saxon England*, ed. C. P. Biggam, Costerus New Series 148 (Amsterdam: Rodopi, 2003), 144.

16. The Latin manuscript used for De Vriend's edition and followed here is MS Ca. Montecassino, Archivio della Badia, V. 97. See De Vriend, *Old English Herbarium*, 81, MS Ca., entry XXXIII.

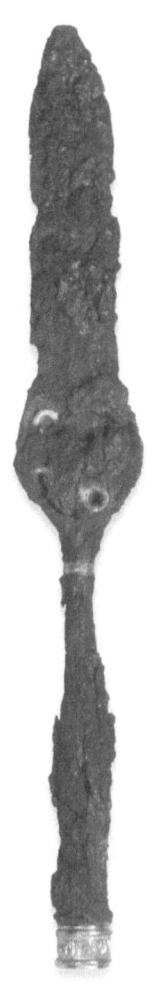

FIGURE 6.1. *Herbarium* entry xxxiii for woodruff, *astula regia*, British Library, Cotton MS Vitellius C iii, fol. 32r. © The British Library Board.

FIGURE 6.2. Leaf-shaped spearhead, early medieval England, British Museum. © The Trustees of the British Museum. All rights reserved.

gloss. But all four of the surviving manuscripts of the Old English *Herbarium* retain *astula regia* while dropping *asphodulus* entirely.[17]

This pattern of emphasizing the plant's connection to a spear makes perfect sense in the entry's new medieval English context, for multiple reasons.

---

17. See De Vriend, *Old English Herbarium*, 80–81, for manuscript variants as well as a Latin exemplar.

First, as we have seen, the use of "spear" to indicate leaf shape was already familiar in the native plant-naming tradition. Just as importantly, leaf-shaped spearheads were common in both Roman and Germanic warfare, giving the name a practical function in both the source language and the new Old English translation. According to M. J. Swanton's definitive study of spearheads in early medieval England, leaf-shaped blades "formed a basic component of all spear series throughout Europe," including Roman and English, and among the leaf-shaped variants those with a slender shape and longer length—not unlike the leaves of the herb known as *astula regia*—were "by far the commonest leaf-shaped blades found" in graves of early medieval England (figure 6.2).[18] Thus, the mnemonic for remembering the plant's shape would seem to have justified the transmission of this particular name from Latin into Old English and across various Old English manuscripts.[19]

The designation "king's spear" arguably carries social connotations as well. While the shape of *astula regia* might not seem especially connected to kings in particular, in Germanic culture possession of a spear did connote status. Swanton explains that, in early medieval England, "the spear was possessive of greater significance than either mere poetic fancy or a convenient and singularly destructive weapon. It was the jealously preserved symbol of a free warrior's status in Germanic society."[20] The spear—and by extension, the plants bearing its name—would thus have carried positive associations not only with victory over adversity but also with higher social stations, associations conferred by extension onto the healer "armed" with such resources.

Weapons (and household implements that could be used as weapons) also served practical and ritual functions in Old English medical texts. For example, the *seax*, a single-edged knife made from iron, appears frequently in the *Leechbooks* and is used in numerous ways. In *Leechbook III* (entry lxii) it is used to mark the location of an herb, *helenium*. In some cases, it is used for surgical cutting, as in entry xiii of *Leechbook II*. In other cases still, the seax serves more of a ritual function, as in a remedy for a horse experiencing sudden pain (lxv). This particular seax is to have a handle made from an ox's horn, on which there are three brass nails and the following inscription: "Benedicite omnia opera domini dominum" [All you works of the Lord, bless the Lord].[21] The inscription called for here elevates a common household tool

---

18. Michael J. Swanton, *The Spearheads of the Anglo-Saxon Settlements* (London: Royal Archaeological Institute, 1973), 46, 51.

19. For more detailed information on this particular spearhead in the British Museum holdings (registration number: 1964,0702.491), see "Spear-head," British Museum Collection Online, accessed August 4, 2020, https://www.britishmuseum.org/collection/object/H_1964-0702-491.

20. Swanton, *Spearheads*, 3.

21. See Stephen Pollington's conjectural drawing of this healer's knife (*Leechcraft: Early English Charms, Plantlore, and Healing* [Hockwold-cum-Wilton, UK: Anglo-Saxon Books,

to the position of a ritual object linked to both Latin learning and Christian culture.

The crossover of weapons and tools into the healing tradition is more natural and logical when we consider that it was typical in medieval culture for the same bows, arrows, spears, and knives used in battle to have alternative uses in hunting and even everyday household work. Richard Underwood explains that the use of the bow in warfare "appears to have been limited to a few specialists," though most men would have been trained in archery for hunting purposes.[22] John Manley describes the difficulties in isolating arrowheads used for military rather than civilian purposes, offering the view that "the same arrowhead could be employed for both hunting and warfare in early medieval England."[23] N. P. Brooks notes that the spear was "important as a throwing weapon in hunting and in battle."[24]

But the seax—the most frequently appearing weapon in the *Leechbooks* and *Lacnunga*—is by far the most versatile and ubiquitous such implement in real-world contexts. While there was certainly specialization of use between the long-seax and the common seax, as well as differentiation of blade type, there was much overlap as well. As David A. Gale explains, the "long seaxes have obvious uses as swords"; however, "the seax must have played a very secondary role" as a weapon, and "in everyday life on the farm and in the ordinary household, the ubiquitous domestic knife was used for eating, skinning, whittling, etc."[25] Underwood notes that the majority of individuals in early medieval England, "both men and women, appear to have carried a knife on a daily basis, presumably used for eating and other domestic tasks. While they were not weapons *per se*, warriors presumably took their knives with

---

2000], 480). The archaeological record supports the existence of such handles in actual practice. Kevin Leahy's work on Anglo-Saxon bone craft tells us that the tangs (the portions of knives that fit into their handles) of some Anglo-Saxon knives "retain traces left by horn handles with which they were once fitted" (Kevin Leahy and Roger Bland, *The Staffordshire Hoard*, 2nd ed. [London: British Museum, 2014], 449).

22. Richard Underwood, *Anglo-Saxon Weapons and Warfare* (Stroud: Tempus Publishing, 1999), 13.

23. John Manley, "The Archer and the Army in the Late Saxon Period," *Anglo-Saxon Studies in History and Archaeology* 4 (1985): 223. This is not to say that specialized spears, arrows, and knives created with battle purposes in mind did not exist, but rather that specialized weapons were less widely accessible and that these objects were frequently multi-use. N. P. Brooks explains that "as a standard tool in general use the knife (*seax*) in warfare developed into a single-edged dagger (known by Gregory of Tours as the *scramasax*) or into fine-edged swords, with blades up to 80 cm in length" ("Arms and Armour," in *The Blackwell Encyclopedia of Anglo-Saxon England*, ed. Michael Lapidge et al. [Oxford: Blackwell, 1999], 46).

24. Brooks, "Arms and Amour," 46.

25. David Gale, "The Seax," in *Weapons and Warfare in Anglo-Saxon England*, ed. Sonia Chadwick Hawkes (Oxford: Oxford University Committee for Archaeology, 1989), 80.

them when they went to battle."²⁶ The multifunctional seax even makes its way into epic poetry as the weapon with which Beowulf delivers the dragon's final death blow.²⁷

Even the sword, typically associated with higher rank and nobility, acquires ritual functions in certain remedies. Remedy lxii in *Leechbook III*, for instance, requires crosses to be inscribed specifically "mid sweorde" [with a sword] as part of the preparation before drinking an herbal remedy. The power of the sword's victory in battle is thus transferred to victory over physical ailment, lending ritual force to the final promise of the remedy's power and effectiveness: "him bið sona sel" [it will soon be better for him].

In a culture that makes less distinction between weapons and domestic tools across situations of use, it is perhaps more logical and natural for the sword, spear, and seax to figure prominently in the remedies, the seax used for cutting herbs and for surgical procedures invested with warlike power against disease and the sword conversely brought into the domestic sphere as part of a ritual preparation of an herbal drink. The evocation of weapons in poetic incantations referring to weapons can be viewed as an extension of this multifunctionality and multivalence. If we recognize the logic linking healing and battle across these remedies generally, then we are in a much better position to understand the weapons appearing in poetic incantations as far more than mere superstition.

Arming the Traveler: Weaponry in the *Journey Charm*

A 42-line poem inscribed in the margins of an eleventh-century copy of Bede's *Ecclesiastical History*,²⁸ most frequently referred to as the *Journey Charm*, calls upon God and various saints and beings for aid and protection while traveling.²⁹ Though lacking the instructions typically found with healing reme-

---

26. Underwood, *Anglo-Saxon Weapons*, 71.

27. Line 2703. In addition, Grendel's mother uses a seax against Beowulf, though he is protected by his mail-shirt (line 1545). Her choice of weapon is appropriate for both her status as female and her assumed role as avenging warrior.

28. CCCC MS 41, 350–53; included in Dobbie, *Anglo-Saxon Minor Poems*. In the standard numbering system used by Dobbie (1942: cxxx) in the Anglo-Saxon Poetic Records (ASPR), this poem is Metrical Charm 11, one of twelve charms in traditional alliterative verse included in that collection.

29. The journey has frequently been understood as metaphorical. See, for instance, Lea Olsan, "The Marginality of Charms in Medieval England," in *The Power of Words: Studies on Charms and Charming in Europe*, ed. James Kapaló, Eva Pócs, and William Ryan (Budapest: Central European University Press, 2013), 149; Heather Stuart, "'Ic me on þisse gyrde beluce':

dies, the standard *wið* construction that pits remedy (in this case preventive) against ailment is recurrent in the text,[30] and this agonistic relationship with adversity is dramatically and powerfully reinforced through battle imagery.

Weaponry and Social Status

In lines 26–29, several costly weapons and items of war gear are invoked metaphorically to correspond to each of the four Gospel authors called upon for protection:

> Biddu ealle bliðu mode þæt me beo hand ofer heafod[31]
> Matheus helm, Marcus byrne,
> leoht, lifes rof, Lucos min swurd,
> scearp and scirecg, scyld Iohannes,
> wuldre gewlitegod.

> I pray to all, glad in mind, that for me—hand over head—Matthew may be a helmet; Mark a mailcoat, light, strong of life; Luke my sword, sharp and bright-edged; John a shield, wondrously made.[32]

Biblical parallels have been extensively noted,[33] especially with the epistle of Paul to the Ephesians:

The Structure and Meaning of the Old English *Journey Charm*," *Medium Ævum* 50 (1981): 268. The reading of weaponry presented here is compatible with both literal and metaphorical travel.

30. See especially lines 4–5 and line 37, "wið þara sara stice, wið þane sara slege" [against the stab of the pains / against the blow of the pains]. See also Thomas D. Hill, "The Rod of Protection and the Witches' Ride: Christian and Germanic Syncretism in Two Old English Metrical Charms," *Journal of English and Germanic Philology* 111 (2012): 145–68. Additionally, the poem refers to itself as a *gealdor* (line 6), a term applied to songs and poems, including those in the healing tradition.

31. For reasons outlined below, I have restored the manuscript reading *hand ofer head*, omitted from Dobbie's long standard ASPR edition. I have followed the line breaks in Frederick Tupper, "Notes on Old English Poems," *Journal of English and Germanic Philology* 11 (1912): 82–103, who retains the manuscript reading.

32. This charm appears in the outer margins of fols. 350–53 and can be viewed directly via Stanford's Digital Manuscripts index, accessed June 2, 2020, https://parker.stanford.edu/parker/catalog/qd527zm3425. The lines discussed here appear on page 352.

33. Richard Marsden, for instance, observes that these "military metaphors convey the key idea of the spiritual fight which the true wayfaring Christian . . . must wage" ("Biblical Literature: The New Testament," in *The Cambridge Companion to Old English Literature*, ed. Malcolm Godden and Michael Lapidge, 2nd ed. [Cambridge: Cambridge University Press, 2013], 235). John P. Hermann refers to these lines as "an Old English poetic version of the Pauline figure

> Stand therefore having your loins girded in truth, and clothed with the breast-plate of justice, and having your feet shod to the preparation of the Gospel of peace: in all things taking the shield of faith, wherewith you may extinguish all the fiery darts of the most wicked one; and take unto you the helmet of salvation: and the sword of the spirit (which is the word of God).[34]

However, connections to actual warfare of the period have not been as fully explored, thus limiting our understanding of how the widely acknowledged spiritual metaphor would have been understood by the poem's earliest audiences. As Leslie Arnovick observes, the charm references some of the same weapons as Ephesians 6, but speaks much "more concretely of holy defense."[35] And perhaps unsurprisingly, these concrete details differentiating the Old English poem from the biblical analogue do indeed take on important meaning when considered within the context of early medieval military culture.

Taken together, these four battle items—helmet, mailcoat, sword, and shield—are markers of a highly elite status in early medieval England. The best-known assemblage of these items is the kingly Sutton Hoo ship burial, which has one of the richest and most intact collections of grave goods from the early medieval period. While weaponed graves cannot serve as an ultimate authority on actual warfare,[36] the selections can certainly enhance our understanding of the symbolic meanings of weapons, meanings that could be—and clearly were—invoked in literary and metaphorical depictions as well. The sword—linked in the charm to Luke—was "the most prestigious of offensive weapons."[37] Labor-intensive and costly, swords are found in only about 10 per-

---

of spiritual armor" (John P. Hermann, *Allegories of War: Language and Violence in Old English Poetry* [Ann Arbor: University of Michigan Press, 1989], 38).

34. Eph. 6:14–17 (Vulg. DV).

35. Arnovick notes that "to admit a literate intertextuality does not deny the oral-traditional context of the charm passage; the practical impetus behind the 'Journey Charm,' safe passage, is consistent with poetic associations," *Written Reliquaries*, 116.

36. John Hines, for instance, reminds us that the deceased in these graves "would appear to be those who did not die on the battlefield, and their weapons, to judge by the criterion of cuts, seem normally to have been unused" ("The Military Context of the *Adventus Saxonum*: Some Continental Evidence," in *Weapons and Warfare*, ed. Chadwick Hawkes, 26). We must "bear in mind the practicality of weapon sets in conditions of battle, and that grave assemblages may well represent symbolic rather than practicable weapon assemblages" (Hines, "Military Context," 36). Heinrich Härke, too, notes the "likelihood that there was a discrepancy between weapons used in the burial rite, and weapons used in real life" ("Early Saxon Weapon Burials: Frequencies, Distributions and Weapon Combinations," in *Weapons and Warfare*, ed. Chadwick Hawkes, 55).

37. Gale R. Owen-Crocker, "Weapons and Armour," in *The Material Culture of Daily Living in the Anglo-Saxon World*, ed. Maren Clegg Hyer and Gale R. Owen-Crocker (Liverpool: Liverpool University Press, 2011), 210.

cent of weaponed graves and were often passed down as heirlooms through multiple generations.[38]

Likewise, helmets and mail corselets have been found in only a small number of "very rich" burials, "indicating that their role as symbols of rank or status may have been much more important than their role in war."[39] The helmet—the equipment connected to Matthew—occupied a very "high place in the hierarchy of male military equipment," and only about five have been found to date.[40] Mail—the gear equated with Mark—was also "a rare luxury" in early medieval England.[41] In fact, "the rusted remains of only one mailcoat survive" from the period "and this from the richest deposit ever discovered."[42] Following this same pattern, the "wuldre gewlitegod" (gloriously made) shield metaphorically equated with John would seem to indicate a decorated shield of the type that also indicates high status. Like mail, helmets, and swords, "decorated shields circulating in society are almost exclusively high-status items."[43]

Evidence from weapon burials, heroic poetry, law codes, letters, and wills reveal that though weapons are included in over half of all gift-giving cases with named recipients, "the only weapon types listed as gifts are swords, mailcoats, and helmets,"[44] precisely those weapons attributed to three of the four gospel authors. The will of Æthelred's son Æthelstan, which included among other valuable artifacts eleven swords, a coat of mail, and two shields, provides further evidence that these particular items circulated together as high-status treasures.[45] A traveler armed with such gear thus would be not only well-protected but also extremely high-ranking. The metaphorical weaponry here manifests a fascinating syncretism of Christian learning and Germanic warrior culture, and the particular weapons chosen effectively fulfill the biblical mandate to arm oneself with Christian ideals, while at the same time conveying a very specific social station in early medieval England.

---

38. Heinrich Härke, "'Warrior graves'? The Background of the Anglo-Saxon Weapon Burial Rite," *Past & Present* 126 (February 1990): 24, 34.
39. Härke, "'Warrior graves'?," 26.
40. Owen-Crocker, "Weapons and Armour," 219. For detailed descriptions of all five helmets, see page 226.
41. Owen-Crocker, "Weapons and Armour," 226.
42. Owen-Crocker, "Weapons and Armour," 226.
43. Heinrich Härke, "The Circulation of Weapons in Anglo-Saxon Society," in *Rituals of Power from Late Antiquity to the Middle Ages*, ed. Frans Theuws and Janet L. Nelson (Leiden: Brill, 2000), 388.
44. Härke, "Circulation of Weapons," 377, 380.
45. Härke, "Circulation of Weapons," 385.

Battling Emendations: Lines 27 and 30

Interestingly, the strong associations this passage has with elite military culture argue against two widely accepted emendations to the manuscript text, the frequent alteration of *wega* to *wælgar* (line 30) and the common deletion of the half-line "hand ofer heafod" (line 27). The first of these emendations was originally made by Holthausen, who altered the manuscript's "wega Seraf hin" (seraphim of the ways) to instead read as "wælgar Serafhin" (the Seraphim a slaughter-spear) in a passage that immediately follows the extended metaphor of the evangelists as protective war gear.[46] However, the emendation's tremendous impact on modern translations, editions, and interpretations comes from its acceptance by Dobbie, whose edition in the *Anglo-Saxon Poetic Records* has long served as the default standard. In recent years, this version has become even more ubiquitous as it has been copied on numerous websites and thus is often a first-stop for many seeking an online text.[47] In most cases, this emendation has either been quietly accepted or countered only inconspicuously in footnotes or endnotes, and the proliferation of this emendation has led to numerous potential mistranslations and problematic scholarly readings.[48] Dobbie found the manuscript "wega" "very unsatisfactory" and explained his decision to follow Holthausen thus: "Following the identification of the four evangelists with weapons of defence, we expect the

---

46. F. Holthausen, "Zu altenglischen Dichtungen," in *Beiblatt zur Anglia XXXI* (1920): 31.

47. E.g., The Online Corpus of Old English Poetry, http://www.oepoetry.ca and "Metrical Charm 11: A Journey Charm," Internet Sacred Text Archive, accessed June 2, 2020, http://www.sacred-texts.com/neu/ascp/a43_11.htm.

48. Marsden accepts Dobbie's emendation, translating as "deadly spear" ("Biblical Literature," 235). Heather Stuart provides the emended ASPR reading in the text of her article, but in an endnote expresses reservations about Dobbie's reading, which "although quoted here is not accepted as suitable" ("Old English *Journey Charm*," 273n20). Judith Vaughan-Sterling gives the text as *wælgar*, and includes this line as part of a larger point about the poem's "penchant for heroic imagery" ("The Anglo-Saxon *Metrical Charms*: Poetry as Ritual," *Journal of English and Germanic Philology* 82 [1983]: 190). Lois Bragg likewise translates as "Seraphim my spear," noting in her analysis "the depiction of the four evangelists and the seraphim as armor and weapons" ("The Modes of the Old English Metrical Charms," *Comparatist* 16 [1992]: 16–17). S. A. J. Bradley's is one of numerous translations following the emendation, "my spear" (*Anglo-Saxon Poetry* [London: Dent, 1982], 549). The potential for confusion and misreading is especially apparent in Peter Sirr's "Charm for a Journey," in *The Word Exchange: Anglo-Saxon Poems in Translation*, ed. Greg Delanty and Michael Matto (New York: W. W. Norton & Company, 2012), 496–97, dual-language version. The Old English text here gives the emended form "**wælgar**" in bold, consistent with a common online manner of indicating that an emendation of some sort has occurred; the facing-page translation, however, gives "path," which would seem to follow the manuscript *wega* instead. Clearly, more consistency and greater understanding are needed with regard to these lines.

Seraflhin (taken by the poet as a singular) to represent a weapon also."⁴⁹ For interpretations that stop at a basic military analogy, the addition of the seraphim to the military arming metaphor might seem to present no immediate problem. By looking at the poem's weapons as material artifacts, however, the addition of the 'spear' becomes quite problematic for several reasons.

While Germanic literature does include examples of warriors armed with a spear or other thrusting weapon along with a sword,⁵⁰ the status marker is clearly the sword, and the spear disrupts the social hierarchy established by the poem. Swanton notes the spear's position as a "symbol of a free warrior's status in Germanic society,"⁵¹ and Owen-Crocker also suggests that "possibly only freemen, of the rank of *ceorl* upwards" would have had the right to carry or be buried with a spear.⁵² Nonetheless, "the spear is the commonest of weaponry found" in graves of early medieval England,⁵³ possessing nowhere near the level of prestige of a helmet or sword. Within the social context established by the poem, it would seem incongruous for one of God's own seraphim to be equipped with a significantly lesser weapon—a possession available to any freedman—than the human evangelists bearing weapons of the highest elite.

On biblical grounds, too, the emendation has been shown to be unnecessary. Thomas Hill makes the excellent observation that the manuscript reading *wega* not only avoids "radical emendation" but also retains the poem's treatment of the four evangelists as a unit: "To the best of my knowledge, the Seraphim are not associated with a spear or spears in any other Insular text of the period, and an emendation that creates an otherwise unattested metaphorical association is problematic."⁵⁴ Heather Stuart objects to the emendation on similar grounds: "The four Evangelists are mentioned as a structural unit in vv. 27–30, and to introduce *Seraflhin* as an extra figurative weapon is to destroy that unit by extending it."⁵⁵ For all of these reasons, then, a return to the manuscript reading *wega* seems the more responsible choice, and indeed the rendering of *wega* is arguably clear as it stands, "seraphim of the ways."⁵⁶ For instance, as some have indicated, the phrase can be read as a paratactic

---

49. Dobbie, *Anglo-Saxon Minor Poems*, 218.
50. *Egil's Saga*, for instance, describes Egil and his opponent Berg-Onund each carrying a spear or halberk in hand and also girded with a sword. Bernard Scudder, trans., *Egil's Saga* (New York: Penguin, 1997), 116–17.
51. Swanton, *Spearheads*, 3n5.
52. Owen-Crocker, "Weapons and Armour," 205.
53. Owen-Crocker, "Weapons and Armour," 205.
54. Hill, "Christian and Germanic Syncretism," 149.
55. Stuart, "Old English Journey Charm," 273n20.
56. Or, as Godfrid Storms translates, "Seraphim of the roads" (*Anglo-Saxon Magic* [The Hague: Martinus Nijhoff, 1948], 218–19).

construction referring back to John.⁵⁷ Though this solution does risk disrupting the social hierarchy discussed above by equating John with the seraphim, the line can also be read as a general wish for the seraphim to be along the traveler's path, a reading that would be fully in line with the spirit of the Old English maxims: "Wel mon sceal wine healdan on wega gehwylcum" [It is well for one to have a friend on each of ways].⁵⁸

The second emendation commonly performed on this section of the poem—the decision to omit "hand ofer heafod"—is even more widely accepted (and less frequently acknowledged).⁵⁹ Grendon stated early on that "*hand ofer heafod* appears to me to be an accidental repetition of line 23," the same logic later accepted by Dobbie.⁶⁰ However, reading the text in the context of the warrior culture invoked here suggests that the phrase is not necessarily repeated in error. It can instead be understood as a formulaic repetition, as part of a ritualized request for aid from two distinct groups, first from the "haligra rof" (valiant host of holy ones), which has often been understood as a reference to saints,⁶¹ and then, in the second instance, from the evangelists. As Anne Klinck has noted in her edition of Old English elegies, *Journey Charm* 24a can be connected with two other poetic passages linking head and hands: *The Wanderer*, lines 41–44, in which the speaker describes laying his head and hands, "honda ond heafod," on his lord's knee, and *Maxims I*, lines 67–68, in which *hond* and *heafod* are associated with the *gifstol* and treasure-giving.⁶² "The gesture of placing head and hands on the knee," Klinck argues, "certainly

---

57. Though a full treatment of this reading is somewhat outside the scope of the present analysis, see, for instance, Felix Grendon, "The Anglo-Saxon Charms," *Journal of American Folklore* 22 (1909): 179; and Storms, *Anglo-Saxon Magic*, 219, for examples of translators presenting the seraphim in apposition with John.

58. *Maxims I*, line 144. Cited from George Philip Krapp and Elliott Van Kirk Dobbie, eds., *The Exeter Book*. Anglo-Saxon Poetic Records 3 (New York: Columbia University Press, 1936).

59. The emendation is frequently accepted in scholarship on the *Journey Charm* (e.g., Stuart, "Old English Journey Charm," 262; Hill, "Christian and Germanic Syncretism," 147; Katrin Rupp, "The Anxiety of Writing: A Reading of the Old English Journey Charm," *Oral Tradition* 23 [2008]: 259; Vaughan-Sterling, "Anglo-Saxon *Metrical Charms*," 190) and editions (e.g., Louis J. Rodrigues, trans. and ed., *Anglo-Saxon Verse Charms, Maxims and Heroic Legends* [Pinner, UK: Anglo-Saxon Books, 1994], 156–57). Unlike words or characters that are added or modified, an omission cannot be italicized or put in bold and thus frequently leaves no trace. "Hand ofer heafod" is left untranslated without comment, for instance, in Robert K. Gordon, trans. and ed., *Anglo-Saxon Poetry* (London: Dent, 1954), 91; and also Sirr's "Charm for a Journey."

60. Grendon, "Anglo-Saxon Charms," 221; Dobbie, *Anglo-Saxon Minor Poems*, 217.

61. See, for instance, Hill, "Christian and Germanic Syncretism," 148.

62. See further R. F. Leslie, ed., *The Wanderer* (Manchester: Manchester University Press, 1966), 74; and Tupper's extended treatment of this half-line, Tupper, "Notes on Old English Poems," 97–100.

seems to have the implication of submission on the one side and protection on the other."[63]

Such a reading builds upon Tupper's earlier but generally overlooked treatment of the phrase in 1912, in which he concluded that "*hand ofer heafod* in the *Journey Spell* carries then the idea of 'guardianship' and protection."[64] If the phrase *hand ofer heafod* does in fact traditionally index a ritualized exchange of loyalty for protection similar to that implied in *The Wanderer* and *Maxims I*, then the repetition is far from redundant, but rather perfectly appropriate in the request for protection from both groups, perhaps even especially so before the explicit connection is made in the succeeding lines between the evangelists and protective armor. A phrase implying an oath of loyalty would serve to validate the speaker's request for protection by framing it within the context of the heroic warrior culture.

This reading does not preclude, but rather can serve to further affirm, interpretations based on religious contexts. Leslie Arnovick (following Godfrid Storms), for instance, offers an equally convincing reading of the image as referring to a hand extended over another's head in a ritual blessing.[65] As with the battle imagery associated with the evangelists, these lines manifest a deep syncretism and invite us to think about such images in terms of both Christian typology and Germanic battle. At every stage, the text supports—even depends upon—this multivalence. As Heather Stuart reminds us, the working title *Journey Charm* is not in the manuscript, and the poem refers to itself as a *syggegealdor* [victory song].[66] The metaphorical victory depends upon metaphorical armor and weapons; thus, to understand the metaphor, we must first understand the weaponry.

Stages of Battle in *Wið Færstice*

Perhaps it is because poems such as the *Journey Charm* do not conform neatly to modern categories of either literature or science, and are thus often dismissed as superstition-fraught products of lesser minds, that the metrical charms have been subject to such free emendation, with assumptions of error going widely unchallenged. But the charm remedy *Wið færstice* (*Against a*

---

63. Anne Klinck, ed., *The Old English Elegies: A Critical Edition and Genre Study* (Montreal: McGill-Queen's University Press, 1992), 114.
64. Tupper translates the relevant lines as follows: "In sanguine mood I solicit, that mine be sovereign protection: Matthew my helmet . . ." ("Notes on Old English Poems," 100).
65. Arnovick, *Written Reliquaries*, 115–16.
66. Stuart, "Old English Journey Charms," 268.

Sudden Pain) provides another example of how close attention to material artifacts can help counter such tendencies.[67] This remedy, which appears in the *Lacnunga* (entry cxxvii), depicts not an individual idealized warrior on a solitary journey, but a full-scale battle, one fought with much more common weaponry. The entry opens simply enough with instructions involving an herbal remedy: "Wið færstice: feferfuige and seo reade netele ðe þurh ærn inwyxð, and wegbrade, wyll in buteran" [Against a sudden pain: feverfew and the red nettle, which grows in through a building, and waybroad; boil in butter]. Next comes a 26-line poem in alliterative verse, presumably a ritual incantation, narrating a fierce attack of approaching female riders and the speaker's own attempts to retaliate:

> Hlude wæran hy, la, hlude,   ða hy ofer þone hlæw ridan,
> wæran anmode,   ða hy ofer land ridan.
> Scyld ðu ðe nu, þu ðysne nið   genesan mote.
>   *Ut, lytel spere, gif her inne sie.*[68]
> Stod under linde,   under leohtum scylde,
> þær ða mihtigan wif   hyra mægen beræddon
> and hy gyllende   garas sændan.
> Ic him oðerne   eft wille sændan,
> fleogende flane   forane togeanes.
>   *Ut, lytel spere, gif hit her inne sy.*
> Sæt smið,   sloh seax,
> lytel iserna,[69]   wund swiðe.
>   *Ut, lytel spere, gif her inne sy.*
> Syx smiðas sætan,   wælspera worhtan
>   *Ut, spere, næs in, spere*
> Gif her inne sy   isenes dæl,
> hægtessan geweorc,   hit sceal gemyltan.
> Gif ðu wære on fell scoten   oððe wære on flæsc scoten
> oððe wære on blod scoten
> oððe wære on lið scoten,   næfre ne sy ðin lif atæsed;
> gif hit wære esa gescot   oððe hit wære ylfa gescot
> oððe hit wære hægtessan gescot,   nu ic wille ðin helpan.

---

67. MS Harley 585, fols. 175a–76a.

68. This treatment of the "ut, spere" lines as offset from the main text (a decision that deviates from previous editorial practice) underscores the refrain's role in punctuating the stages of battle, as will be discussed below.

69. ASPR edits with "lytel" on previous line. Rationale below for my departure from this line break.

Þis ðe to bote esa gescotes,   ðis ðe to bote ylfa gescotes,
ðis ðe to bote hægtessan gescotes;   ic ðin wille helpan.
Fleo⁷⁰ þær   on fyrgenhæfde.
Hal westu,   helpe ðin drihten.

Loud were they, lo, loud, when they rode over the mound,
were single-minded, when they rode over land.
Shield yourself now, you are able to survive this evil.
   Out, little spear, if it be in here.
[He/she/it/I]⁷¹ stood under linden, under a light shield,
where the mighty women readied their strength
and they yelling spears sent.⁷²
I will send them another back,
a flying arrow back in the other direction.
   Out, little spear, if it be in here.
A smith sat, forged a knife,
a small piece of iron,⁷³ severe wound.
   Out, little spear, if it be in here.
Six smiths sat, made slaughter-spears
   Out, spear, not in, spear.
If herein be a piece of iron,
work of a hag, it must melt.
If you were shot in the skin or were shot in the flesh,
or were shot in the blood
or were shot in a limb, may your life never be harmed;
if it were gods' shot, or it were elves' shot
or it were a hag's shot, now I will help you.
This to you as a remedy for gods' shot, this for you as a remedy for elves' shot,
this for you as a remedy for hag's shot; I wish to help you.

---

70. Manuscript *fled*. *Fleon* and *fleogan* both being strong verbs, *fled* requires emendation. On various proposed emendations, see Dobbie, *Anglo-Saxon Minor Poems*, 213. I am here adopting the emendation to *fleo* (first proposed by Grimm and Sweet in the 19th century), taking the form as the present subjunctive singular of *fleon*. *Fleo* requires less intervention than other common proposals, such as *fleoh* or *fleah*. See *DOE*, s.v., *fleon*.

71. As will be discussed below, the subject of *stod* is ambiguous.

72. Although the syntax is undeniably awkward in modern English, the word order here retains the semantic ambiguity of the original Old English, as discussed further below.

73. Taking the meaning metonymically, some have translated *isern* as "sword." See, e.g., Alaric Hall, *Elves in Anglo-Saxon England: Matters of Belief, Health, Gender and Identity* (Woodbridge, UK: Boydell Press, 2007), 3; Michael Collier, "Against a Sudden Stitch," in *The Word Exchange*, ed. Delanty and Matto, 483. See below on the choice here to read *iserna* literally, in apposition with *seax*.

> May it fly there to the mountaintop.
> Be whole, may your lord help you.

Following this incantation is a final instruction in prose to place a knife in liquid, most likely for the application of a salve made from the herbs in the opening.

Stephen Glosecki observes that "quibbles creep in over almost every line of this lyrical charm,"[74] with much of the criticism connected in various ways to the poem's treatment of weaponry. In the pages that follow, I wish, then, to work through the incantation not in terms of how it contains vestiges of "primitive" magic,[75] but as it depicts stages of an actual battle fought with actual weapons. Approaching the weapons in the poem as material artifacts not only helps resolve seeming ambiguities in the poem but also reveals a coherent logic underlying the remedy's healing power, one that powerfully links the cryptic incantation to the surrounding instructions for herbal preparation.

The Chaos of Early Battle and Poetic Ambiguity: Lines 1–10

The first stage of this battle is, quite naturally, an attack from approaching enemies, in this case "mihtigan wif" (line 6) [mighty women]: "Hlude wæran hy, la, hlude, ða hy ofer þone hlæw ridan" (line 1) [Loud were they, lo, loud, when they rode over the mound]. The folk epidemiology underlying this and many other Old English remedies assumes that ailments without otherwise known causes result from attacks of "invisible or hard-to-see creatures who shot their victims with some kind of arrow or spear."[76] Not to be defeated in this medical battle, the healer orders the sufferer to "shield yourself now" (line 3). The next half line, "stod under linde" [stood under a (linden) shield[77]], has, however, raised many questions about the narrative context, since *stod* can be

---

74. Stephen Glosecki, *Shamanism and Old English Poetry*, Albert Bates Lord Studies in Oral Tradition 2 (New York: Garland Publishing, 1989), 109. For a list of translations and editions along with a detailed overview of scholarship on this text prior to 2001, see Pettit, *Anglo-Saxon Remedies*, 212–61.

75. Storms, *Anglo-Saxon Magic*, 143.

76. Karen Jolly, *Popular Religion in Late Saxon England: Elf Charms in Context* (Chapel Hill: University of North Carolina Press, 1996), 134.

77. While a minority translate *linde* as linden tree, the majority assume a metonymic reference to a shield made from linden or a similar wood.

third or first person, and can thus be variously translated as "I stood" or "he/she/it stood."[78]

Parallels in historical and literary battles, though, suggest that this ambiguity would not have been as problematic for early medieval audiences as for modern scholarship and that it even contributes to the battle's realism. For instance, this opening battle of the healer against the mighty women is paralleled by the *Battle of Maldon*'s description of the historic 991 battle against a Viking invasion, which also begins in earnest with a fierce exchange of flying arrows and spears, and protection from wooden shields: "Bogan wæron bysige. Bord ord onfeng" (line 110) [Bows were busy. Shield caught point]. Like the metrical charm, *Maldon* does not specify whose shield caught whose point, the seeming implication being that in this early stage of fighting, arrows and spears are flying everywhere, and each side is shielding itself from the other.

What is important is the fierceness of this initial onslaught: "Biter wæs se beaduræs" (line 111) [Bitter was the attack]. Brooks's discussion of weaponry in *Maldon* notes that "preliminary bombardments" occurred "before the two armies closed for hand-to-hand fighting" and that "the practice was to reuse the enemy's projectiles";[79] this strategy is also paralleled in the charm speaker's oath to "him oðerne eft wille sændan" (line 8) [send them another back]. In this context, the ambiguity of the subjectless *stod* grammatically contributes to the chaos in a fierce and fast-paced battle where individuals are difficult to distinguish and everyone on both sides is seeking protection from shields.

Another source of confusion in the charm, the relative interchangeability of words referring to missile weapons like darts, javelins, and arrows, is also shared with *Maldon*. The charm speaker, for instance, returns "garas" (line 7) [spears] with a "flane" (line 9) [arrow]; *Maldon*, too, intensifies the chaos of early battle through the inclusion of flying "speru" (line 108) and "garas" (line 109), as well as the "flanes flyht" (line 71) [flight of arrow] and Æscferð's shooting of "flan" (line 269). The Old English poem *Judith* also exhibits this kind of alternation, as the battle between the Bethulians and Assyrians begins with archery, the missile flying from the hornbow variously referred to as a *flan*, *gar*, or *stræl* (lines 220–25). This interchangeability not only gives poets of these and other texts flexibility with regard to alliterative requirements; the

---

78. "I" is the most commonly proposed subject (e.g., Michael Collier, "Sudden Stitch," 483; Pollington, *Leechcraft*; Rodrigues, *Verse Charms*; Glosecki, *Shamanism*); "it" is preferred by Hall, *Elves*. Karen Jolly leaves the subject unstated, noting that "*stod* is unclear, whether it is 'he stood,' invoking a heroic story sympathetically, or 'I stood,' the speaker of the charm who uses his own voice below to fight the attackers" (*Popular Religion*, 205).

79. Brooks, "Weapons and Armour," 208.

variation on kinds of arrows and throwing spears also adds to the sense of chaos that each of these texts conveys during missile warfare.

The chaotic tension of missile warfare in the charm is furthered by the syntactical ambiguity in its description of the attack in which "hy gyllende garas sændan" (line 7), which literally means "they yelling spears sent," in which *gyllende* could easily modify either the mighty women or the spears they sent, both being possible in the context of early medieval battle.[80] The lines above in *Judith*, for instance, offer one of many examples of fierce warriors approaching loudly, *hlude* (line 223). Thus, the women could indeed be yelling, but perhaps even more plausible in the context of actual battle patterns is that the flying spears and arrows are *gyllende*. John Manley notes that while some Germanic cultures did employ archery at close-range, warriors in England used bows and arrows more exclusively for long-range fighting, and, of course, the longer an arrow remains in the air, the stronger, faster, and louder it gets, making this image quite apt for the arrows flying from approaching—but still somewhat distant—attackers. Alaric Hall supports his translation "shrieking spears" with evidence from *Widsið*, in the half-line "giellende gar" (line 128).[81] In the context of the battle chaos being depicted, either reading is appropriate, and, as Edward Pettit has stated, "an oral performance might well exploit the potential ambiguity of the syntax and render both senses available at the same time."[82]

What is more important to keep in mind here is that literary and historical evidence suggests that the missile weapons so prominent in the early lines of *Wið færstice* mark an enemy's approach and the beginning of battle. Richard Underwood explains that "before battle lines joined and warriors risked all," warriors of early medieval England "would attempt to thin the enemy ranks with missiles. This would begin with archery," eventually leading up "to the hand-to-hand combat."[83] If we think of archery and the use of projectile weapons as preliminary to close combat, the poem's next section becomes more logical.

---

80. The variation in translation reflects this ambiguity as well: Hall, Hill, Bjork, and Rodrigues translate as *gyllende* modifying *garas* (Hall, *Elves*; Hill, "Christian and Germanic Syncretism"; Robert E. Bjork, trans. and ed., *Old English Shorter Poems*, Dumbarton Oaks Medieval Library 32 [Cambridge, MA: Harvard University Press, 2014]; Rodrigues, *Verse Charms*); Pollington and Collier are among those who have *gyllende* modifying women (Pollington, *Leechcraft*; Collier, "Sudden Stitch," 483); Jolly retains the ambiguity, "they screaming spears sent" (*Popular Religion*, 139).

81. Hall, *Elves*, 2.

82. Pettit, *Anglo-Saxon Remedies*, 240.

83. Underwood, *Anglo-Saxon Weapons*, 23.

Close Fighting, Close Reading: Lines 11–17

In lines 11–14 the charm introduces first a single smith and later six smiths forging weapons more appropriate for close fighting. This section of the poem has caused much debate as to which side these smiths are assisting. Glosecki, for instance, argues convincingly that the smiths are "the forgers of pain,"[84] whereas Storms asserts that the individual smith and the group of smiths are all forging weapons for the healer.[85] Minna Doskow makes a strong case for seeing a division of the smiths "into two groups, the single good one followed by the six evil ones."[86] In fact, all of these readings are plausible. If we continue to see the battle as relatively balanced between the two sides, with shared war tactics, as indicated above, then we can perhaps more readily accept the ambiguity that the text presents, assuming that after the furious preliminary exchanges of various flying weapons both sides would be preparing for the next stage of battle, hand-to-hand combat.

Another much-debated question regarding this section of the text involves precisely what weapon the first smith is forging. The manuscript reads, "sæt smið sloh seax lytel iserna" [(literally) a smith sat, forged a *seax*, small, of iron/s]. As with the *Journey Charm*, assumptions of scribal error have led to editing and translation choices that are arguably unnecessary and that sometimes work against the specific type of battle set up by the poem's elaborate imagery. Grendon and Dobbie, for instance, insert an ellipsis between *lytel* and *iserna* in an attempt to correct perceived irregularities in the meter.[87] However, if we accept Alan J. Bliss's argument for the integrity of the half-line as a viable—albeit uncommon—metrical unit, rather than an abnormality driven by error, we can see that the manuscript reading is quite viable.[88] More importantly for present purposes, the manuscript reading is completely in keeping with the battle ethos of the poem. If we see "lytel iserna" in apposition with "seax," we can understand the line thus: "a smith sat, forged a knife,

---

84. Glosecki, *Shamanism*, 108.

85. Storms, *Anglo-Saxon Magic*, 146.

86. Minna Doskow, "Poetic Structure and the Problem of the Smiths in *Wið Færstice*," *Papers on Language and Literature* 12 (1979): 325.

87. See MS Harley 585, fol. 130ʳ, lines 4–5, British Library, accessed June 2, 2020, http://www.bl.uk/manuscripts/Viewer.aspx?ref=harley_ms_585_f130r. One of several such attempts to resolve a perceived irregularity in meter can be found in Murray McGillivray, ed., *Old English Reader* (Peterborough, ON: Broadview Press, 2011), which supplies *wæpen* in the presumed gap.

88. Alan J. Bliss, "Single Half-Lines in Old English Poetry," *Notes and Queries* 18 (1971): 448. On the integrity of single half-lines in Old English charms, see John Miles Foley, "Hybrid Prosody: Single Half-Lines in Old English and Serbo-Croatian Poetry," *Neophilologus* 64 (1980): 284–89.

a small one, [made] of iron pieces."[89] The *seax* "occurred in long and short varieties (54–76 cm and 8–36 cm respectively)";[90] thus "lytel iserna" would be important in clarifying the nature of the seax being forged and indicating precisely what type of combat was forthcoming.

A more literal reading of this poetic battle can also help resolve another source of confusion in the line—the meaning of *iserna*, which has been translated by some as the material iron and metonymically by others as a reference to swords.[91] The specific battle context here—which employs common rather than elite weaponry—would argue strongly for a small knife made of iron, indicated by genitive *iserna*, rather than a sword. While it is possible that the poem is invoking a sword as a symbol of elite power (or that some audiences may have understood the multivalent text in this way), all other evidence in the poetic battle would seem to suggest a much more common warfare, with spears, bows, arrows, and knives.

Further, as noted above, there is a reciprocal and balanced nature in the poetic battle between the "mihtigan wif" and the healer, who in the first stage of battle exchanged equally powerful missile weapons. If the next stage of battle remains balanced, with smiths forging on both sides, sword makes far less sense than iron seax, a tool/weapon frequently carried by women as well as men. There is also evidence of small spears being worn and carried by women as trinkets,[92] so the *wælspera* [slaughter spears] depicted as being forged a few lines later in the poem, are also appropriate for both sides as the battle between the healer and the mighty women escalates from missile warfare to direct combat.[93]

Let us turn now to the "ut lytel spere" refrains. The seemingly random spacing at lines 4, 10, 13, and 15 have led to perceptions of a structural "irregularity" that "leaves much to be desired."[94] However, when we keep in mind the poem's systematic progression toward hand-to-hand fighting with spears

---

89. See also Doane, who translates as "little knife of iron parts" (A. N. Doane, "Editing Old English Oral/Written Texts: Problems of Method [With an Illustrated Edition of Charm 4, *Wiþ Færstice*]," in *The Editing of Old English: Papers from the 1990 Manchester Conference*, ed. Donald G. Scragg and Paul E. Szarmach [Woodbridge, UK: D. S. Brewer, 1994], 143). Pettit likewise sees *lytel iserna* in "apposition to seax" (Pettit, *Anglo-Saxon Remedies*, 244).

90. Owen-Crocker, "Weapons and Armour," 203.

91. See, for instance, Hall, *Elves*, 2, and Collier, "Sudden Stitch," 483, which show the smith forging a small sword. Jolly, *Popular Religion*, 139, and Hill, "Christian and Germanic Syncretism," 159, are among those who translate *iserna* as the material iron.

92. Gale R. Owen-Crocker, "Dress and Identity," in *The Oxford Handbook of Anglo-Saxon Archaeology*, ed. Helena Hamerow, David A. Hinton, and Sally Crawford (Oxford: Oxford University Press, 2011), 106.

93. For discussion of this issue, see, for example, Pettit, *Anglo-Saxon Remedies*, 242–46.

94. Storms, *Anglo-Saxon Magic*, 143.

and knives, the refrain spacing acquires a clear and compelling logic. These imperatives, directed toward the singular, specific source of the pain (the little spear), punctuate the incantation with increasing frequency, first with five lines between refrains, then two, then just one, serving as more and more urgent reminders of the battle's most important goal, to send the source of pain away and restore balance and healing. In this context, the assurance the speaker gives to aid against pain in flesh, blood, or limbs caused by shots from a wide array of supernatural beings becomes a powerful *beot,* a formalized oath commonly uttered before heroic battle.[95]

Note that we do not see the actual hand-to-hand combat in the poem. It is here where I see the surrounding physical actions of the charm working in tandem with the poem to complete the battle. The charm's lengthy explication on the early, preparatory stage of battle is recited precisely during the preparation of herbs. As Cameron explains, incantations that "appear superficial" could often serve time-keeping functions in the absence of modern watches and clocks, ensuring that herbs or liquids were boiled or mixed for the proper amount of time.[96] Then, at the end of the charm's recitation, the remedy calls for a knife to be plunged into liquid: "Nim þonne þæt seax, ado on wætan" [Then take that knife, put in liquid]. Most likely, the herbs would have then been applied as part of a salve directly to the skin, with a knife—the medical equivalent of direct and close-up combat with the ailment itself.[97] In the logic provided by the charm, the herbs *themselves* become weapons, consistent with the plants named after weapons seen in all of the major medical texts, as discussed previously.[98]

---

95. Cf. Beowulf's promise to Hrothgar that he would defeat the monstrous Grendel (lines 679–85). On the traditional force of the *beot,* see further Amodio, *Writing the Oral Tradition,* 146–56. For excellent discussions of the supernatural beings that appear in these lines, see especially Glosecki, *Shamanism,* 106–31; Hall, *Elves,* 1–3; and Pettit, *Anglo-Saxon Remedies,* 247–55.

96. M. L. Cameron, *Anglo-Saxon Medicine* (Cambridge: Cambridge University Press, 1993), 38–39.

97. Cameron offers a detailed discussion of the uses of the herbs used in this remedy, concluding that "all three herbs have been recommended for muscular and joint pains, hence useful against 'sudden stitch,' when applied as a salve to the aching parts" (*Anglo-Saxon Medicine,* 143–44). While Cameron's explanation is certainly convincing, the logic is still consistent if the knife is used for other purposes, such as surgical incision or a ritual of sympathetic magic. However the *seax* might be used, it ends the battle through close-range fighting. For discussion of various theories regarding this final instruction, see Pettit, *Anglo-Saxon Remedies,* 259–60.

98. Even some of our most basic vocabulary speaks to a long-standing overlap connecting the worlds of plants and weapons, and historical linguistics shows that some of our earliest metaphors go from plants to weapons rather than the other way around. Our word blade—used for blades of grass and blades of swords alike—ultimately derives from Proto-Indo-European *bhel-, "thrive, bloom," *American Heritage Dictionary,* 5th ed., "Indo-European Roots," s.v. *bhel-³.

Battles against illness—like battles against military opponents—have stages, and the poetry in *Wið færstice* beautifully and powerfully reminds us of the importance of careful preparation without ever losing sight of the ultimate goal. And the link, of course, is the simple *seax*, which functions as a powerful weapon forged by smiths in the inset heroic poem and a healer's curative implement in the outer preparation of the medicine.

Conclusions

Far from mere vestiges of superstition, the weaponry employed here and throughout the Old English medical tradition follows a fairly clear and consistent logic. The leaf-shaped spearhead—a common weapon in Roman and Germanic warfare—quite naturally figures prominently in the Latin-derived *Herbarium* as well as in the Old English *Lacnunga* and *Leechbooks* as accessible aids to identification. Likewise, the *seax*, ubiquitous as a domestic tool and military weapon across early medieval England, displays an equally wide range of uses in the *Leechbooks* as a surgical tool, a harvesting implement, and ritual object. The *Journey Charm*, inscribed in the margins of Bede's *Ecclesiastical History*, reflects the manuscript's implied audience of higher learning through its metaphorical weapons, which would have been associated with only the most elite warriors, equipped with sword, mailcoat, shield, and helmet. In contrast, *Wið færstice* appears in a commonplace medical text and employs commonplace weapons, primarily arrows and flying spears, hunting equipment that readily transferred to the battlefield and that traditionally marks the beginning of great battles in much epic poetry. These different kinds of power from distinct types of weapons are all channeled into herbal remedies and ritual practices for healing.

As these examples illustrate, the Old English medical texts creatively infused already powerful metaphors of battle with rich associations from an array of weapons that would have been known and understood in early medieval England. By combining our knowledge of material culture, military tactics, and historical context with the seemingly far-removed fields of oral poetry and traditional medicine, we come to a much richer understanding of how traditional healers negotiated power over illness and adversity in early medieval England.

CHAPTER 7

Saracens at St. Albans

The Heart-Case of Roger de Norton

NAOMI HOWELL

Discovery, Origins, and Context of the De Norton Heart-Case

The year 1872 saw a massive overhaul and restoration in St. Albans Abbey as the people of St. Albans and others sought to transform the crumbling parish church into a living cathedral, an effort that was soon to prove successful. The great architect Sir George Gilbert Scott directed the works until his death in 1878, and it was fortunately under his guidance that a curious discovery was made. While excavating the floor before the altar of St. Mary of the Four Tapers, in the antechapel of the Lady Chapel at the southeast end of the church, a cylindrical hole was found in the stone. About a foot in diameter, it contained the remains of a fragile wooden box, delicately painted and decorated with Arabic lettering (figure 7.1). The stone cavity was re-covered by paving stones, while what remained of the box was removed for careful inspection and preservation. It may be that the dust left behind by the crumbling wooden box and its contents were left *in situ* and still lie under the paving awaiting future analysis; more probably, most of the residual particles were swept away. The box would eventually be identified as the heart sepulcher of the thirteenth-century abbot, Roger de Norton (d. 1290).[1] Beyond even what we now know

1. The discovery was reported by G. G. Scott, "Notes upon the Burial of the Body and Heart of Abbot Roger de Norton in St Albans Abbey," *Archaeological Journal* 31 (1874): 293–95,

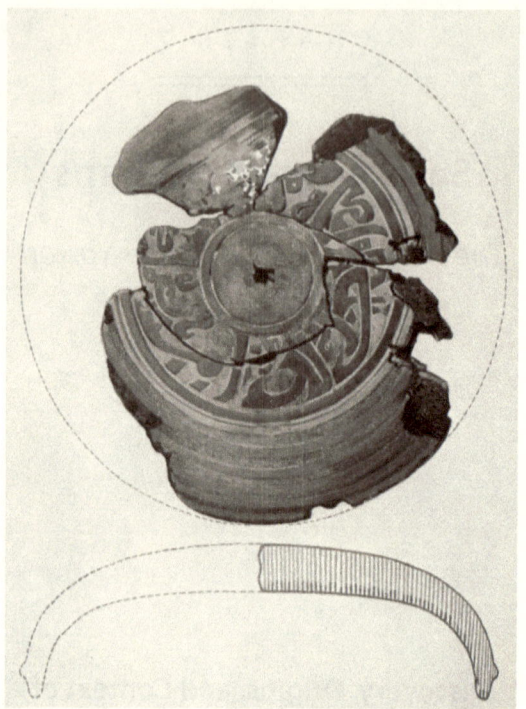

FIGURE 7.1. Depiction of the heart-case by Charles William James Praetorius RA, published with William Page's "Notes on the Heart-Case of Roger Norton," *Proceedings of the Society of Antiquaries* 22, 2nd series (1909): 253–54.

about its extraordinary origins and its unprecedented reuse, the heart-case of Roger de Norton deserves our attention because of the light it can shed on a number of different narratives and traditions that intersect in and around it. Commencing with a discussion of the probable origins and multiplying meanings of the box itself (its roots and its routes), this chapter will proceed to situate its discovery in relation to the long history of archaeological excavations and revelations at the abbey, developing a reading of this unique artifact in light of other texts and objects from thirteenth-century St. Albans, including Matthew Paris's *Vie de St. Auban* and a spectacular Roman cameo, described and drawn by Matthew, which likewise became the nexus of interwoven narratives regarding the abbey's origins and identity. Like many of the objects and artifacts examined in this volume, the heart sepulcher affords a case study in which place, text, movement, and materiality reveal themselves as mutually

and further discussed in William Page, "Notes on the Heart-Case of Roger Norton," *Proceedings of the Society of Antiquaries* 22, 2nd series (1909): 253–54.

shaping and engendering one another. The rhythm of this relationship seems tidal: shifting, subsiding, regenerating, and resurging over time.

Scott presented a brief account of the discovery, accompanied by a careful drawing of the heart-case, to the Royal Archaeological Institute. After diligently seeking the advice of specialists, the architect had to fall back on his own observations: "The apparently oriental character of the box-cover, and the resemblance of some of its ornaments to an inscription, I submit to the consideration of the members of the Institute."[2] Scott's acquaintance, the Bishop of Brechin, saw in the inscription the name of God, or Allah.[3] More recently, thanks chiefly to the work of Barry Knight in consultation with an array of specialists in Islamic art, we understand a great deal more. The inscription on the lid is benedictory, imparting "everlasting glory, enduring wealth" to the possessor. Comparison with similar boxes (a collection containing medicinal substances) indicates that it may have originated in the mountains of Northern Afghanistan in the second half of the twelfth century.[4] It may thus have been over a hundred years old at the time of its reuse and burial. What is beyond doubt is that it traveled thousands of miles before it came to rest before the altar of Mary of the Four Tapers at St. Albans, where it would remain undisturbed for the next 600 years.

Scott's identification of the box as the heart-case of Roger de Norton led to the resolution of an understandable but persistent textual error. The St.

---

2. Scott, "Notes upon the Burial," 294.

3. Page, "Heart-Case," 253–54. In 1855, Scott had designed what would become the Cathedral of St. Paul in Dundee at the invitation of Alexander Penrose Forbes, Bishop of Brechin (d. 1875), an orientalist and Sanskrit scholar who had been profoundly influenced by Henry Newman. Recalling Newman's claim that revelation was various and diverse, and that divine "seeds of truth" were to be found "far and wide over [the world's] extent," Forbes's suggestion that the heart-case bore the name of God emerges as a theological affirmation. See Terrence Merrigan, "Revelation," in *The Cambridge Companion to John Henry Newman*, ed. Ian Ker and Terrence Merrigan (Cambridge: Cambridge University Press, 2009), 52n29 and 53n37.

4. Barry Knight, "The Heart Case of Abbot Roger de Norton from St. Albans Abbey: An Islamic Object in a Medieval English Context," *Muqarnas* 36, no. 1 (2019): 221–28. I am grateful to the late David Kelsall, archivist of St. Albans, for putting me in touch with Barry Knight. As Knight observes, several boxes in the "basket find" of the David Collection (IDs 89a-y 2003; the wooden boxes being designated 89a-j) provide points of comparison with the heart-case, as well as indications of date and provenance. These boxes, probably once belonging to an apothecary, have been carbon dated to the second half of the twelfth century. The four largest wooden boxes especially (David Collection 89a–d, 2003) are those which bear the most striking resemblance to the heart-case. Of similar size and round, spherical shape, topped by knobbed lids, they are painted with the same orange, yellow-ochre, grey, and black palette. One of them (David Collection 89c, 2003) is adorned on the lid with concentric circles and Kufic or pseudo-Kufic script. See also K. von Folsach, "What the Basket Contained: Some Dateable Glass Bottles from the Eastern Islamic World," in *Facts and Artefacts: Art in the Islamic World; Festschrift for Jens Kröger on his 65th Birthday*, ed. A. Hagedorn and A. Shalem (Leiden: Brill, 2007), 3–11.

Albans *Gesta Abbatum* (the *Deeds of the Abbots*) records that Roger de Norton died on November 3, 1290, and was buried on November 6 in the presbytery before the high altar. But another St. Albans document, John of Amundesham's account of the tombs and monuments in the abbey written in 1428, appears to place the body of Roger de Norton both in the presbytery and also "near the last step of the altar of St Mary called that of the Four Tapers in the middle beneath a small stone with the figure of abbot Roger bearing within his hands a heart."[5] This apparent double burial does not result from an unrecorded translation of the whole body from one spot in the abbey to another, as some had assumed. Rather, the discovery of the small box before the altar of St. Mary clarified confusion resulting from the ambiguity of the Latin *cor*, which could signify both *body* (*cor* as in *corpus*) and *heart* (*cor* as in *corde, cordis, cordi*). In this way the effort, expense, and meanings of the de Norton heart burial had been quite literally lost in translation.[6]

Yet to mistake the *cor* (heart) for the *cor* (body) is not *merely* an error. The separated heart recalls and stands synecdochically for the body as the surviving lid of the heart-case recalls the lost box; the part recalls the whole. Delivering his findings, Scott mused on "the solemn feeling which must arise upon the contemplation of a long list of hearts, the sources of sentiment and feeling, separated from the bodies in which they once had life."[7] It seems fitting that Matthew Paris, a thirteenth-century monk of the abbey, also employs the imagery and homophony of heart and body (*quor* and *cor*) to meditate on parts and wholes, essences and extracts, influences and effusions, when describing the heart of its patron saint. On at least three separate occasions in the *Vie de St. Auban*, the identity and distinction between the heart and the body are emphasized, playing on the homophony of *cors* and *quor* to underline the heart's function as a nexus between shifting, paradoxical, and inter-

---

5. John Amundesham, *Annales monasterii S. Albani, a Johanne Amundesham, monacho ut videtur, conscripti (AD 1421–1440)*, ed. Henry Thomas Riley, Rolls Series 28 (London: Longmans, Green, and Co., 1870–71), 1:434, 438; see Scott, "Notes upon the Burial," 294, where *corpus* is corrected to *cor*.

6. Not all were instantly convinced. Ridgway Lloyd reports the discovery of the heart-case but insists that the "prevalent theory, that it was intended to contain the heart of Abbat [sic] Roger de Norton, is founded on a mistranslation." Lloyd argues that "his body seems to have been at first buried here, and afterwards removed to the Presbytery" (John Amundesham, *Account of the Altars, Monuments, and Tombs, Existing A. D. 1428 in Saint Alban's Abbey*, trans. Ridgway Lloyd [Saint Albans: Langley, 1873], 38, 43). Lloyd's position is followed by Fred B. Mason, *Gibbs' Illustrated Handbook to St Albans: Containing a Sketch of Its History, and a Description of Its Abbey, Its Antiquities, and Other Objects of Interest* (St. Albans: Gibbs and Bamforth, 1884), 96–97.

7. Scott, "Notes upon the Burial," 294, paraphrasing Emily Sophia Hartshorne, *Enshrined Hearts of Warriors and Illustrious People* (London: Robert Hardwicke, 1861).

dependent binaries. Each instance is imbued with nostalgia, awe, and solemn feeling. Before the saint is baptized, his confessor, Amphibalus, perceives that he has been touched and made receptive by divine light: "ne vus serra celé: / Seint esperitz ad tun quor eslumé"[8] (lines 339–40) [(answers) shall not be hidden from you: / the Holy Spirit has illumined your heart]. As the following lines clarify, this illumination imparts an understanding of the immortality of the soul, even while the body and the heart remain vulnerable to pain and injury here on earth: "ne soiez esmeüz par nule adversité / ke hem vus face au cors u au quor mauffé" (lines 364–65) [fear no adversity which the wicked can inflict on your body and heart]. This vulnerable permeability is complicated later on, when the heart and the body are again aligned. As his converts are being tortured, their confessor (Amphibalus) suffers even more than they do as he witnesses their bodily torments: "cist sunt martir de cor, cist de quor duluser" (line 1350) [(as) they are martyred in their bodies, he suffers in his heart]. Here, the experiences of the bodies of others are intensified in the heart of the viewer. Yet elsewhere, the heart seems to share in the soul's invulnerability when "si cors est las, mais sis bons quors tut frais est e nuveus" (line 1470) [the body is exhausted, but the heart is fresh and new]. The heart in the *Vie de St. Auban* can be imagined as a vessel for eternity on the one hand and fleeting temporality on the other. Uniting the transcendent soul in the contingent mortal body, the heart is the vessel containing both distilled individual essence and the capacity to mingle with other beings, human and divine. Thus the heart (*quor*) lies at the *core* of the body (*cors*) for which it stands, but also marks the body's boundary or periphery, where it interacts with things external and eternal. This conflation or co-location of core and periphery will be central to my interpretation of the de Norton heart-case.

Although heart burial was a common practice in the thirteenth century, separate burial of the heart and body only a few meters away within the same religious building was extremely unusual, even for bishops, and it was almost unheard-of for monks in Britain, whose rules discouraged such expense and self-promotion.[9] Nor is this the only respect in which de Norton's heart-case

---

8. Matthew Paris, *"Vie de Seint Auban": A Poem in Old French*, ed. Robert Atkinson (London: John Murray, 1876), cited in text as *VA*; translations are my own except where noted. Alban's newly acquired comprehension of his immortal soul can counteract the terror of torture and pain inflicted on his body and his heart.

9. Scott, "Notes upon the Burial," 295, cites the non-monastic example of Hugh de Balsham, Bishop of Ely (d. 1286), whose body and heart were buried separately in his cathedral. Heart-burial in the same city (but not the same building) as the body was customary for the prince-bishops of Würzburg; see Estella Weiss-Krejci, "Heart Burial in Medieval and Early Post-Medieval Central Europe," in *Body Parts and Bodies Whole*, ed. Katharina Rebay-Salisbury, Marie Louise Stig Sørensen, and Jessica Hughes (Oxford: Oxbow, 2010), 119–34. It

departs from medieval norms. The box, of which only the lid survives, was not intended as a heart casket. Originally intended as a container for precious spices or medicinal herbs, possibly fitting as a gift, its repurposing as a heart-case is surprising and perhaps unparalleled.

Arriving in Europe, this Afghan box would have been perceived as belonging to a group of high-status portable objects marked with eastern motifs and lettering. Whenever they could be obtained, such objects were treasured throughout Europe and Britain, sometimes finding their way to shrines and holy places. In Maastricht, the remains of St. Servatius were found wrapped in precious silks originating from the seventh century and later, and having traveled from as far away as China. Also preserved in the treasury of St. Servatius are several thirteenth-century ivory relic-boxes, including a casket of Arabic craftsmanship with a set of combination locks.[10] In some cases, the inscribed object could itself become an object of veneration. The fragment of linen gauze venerated as the Veil of St. Anne, still in the treasury of St. Anne's Cathedral in Apt, Provence, features benedictory words in Arabic. A relic believed to have been the shroud of Christ, still in the monastery of Cadouin in the Dordogne where it was presented in the thirteenth century, is adorned with Arabic script.[11] Woven in the late eleventh century in Fatimid Egypt, its text begins: "(In the name of God) the Compassionate, the Merciful. There is no god but Allah [i.e., God] alone, who has no equal. Muhammad is the messenger of Allah [i.e., God]."[12]

Objects inscribed with Arabic lettering were so closely associated with status, authority, and authenticity that they were sometimes forged, copied, or imagined in Christian contexts. In an early example, a gold coin minted in Mercia between 773 and 796 CE (also discussed in Andrew James Johnston's contribution and the introduction to this volume), during the reign of Offa,

---

is worth noting that de Norton was not the only abbot with two memorials at St. Albans. His predecessor William de Trumpington (d. 1235) had his entrails buried in the cemetery a few feet away (Charles Angell Bradford, *Heart Burial* [London: Allen and Unwin, 1933], 23–24). But heart ablation was of a different order from entrail extraction. The sternum needed to be sawed through with some force and expertise so as to keep the organ intact.

10. Xinru Liu, *Silk and Religion: An Exploration of Material Life and the Thought of People* (New Delhi: Oxford University Press, 1996), 126, 155; Avinoam Shalem, *Islam Christianized: Islamic Portable Objects in the Medieval Church Treasuries of the Latin West* (Bern: Peter Lang, 1998), 289.

11. Janet E. Snyder, *Early Gothic Column-Figure Sculpture in France: Appearance, Materials, Significance* (Farnham, UK: Ashgate, 2011), 181.

12. "Saint Suaire de Cadouin," *Qantara: Patrimoine méditerranéen*, accessed June 2, 2020, https://www.qantara-med.org/public/show_document.php?do_id=1113, line A; discussed in Isabelle Dolezalek, *Arabic Script on Christian Kings: Textile Inscriptions on Royal Garments from Norman Sicily*, Das Mittelalter, Perspektiven mediävistischer Forschung, Beihefte 5 (Berlin: de Gruyter, 2017), 87–89.

copied an Arabic dinar. Though imperfect, and clearly produced by a non-Arabic speaker, the copy is accurate enough to still be legible in both Latin and Arabic. "Offa Rex" is imprinted upside down in relation to the Arab lettering, which has been translated as "Muhammad is the messenger of God."[13] A fashion for objects adorned with pseudo-Kufic script flourished in the thirteenth century. Real and pseudo-Islamic objects and texts were seen as perfectly compatible with Christian religious imagery and ritual functions from a very early date, and across Europe, Kufic and pseudo-Kufic script enhanced the beauty and desirability of secular and sacred objects (figures 7.2–7.3).[14] The costly Islamic "Peacock Silk" enfolding St. Cuthbert's relics in Durham from the time of their translation in 1104 features Kufic script prominently.[15] Medieval works of art feature halos—particularly, it seems, of the Virgin Mary and the Holy family—filled or bordered with Kufic or pseudo-Kufic script. Duccio di Buoninsegna's *Rucellai Madonna* from ca. 1285, now in the Uffizi Gallery in Florence, features pseudo-Kufic script in the Virgin's halo and along the gold hem of her robe.[16] In Gentile de Fabriano's *Adoration of the Magi* (1423), also in the Uffizi, the robes of an attendant and all the haloes of the holy family are filled with pseudo-Kufic script as they greet their Eastern visitors.[17] It has

13. Offa's dinar is in the British Museum (registration number: 1913,1213.1), "Gold imitation dinar of Offa," British Museum, accessed June 2, 2020, https://www.bmimages.com/preview.asp?image=00031108001. See the introduction to this volume concerning the translation of the Arabic inscriptions on the coin.

14. Other splendid examples include the enamel ciborium from ca. 1215–30, now in the British Museum, (registration number: 1853,1118.1). "Ciborium," British Museum, accessed June 2, 2020, http://www.britishmuseum.org/research/collection_online/collection_object_details/collection_image_gallery.aspx?assetId=12213001&objectId=49664&partId=1.

15. See Anna Muthesius, "Silks and Saints: The Rider and Peacock Silks from the Relics of St. Cuthbert," in *St. Cuthbert, His Cult and His Community to AD 1200*, ed. Gerald Bonner, David W. Rollason, and Clare Stancliffe (Woodbridge, UK: Boydell Press, 1989), 363–64. Though the "Nature Goddess Silk" also associated with Cuthbert's relics is Byzantine, the discussions by Clare Higgins ("Some New Thoughts on the Nature Goddess Silk") and Hero Granger-Taylor ("The Inscription on the Nature Goddess Silk") in the same volume provide an astonishing array of comparisons with other Eastern and Islamic silks used to envelop relics across Christendom.

16. Duccio di Buoninsegna, "Virgin and Child Enthroned, Surrounded by Angels," Uffizi Gallery, Florence, accessed June 2, 2020, https://www.uffizi.it/en/artworks/virgin-and-child-enthroned-surrounded-by-angels-known-as-the-rucellai-madonna. Duccio repeatedly includes pseudo-Kufic script in his paintings of the Virgin. See for example his "Virgin and Child with Saint Dominic, Saint Aurea, Patriarchs and Prophets" (now in the National Gallery in London, ID: NG 566). Giotto also does this. See his "Madonna and Child," ca. 1310/1315, National Gallery of Art, Washington, DC, Samuel H. Kress Collection, ID: 1939.1.256, accessed June 2, 2020, https://www.nga.gov/collection/art-object-page.397.html.

17. Gentile da Fabriano, "Adoration of the Magi," Uffizi Gallery, Florence, Inv. 1890 no. 8364, accessed June 2, 2020, https://www.uffizi.it/en/artworks/adoration-of-the-magi. It is as if the wise men from the East—turbaned strangers representing the full array of human ages, their retinue indicating varied ethnicities—reach the culmination of their voyage only to find

FIGURE 7.2. Cross fragment of the Mourning Virgin, early thirteenth century, champlevé enamel on gilded copper, glass, Walters Art Museum, Baltimore, acquired by Henry Walters, 1927 (accession number 44.22). © The Walters Art Museum.

been suggested that the circular form of this "writing" takes its inspiration from bowls and other vessels and round portable inscribed objects from the East, such as our heart-case.[18]

The Eastern origins of these objects and the writing on them were charged with authority, glamour, and sanctity not merely for the recognized consistency of their superlative craftsmanship, but for their geographic proximity to the Holy Land and to Eden. The reception and repurposing of the Afghan box in a Christian monastic context was thus not (or not *only*) determined by a

---

divine truth emanating from the Virgin and Child in their own native tongue. For Christian viewers of the altarpiece, on the other hand, the Saracen text—like the ultramarine blue and costly gold, imbue the familiar domesticity of the scene with grandeur, spaciousness of reference, and awe.

18. See "Beautiful Gibberish: Fake Arabic in Medieval and Renaissance Art," *Encyclopedia Britannica*, accessed June 2, 2020, https://www.britannica.com/story/beautiful-gibberish-fake-arabic-in-medieval-and-renaissance-art.

FIGURE 7.3. The Resurrection of the Dead, thirteenth century, champlevé enamel on gilded copper; possibly once part of the same crucifix as Figure 2, Victoria and Albert Museum, London (museum number M.104–1945). © Victoria and Albert Museum, London.

failure of understanding, but by a sense of untold richness, promise, and mystery, which we can surmise accorded reasonably well with the maker's intentions.[19] The associations with origins could also be conceived of in temporal terms. Christians habitually regarded all non-Christians as potential converts, and in that sense both historical and contemporary pagans and unbelievers could be considered pre-Christian, stuck, in different ways, in the past. The point here is not that medieval Christians failed to grasp the distinction between ancient pagans and contemporary ones, but that they often (though not always) considered these differences relatively unimportant.

Objects like the Islamic box, together with the texts I will consider in this chapter, might well be understood in terms of a Christian narrative of triumphalist supersession over the pagan past. In other words, it would be tempting to consider the heart-case of Roger de Norton in terms of real or imagined *spolia*; but this is a temptation I hope to resist or at least complicate. David Ludden has termed such readings "civilisational histories," which "nec-

---

19. If the monks of St. Albans valued the letters' ornamental form rather than the presumably illegible content, so too would many in the Islamic community that produced it. Kufic script was often employed for its decorative qualities, imbuing the object inscribed with a sense of elevated purpose, meaning, and beauty. Even Islamic artifacts that never left and were never intended to leave their original linguistic sphere frequently featured pseudo-Kufic in which the forms of the script were imitated decoratively, without forming recognizable words or letters. Examples of pseudo-Kufic script appear, for instance, on a number of the boxes in the David collection that helped date de Norton's heart-case.

essarily (if not intentionally)" read back "present-national sentiments into a timeless past."[20] In the multiple foundation narratives of St. Albans that this chapter will explore, the identity of the institution, its rootedness in its precise location, and its importance in the supercessionary Christian drama, are all reasserted and reiterated in a way that privileges the narrative arc of that drama. Yet if we as readers stop there, we risk flattening and overlooking the complexities in our source texts and objects, and moreover "prevent[ing] history from working against cultural hegemonies in the present by stultifying our analysis of mobility, context, agency, contingency and change."[21] Unexamined "civilizational histories" have too long shaped medieval scholarship, and continue to do so, but analysis of the kind Ludden calls for has in recent years been opening critical debates and discourses. In an era when medieval notions, symbols, and narratives are being seized upon and deployed in the interests of racist and fascist agendas privileging racial, ethnic, and cultural purity, these debates are at once relevant and overdue, and the heart-case of Roger de Norton rewards such analysis in a way that is both illuminating and timely. Focusing on this object generates further questions about how it might have been perceived and further challenging reflections on what "civilizational histories" have encouraged us to see (or overlook) in such objects. Entangled as they are in the on-going histories of racial/cultural/religious antipathy and violence, the objects and events discussed in this chapter emerge as not *only* shaped by hostility, ignorance, and an urge to dominate.

As Finbarr Flood has observed, "Like most teleologies, these scenarios [of civilizational histories] operate through a collapse of all possible identities into a single monolithic identification, producing as singular, static, and undifferentiated what was often multiple, protean, and highly contested."[22] Seeking to "deconstruct these monoliths," Flood traces dynamic patterns of intercultural engagement "over several centuries, emphasizing relations rather than essences, 'routes' rather than 'roots.'" Focusing on "practices of circulation, displacement, and translation," Flood demonstrates "the contingent and unstable nature of premodern identity."[23] While texts have long served the interests of territorial claims ("roots"), portable objects invite the consideration of practices of circulation, displacement, and translation; in other words,

---

20. David Ludden, "History Outside Civilisation and the Mobility of South Asia," *South Asia: Journal of South Asian Studies* 17 (1994): 3, 6–7.

21. Ludden, "History Outside Civilisation," 7–9.

22. Finbarr Barry Flood, *Objects of Translation: Material Culture and Medieval "Hindu-Muslim" Encounter* (Princeton, NJ: Princeton University Press, 2009), 3.

23. Flood, *Objects of Translation*, 3. For the terminology of "routes" versus "roots," Flood cites James Clifford, *Routes: Travel and Translation in the Late Twentieth Century* (Cambridge, MA: Harvard University Press, 1997).

"routes."²⁴ In this light, texts appear deeply implicated in deadly, present-day ethnic and political conflicts. As Flood argues, attention to itineraries (paths, directions) and the haptic, multisensory objects that traveled them illuminate networks of interrelation that resist the exclusionary scenarios of origin and foundation evoked in texts, at least as they have often been understood.²⁵

Taken too rigidly, this set of terms, metaphors, and distinctions would have fairly obvious limitations. By focusing on *translation,* that is, the translation and relocation of both texts and objects, Flood emphasizes the complex networks of movement and transmission that emerge when texts and objects are explored in relationship to each other. Thus, "the relationship between strategies of translation associated with the circulation of objects and processes of transculturation" can be understood as "a mode of facilitating communication between premodern elites," which highlights "the ambivalences and ambiguities that often characterized transcultural exchanges."²⁶ Flood advocates interpreting texts as things and vice versa, resisting the impulse to draw distinctions too neatly or privilege one medium over another: "This dynamic aspect of translation confounds any attempt to draw hard-and-fast boundaries between cultural formations.... Appreciating this calls for a willingness to engage both media simultaneously, to read between and beyond text and image rather than privileging one over and above the other."²⁷

---

24. In exploring another precious object with contemporary Christian and Muslim associations, Oleg Grabar traces an entire genre of such items traded around the Mediterranean and beyond ("The Crusades and the Development of Islamic Art," in *The Crusades from the Perspective of Byzantium and the Muslim World,* ed. Angeliki E. Laiou and Roy Parviz Mottahedeh [Washington, DC: Dumbarton Oaks, 2001], 235–45; "About a Bronze Bird," in *Reading Medieval Images: The Art Historian and the Object,* ed. Elizabeth Sears, Thelma K. Thomas, and Ilene H. Forsyth [Ann Arbor: University of Michigan Press, 2002], 117–25). The bronze vessel in the shape of a bird is known as the "Peacock Acquamanile" (though some art historians have convincingly suggested a hoopoe) and is enigmatically inscribed in Latin and Arabic, the languages and ornaments artfully juxtaposed to generate multiple but divergent meanings, imparting different information to different readers (as explored more fully by Grabar): "✢ OPVUS · SALOMONIS · ERᴬT ✢ / عمل عبد الملك النصراني [amal 'abd al-malik al-nasrânî]." Possible translations include: "A work of Solomon [/ Solomonic beauty], year 962, made by the servant of the Christian King [or '... by Abd al-Malik the Christian']." Possibly dating from as early as the ninth century, the object attained its present form by 1250 CE; it is now in the Louvre.

25. "If, therefore, 'routes not roots' and 'networks not territories' are two fundamental themes of this book, a third, related concern might be characterized as 'things not texts'" (Flood, *Objects of Translation,* 9).

26. Flood, *Objects of Translation,* 9, 6–7. "In the first place, the value of the desired texts is related not only to their content but also to their foreignness, to the long and dangerous voyage that their acquisition necessitated.... In this regard, it is noteworthy that the texts acquired from India and other lands by the Sasanian kings of Iran were reportedly deposited in the Royal Treasury along with more material riches" (Flood, *Objects of Translation,* 7).

27. Flood, *Objects of Translation,* 9.

The heart-case of Abbot Roger de Norton requires us to consider objects and texts together—as *routes* and *roots*—because the monks of St. Albans were intensely, exceptionally conscious of how these could represent and impinge on the prestige of their abbey. The abbey's role (as many saw it) at the heart of networks of learning, trade, and political power was demonstrated and visualized in many ways, including the production of maps. By the time of Abbot Roger de Norton's death in 1290, St. Albans had become a center of mapmaking, and would remain so for the following century—thanks in large part to the wide-ranging interests and innovative talents of Matthew Paris who, by the time of his death in 1259, had produced a Mappamundi, a splendid and detailed map of Britain, and a large number of itinerary maps.[28] The numerous maps produced at St. Albans—linear, itinerary maps and two-dimensional maps, as well—emphasize links with pilgrimage sites, religious (especially Benedictine) houses, and important political centers, as well as the place of St. Albans in relation to these. Map production thus participates in a conception of St. Albans, asserted by the monks in a number of ways, as being both a site of origins, and the center of a number of larger networks. Continuing well into the fourteenth century, this perception is witnessed in the famous *Mandeville's Travels*, whose author identified himself as a native of St. Albans and whose tomb was said to lie in the abbey.[29]

The outward-looking self-consciousness of the monastic culture of St. Albans did not necessarily mean that the abbey was any more well disposed to cultural "others" than any other Christian community of the time. The thirteenth-century chronicles of Matthew Paris are full of excoriations of the Jews.[30] Rather more distinctive was the relationship with "Saracens," yet even

---

28. Daniel K. Connolly, *The Maps of Matthew Paris: Medieval Journeys Through Space, Time and Liturgy* (Woodbridge, UK: Boydell Press, 2009).

29. See John Mandeville, *The Book of Marvels and Travels*, trans. and ed. Anthony Bale (Oxford: Oxford University Press, 2012), xv.

30. The particular hostility to the Jews can be partly attributed to the considerable debts owed by the abbey to Jewish moneylenders. The fabulously wealthy Aaron of Lincoln, on viewing the abbey church, reportedly remarked that he had provided the saint with lodging. This generous provision of shelter by a non-Christian to a Christian recalls the *Life of St. Alban*, the narrative of foundational importance to the abbey, and strongly indicates Aaron's familiarity with it. In the narrative, the pagan Alban provides lodging in his own home for the fugitive Christian missionary Amphibalus. As Aaron implies, it was now Alban who was offered lodging by a non-Christian. Had the monks been less aggrieved by their debts, they might have been impressed by Aaron's intimate acquaintance with their foundational narrative. If Aaron cast himself in the role of the not-yet-converted host Alban, a monastic ear might have even inferred the possibility of a future convert. A number of valued monks of St. Albans were converts enjoying ongoing ties with the Jewish community. Matthew Paris recorded the 1259 conversion of Elias of London, known as *episcopus*, "the bishop" (Matthew Paris, *Chronica Majora*, ed. H. R. Luard [London: Longman, 1872–83], 5:730). Solomon the Goldsmith, who also worked

these were considered sufficiently "miscreant" (of false belief) to make the use of a Saracen box for heart burial surprising at first glance. It would be misleading, however, to cherry-pick the denunciation of Jews and Muslims in texts from St. Albans without noting the abbey's conflicts with fellow Christians. The papacy was frequently deplored in passages that would be often reprinted during the Reformation. King John was invariably described with deep disgust. In other words, Matthew Paris and his fellow monastic chroniclers were committed to defending St. Albans's interests against outsiders, both Christian and not. Profoundly committed to the abbey and its foundational narratives, they were loyally "rooted" there, no matter how far flung their networks and their travels. With this in mind, the use of an Islamic artifact as a heart sepulchre is only remarkable if we assume that the object would have been associated with inimical *outsiders*. As I shall argue in the next section, the monks of St. Albans may well have associated the box instead with a particularly local kind of Otherness, an alterity with paradoxically deep roots in the history of the abbey. The heart burial marking the end of the life of Roger de Norton is complexly intertwined with the traditions and narratives concerning the origin of the institution of which he was abbot.

Excavations and Foundations at St. Albans

Roger de Norton served as abbot of St Albans from 1263 until his death in 1290. He had previously been a monk of St. Albans and would have known the old Matthew Paris before Matthew's death in 1259. De Norton's abbacy was characterized by heated litigation—including a successful case against the queen, Eleanor of Castile.[31] Roger aggressively reasserted and defended the abbey's territorial claims, and also had barriers, gates, and ditches constructed around abbey boundaries. (The point is worth highlighting because heart burial was not infrequently associated with disputed territorial claims.) His gifts to the abbey, including a precious silver candle stick, reflect the importance of the liturgy, which we also saw reflected in the placement of his heart-

---

on Thomas Becket's shrine, was almost certainly one of these. As it was, Aaron's remarks were recorded as expressive of his gloating vanity at having funded (and being owed) so much. See Kathy Lavezzo, *The Accommodated Jew: English Antisemitism from Bede to Milton* (Ithaca, NY: Cornell University Press, 2016), 106–7; see also Matthew Paris, *The Life of Saint Alban*, trans. and ed. Jocelyn Wogan-Browne and Thelma S. Fenster (Tempe: Arizona Center for Medieval and Renaissance Studies, 2010), 26–27.

31. H. M. M. Lane, "Queen Eleanor of Castile," *Transactions of the St Albans and Hertfordshire Architectural and Archaeological Society* (1928–30): 255–73.

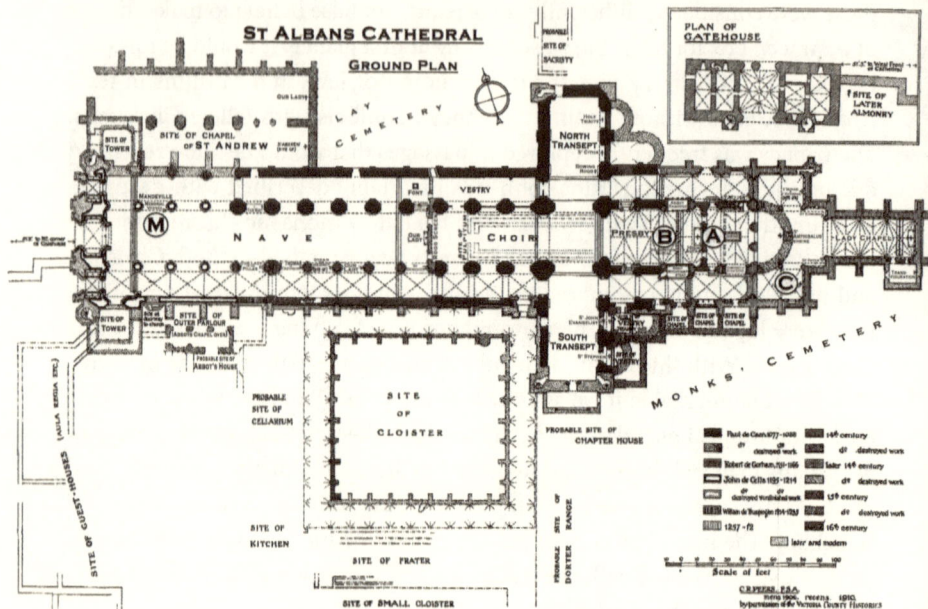

FIGURE 7.4. Ground plan of St. Albans Abbey, showing [A] the Shrine of St. Alban; [B] the burial place of Abbot Roger de Norton's body; and [C] the burial of his heart within the heart-case, in front of the altar of Mary of the Four Tapers; and [M] the supposed site of John Mandeville's tomb. Based on the plan in *An Inventory of the Historical Monuments of Hertfordshire* (London: HM Stationery Office, 1910), with labels enhanced and added for clarity.

case. He is best remembered for pursuing the repair of the eastern end of the abbey church damaged in the earthquake of 1250.[32]

At the time of his death, the Lady Chapel was not yet completed: the walls would only have been about waist- or shoulder-high. Abbot Roger had his heart placed in the easternmost part of the completed church, a part *he* had seen rebuilt, before an altar—with four candles, or tapers—which he had founded (figure 7.4). The heart sepulcher was situated at a point crossed by several routes through the abbey. In sight of St. Alban's magnificent, jewel-encrusted shrine, it occupied a place imbued with the sanctity of the founding saint, without being so obtrusive as to draw censure. Pilgrims, who would

---

32. Matthew describes the earthquake in detail in the *Chronica Majora*, 5:187. Details of Roger de Norton's energetic and litigious abbacy are recorded in Thomas Walsingham, *Gesta Abbatum Monasterii Sancti Albani*, ed. Henry Thomas Riley (London: Longmans, 1867), 1:399–485. *Gesta Abbatum*, the domestic chronicle of St. Albans, was compiled by Matthew Paris up to the middle of the thirteenth century and continued by Thomas Walsingham and others thereafter. Although credited to Walsingham, Riley's edition encompasses the complete chronicle.

pause to kneel along their progress to the shrine and often approached entirely on their knees, would perceive the heart monument as they passed over it. Slowed by their own reverence, if not by the congestion of other thronging pilgrims, they might offer a brief prayer for de Norton's soul even as their living bodies pressed against the paving above his heart. We also know that for the monks it lay on the path to "a very curious passage" by which the monks could get to the Lady Chapel or the monastery.[33] Even as the sandaled feet and all-too-busy minds of succeeding monks passed over the spot, the monument might fleetingly remind them—perhaps of the life and works of their predecessor recorded in their annals, certainly of the regular masses performed for his soul at this very spot.

After the Reformation, the abbey church was partitioned and repurposed as a humble protestant parish church on the west side, and—perhaps fittingly (given the Virgin's care of children, as in the *Prioress's Tale*)—a school at the east end, where the Lady Chapel has now resumed its place. The school and the parish church were divided by a road that tunneled its way through the building. The de Norton heart burial was located just under or behind the wall. Where previously the liturgical passageways had made the heart burial visible, the post-Reformation passageway obscured it entirely. By the nineteenth century, the vicissitudes of time, the Reformation and repurposing, and centuries of neglect had left St. Albans structurally unsound and in imminent danger of demolition. The great renovator Sir George Gilbert Scott, who dismantled the partition wall in the course of his repairs, was hailed as the "Saviour of the Abbey."[34] The discovery of the heart-case in 1872 thus participated in a moment of refoundation that culminated in 1877 when the parish church was promoted to its new status as a cathedral.

In this sense, the revelation of the heart-case quite pleasingly echoes medieval *inventio* narratives, which heralded events of (re-)foundation and renewal at St. Albans. St. Albans has a long history of finding both Christian and non-Christian objects in its earth. Far from being "inventions" in the modern sense, these astonishing discoveries—once dug up and brought to light—recalled, embodied, and confirmed truths that were seen to have endured in spite of having been forgotten. As I'll suggest below, the digging and excava-

---

33. Mason, *Gibbs' Illustrated Handbook*, 96.
34. At St. Albans, Scott is still favorably contrasted with Edmund Beckett, Baron Grimthorpe, who funded and directed subsequent work. The structures most radically redesigned under his direction (e.g., the West Façade), are now disparagingly said to have been "Grimthorped." For Scott as "saviour," see Eileen Roberts, *The Hill of the Martyr: An Architectural History of St. Albans Abbey* (Dunstable, UK: Book Castle, 1993), 205.

tion that is integral to foundation can be (and perhaps was) imagined as the planting and rooting of a living institution, its memories, and its narratives.[35]

St. Albans takes its name from Britain's third-century protomartyr, the first to shed his blood on British soil for the Christian faith. According to most traditions, Alban was a Roman, a high official in the city of Verulamium, or, in some versions, a "prince."[36] Matthew Paris reports in his *Vie de St. Auban*, "N'i out plus cuneüz, ne plus communal" (line 22) [There was no one more well-known or more sociable]. When the fugitive Christian missionary Amphibalus came to him for shelter, he was received and welcomed: "[Est en] sun ostel entrez e receüz" (line 72) [He entered into his lodging and was received]. When his role in aiding the escape of St. Amphibalus was discovered, Alban was tried and beheaded. Described as ruby-red, as crystalline as the miraculous spring that Alban had caused by his intercession to well up, his blood spattered the cross he was holding and saturated the earth.[37] Alban was buried on the hill overlooking the Roman city near the spot, it is asserted, where the abbey church would later be built.

In the eighth century, an angel was said to have come to King Offa in a dream, pointing out the location of Alban's body; in 793, Offa founded the abbey in his name. This sequence of events would be echoed in the twelfth century when—conveniently in the wake of Becket's martyrdom and the diversion of pilgrims from St. Albans to Canterbury—the body of Amphibalus was found and enshrined in the abbey.[38] The abbey church was built from the bricks and stones quarried from the ruined remains of Verulamium; according to Matthew Paris, these ruins eventually also yielded up an "ancient book"

---

35. My discussion of *inventiones* and (re)foundations at St. Albans builds in particular on Monika Otter, "'New Werke': St. Erkenwald, St. Albans, and the Medieval Sense of the Past," *Journal of Medieval and Renaissance Studies* 24 (1994): 387–414; Monika Otter, *Inventiones: Fiction and Referentiality in Twelfth-Century English Historical Writing* (Chapel Hill: University of North Carolina Press, 1996); Julia Crick, "Offa, Aelfric and the Refoundation of St Albans," in *Alban and St Albans: Roman and Medieval Architecture, Art and Archaeology*, ed. Martin Henig and Phillip Lindley (Leeds: British Archaeological Association, 2001), 78–84. See also the chapters by Sarah Salih and Philip Schwyzer in this volume.

36. The lives of Alban produced at St. Albans in the Middle Ages describe him as a Roman official. In the *Golden Legend*, however, he is the steward of all of Britain and "prince of knights," and John Lydgate's version, printed at St. Albans in 1534, follows this alternative tradition.

37. The holy blood-saturated soil of St. Albans is a repeated trope, occurring in the *Vita Germani*, repeated by Bede (1.18) and further developed by Matthew: "du seint sanc glorïus ki du cors est flaschiz / la croiz k'Auban porta e li tertre est fluriz" (*VA*, lines 896–97) [with the glorious holy blood gushing from his body / The cross Alban carried and the (whole) hill blossomed].

38. Diana Webb, *Pilgrimage in Medieval England* (London: Hambledon and London, 2000), 58; Benjamin Nicholas Gordon-Taylor, "The Hagiography of St Alban and St Amphibalus in the Twelfth Century," Master's thesis, Durham University, 1991.

recording Alban's martyrdom (discussed further below).³⁹ It is near the site of St. Alban's shrine that the heart-case of Roger de Norton would be found more than a millennium after the abbey's foundation, a discovery that coincided closely with the discovery of fragments of the shrines of Alban and Amphibalus in the internal wall constructed in the sixteenth century. The history of St. Albans is thus punctuated by a series of miracles, *inventiones*, and *translationes*, all of which refer back to, reimagine, and recreate the abbey's founding moment or moments:

- Alban's martyrdom and burial
- Offa's discovery of the body and foundation of the abbey
- The discovery under Abbot Eadmar (early eleventh century) of a *Life of St. Alban* in the ruins of Verulamium
- The discovery and enshrinement of Amphibalus
- The numerous and repeated redesigns of the shrines on the occasions of their translations and anniversaries to more fittingly reflect the virtues and sanctity of these bodies

Most of these *inventiones* and *translationes* were heralded by visions or dreams.⁴⁰ Each of them required digging or excavation. Each also served multiple purposes. On the one hand, they heightened the devotion of the faithful and manifested the abbey's historical significance to its members in ways at once shared and deeply personal. Another related but distinct result (and, arguably, cause) was that they increased revenues, so that the abbey's endless building works could be advanced.⁴¹ Each fresh discovery also asserted the abbey's unique and important role as it looked sometimes anxiously at the two other eminent Benedictine abbeys of Britain: Glastonbury and Canterbury.⁴² The sacred, the suitable, and the strategic can be difficult to distinguish in these cases. Centering on bodies, body parts, and their containers,

---

39. Terence Paul Smith, "Early Recycling: The Anglo-Saxon and Norman Re-Use of Roman Bricks with Special Reference to Hertfordshire," in *Alban and St Albans*, ed. Henig and Lindley, 111–17; Walsingham, *Gesta Abbatum*, 1:24–28.

40. See the discussion of dreams in Otter, *Inventiones*.

41. Matthew Paris would remark on the interminable building works begun by Abbot John de Cella in 1185, "Sed infaustum opus istud, quasi mare flumina, amnio absorbuit, nec adhuc incrementum ceperat fortunatum" (Walsingham, *Gesta Abbatum*, 1:219) [But like a river by the sea, everything was absorbed by that unfortunate work, but without any progress].

42. On St. Alban's vying for eminence, see Brenda Bolton, "St Albans' Loyal Son," in *Adrian IV, The English Pope (1154–1159): Studies and Texts*, ed. Brenda Bolton and Anne J. Duggan (Abington, UK: Routledge, 2016), 75–104. The English Pope Adrian IV (1154–59) bestowed a great deal of independence on St. Albans, declaring that the abbot was to enjoy all pontifical rights and don the episcopal pontificalia still to be seen on many seals and monuments of St.

inventio and *translatio* asserted the place and prosperity of St. Albans Abbey in history and in the wider world; remembering and even reenacting the foundation of the abbey, they could in some cases be considered occasions of *re*-foundation. Implicitly echoing Fortunatus's oft-quoted verse, "Albanum egregium foecunda Britannia profert" [Fertile Britain boasts the noble Alban], these excavations and exhumations can be understood as a reflowering of the abbey's foundational past in moments of present need, the objects and artifacts springing from the fertile soil like seeds planted long before.[43] The burial and rediscovery of Abbot de Norton's heart-case can be best interpreted in the light of this series of exquisitely well-timed "untimely" moments.[44]

The burials of subsequent generations and their intermittent rediscovery have continued to participate (albeit in a more peripheral way) in the tradition of burial, discovery, and renewal at St. Albans. In 1703, the marvelously preserved body of Humphrey, Duke of Gloucester (d. 1447) was discovered, attracting throngs of visitors.[45] In 1978, the remains of eleven medieval abbots were uncovered in the course of the excavation of the old chapter house and reburied with great ceremony before the high altar in the following year. Most recently (in early December 2017), the remains of Abbot John Wheathampstead were rediscovered. Where in the medieval period such discoveries might arouse religious devotion and contemplation, today they attract media attention as events of archaeological, historical, and even national importance. As the Very Rev'd Dr. Jeffrey John (Dean of St. Albans since 2004) remarked, "It is a wonderful thing to have found the grave and relics of John of Wheathampstead." Recalling the abbot's "own national and international influence on the Church at a time when (not unlike today) it was faced with threats of division and decline," the Dean described Abbot John's contributions to "the

---

Albans. The de Norton heart burial, unusual in a monastic context, could be read as a further assertion of episcopal status and privilege.

43. The verse is quoted by Bede (*Historia Ecclesiastica*, 1.7), and subsequently by others including Matthew Paris, the Scottish historian Thomas Dempster, and the antiquary William Camden; see Jennifer Summit, *Memory's Library: Medieval Books in Early Modern England* (Chicago: Chicago University Press, 2008), 177.

44. "Untimely" here does not connote inappropriateness, but a point of conjunction between two moments in history; see Jonathan Gil Harris, *Untimely Matter in the Time of Shakespeare* (Philadelphia: University of Pennsylvania Press, 2008). To Harris's untimely temporalities of "supersession," "explosion," and "conjunction," we might add the temporality of dormancy and reflorescence.

45. Visitors would purchase the liquid in which the body had been embalmed as medicine. Many left their names and initials carved in the stones around his coffin. See Jane Kelsall, "The Chantry of Humphrey Duke of Gloucester (1391–1447) at the Cathedral and Abbey Church of St Alban," Church Monuments Society: Monument of the Month, May 2010, accessed June 2, 2020, https://churchmonumentssociety.org/monument-of-the-month/the-chantry-of-humphrey-duke-of-gloucester-1391-1447-at-the-cathedral-and-abbey-church-of-st-alban.

renown and the beauty of the Abbey, [which] attracted many new pilgrims from Britain and overseas." Noting his defense of the abbey during the Wars of the Roses, the Dean said,

> [Abbot John] was proud to say that he had preserved its treasures for future generations. It seems appropriate that he should appear just as we are trying to do the same through the "Alban, Britain's First Saint" project, which aims to make the Abbey much better known, and to provide better resources to welcome and inform new visitors. As John would certainly wish, in due course his body will be laid to rest again, with proper prayer and ceremony, along with his fellow Abbots in the Presbytery of the Cathedral and Abbey Church. We trust he prays for us, as we do for him.[46]

The discovery of the Abbot's remains serves as an occasion to recall the national and international importance of St. Albans. At the same time, the resonances between distinct historical moments—the era of Alban's martyrdom, the Wars of the Roses, and the present—are underlined. Situated between the past of John's abbacy and the future of "future generations," the discovery of his remains serves as a temporal nexus of intersecting narratives.

The multiple miraculous and sacred *inventiones* and *translationes* at St. Albans, cited above, participate in a wider pattern of archaeological discovery throughout its history. The earth of old Verulamium has continued to give up treasures that have often become intertwined with the history of the abbey. The magnificent mosaic floor and hypocaust now displayed in Verulamium Park were only discovered in 1930. A number of Roman burials with delicate glass and ceramic vessels were unearthed in the nineteenth century, including the beautiful Kingsbury Jug, found with a skeleton in a sarcophagus from the third century. Individual finds in the medieval period generally went unrecorded, but at St. Albans, as elsewhere, coins, jewels, and cameos yielded by the soil of former Roman settlements were treasured both for their beauty and for their purported magical or supernatural properties.[47]

---

46. Matt Adams, "St Albans Cathedral Archaeological Dig Uncovers the Lost Grave of Abbot Wheathampstead," *Herts Advertiser*, December 7, 2017, accessed June 2, 2020, http://www.hertsad.co.uk/news/st-albans-cathedral-archaeological-dig-uncovers-the-lost-grave-of-abbot-wheathampstead-1-5312692; Paul Wilkinson, "Rare Seals Identify Significant Remains at St Albans Abbey," *Church Times*, December 17, 2017, accessed June 2, 2020, https://www.churchtimes.co.uk/articles/2017/15-december/news/uk/rare-seals-identify-remains; and the St. Albans Cathedral website, accessed June 12, 2018, https://www.stalbanscathedral.org/news/archive/2017/st-albans-cathedral-finds-lost-abbot.

47. The prevalence of such discoveries is reflected in the textual tradition of lapidaries. Whereas classical lapidaries indicated what needed to be engraved or sculpted on a gem to

Matthew Paris provides a key example in his depiction of a now-lost engraved gem in his inventory of precious gems belonging to the abbey.[48] The gem is described as very large—half a foot in length—and the drawing, certainly the largest in the series, may be life-sized. Matthew reports that the stone is called *Kaadmau* by the common people. A lengthy text providing a verbal description and several narratives regarding its acquisition accompanies the drawing. In his meticulous drawing, Matthew depicts what was clearly a large late antique cameo (figure 7.5). He describes it as oblong, a precious stone of sardonyx, chalcedony, and onyx. The colors are remarkable. On a dark field ("campum . . . fuscum"), edged with rainbow colors ("limbum quoque ad instar iris"), the "true image" ("ymagijnum vero") is also described as comprising several colors: partly red in hue, partly sky-blue (or bronze: "pars aerei coloris est"). The drawing shows a standing male figure holding a staff (or spear: "hastam") entwined by a crawling, ascending serpent ("repens, ascendensque serpens" in the *Gesta Abbatum*) in his right hand. A tiny human figure with a raised arm perches on his left, and an eagle sits at his feet.[49] The man sports an imperial diadem or fillet, and wears what is recognizable as Roman military attire, including a *pteroges* or *cingulum* (the skirt-like leather or fabric hanging from the waist to protect the loins), a sword-belt and sword (the hilt of which can be seen on the left hip), and a number of straps customary for keeping the armor in place over a tunic. Over his shoulders and behind him is draped a *paludamentum*, a cloak reserved for military commanders worn over one shoulder.

Comparison with other Roman carvings reveals that the cameo clearly owes most of its iconographical elements to similar carvings of Jupiter or a surrogate as *Iovis Conservator*. Like the Chartres or "Jupiter Cameo" (41–45 CE) offered by Charles V of France to adorn the shrine of the reliquary of the Virgin's *chemise*, the central figure stands with a cloak draped over one shoulder, holding a staff and looking to his right.[50] An eagle, Jove's messenger

---

achieve desired results, from the late antique period the wording changed from "if you engrave" to "if you find" ("Se tu treuve" in Anglo-Norman lapidaries, for example). See Fernand de Mély, *Du rôle des pierres gravées au Moyen Âge* (Lille: Desclée & De Brouwer, 1893), 7, 27.

48. Matthew Paris, *Liber additamentorum* [mid-thirteenth century], MS BL Cotton Nero D I, fols. 146ᵛ–147ʳ; Matthew Paris, *Chronica Majora*, 6:387–88. The object is also described in a shorter passage in Walsingham, *Gesta Abbatum*, vol. 1. See M. R. James, "The Drawings of Matthew Paris," *Volume of the Walpole Society* 14 (1925–26): 23–24.

49. The eagle is not mentioned in the *Liber additamentorum*. Matthew's *alas expandens elevates* (only in *Gesta*) describes the "mantling" posture of the eagle: not stretched out in flight, but fanned with (in this instance) head raised, turning over its back to look upward. See David H. Ellis, "Development of Behaviour in the Golden Eagle," *Wildlife Monographs* 70 (1979): 25.

50. The Chartres Cameo, now in the Cabinet de Medailles of the BNF (ID camée.1, Chabouillet.4), was carved from sardonyx and reset in the fourteenth century. It remained at Chartres until the Revolution.

FIGURE 7.5. Matthew Paris's drawing of the "Kaadmau" cameo. Matthew Paris, *Liber additamentorum*, British Library, Cotton MS Nero D I, fol. 146v (detail). © The British Library Board.

and one of his most recognizable identifying attributes, gazes up at him. But while Jupiter often appears—as on the Chartres cameo—bearded and naked except for a cloak, the fully dressed, clean-shaven figure on the St. Albans cameo bears all the trappings of an emperor and military leader. Leaders as early as Alexander the Great had sought to identify themselves with the chief of the gods, but Romans claimed Jupiter (along with Mars) as a patron of their city.[51] Diocletian adopted Jupiter as his patron and assumed the title *Diocletian Iovius*.[52] In the reigns of Constantine and Licinius, such imagery prolifer-

---

51. Caligula claimed Jovian status (see Philo of Alexandria, *On the Embassy to Gaius* 29.188, 35.265, and 43.346), and Claudius, too, had himself represented in this way, for instance, on a cameo depicting him as the god, clean-shaven, holding a staff or scepter in his left hand, an eagle at his feet (The Art Institute of Chicago, gift of Marilynn B. Alsdorf, 1991.375, Cat. 138). See Sandra E. Knudsen, "Cat. 138 Cameo Portraying Emperor Claudius as Jupiter: Curatorial Entry," The Art Institute of Chicago, accessed June 2, 2020, https://www.artic.edu/artworks/111809/cameo-portraying-emperor-claudius-as-jupiter.

52. Bernard Green, *Christianity in Ancient Rome: The First Three Centuries* (London: A&C Black / T&T Clark, 2010), 210.

ated, particularly on coinage minted throughout the empire, on which each of these emperor-generals had themselves depicted as *Iovis Conservator* and *Iovis Victor*, ever more frequently in military regalia. These figures were often shown being crowned by Victoria, or Nike, usually depicted as a small, winged woman in full-length attire, reaching up to crown the victorious conqueror. She is often alighted on a globe held in the left hand of the emperor. Sometimes the eagle holds a garland in his beak. On Constantinian coins, a Chi Rho symbol and labarum often adorns the top of the staff/scepter held by the victor, and frequently, a bound captive kneels below.

We can thus be relatively certain that Matthew's drawing does not represent Mercury or Aesculapius, as has been suggested, but rather an emperor in the pose of *Iovis Conservator* from the late third or fourth century. What Matthew understood to be a little child turning away from the central figure was in fact winged Nike or Victoria, reaching up toward the emperor/god to crown him with laurels of victory. What Matthew took to be the *ancile* or shield would probably have been the wings. The only element of Matthew's drawing that remains unaccounted for is the snake or serpent ascending the staff. Snakes did frequently appear entwining staffs with figures of Asclepius and Salus, and also—sometimes in association with these—Mercury, but no known iconographic program also includes the eagle, winged Victory, and a figure in armor. This is not to say that Matthew invented the snake. Licinius, Constantine's rival (and ultimately defeated victim) was considered serpentine by Eusebius and Constantine in the most vehement and public rhetoric.[53] Numerous coins depicting the *labarum* with a Chi Rho symbol impaling a writhing Licinian serpent were minted in celebration of Constantine's victory, and it is possible that Matthew's cameo combined these images, though I am not aware of another program arranged in this way. It is also worth observing that in many representations of *Iovis Conservator* the *paludamentum* undulates behind the scepter in a way that could easily be mistaken for a snake.

Mysteriously, Matthew describes the carving on the stone in ways that contradict his careful drawing. In his description, the central figure's armor, sword, diadem, and cloak are omitted; instead, he merely mentions that the figure is "pannosa" [dressed in rags]. Counterintuitively, Matthew repeatedly refers to the central male figure as the "ymago" [image], while the small image in his left hand is described as a "puerum vestitum" [clothed child]. This child is described as wearing a shield or target (*ancile* or *clypeum* in the *Gesta*

---

53. Eusebius, *Life of Constantine*, ed. Averil Cameron and Stuart G. Hall (Oxford: Clarendon Press, 1999), 3.1–3, 94, 122. For a discussion and examples of Eusebius's descriptions of Licinius as a serpent and the many depictions of this image, including on coinage and relief sculpture, see the commentary in Eusebius, *Life of Constantine*, 255–56.

Abbatum) over one shoulder, extending the other hand towards the *imago* (the large central figure). The "serpens repedo ascendit" [crawling serpent ascends] the figure's staff (as if toward the child's target?), and the child turns away, its arm raised as if defensively toward (or against: *versus*) the image. Remarkably, Matthew takes pains to emphasize precisely those characteristics that he seems to get wrong, or that present problems for identification. He even asserts that his description exactly corresponds to the drawing "prout in antecedenti pagina figuratur" [figured on the opposite page], which is clearly not the case.

Ulrich Rehm has convincingly explained these inconsistencies by observing that the description immediately follows and illustrates the account of the folk-medicinal properties the stone was said to possess.[54] Renowned for its power to assist in childbirth, the stone, as Matthew tells us, would be placed on the breast of the pregnant woman, and, as the birth progressed and the child descended, the stone was to be placed lower and lower on the woman's body, little by little, because "infantulus enim nasciturus lapidem subterfugit appropinquantem" [the child about to be born retreats from the approach of the stone]. In keeping with its puerperal functions, the cameo in Matthew's description was provided with a rich iconography relevant to childbirth, incorporating the eagle and serpent associated with St. John the Evangelist as well as the staff and ragged clothing of John the Baptist, figures often depicted flanking the infant Jesus.

Here I'd like to build on this observation by suggesting that Matthew's detailed account and drawing of this object may have been impelled by a need to lay claim to and manage popular stories about this precious object—stories that might have challenged the abbey's claim to the stone. Matthew explains that the cameo was once borrowed by an elite woman, who treacherously kept it for herself and passed it on to her daughter, who confessed the theft on her deathbed and returned the object to the abbey. The abbot in whose time this (re?-)appropriation took place claimed to have donated the cameo himself. Matthew sagely comments that it is common for those who recover or restore lost things to be credited in this way, an observation that allows him to reconcile the abbot's statement with his earlier assertion that the object had been given to the abbey several centuries earlier by King Æthelred. It seems plausible that in Matthew's time some citizens of St. Albans were still inclined to contest what they perceived as the abbey's appropriation of a family heirloom.

---

54. Ulrich Rehm, "Diachrone Dialoge: Zur Interpretation antiker Gemmen mit mythologischen Motiven im Mittelalter," in *Dialog—Transfer—Konflikt: Künstlerische Wechselbeziehungen im Mittelalter und in der Frühen Neuzeit*, ed. Wolfgang Augustyn and Ulrich Söding (Passau: Dietmar Klinger Verlag, 2014), 76–78.

Matthew counters their claims by writing the cameo into the abbey's early history. The association of the object with the abbey's earliest origins is heightened by the inscription on the mounting, which identifies Alban himself as the owner of the cameo, with Æthelred named merely as the donor. As Laura Cleaver notes, the catalogue of gems, including the cameo, "was ultimately bound with Matthew's copies of the abbey's documents, further suggesting that these objects were conceived of as part of the abbey's history, and a form of record that could be associated with rich narratives about the past."[55] As I shall argue in the last section of this paper, something similar could be said of the heart-case of Roger de Norton, another object that, in spite of having been acquired only recently and in spite of bearing the clear hallmarks of an alien culture and religion, was subsumed and enfolded in the abbey's foundational narratives.

Saracen Roots

As I briefly mentioned above, one of the various *inventiones* at St. Albans was that of the *vita* of the protomartyr himself. Allegedly discovered among the stones of Verulamium in the early eleventh century, written in an ancient language understood by only one of the monks, it crumbled to dust upon the completion of its translation into Latin.[56] When composing this passage in the *Gesta Abbatum*, Matthew may have been thinking of his twelfth-century predecessor William of St. Albans's *Passio Sancti Albani*, which claims to be a translation of an Old English text whose alleged author found the story carved on the crumbling walls of Verulamium. Yet when Matthew came to write his own *Vie de St. Auban,* largely based on William's *Passio,* he provided a different set of details about the text's origins, language, and narrator, all of them compatible with the archaeological story in *Gesta Abbatum* but not with William's version. Where William imagined a Saxon author writing some centuries after the fact, Matthew's narrator is as an eyewitness to Alban's martyrdom. And where William's narrator describes his people as "heathens" (*gentili*) and "pagans" (*pagani*), Matthew's unnamed narrator identifies himself and his fel-

---

55. Laura Cleaver, *Illuminated History Books in the Anglo-Norman World, 1066–1272* (Oxford: Oxford University Press, 2018), 138. Cleaver also notes that the description of Alban as the owner relates to the capacity of saints to "transcend normal human lifespans" since the saint had "not owned the stone in his lifetime, but only when it was given to the abbey by Æthelred" (*Illuminated History Books,* 137–38).

56. Walsingham, *Gesta Abbatum.* See Philip Schwyzer, *Archaeologies of English Renaissance Literature* (Oxford: Oxford University Press, 2007), 55–57.

low Romano-British Verulamian natives repeatedly as "Saracens."[57] The persecutors of Christians in this text worship "Mahum e Tervagant" (*VA*, line 1737) [Muhammad and Tervagant], as well as Pallas and Phoebus, gods whom Alban implores them to renounce in favor of Jesus. The Saracens lament that those who have fallen into the error of Christianity cannot be reclaimed "pur tut l'or de Damas" (line 1497) [for all the gold of Damascus], pointedly locating the heartland and mainstay of their faith in a distant city that never fell to the Crusaders.

The *Vie de St. Auban* concludes with the Saracen narrator prophesying that his barbarian text (implicitly, the very text that will be discovered 700 years later in the ruins of Verulamium) will one day be translated into both Latin and French:

> Jo, ki à ceu tens estoie mescreant sarrazin,
> de ceste estoire vi le cumençail e fin,
> . . . .
> la geste ai, cum la vi, escrit en parchemin.
> uncore vendra le jur, ben le di e devin,
> la estoire ert translatée en franceis e latin.
> ne sai autre language fors le mien barbarin,
> mais fei ke doi porter lui ki fist d'ewe vin,
> ne i deise fauseté pur tut l'or Costentin.
> (*VA*, lines 1811–25)

> I, who was at that time a Saracen of false belief, saw the beginning and end of this story. . . . The day will yet come, I say and indeed predict, when the story will be translated into French and Latin. I know no other language outside my own barbarian one, but by the faith that I owe him who made wine from water, may I not have uttered a falsehood for all the gold of Constantine.[58]

Here the transformative powers of translation are associated with the transformation of water into wine. Just as the Eucharistic feast that transforms wine into the blood of Christ echoes Christ's transformation of water into wine at the wedding at Cana; so the prophesied translation of the account of St. Alban's martyrdom echoes and reenacts the original testimony, transcribed on parchment by the Saracen eyewitness who personally experienced it. The truth of the account—in spite, or because of the "barbarian tongue"

---

57. Matthew Paris, *Life of Saint Alban*, 8, 27–28.
58. Translation from Matthew Paris, *Life of Saint Alban*, 103.

that mediates it—is attested by the humble faith and Christological awareness that motivates it, as well as by the prophecies that have indeed come to pass by the time the account becomes generally known. The rejection of falsehood is aligned with the hypothetical rejection of "all the gold of Constantine," an emblem of earthly wealth that itself stands in telling opposition to "all the gold of Damascus."

In the *Vie de St. Auban*, the prophecies of a Saracen powerfully substantiate the claims of a Christian institution about its origins. Clearly, the term *Saracen* in this period did not always apply specifically or exclusively to Muslims; the term could be employed much more widely to denote the non-Christian Other. But this is precisely the point: that the monks of thirteenth-century St. Albans were capable of and interested in tracing connections between the Muslim cultures of the East and their own pagan predecessors. As I have argued above, the incorporation of Kufic and pseudo-Kufic script in medieval Christian art often supplied a means of drawing links between the present and the past. Inscribed on a coin, a piece of silk, or the halo of the Virgin, Islamic script and motifs could signify not an alien and malignant force but a valued (albeit subordinated) aspect of Christian history and identity. This habit of thought carried particular force at St. Albans, where the Saracen Other could be seen not only as a distant present threat, but as a denizen of the abbey's own past and a witness to its origins. As such, Saracens and their artifacts have an important role to play in the multiple stories of origins, burials, excavations, and refoundations that St. Albans has told about itself across the centuries. These local traditions provide a crucial context for the ways in which a little Afghan box with an inscrutable inscription was interpreted and repurposed by the monks of the abbey at the close of the thirteenth century.

The story of Roger de Norton's heart-case must be understood in terms of both routes and roots. It is a story, on the one hand, of the geographical routes that carried the box from Afghanistan to England and, on the other, about the textual roots of St. Albans. These two kinds of roots/routes come together in the images of Saracen objects rising up from and being restored to the ground. I would argue that the triumphalist term *spolia* is clearly insufficient to capture everything that may be at stake in a traveling object of this kind. The heart box demands to be read in multiple and ambivalent ways. The use of an Afghan artifact to contain the heart of an English abbot can certainly be seen as an act of appropriation. Yet the burial of a "Saracen" box in almost the same earth as that from which the "Saracen" life of Alban emerged might also suggest a kind of reparation or reciprocity, returning the object of the Other, now united with a Christian heart, to the soil from which it came. As they paid a debt to the past, the monks at Roger de Norton's burial were also paying forward, seeding the fertile earth of St. Albans to flower again in future moments of discovery, reconnection, and refoundation. The monks who were so practiced in digging, finding, refounding, and translating knew that what they planted before the altar of Mary of the Four Tapers would probably come to light well before Judgement Day—and that whatever message it conveyed to future discoverers would doubtless seem as prophetic, fitting, and uncanny as their own discoveries seemed to them.

CHAPTER 8

The Ruthwell Cross and the Riddle of Time

JAN-PEER HARTMANN

The church of *Ruthwell* contains the ruins of a most curious monument; an obelisk once of a great height, now lying in three pieces, broken by an order of the general assembly in 1644, under pretence of being an object of superstition among the vulgar. . . . The pedestal lies buried beneath the floor of the church: I found some fragments of the capital, with letters similar to the others; and on each opposite side an eagle, neatly cut in relief. There was also a piece of another with *Saxon* letters round the lower part of a human figure, in long vestments, with his foot on a pair of small globes: this too seemed to have been the top of a cross.[1]

This is an extract from Thomas Pennant's best-selling travelogue *A Tour in Scotland, and Voyage to the Hebrides,* published in 1774. The passage describes the monument nowadays referred to as the "Ruthwell Cross" or "Ruthwell monument." Since Pennant's day, the monument has been reerected and reconstructed; first without, and later, in 1887, within the church. There is no clear evidence as to where the cross was originally erected, nor where it stood when it was destroyed in the seventeenth century. Nor is the nineteenth-century reconstruction historically accurate: new stones were used to replace

---

1. Thomas Pennant, *A Tour in Scotland, and Voyage to the Hebrides; MDCCLXXII* (Chester: John Monk, 1774), 85–86.

parts missing from the original monument—most prominently the crossbeam, which displays modern iconography[2]—and the whole monument was turned around so that the front and back, originally facing East and West, now look South and North, respectively, with the main sides of the cross-head reversed. Other parts were possibly misplaced, too.[3] Indeed, it has been suggested that the original monument represented a simple obelisk rather than a cross—Pennant even seems to have believed that the pieces belonged to two different monuments: an obelisk and a cross.[4]

Hence, as it is now displayed in Ruthwell church, the cross is the product of different ages. Its present shape reflects the attitudes of seventeenth-century Scottish puritanism and nineteenth-century antiquarianism just as much as those of the time that originally produced it—whenever that may have been. Intriguingly, there are hints that this multitemporal aspect has been part of the monument's character far longer than my historical sketch suggests. Paul Meyvaert has drawn attention to an eighteenth-century depiction seeming to suggest that evidence of an earlier—possibly medieval—repair was visible at that

---

2. On the shaft, missing images were left blank. The transom, by contrast, displays what Brendan Cassidy interprets as Masonic iconography ("The Later Life of the Ruthwell Cross: From the Seventeenth Century to the Present," in *The Ruthwell Cross: Papers from the Colloquium Sponsored by the Index of Christian Art, Princeton University, 8 December 1989*, ed. Brendan Cassidy, Index of Christian Art, Occasional Papers 1 [Princeton, NJ: Index of Christian Art, Department of Art and Archaeology, Princeton University, 1992], 15–19). He suggests that the Rev. Henry Duncan, who commissioned the reerection of the monument in 1802 and had the transom added in the 1820s, chose symbols that were acceptable to his parishioners and superiors, at a time when suspicion of Roman Catholic (and hence also of medieval) iconography was still strong in Scotland. Éamonn Ó Carragáin, however, notes that all of the images added by Duncan can also be read as Christian symbols (*Ritual and the Rood: Liturgical Images and the Old English Poems of the "Dream of the Rood" Tradition*, British Library Studies in Medieval Culture [London: British Library / University of Toronto Press, 2005], 19, 64n31).

3. See Robert T. Farrell, "The Construction, Deconstruction, and Reconstruction of the Ruthwell Cross: Some Caveats," in *Ruthwell Cross*, ed. Cassidy, 43–44; Paul Meyvaert, "A New Perspective on the Ruthwell Cross: Ecclesia and Vita Monastica," in *Ruthwell Cross*, ed. Cassidy, 100, 102–4.

4. Pennant's account is somewhat ambiguous (it is not clear whether "another" in the last sentence of the quotation refers to another fragment or another monument), as is the one given by antiquarian and grammar school headmaster Reginald Bainbrigg, preserved in a letter to William Camden, for whom he was collecting materials. Bainbrigg's description, based on his visits to Ruthwell in 1599 and 1601, and the only one to predate the monument's destruction, was interpreted by Fred Orton as suggesting that Bainbrigg saw an obelisk rather than a cross ("Rethinking the Ruthwell Monument: Fragments and Critique; Tradition and History; Tongues and Sockets," *Art History* 21 [1998]: 65–106; and in Fred Orton and Ian Wood, with Clare A. Lees, *Fragments of History: Rethinking the Ruthwell and Bewcastle Monuments* [Manchester: Manchester University Press, 2007], 46–61). Orton's interpretation has been rejected by Ó Carragáin (*Ritual and the Rood*, 13–15, 63n10).

time, evidence now concealed by the nineteenth-century reconstruction.[5] It has also been suggested that some of the monument's images and inscriptions were added after it was first erected.[6] If this were true, the Ruthwell monument is, and has been for most of its existence, a temporally ambiguous object.

In this paper, I will argue that temporal asynchrony is in fact inherent in the monument's iconographic and literary program. The monument's poetic inscription, which I read as a riddle on the Holy Cross, suggests that it is the monument itself that addresses the observer. The text thus cleverly plays on the formal accord between Christ's original cross and its representation in

---

5. Meyvaert, "New Perspective," 100–102. The engraving, produced by Adam de Cardonnel to accompany Richard Gough's account in the 1789 volume of *Vetusta Monumenta: Quae ad rerum Britannicarum memoriam conservandam Societas Antiquariorum Londini sumptu suo edanda curavit*, is reproduced in *Ruthwell Cross*, ed. Cassidy, as plate 38. According to Ó Carragáin, the symmetrical hole depicted in Cardonnel's drawing, which Meyvaert takes to be evidence of repair, is in fact the indentation between the feet of Mary and Elizabeth in the Visitation panel, the upper part of which had not yet been found when the drawing was made—hence Cardonnel's and Gough's inability to make sense of it (*Ritual and the Rood*, 17).

6. This was first suggested by R. I. Page in an attempt to account for the unusual arrangement of the runes, which he found "so odd . . . that I incline to think it may not be a part of the original design for the cross, and to wonder if these runes were added by a later carver who had less command over the space he had to fill" (*An Introduction to English Runes* [London: Methuen, 1973], 150). In contrast to the vast majority of runic inscriptions (as well as the Ruthwell monument's Latin inscriptions), the Ruthwell rune inscriptions are aligned horizontally throughout, resulting in very short lines of two to four letters along the upright borders. In 1982, Paul Meyvaert put forward an explanation for this, based on the hypothesis that the monument was already standing when the runes were added ("An Apocalypse Panel on the Ruthwell Cross," in *Medieval and Renaissance Studies, Proceedings of the Southeastern Institute of Medieval and Renaissance Studies, Summer 1978*, ed. Frank Tirro [Durham, NC: Duke University Press, 1982], 26). According to Meyvaert, while it would have been easy to cut the runes vertically while the monument was still lying on the ground, it would have been more difficult to do so once the monument was standing upright. This explanation suggests a time lag between the erection of the monument and the addition of the runes, the duration of which Meyvaert does not attempt to specify; however, in 2007 Patrick Conner argued for a tenth-century date of the runes on linguistic grounds ("The Ruthwell Monument Runic Poem in a Tenth-Century Context," *Review of English Studies* n.s. 59, no. 238 [2008]: 26). Conner links the poem to antiphons recorded in the *Regularis Concordia* and suggests that the runic distinction between velar and palatal allophones of /g/ and /k/, usually considered to be an early feature, may be explained by antiquarian practice ("Ruthwell Monument Runic Poem," 38–51). The traditional view that the runic inscription forms an integral part of the monument's original design is defended by Ó Carragáin, who cites a 1978 study by Ute Schwab that draws attention to Latin and Greek inscriptions on crosses and reliquaries that parallel the Ruthwell arrangement (*Ritual and the Rood*, 52–53). Meyvaert has recently retracted his earlier view, arguing instead that the unusual arrangement has to do with the fact that it can accommodate more text ("Necessity Mother of Invention: A Fresh Look at the Rune Verses on the Ruthwell Cross," *Anglo-Saxon England* 41 [2012]: 409). While the above theories are persuasive to varying degrees, none of them present conclusive proof, as stone resists carbon dating and both art historical and linguistic evidence are prone to circular argumentation (see, for instance, the discussion of style as a means of dating in Orton, Wood, with Lees, *Fragments of History*, 62–66).

a liturgical work of art. In so doing, the poem identifies the monument as the original cross's *figura*, as defined by Erich Auerbach, i.e., as historically distinct yet spiritually identical with the original object. In highlighting this tension inherent in the *figura* concept, the poem identifies the monument as a temporally ambiguous object, with an iconography that points the observer to a single historical moment, a moment whose suggested presence is belied by the object's own historicity.

Liturgical Art as *Figura*

According to Erich Auerbach's famous definition, *figura* denotes a relation between two concrete historical entities or events that stand in a relationship of promise and fulfilment: "Figural interpretation establishes a connection between two events or persons, the first of which signifies not only itself but also the second, while the second encompasses or fulfils the first."[7] The connection is established by an outward similarity or accord that exists between the two poles independent of their actual historical situation.[8] And yet, Auerbach claims, the poles are to be understood first and foremost as concrete historical realities; it is only through their interpretation that they come to be perceived as spiritually linked. On the other hand, the spiritual relationship can itself be regarded as a historical reality, since it is based on an actual accord that is part of God's vision, in which all times exist simultaneously. Thus the two poles, figure and fulfilment, are not identical but persist as singular, historical entities, yet they also participate in each other through the spiritual accord that exists between them.[9] As Heike Schlie points out, "in *figura*, 'sign' and 'presence' are no contradiction but constitute a dual principle that is constitutive of the whole concept."[10] Nevertheless, this duality generates a tension that makes the concept highly productive for the interpretation of liturgical art.

---

7. Erich Auerbach, "Figura," trans. Ralph Manheim, in *Scenes from the Drama of European Literature: Six Essays by Erich Auerbach* (New York: Meridian, 1959), 53.

8. Auerbach, "Figura," 29.

9. Christian Kiening, introduction to *Figura*, ed. Christian Kiening and Katharina Mertens Fleury, Philologie der Kultur 8 (Würzburg: Königshausen & Neumann, 2013), 16.

10. "'Zeichen' und 'Präsenz' sind in der *figura* kein Widerspruch, sondern als duales Prinzip bereits als Grundeigenschaften angelegt" (Heike Schlie, "Der Klosterneuburger Ambo des Nikolaus von Verdun: Das Kunstwerk als *figura* zwischen Inkarnation und Wiederkunft des Logos," in *Figura*, ed. Kiening and Fleury, 205). Unless noted otherwise, translations are my own.

Figural interpretation in this sense was first used in patristic literature as a means of integrating the Old and New Testaments into a single coherent vision of history in which both kept their concrete historical reality but were also linked within the wider scheme of providential history in which they signified a third, still absent, reality, which they partly reveal but that will only manifest itself fully in the second *parousia*. *Figura* thus establishes a model of history based on three points of reference: first, promise; second, first fulfilment and second promise; and third, ultimate fulfilment. While the vision is ultimately teleological in that it looks forward to a transcendental truth at the end of history, it is also nonlinear since it privileges spiritual significance over cause and effect: the connection between the poles is spiritual rather than causal. In a certain sense, Schlie points out, *figura* is even a-temporal, since it suggests that the events, in participating in each other, are contemporaneous: "In God, there is no *differentia temporis*."[11] Even more important for the purpose of this paper, the three-stage model opens up the possibility for post-biblical events to participate in providential history, since any event can be perceived, simultaneously, as figure and fulfilment, and hence as referring back to an event in the past and as looking forward to something that has yet to come to pass.

With respect to medieval liturgical art, Schlie argues, this means that the work of art refers back to the New Testament antitypes of Old Testament events but also has the potential of prefiguring the Second Coming of Christ.[12] The work of art, she states, "constitutes a membrane on which is projected and captured that which only becomes representable postfigurally after the incarnation of the Logos and which can only be indicated prefigurally before the Second Coming, because it is unfathomable." As a material and hence historical reality that simultaneously references something else, the artifact is itself a *figura*.[13] The medieval work of art can thus be regarded as a historical entity that represents—and, as Christian Kiening points out, also participates in—something even more valid than itself: it becomes a medium, as Aquinas defines it, that mediates between the two poles it represents.[14] Kiening's notion of *figura* goes beyond Auerbach's, yet it draws attention to a tension already

---

11. "Bei Gott gibt es keine *differentia temporis*" (Schlie, "Klosterneuburger Ambo," 205).
12. Schlie, "Klosterneuburger Ambo," 242.
13. "[Das Kunstwerk] bildet eine Membran, an der sich durch die Zeiten hindurch das abbildet und anschaulich einfängt, was postfigurativ nach der Inkarnation des Logos darstellbar wird und präfigurativ vor der Wiederkunft nur angedeutet werden kann, weil es unauslotbar ist. Auch das Bild ist als materielles, verweisendes Ereignis in einem innergeschichtlichen Zusammenhang *figura*" (Schlie, "Klosterneuburger Ambo," 246).
14. "Sie repräsentiert ein Anderes, Gültig(er)es, partizipiert aber auch an diesem—das wäre die Definition des *medium*, das nach Thomas von Aquin etwas von den Extremen, zwischen denen es vermittelt, haben muss" (Kiening, introduction to *Figura*, 16).

FIGURE 8.1. W. Penny, engraving published with Henry Duncan's "An Account of the Remarkable Monument in the Shape of a Cross, Inscribed with Roman and Runic Letters, Preserved in the Garden of Ruthwell Manse, Dumfriesshire," *Archaeologica Scotia: or, Transactions of the Society of Antiquaries of Scotland* 4 (1857): 313–36 (Plate XIII). Image © National Museums Scotland.

present in Auerbach's concept: if the two poles of the *figura* can represent each other, as well as a transcendental third, there must exist some element of spiritual identity between them, in spite of their historical—and hence material—distinctness. From this perspective, *figura* thus derives its significance from the special tension that exists between the historical and the spiritual dimensions of the two poles of reference. This makes it ideal for the interpretation of the *Ruthwell Poem,* whose double reference to the original cross and its representation in the monument, I suggest, displays a similar tension.

The *Ruthwell Poem* as Riddle

As it stands in Ruthwell Church today, the monument is some eighteen feet high and consists of two parts, a column and a cross, of differently colored sandstone.[15] Both column and cross are adorned with reliefs framed by raised borders inscribed with text (figure 8.1; Penny's drawing is not always accurate, but gives a better impression of the monument's overall program and alignment than could be conveyed by photographs). The front and back of the monument each display four large panels with biblical scenes bordered by Latin descriptions, as well as two smaller ones, directly above and below the crossbeam. On the north face, these are, bottom to top: the Holy Family; the hermit saints Paul and Anthony; Christ acknowledged by the beasts in the desert; St. John the Baptist bearing the Lamb of God; and, above and below the crossbeam, a bird on a branch and two men. On the south face, we find the Annunciation; Christ healing the blind man; Christ and Mary Magdalen; Mary and Martha; and, above and below the crossbeam, a man with a bird and an archer.[16] The east and west faces of the monument, as far up as the crossbeam, are adorned with plant scrolls surrounded by a border inscribed with

---

15. For analyses of the types of stones used in the monument and its reconstruction, see Orton, Wood, with Lees, *Fragments of History,* 40–46; and Farrell, "Some Caveats," 41, fig. 2. To Orton, the obvious visual differences between the two kinds of sandstone constitute important evidence for his view that the column and cross parts did not originally belong together. However, Ó Carragáin has pointed out that medieval stone monuments were often covered with gesso and painted in bright colors, which would have obscured the visual difference (*Ritual and the Rood,* 27). According to Ó Carragáin, the Ruthwell monument may have shown traces of the protective gesso as late as the nineteenth century.

16. The top stone was mistakenly reversed in the reconstruction (Meyvaert, "New Perspective," 103; David Howlett, "Inscriptions and Design of the Ruthwell Cross," in *Ruthwell Cross,* ed. Cassidy, 74). Hence, the two men would originally have been on the same side as the man with the bird, on the opposite side of the archer and the bird on the branch. Howlett interprets the man with the bird as St. John with his eagle and the two men as Matthew and the angel, arguing that the original crossbeam would probably have depicted the two missing evangelists

runes. Transcribed, these yield the following alliterative text in the Northumbrian dialect of Old English:[17]

East Side
I. North Border
[+ *ond*]geredæ hinæ ḡod alme3ttig [·] þa he walde on ḡalḡu gistiḡa
"God almighty prepared himself when he wanted to mount the gallows"
modig f[*ore allæ*] men
"brave before all men"
[*b*]ug̅[a] {*ic ni dorstæ*} [. . .]
"[I did not dare] to bow"

II. South Border
[*ahof*] ic riicnæ k̄yniŋc [·]
"I lifted up a mighty king"
hēafunæs hlafard hælda ic ni dorstæ
"I did not dare to hold Heaven's Lord"
[*b*]ismæradu uŋk̄et men ba æt[g̅]ad[*re*] [*i*]c [*wæs*] *mi*þ blodi *b*ist[*e*]mi[*d*]
"men defiled the two of us, both together, I was drenched in blood"

---

with their attributes, Mark with the lion and Luke with the ox ("Inscriptions and Design," 76). Howlett's reconstruction is accepted by Ó Carragáin (*Ritual and the Rood*, 143–44).

   Various interpretations of the monument's iconographic program have been put forward. Thus it has been suggested, first by Meyvaert ("New Perspective") and later by Orton, Wood, with Lees (*Fragments of History*, 186–88), that the reliefs on the north side have specifically monastic concerns, while the ones to the south, depicting scenes of conversion and a growing commitment to Christianity, might more generally represent the *ecclesia*. Margaret Jennings has likewise argued that the desert scenes on the north side suggest the monastic themes of denial and withdrawal from the world, while the images on the opposite side depict Christ's involvement in society ("Rood and Ruthwell: The Power of Paradox," *English Language Notes* 31 [1994]: 10). She links these to Christ's two natures, divine and human, that are also stressed in the runic poem. In a magisterial discussion that draws on a large array of liturgical and theological sources, Ó Carragáin develops a complex program centered on the themes of annunciation, passion, baptism, and the Eucharist that involves and accounts for all images and inscriptions found on the monument (*Ritual and the Rood*, 79–222). Ó Carragáin's is the most detailed and comprehensive discussion of the monument to date. He attempts to trace its themes—often persuasively—to contemporaneous liturgical developments and suggests a date of creation in the 730s (Ó Carragáin, *Ritual and the Rood*, 283).

   17. The Old English text is based on Ó Carragáin (*Ritual and the Rood*, 79–81, 180–81), with <3> substituted for <i>. Italicized letters represent runes still partially visible or, when put in square brackets, collated from earlier transcriptions or drawings. Curly brackets denote emendations based on the *Dream of the Rood*. When the available space on the border suggests that more text is missing, this is indicated by three dots in square brackets. A persuasive—but nonetheless conjectural—reconstruction based on the *Dream of the Rood* can be found in Howlett, "Inscriptions and Design," 82–88.

bi{goten of þæs gumu sida} [. . .]
"[from that man's side]"

West Side
III. South Border
[+] krist wæs on rodi [·]
"Christ was on the rood."
hweþræ þer fusæ fearran kwomu
"Yet readily there came from afar"
æþþilæ til anum ic þæt al bi[heald]
"nobles to the one, I beheld all that"
s[aræ] ic w[æ]s [·] mi[þ] so[r]gu[m] gidrœ[fi]d h[n]a[g] {ic þam secgum til handa}
"Sorely I was troubled by grief, I bent [to the men's hands]"

IV. North Border
*mi*þ stre*l*um giwundad
"wounded by arrows"
alegdun hiæ hinæ limwœrignæ [·] gistoddu[n] him [æt his lic]æs [hea]f[du]m
"they laid the limb-weary down, stood at his body's head."
[bih]ea[ld]u[n] [h]i[æ] [þ]e[r] {heafunæs dryctin} [. . .]
"They beheld there the [Heavens' Lord]"

This poetic inscription stands in a complex relationship, textually as well as regarding its modern reception, to a poem known today as the *Dream of the Rood,* preserved in the late tenth-century Vercelli Book. This poem is much longer than the Ruthwell inscription, totaling more than 150 lines, and includes a frame narrative in which a first-person narrator tells of a dream in which the Holy Cross spoke to them. Most of the poem consists of the Cross's narrative, in which it describes how as a tree in a forest it was cut down, shaped into a cross, used as a means of executing criminals and thus experienced Christ's crucifixion at first hand, how it was afterward buried and later recovered, adorned with gems and set up as an object for adoration. The poetic inscription on the Ruthwell monument is close enough to lines 39–49 and 56–64 of the *Dream of the Rood* to have given editors the confidence to use either poem to emend the other. But there are also a number of differences. Most of these relate to the actual wording of what is by all accounts the same content, but there are also a number of omissions, most significantly the one instance in the speech of the Cross in which the Cross identifies itself, the half-line "rod wæs ic geræred" (*Dream of the Rood,* line 44) [I was raised (as) a cross], which in the *Dream of the Rood* forms a metrical unit with the half-line "ahof ic riicnæ k̄yniŋc" [I lifted up a mighty king]. In the Ruthwell inscription, the first phrase is notably absent, rendering the line metrically incomplete.[18]

The exact relationship of the two poems is thus far from clear: too different to establish a direct influence of one upon the other, and yet too similar not to suspect some kind of connection. Yet whatever their exact relationship, it is obvious that the *Ruthwell Poem*—so much shorter and inscribed into a stone monument—must be read in a context very different from that of the *Dream of the Rood*. Moreover, even if it were a case of one poem quoting the other, knowledge of the "original version" cannot be presupposed: to most of its readers, at any given point in time, each of the two poems would have appeared as a self-contained text. Hence, suspending all knowledge of the *Dream of the Rood*, let us consider what the *Ruthwell Poem* itself tells us.

To the Christian observer, given that he or she is able to decipher the runes and understand the language, the references to "God almighty" and "Christ," as well as the terms *galga* and *rod*, conventional appellations of the cross, would immediately conjure up a crucifixion scene. The real question, then, is not about what is happening in the poem or about identifying Christ: the real question, as Fred Orton, Ian Wood, and Clare Lees note, concerns the unnamed first-person speaker, "Who speaks this 'I'?"[19] From what the text tells us, the speaker is not a mere observer, but takes on a more active role: "I dared not withdraw," "I lifted up a mighty king," "I bent forward to their hands." Indeed, the speaker seems, by implication, to be claiming almost equal participation and suffering as Christ himself: "Men defiled the two of us, both together," "I was drenched in blood," "I was sorely troubled by grief," and "[I was] wounded by arrows."[20] These references suggest the Holy Cross itself as

---

18. Meyvaert, in the same contribution in which he retracts his earlier view of the runic poem as a later addition, surmises that the textual differences between the *Dream of the Rood* and the *Ruthwell Poem* can be ascribed to the limitations of space on the monument ("Necessity Mother of Invention," 413–14). Obviously, the result would still be a new and different textual item whose textual and aesthetic unity—not least in the context of a different medium, a stone monument rather than a manuscript folio—generates meaning and significance independent of its supposed source. See also John Hines, "The Ruthwell Cross, the Brussels Cross, and *The Dream of the Rood*," in *Transitional States: Change, Tradition, and Memory in Medieval Literature and Culture*, ed. Graham D. Caie and Michael D. C. Drout, Medieval and Renaissance Texts and Studies 530 (Tempe: Arizona Center for Medieval and Renaissance Studies, 2018), 175–92, for a recent discussion of the *Ruthwell Poem*, *The Dream of the Rood*, and the related inscription on the Brussels Cross that draws attention to the way the differences between these texts and their material contexts generate independent meanings.

19. Orton, Wood, with Lees, *Fragments of History*, 168.

20. It is not clear whether the last phrase refers to the preceding line—and hence to the speaker—or to Christ in the following line.

the speaker—who else carried Christ and was close enough to be drenched in blood? But this identification is obscured by the anomaly of a cross capable of feeling and expressing emotions, as well as by the fact that the cross is referred to in the third person: "þa he walde on galgu gistiga" and "Krist wæs on rode" rather than *þa he walde on me gistiga* and *Krist wæs on me*. In this light, the missing self-identification of the Cross noted above, with the resulting metrical inconsistency, looks like a deliberate suppression.[21]

If the speaking cross's identity has been deliberately obscured, then it makes sense to read the poem as a riddle and to regard the differences between the *Dream of the Rood* and the *Ruthwell Poem* as primarily a difference in genre, the former a dream vision and the latter a riddle.[22] This is also suggested by the different material contexts in which the two texts have been transmitted and by their respective forms of intermediality. For while the *Dream of the Rood* is preserved in a codex of religious verse and prose, undistinguished from the rest, a text among texts, the *Ruthwell Poem* is distinguished from the other writings on the monument through its different layout, language, and script.

There is some disagreement among scholars as to the exact status of runes as a medium of writing among the Anglo-Saxons, and usage must, of course, have varied over time and between different contexts. But in Anglo-Saxon manuscripts, as John D. Niles has argued, runes seem to have been used chiefly for antiquarian and/or cryptographic purposes.[23] The latter function

---

21. This is admittedly only one of several metrical inconsistencies in the *Ruthwell Poem*, some of which result from damage to the monument, while other lines "are apparently deliberately incomplete, at least according to later, normative standards of metre" (Orton, Wood, with Lees, *Fragments of History*, 162). It should also be noted that the references to the cross in the third person also occur in *The Dream of the Rood*, where, however, the identity of the speaker is known from the outset. It is only in the *Ruthwell Poem*, where the speaker is never introduced, that these take on a special significance.

22. Orton, Wood, with Lees, *Fragments of History*, 156 and 167–69, respectively. *The Dream of the Rood* has long been associated with riddling. This association rests chiefly on the poem's use of prosopopoeia, the personification of inanimate objects (Margaret Schlauch, "The *Dream of the Rood* as Prosopopoeia," in *Essential Articles for the Study of Old English Poetry*, ed. Jess B. Bessinger Jr. and Stanley J. Kahrl [Hamden, CT: Archon Books, 1968], 428–41; Peter Orton, "The Technique of Object Personification in *The Dream of the Rood* and a Comparison with the Old English *Riddles*," *Leeds Studies in English* 11 [1979]: 1–18). This is a frequent feature in Old English riddles, where the object is either described in the third person as *wiht* [a creature], and usually accorded the ability to act of its own accord, or speaks for itself and tells its story. In the case of the *Dream of the Rood*, however, the similarity starts and ends with the device of prosopopoeia, since the reader is never left in doubt as to who is speaking. In the *Ruthwell Poem*, on the other hand, the additional suppression of the speaker's identity suggests a closer kinship with prosopopoeic riddles.

23. John D. Niles, *Old English Enigmatic Poems and the Play of the Texts*, Studies in the Early Middle Ages 13 (Turnhout: Brepols, 2006), 221. The earliest cryptographic and orna-

can be observed in a number of Old English riddles, as well as in poems such as *The Husband's Message, The Ruin,* or the *Cynewulf* signatures. According to Niles, instances such as these can be regarded "as a literary ploy, a special type of defamiliarization that appeals to writers who wish to cast a cloak of real or apparent mystery over their text."[24] Similarly, Ray Page has suggested that "runes could be used in contexts where they stand distinct from Roman [letters], for display and riddling/cryptic purposes, as an unusual and 'learned' script, to make certain passages stand distinct."[25] In comparison to Latin script, runes were possibly even more elitist in that even fewer readers would have been able to decipher them.[26] On the Ruthwell monument, the presence

---

mental use of Anglo-Saxon runes is known from early eighth- and ninth-century continental manuscripts (David Parsons, "Anglo-Saxon Runes in Continental Manuscripts," in *Runische Schriftkultur in kontinental-skandinavischer und -angelsächsischer Wechselbeziehung,* ed. Klaus Düwel, Ergänzungsbände zum Reallexikon der germanischen Altertumskunde 10 [Berlin: de Gruyter, 1994], 195–96); similar usage in manuscripts of insular provenance is late (tenth to eleventh century). Parsons, following René Derolez, assumes "a widespread and essentially uniform runic literacy amongst the educated in eighth- and ninth-century Anglo-Saxon society" and explains the absence of runes in early insular manuscripts by arguing that, since runes were commonplace, they held no fascination for Anglo-Saxons scribes, whereas continental scholars would have been intrigued by the foreign script (Parsons, "Anglo-Saxon Runes," 199, 215–16; cf. Derolez, "Epigraphical versus Manuscript English Runes: One or Two Worlds?," *Academiae Analecta. Mededelingen van de Koninklijke Academie voor Wetenschappen, Letteren en Schone Künsten van België, Klasse der Letteren* 45 [1983]: 70–93). Niles's suggestion is seconded by Page (*English Runes,* 116–17; "Runic Writing, Roman Script and the Scriptorium," in *Runor och ABC: Elva föreläsningar från ett symposium i Stockholm, våren 1995,* ed. Staffan Nyström [Stockholm: Sällskapet Runica et Mediævalia, Riksantikvarieämbetet, Stockholms Medeltidsmuseum, 1997], 135, see below).

24. Niles, *Enigmatic Poems,* 223. Intriguingly, Christine Fell notes, Old English *run* [rune] and related words such as *geryne* are frequently used to refer to Christian mysteries ("Runes and Semantics," in *Old English Runes and Their Continental Background,* ed. Alfred Bammesberger, Anglistische Forschungen 217 [Heidelberg: Carl Winter Universitätsverlag, 1991], 206), which resonates with the specific use the runes are put to in the context of the *Ruthwell Poem.* While Fell's argument is primarily directed against the notion that Anglo-Saxons regarded runes as chiefly pagan and magical, insisting that runes were, on the contrary, "thoroughly absorbed into the Christian culture" (Fell, "Runes and Semantics," 228), this does not necessarily speak against the interpretation proposed here, that the use of runes enhances and mirrors the riddlic character of the poem.

25. Page, "Runic Writing," 135.

26. For an opposing view, see Derolez ("Epigraphical versus Manuscript") and Parsons ("Anglo-Saxon Runes"), quoted in footnote 23 above, who argue for a widespread runic literacy in the eighth century. On the Ruthwell monument, however, the unusual alignment of the runes makes the text, to paraphrase Page, "maddeningly hard to read" even to experienced readers (*English Runes,* 150). I made the experiment of arranging a translation of the poem in the same way and showing it to a number of people, all of whom it took a long while to find out how the text worked. Ó Carragáin, who cites Roman and Greek examples of similarly (though not quite identically) arranged inscriptions, argues that eighth-century readers would have been used to decipher and process inscriptions in *scriptura continua* through the act of *praelectio,*

of Latin writing suggests that the runes were certainly *not* used because they constituted the most natural medium of writing. On the contrary, the use of a different, less usual, and possibly "marked" writing system separates and distinguishes the runic text from the Latin inscriptions and, I would argue, mirrors the riddlic quality of the language on the visual level of writing.

This situation is paralleled in the monument's pictorial program. Just as the *Ruthwell Poem* fails to mention the identity of its speaker, and actually encrypts the whole account of the crucifixion scene, so the reliefs and accompanying Latin inscriptions, in spite of predominantly depicting scenes from Christ's life, do not reference the crucifixion—with one exception that I have hitherto neglected to mention: an additional panel situated beneath the Annunciation, almost completely obliterated or left unfinished, with no trace of an accompanying text, showing a crucifixion scene.[27] This panel was probably hidden during the Anglo-Saxon era, buried in the ground to provide necessary hold for the monument.[28] The absence of any reference to the crucifixion in the other panels grants this image a central place in the monument's

---

the chewing over of a text until it is known by heart (Ó Carragáin, *Ritual and the Rood*, 44, see 52–53 and plates 6 and 8 for the discussion of parallels). However, in contrast to the examples cited by Ó Carragáin, the sheer length of the Ruthwell text and hence the number of runes, as well as the overall arrangement of the text (horizontally along the top bar, then vertically down the right bar, and finally vertically down the left bar), further complicate the reading process.

27. Robert B. K. Stevenson argues that the crucifixion panel was only added in the late ninth century. He suggests that the shaft beneath the Annunciation and Holy Family panels was originally buried, but that the monument was raised in the late ninth century, at which point the crucifixion scene was added ("Further Thoughts on Some Well Known Problems," in *The Age of Migrating Ideas: Early Medieval Art in Northern Britain and Ireland*, ed. Michael Spearman and John Higgitt [Edinburgh and Stroud: National Museums of Scotland and Alan Sutton, 1993], 16–26). Orton, Wood, with Lees (*Fragments of History*, 56–57) propose that it was at this time that the monument was transformed from a column into a cross through the addition of the crosshead. One feels tempted to link the addition of the runic poem—if indeed later—to this hypothetical event, and to hypothesize that the monument's iconographic and written program was deliberately changed so as to take this transformation into account. The interpretation proposed here would fit well with such a scenario but in no way depends on it.

28. As was the case during the time the monument stood in the vicarage garden and still is with the monument at Bewcastle, in many respects the closest existing parallel to the Ruthwell monument. Much speaks for the assumption that this was also the way the monument was originally conceived: the shaft broadens beneath the panel depicting the Annunciation and is much more roughly hewn (Stevenson, "Further Thoughts," 21), nor is there evidence of a block on which it could have stood. On the contrary, in order to erect the monument in its present position within the church, the mason John W. Dods had to carve away a considerable part of the original shaft in order to create a tongue with which it could be fitted into the pedestal. This might speak against Stevenson's theory that the monument was raised during the Middle Ages, though it does not preclude changes, repairs, or additions to the monument. See Farrell, "Some Caveats," 38–43; and Orton, Wood, with Lees, *Fragments of History*, 56–61 for discussions of Dods's account and drawing.

overall program: placed on a part of the monument that was hidden but nevertheless central to its stability—the base that kept it from falling over—it may have wittily referred to the centrality of the crucifixion both to the Christian faith and to the monument's visual and written program.

The same can be said of the runic poem: by providing the one reference that is so obviously missing from the rest of the monument's visual and literary content, the poem not only neatly fits into its overall program but even takes its central place. The fact that the poem's meaning is hidden, both graphically and linguistically, might then be a reference to the significance of the crucifixion, which is likewise a sacred mystery.[29]

The Ruthwell Monument as *Figura*

If the *Ruthwell Poem*, as an account of the crucifixion and a riddle on the Holy Cross, takes such a central place in the monument's program, surely it is no coincidence that it is inscribed into an object that either was, or, as Orton, Wood, and Lees suggest more cautiously, might have been conceived of as a representation of the cross.[30] Through the riddlic persona of its speaker, the poem on the monument might then not only refer to the original cross but also, by extension, to the monument itself as the original cross's representation: in the absence of a frame narrative that introduces the speaker, the poem seems to suggest that it is the monument itself, the silent bearer of the message, that is speaking to the observer.[31]

---

29. The crucifixion, which points both to Christ's death and his resurrection, arguably constitutes Christianity's central paradox. As Jennings explains, "The early Christians understood that their way of living in the world was characterized by the paradox of the cross in that the instrument of defeat had become the instrument of victory. . . . The cross was never presented as simply an instrument of suffering; belief in the cross necessarily included resurrection symbolism and assent thereto. At the eighth century's dawn, then, the all-encompassing symbolic structure of the Christian Church was the cross of the one who was paradoxically put to death and raised up" ("Rood and Ruthwell," 7–8).

30. "Though there are few persons who would admit to *seeing* crosses *as* columns, there are many who tend to *see* columns *as* crosses, rather than as objects that may or may not once have been crosses" (Orton, Wood, with Lees, *Fragments of History*, 50).

31. See also Ó Carragáin: "The runic verse *tituli* employ the rhetorical device of prosopopoeia to give the monument an articulate personality: they make this cross tell us, in the English vernacular, of itself" (*Ritual and the Rood*, 60). Obviously, many objects are inscribed with text and thus seem to "speak" to the reader, but the *Ruthwell Poem* is distinguished from the majority of inscriptions in that it self-reflexively draws attention to the formal accord between the speaker of the text and the medium it is inscribed onto. Indeed, the form of the monument, its literal *figura*, already gives away the solution to the riddle: as in the process of riddling, where the solution already exists in the hints given by the text, the answer to the

This brings us back to Auerbach's concept of *figura*. The double identification of the poem's speaker with both the original cross and the monument as its representation is made possible through a figural relationship between the original cross and its representation: the liturgical object, as the cross's *figura*, both represents the original and participates in its reality. At the same time, the liturgical cross prefigures an even more universal truth, the resurrection of the flesh at the end of historical time, which has yet to come to pass and whose full significance is still hidden. In addition, the cross as a Christian symbol and a liturgical object is also partial fulfilment of the promise of universal salvation, since it represents one of the immediate effects of the crucifixion, namely the development of a Christian faith and church. Understood as a *figura*, the Ruthwell monument is thus able to participate in salvation history by referencing the past and the future—the historical moment of Christ's crucifixion and Isaiah's promise of universal conversion, to be fulfilled before the end of historical time.

According to Schlie, it is this temporal relationship between phenomenal prophecy and the revelation of its significance that is expressed by St. Paul in the First Letter to the Corinthians (13:9–12):[32]

> 9 Ex parte enim cognoscimus, et ex parte prophetamus. 10 Cum autem venerit quod perfectum est, evacuabitur quod ex parte est. . . . 12 Videmus nunc per speculum in ænigmate: tunc autem facie ad faciem. Nunc cognosco ex parte: tunc autem cognoscam sicut et cognitus sum.

> For we know in part, and we prophesy in part. But when that which is completed comes, the partial will disappear. . . . Now we look through a mirror into a riddle; then, however, face to face. Now I know in part; then, however, I will know even as I also am known.

---

riddle of the *Ruthwell Poem* is "already there" in the monument. Strikingly, while the Ruthwell monument employs such extra-textual means to draw attention to the formal identity of the monument and the speaker of the poem, in the *Dream of the Rood* the identity of the speaker is revealed by purely textual means, i.e., in the frame narrative, rather than visually, as for instance in the cruciform acrostics of Venantius Fortunatus, Hrabanus Maurus, Alcuin, and others (cf. George S. Tate, "Chiasmus as Metaphor: The 'Figura Crucis' Tradition and *The Dream of the Rood*," *Neuphilologische Mitteilungen* 79, no. 2 [1978]: 120–21; and Seeta Chaganti, "Vestigial Signs: Inscription, Performance, and *The Dream of the Rood*," *PMLA* 125 [2010]: 61). It is intriguing to note that both the *Dream of the Rood* and the *Ruthwell Poem* make extensive use of chiasmus and thus structurally play on the form of the cross; see Tate ("Chiasmus as Metaphor") and Howlett ("Inscriptions and Design," 76–78), who also discuss the use of chiasmus in the Latin inscriptions on the Ruthwell monument.

32. Schlie, "Klosterneuburger Ambo," 206.

Until the second *parousia*, a full understanding of the figural relationship must by necessity remain fragmentary; any attempt to unveil it therefore appears as if one were looking "through a mirror in a riddle." It is tempting to see a connection between the *enigma* aspect of *figura* and the riddlic style of the *Ruthwell Poem*, whose speaker's veiled identity points out the link between the Holy Cross and the monument as its *figura*.[33] Indeed, the fact that the poem's solution is already present in the shape of its medium suggests a play on the hermeneutic process of riddling, in which the riddle's subject only comes into existence at the moment the riddle is solved, and yet is also already there, fragmented and veiled, in the textual hints that lead the reader to the solution.

In this dynamic structure, the monument takes a central place, since it is experienced by the observer as a sort of performance, a performance that reproduces but also participates in it, and in which the recipient him- or herself likewise participates.[34] Thus, the Ruthwell monument, as a (postfigural) *figura* of the Holy Cross, not only participates in the figural scheme of providential history but also actively involves the recipient, given that he or she has grasped the relationship between text, object, and biblical event. The simultaneous identification of the speaker with the historical cross and with the monument as its symbol and representation implies a performative situation in which the object appears to be speaking directly to the observer. In a strange parallel to the situation described in the frame narrative of the Vercelli poem, the observer thus finds him- or herself on the same level as the dreamer in the *Dream of the Rood*, being lectured—by whom? Historically speaking, not the Holy Cross itself, but a representation: a product of the *imaginatio* in the *Dream of the Rood*, a material work of art in the Ruthwell Cross. Yet from a figural perspective, the representation *is* the Holy Cross, in a fashion similar

---

33. Ó Carragáin, who also associates the runic poem with riddling but sees the central challenge in the need "to reconcile the tragic vernacular narrative with its joyful vine-scroll setting," likewise draws attention to the relevance of 1 Cor. 13:9-12 with regard to riddles: "For them [the literate ecclesiastics who commissioned the cross], riddles could recall 'in a glass darkly' the central mystery of the faith" (Ó Carragáin, *Ritual and the Rood*, 60).

34. According to Schlie, the work of art—or rather, the viewer's experience of the work of art—appears as an event that can only be experienced as a performance ("Klosterneuburger Ambo," 246). Similarly, Catherine E. Karkov sees the Ruthwell monument as an object performed by its viewers ("Naming and Renaming: The Inscription of Gender in Anglo-Saxon Sculpture," in *Theorizing Anglo-Saxon Stone Sculpture*, ed. Catherine E. Karkov and Fred Orton [Morgantown: West Virginia University Press, 2003], 52). Seeta Chaganti ("Vestigial Signs," 59) and Ó Carragáin (*Ritual and the Rood*, 296-98) likewise draw attention to the monument's performative potential. John Hines calls the Old English texts on the cross "affective" and argues that they "invite the reader into a more immediately dramatic relationship with the monument itself in a way that the Latin texts never aim to bring about" ("Ruthwell Cross," 187; see also 189-90).

to later medieval mystery plays, where the performer *becomes*, quite literally, the person he or she represents.

In the case of the *Ruthwell Poem*, the identification even goes so far as to include the original object's historical perspective. As far as the poem is concerned, the speaker *is* the Holy Cross, not a representation. And as such, the speaker—and hence the poem—lacks the temporal perspective of the monument, which, as a liturgical object, can place the crucifixion in the historical past. For although the material context suggests that it is the monument that is speaking, the narrator's perspective places the poem precisely at the moment of the historical crucifixion. Although told in the past tense, the narrative has an immediateness to it that culminates in the incompleteness of the account: the strange silence, on the part of the speaker, concerning Christ's resurrection. The *Ruthwell Poem* ends with Christ being taken down from the cross, *limwœrig* [dead].[35] The speaker's historical knowledge, the poem suggests, goes no further than the time of Christ's temporary death; certainly it does not extend as far as the resurrection. The speaker thus remains in doubt as to the outcome. The future, even that of the reader, has yet to come to pass—and the Cross has no knowledge of it. From the observer's perspective, then, the Cross is addressing him or her from the past, in archaic writing and in a language shrouded in mystery. This is again suggested by the contrastive use of Latin and runic scripts: for while the Latin inscriptions with their Scriptural quotations would have appeared timeless to the medieval reader, the runes would have had an archaizing effect in that they would have been perceived, after the conversion, as belonging to an earlier cultural layer. Such an archaizing effect is suggested by Niles with regard to runes more generally: "Since runes derive from a layer of culture older than the Roman alphabet which Christian missionaries introduced to Britain at the end of the sixth century AD, an Anglo-Saxon text that has been runified has at the same time been rendered more

---

35. This interpretation is impeded by the fact that the text at this point is truncated. Bruce Dickins and Alan S. C. Ross estimate that there would have been enough room for another 40 runes (*The Dream of the Rood*, [London: Methuen, 1963], 29, note to line 64). These may have expressed something similar to Howlett's reconstruction of the last line: "bihêaldun hiæ þer Hêafunæs Dryctin; ond He Hinæ þer hwilæ restæ" (Howlett, "Inscriptions and Design," 88). The expression *hwilæ restæ* in the second half-line, if part of the original inscription, may have drawn attention to the temporary nature of Christ's death. Yet *restan* also has the meaning "to rest in death, lie dead, lie in the grave" (Bosworth-Toller, s.v. "*restan*" I,3) and *hwile* could also be understood to mean "meanwhile, at the same time" (Bosworth-Toller, s.v. "*hwil*," example 6), although I admit to special pleading in case of the latter. In any case, it is uncertain whether the second half-line once formed part of the inscription; as we have seen in the case of the half-line "rod wæs ic geræred," the Ruthwell text is prone to suppress important details.

antique."[36] The runic inscription, and hence the Cross's speech, thus have the appearance of being older than the monument, quasi contemporaneous with the biblical events themselves.

In this respect, the *Ruthwell Poem* diverges from the *Dream of the Rood*, where the Cross seems to be speaking from an extra-temporal perspective as a timeless symbol that views past, present, and future all at once, as if participating in God's extra-temporal eternity. The speaker of the *Ruthwell Poem*, by contrast, is not only arrested in a specific temporal moment but is also ignorant of the historical knowledge that the reader possesses. The poem thus seems to stress the immanence of the historical object over the transcendental knowledge of the religious symbol. Historical time is thereby presented as a process that privileges the later moment over the earlier one in that the former possesses knowledge denied to the latter. As both a symbol of the Christian hope of resurrection and a representation of the historical cross, the monument possesses this knowledge, yet the poem inscribed onto the monument does not. Strikingly, while in the *Dream of the Rood* the Rood's speech is presented as part of a literary work by being removed from the reader by several layers of framing devices,[37] the *Ruthwell Poem* feigns direct contact with the reader. The recipient thus becomes, figurally, both an observer of the crucifixion and a witness of its historical impact, since the cross is also a symbol of its promise of conversion, without which the liturgical enactment of the crucifixion that the reader takes part in would be impossible.[38] He or she becomes a *figura* him- or herself—and as such, witness to the concept's inherent tension.

Conclusion

Poem and monument, I have argued, draw part of their meaning from the tension between the historical and semiotic aspects of figural interpretation. As we have seen, this tension can be understood as a tension between similarities and dissimilarities. On the one hand, the formal accord that exists between

---

36. Niles, *Enigmatic Poems*, 223. In a similar vein, Seth Lerer argues that runes, as an archaic script, were used by Anglo-Saxons to draw attention to the "alterity of their own past" (*Literacy and Power in Anglo-Saxon Literature* [Lincoln: University of Nebraska, 1991], 11–12).

37. For a discussion of narrative frames in *The Dream of the Rood*, see Carolyn Holdsworth, "Frames: Time Level and Variation in *The Dream of the Rood*," *Neophilologus* 66 (1982): 622–28.

38. The iterative character of liturgical performance, which reenacts the events of Christ's life, is stressed by Jennings: "The church's public worship, the liturgy is designed to be reiterative, to reflect repeatedly the realities of the Christ and the Christian life" (Jennings, "Rood and Ruthwell," 6).

the historical cross, the monument, and the poem's speaker suggests their identity; it is this accord that makes it possible for the recipient to perceive their figural relationship. On the other hand, there is the historical singularity of cross, monument, and poem, which marks the three as separate and affords each its individual meaning. The tension between the historical vision of the poem and the representative, and hence interpretive, character of the monument mirrors the tension between the historical and semiotic aspects of the *figura* concept, while the fact that the relationship between poem, cross, and monument is veiled in riddlic fashion plays on its hermeneutic dimension.

Yet there is a further tension, or, one might even say, contradiction that marks the relationship between monument, poem, and historical cross. For although the poem, on the one hand, pretends to be the speech of the historical cross, and the monument, on the other, through the absence of other contextualizing features, suggests the speech is its own, it is of course neither. In reality, neither cross nor monument are capable of speaking. The interpretive act that identifies the three as one requires a suspension of disbelief on the part of the recipient that marks the poem as fiction. It is in this respect that the poem goes beyond a purely figural—and, hence, providential—vision of history.

PART III

SPECTACLE AND PERFORMANCE

CHAPTER 9

Archaeo-Theatrics

JONATHAN GIL HARRIS

We often imagine archaeology through the template of the "dig." Poised somewhere between practice and metaphor, the dig presumes a past that is buried and has to be disinterred to be discovered. The object of the archaeological dig is therefore something indisputably prior to and independent of the activity that unearths it. This makes the term *archaeology*, the order of that which originally came before, something of a pleonasm or redundancy. The *logos* of archaeology is by definition *arche*, ancient, originary, or prior. This is as true for the radical archaeology of knowledge theorized by Michel Foucault as it is for actual archaeological practice. Even as Foucault challenges post-Enlightenment understandings of science by thinking not about the primacy of *logos* but, rather, the historical genealogies of discourse itself, he still abides by the depth model of the dig.[1] Any discourse of knowledge is, for Foucault, metaphorically aligned with the three-dimensional soil or clay that the archaeologist works with her spade: it contains within it the sedimented layers of past formations that must be unearthed for them to become available for archaeological analysis in the present.

Yet early modern English counterparts to what we now call archaeology often resist this hermeneutics of occulted depth. They prefer instead to discover the past in immediately visible and, more importantly, legible surfaces.

---

1. See Michel Foucault, *Archéologie du savoir* (Paris: Gallimard, 1969).

Their versions of archaeology do not unearth something ancient or original. Instead, they produce *spectacles* of what supposedly came before. As such, they work metaphorically not with the spade but the stage. Because, if archaeology means "discourse about the ancient," early moderns offer us a highly histrionic form of discourse about antiquity that we might term *archaeo-theatrical*. In the archaeo-theatrical encounter with the past, all the world's a stage, but not in the synchronic way that we now interpret Shakespeare's phrase. Rather, the world is a *theatrum historiae,* in which every material object is potentially a mnemonic that recalls past events, lives, and traditions. Just as importantly, it also prompts stories about who we are now and even predicts what is to come. The present and future as much as the past are discovered through antique material objects, which serve as sets and stage properties for the performance of the contemporary self.

As this suggests, archaeo-theatrics differs from archaeology in one other crucial respect. Not only does it stage rather than unearth the past; by virtue of that staging, it also foregrounds—often against its wishes—the theatrical constructedness of the past. That doesn't mean the antique archaeo-theatrical object is necessarily fraudulent (though in some cases its interpretation can be spurious to an almost hilarious degree). What is more important is that the object explicitly bears the traces of work in the present in a way that archaeology often disavows. The archaeologist regards her spade as a supplement to rather than as an integral part of her archaeological object, which belongs to a temporally quarantined historical moment separate from her. As a result, the archaeological object, once unearthed, must not be touched other than through the most scrupulous of forensic protocols, and preferably with latex gloves. By contrast, the archaeo-theatricalist cannot see the past as having a life independent of her performance in the present. The archaeo-theatricalist's object does not belong simply to the past; it is, like the time it comes from, a potentiality that acquires fullness of its meaning only when it touches, and is touched by, the present and the future.[2]

In this essay I consider four instances of early modern archaeo-theatrics. The first is an example of the ceremonial civic procession, the highly theatrical walk through London—in this case, King James I's coronation procession in 1603—that was designed to discover the city's past as a prologue to the present. The second is an episode in a work of chorography loosely derived from the ceremonial procession: the second edition of John Stow's *Survey of London* (1603), in which the author semi-theatrically walks through the city and

---

2. My discussion here owes a debt to Eve Kosofsky Sedgwick's *Touching Feeling: Affect, Pedagogy, Performance* (Raleigh, NC: Duke University Press, 2003). I have discussed this more haptic, polychronic relation to the past in my book *Untimely Matter in the Time of Shakespeare* (Philadelphia: University of Pennsylvania Press, 2008), especially ch. 6.

stages it for the reader not just as it is but also as it was in antiquity. The third, to which I will pay most attention, also involves a theatrical scene enacted at the site of an ancient structure: the attempt by the English traveler to India, Thomas Coryate, to make sense of the multilingual inscriptions on an ancient pillar he saw in Delhi in about 1616. And the fourth is a scene from Shakespeare's *Hamlet*, one that shows how the act of digging up the past is always already a performed act. Taken together, these four instances can help us better understand how the past is not simply dead matter awaiting archaeological excavation. It is also theatrical matter that we stage with our own hands. And in the process, the archaeo-theatrical entertainment doesn't just tell tales of the past. It also tells tales of the present and the future.

•

The ceremonial civic processions of late medieval and early modern London—ranging from mayors' pageants to royal coronation entertainments—most graphically demonstrate what I am calling the archaeo-theatrical impulse. Progressing through the streets of the city and, in particular, moving between a series of monuments and ancient buildings, the participants in London's ceremonial civic processions "discovered" antiquity as one pole of a historical continuum within which they themselves were situated. And in these processions, seeming differences between then and now could be realigned typologically.[3] That is to say, the past was encountered less as a temporally remote culture than as an anticipatory, if superseded, "type" of the present and the future. It was thus an antique stage property in a historical drama featuring contemporary actors and spectators.

Take, for example, the coronation procession of King James in 1603. This entailed the new king riding from the Tower of London to St. Paul's Cathedral, and then pausing at the ancient city gate of Ludgate before riding on to Westminster Abbey for the coronation proper. His itinerary was the traditional one taken by new English monarchs: in the previous century, Anne Boleyn and Elizabeth had taken the same route in their coronation processions.[4] In each case, the processional locations were transformed into stage sets for elaborate

---

3. My thinking about typology is greatly influenced by Kathleen Biddick, *The Typological Imaginary: Circumcision, Technology, History* (Philadelphia: University of Pennsylvania Press, 2003).

4. Lawrence Manley, *Literature and Culture in Early Modern London* (Cambridge: Cambridge University Press, 1997), 226. For Anne Boleyn's coronation in 1533, for example, Ludgate was "costly and sumptuously garnished with gold, colors, and azure"; Elizabeth's precoronation approach to Ludgate was announced by the playing of music at the site. See Robert Withington, *English Pageantry: An Historical Outline* (Cambridge, MA: Harvard University Press, 1920), 1:184, 202. For a discussion of the symbolic dimensions of the theatrical city progress, see

pageants and performances. For King James, the performances were devised by the playwrights Ben Jonson and Thomas Dekker; a description of the entertainments, along with the scripts of the scenes enacted before its various locations, was published later that year by Dekker.[5] The scenes he and Jonson produced were not just fawning spectacles designed to celebrate the new king. They also deployed the antiquity of the buildings—the Tower, St. Paul's, Westminster, Ludgate—to perform the intimate connection of the present to the past. And that connection was understood typologically: the new king was the true meaning of a polity embodied in ancient buildings that not only preceded but also anticipated his rule. His royal predecessors, moreover, were types of him, which is to say they could signify fully only in relation to him. In the entertainments staged for him, then, King James didn't just see the antiquity of the city. He was also invited to see himself as the ancient city's present and future.

The typological importance of the Tower, St Paul's, and Westminster in King James's coronation procession is immediately clear: they were the ancient markers of (respectively) the royal, the spiritual, and the political power of which he was now the living embodiment. But why was Ludgate—an ancient and rather dilapidated gate near St. Paul's that opened up onto Fleet Street, and that was used by this time mostly as a debtor's prison—also a crucial venue for the theatrics of James's procession?

Ludgate was not just a gate but also a vital component in the symbolic topography of London.[6] It was a nodal point that asserted relations between the city's inside and outside, spiritual and earthly power, and past and present. At the threshold between St. Paul's and Westminster, between two different cities and between two different forms of power, Ludgate assumed an especial significance. The gate was supposedly named for King Lud, the mythical pagan founder of London. (London's name is supposed by some to derive from Lud's.) Statues of Lud and his two sons had been installed, in Roman gear, on the gate's east side within the city some centuries earlier. Ludgate was demolished in 1760, but the statues were preserved and are now housed in St. Dunstan's Church on Fleet Street. Although they had been defaced during the Protestant Reformation as supposedly pagan abominations, the statues were refurbished during the Spanish Armada as patriotic figures who anticipated

---

Steven Mullaney, *The Place of the Stage: Licence, Play, and Power in Renaissance England* (Chicago: University of Chicago Press, 1988), 10–20.

5. See Thomas Dekker, *The Royal Entertainment* (London, 1603).

6. On the symbolic resonances of Ludgate, see my essay "Ludgate Time: Simon Eyre's Oath and the Temporal Economies of *The Shoemaker's Holiday*," *Huntington Library Quarterly* 71, no. 1 (2008): 11–32.

English royalty in the present. Pausing at Ludgate, then, the new king symbolically doubled his English royal predecessors—not only those monarchs who had traced the same route during their coronation processions but also the antique foundational figures commemorated in the gate. And that is why, as James looked up along with the spectators at the statues of King Lud and his sons, actors made dramatic speeches about the antiquity of London, the greatness of the kingdom, and the glorious future about to be ushered in by the new king.

After passing through the gate en route to Westminster for his coronation, James then looked back in the direction of St Paul's Cathedral. On the west side of Ludgate facing away from the city, he saw the statue of another monarch, also installed at the time of the Armada: Queen Elizabeth. In other words, looking away from St. Paul's on the gate's east side, he peered into an antique pagan past and saw an antique pagan king; looking back at St. Paul's on the gate's west side, he peered at a Christian present and saw a recently deceased Christian queen. Guided by the sightline of the cathedral, James was able to transform Ludgate and its meanings. The building became the bearer not only of the ancient past. It was also the site of a Christian present and future of which he was now the successor and custodian.

This is an illustrative instance of an archaeo-theatrical discourse about the ancient, one that depended on the "discovery" of visible surfaces rather than occulted depths. And I employ the term *discovery* advisedly here. First, early moderns used the words *discourse* and *discovery* interchangeably.[7] And second, even though Ludgate was well known to London's citizens, they arguably discovered its antiquity afresh in James's coronation procession, inasmuch as the procession performatively altered the symbolic meanings of the gate and its statues—in particular, the meaning of the statue of Elizabeth—to accommodate the new king as the typological climax of Ludgate's antiquity. The stage properties for these archaeo-theatrics, it is worth noting, were not just antique material objects—the ancient gate, the statues on the east and west sides—but also the king himself, absorbed into a *tableau vivant* that rediscovered and recoded antiquity within a new set of continuities as much as differences between London's past, present, and future.

•

---

7. Ralph Bauer has written effectively about the subtly different meanings of *discovery* in early modern writing. Both to *discover* and to *discourse* meant less to reveal the truth than to bring to light something hitherto secret. See Ralph Bauer, "A New World of Secrets: Occult Philosophy and the Sixteenth-Century Atlantic," in *Science and Empire in the Atlantic Worlds*, ed. James Delbourgo and Nicholas Dew (New York: Routledge, 2008), 99–126.

Early modern English archaeo-theatrical performance was not confined to obviously theatrical rituals, such as King James's coronation procession. It was also part of a larger hermeneutic, a way of understanding the past, the present, and the future through material objects, which we find in other, less obviously performative cultural practices. The hermeneutical dimension implicit in James's procession is spelled out in actual scenes of archaeo-theatrical reading. I am referring here to the practice of reading captions written in ancient scripts on the surfaces of antique buildings and structures. These acts of reading are again typologically inflected: the antique cryptogram or hieroglyph can find its meaning only in the present and the future, thanks to the interpretive skill of the archaeo-theatrical reader who decodes it. As a result, this reader is not just an invisible, anonymous interpreter. Like King James, the reader also becomes a crucial character in the archaeo-theatrical scene, inasmuch as the act of decoding the ancient inscription is understood to fulfill in some way the inscription's destiny.

Antiquarian texts, such as John Stow's *Survey of London*, for example, employ what we might call an archaeo-theatrical method of investigation. Stow not only treats his urban environment as a *theatrum historiae* in which he can view the past. That environment also incites Stow to theatrical action himself: in order that he might make London's past more fully visible, he moves through the city like a participant in a coronation procession or civic pageant, pausing at certain buildings to discourse theatrically on the relations between then and now. The first edition of Stow's *Survey* was published in 1598; the second appeared in 1603, the year of King James's accession. The *Survey* offers a fascinating instance of archaeo-theatrics that, like the entertainment for James's coronation procession, involves Ludgate. This time, however, it entails a scene of reading.

Describing Ludgate, Stow relates a remarkable discovery from 1586. As workmen toiled to restore the gate that commemorated the supposed pagan founder of the city, they found instead the ancient remains of another, unexpected religious past:

> When the same gate was taken downe, to bee newe buylded, there was founde couched within the wal thereof, a stone taken from one of the Jewes houses, wherein was grauen in Hebrew caracters these wordes following.
> חך מצב חר משח בן הרב ר יצהק.[8]

---

8. John Stow, *A Survey of London, by John Stow* (London, 1598), 1:38. My discussion in this section builds on ideas that I had previously explored in *Untimely Matter*.

Stow seems to have transcribed the inscription carefully. But he was not a scholar of Hebrew and his characters do not quite make sense. One word (משח) is the name Moshe; another (יצהק) is Yitzhak. But other words (especially the cluster at the end of the inscription, חך מצב חר) seem to have been garbled in transmission.[9] To gloss the Hebrew, however, Stow chose a language other than English:

> חך מצב חר משח בן הרב ר יצהק. *Haec est statio Rabbi Mosis filii insignis Rabbi Isaac*; which is to say, this is the Station, or Ward of *Rabby Moses*, the sonne of the honorable *Rabby Isaac*, and had beene fixed vppon the front of one of the Jewes house as a note, or signe that such a one dwelled there.[10]

Stow here does not so much translate the Hebrew as supplement it with a Latin tag that he only then translates into English. Using the Latin, he concludes that the Hebrew inscription had been affixed to a rabbi's house in medieval London's Jewish district whose materials were looted and reworked by the barons, during their war with King John in 1215, for the purpose of civic improvement.

Why did Stow furnish the Latin gloss and avoid translating the Hebrew directly into English? The effect is to distance the Hebrew and make it even more remote than a direct translation might have done. Clearly, he wanted his readers to thrill to the strangeness of the Hebrew by including it in his text. That strangeness is all the more pronounced given that Jews had been officially banished from London and England three centuries earlier. There were, however, some Jewish immigrants—mostly refugees from Portugal and Spain after the Christian Reconquista of 1492—living undercover in London during the late sixteenth century. And perhaps their presence affected Stow's decision to include the Hebrew. Antony Bale has speculated that Stow personally supervised the typesetting of the characters in the 1598 edition, taking

---

9. In all likelihood, based on the Latin translation, the inscription was "matzevat rabbi moshe ben harav rabbi yitzhak," which means (literally) "monument of Rabbi Moshe son of Rabbi Yitzhak." I am assuming that what Stow records as "מצב חר" should be "מצבת ר." Hebrew has two related forms for rabbi: (a) "rav" or "harav" (הרב) with definite article "ha" (ה), denoting the occupation with all its gravitas; and (b) "rabbee," as title, abbreviated in writing to "r" [ר]. Note the duplication in relation to Yitzhak of "harav" and "rabbi." The one part of Stow's inscription that remains inscrutable to me is the concluding (or in Hebrew, beginning) word, "חך." It may in fact not be a word but, like the use of "ר" for "rabbee," a pair of initials denoting a phrase. Perhaps Stow has mistranscribed the "ך" (or kof), and it should instead read "ו" (or vav). With Hebrew's tendency to pair adjectives for reinforcement, the possibilities are endless: it could be, for example, "hagadol v'hanechbad" [the great and honored]. I am grateful to Stella Harris for assistance with my translation, and for further speculations.

10. Stow, *Survey of London*, 1:38.

advantage of the recent import of movable Hebrew typefaces from Italy. Bale also proposes that this special care represents a sympathetic attitude on Stow's part to Jews in general, and that he may even have known some undercover Jews.[11] Whether or not this is the case, it still does not explain why Stow felt he needed to translate the Hebrew into Latin.

There is clearly more to Stow's Latin-glossed Hebrew letters. This was not just a theatrical display of a strange typeface from long ago. It was also an archaeo-theatrical episode that involved telling a tale about the present and the future as much as the past. In producing his trilingual text, Stow plotted a familiar religious as well as linguistic path: the dissemination of the word from the Hebrew of Moses, via its Catholic reworking in Latin, to its vernacular redemption in the English of Anglican liturgy. The scene may at first look archaeological—a lost antiquity is uncovered, hidden beneath the surface of the gate—yet Stow's practice is ultimately less archaeological than it is archaeo-theatrical. For Stow not only insists that the matter of London's present contains the legible traces of the past. He also uses those traces to shape the meanings of the present through a logic of typological supersession. Just as Lud is a prototype for Elizabeth, who is a type for James, so is Hebrew fulfilled by Latin, which is perfected by English. In other words, Stow "discovers" the antiquity of Ludgate by rehearsing a well-established Christian script. Christian meaning supersedes Jewish writing; Protestant English vernacular supersedes Catholic Latin.

Archaeo-theatrics in this instance reveals something implicit in King James's coronation pageant. The past isn't just there, waiting to be discovered: it has to be read and interpreted. And interpretation isn't just an act of deciphering the "arche." It also produces the *meaning* of antiquity in relation to a sense of the present moment and also of what is to come. Stow's text places the Jewish past and the Catholic present in relation to a Protestant future. It matters little that Stow is suspected to have entertained Catholic sympathies; he was writing as a chronicler of what had recently become a Protestant-ruled city with a strong sense of itself as "New Troy" or "New Rome."[12] Stow's

---

11. Antony Bale, "Stow's Medievalism and Antique Judaism in Early Modern London," in *John Stow (1525–1605) and the Making of the English Past: Studies in Early Modern Culture and the History of the Book*, ed. Ian Gadd and Alexandra Gillespie (London: British Library, 2004), 79–80.

12. On the medieval and early modern vogue for calling London "Troynovant" or "New Troy," see John E. Curran Jr., *Roman Invasions: British History, Protestant Anti-Romanism, and the Historical Imagination in England, 1530–1660* (Newark, NJ: University of Delaware Press, 2002), 99.

archaeo-theatrics is, in other words, a performance of futurity as much as of antiquity.

•

Early modern English archaeo-theatrical performance was not confined to London. It is evident also in a compellingly strange episode in Delhi from 1616, involving the eccentric early seventeenth-century walker to India, Thomas Coryate. This Indian episode involves many of the elements we have seen in King James's coronation pageant and John Stow's encounter with the Hebrew inscription in Ludgate. Like James's pageant, the episode is a highly theatrical one; and like Stow's interpretation of the inscription, Coryate's archaeo-theatrics is grounded in a mode of typological reading that stages the past, inscribed in the form of inscrutable characters, as a type of the present and future.

Thomas Coryate certainly put the theatrical into the archaeo-theatrical. Known to his London friends and detractors alike as "Odd Tom," he was something of an eccentric.[13] Coryate cheerfully embraced his nickname: born in approximately 1577 and raised in the small Somerset village of Odcombe in west England, he admitted that he embodied the "odd" of his village's name. Of highly diminutive stature, with a large head, he was considered something of a clown. But he was bright: educated at Winchester College and Oxford, he developed an unusual skill in languages—Greek, Latin, French, Italian—and made highly theatrical orations in them. Perhaps this unusual pastime was a means to compensate for (or take advantage of) his odd appearance. In 1603, this skill earned him a position in King James's entourage as a de facto court jester, where he won a reputation for devising strange new multilingual terms; he also became a member of a group of wits at London's Mermaid Tavern, where he honed his reputation as a nonstop talker but also, more specifically, as someone who loved moving between different languages in his never-ending orations. One of his fellows observed, "With Latin he doth rule the roast, / And spouteth Greek in every coast."[14]

---

13. For more on Coryate's biography, see Dom Moraes and Sarayu Srivatsa, *The Long Strider: How Thomas Coryate Walked from England to India in the Year 1613* (Delhi: Penguin India, 2003) and R. E. Pritchard, *Odd Tom Coryate: The English Marco Polo* (Stroud: Sutton Publishing, 2004). I have written on Coryate's time in Ajmer in *The First Firangis: Remarkable Stories of Heroes, Healers, Charlatans, Courtesans, and Other Foreigners Who Became Indian* (New Delhi: Aleph Books, 2015).

14. Thomas Coryate, *Coryats Crudities Hastily Gobbled up in Five Months Travels in France, Savoy, Italy, Rhetia Commonly Called the Orison's Country, Helvetia Alias Switzerland, Some Parts of High Germany and the Netherlands, Newly Digested in the Hungry Air of Odcombe in*

In 1607, Coryate left the King's service to perform another theatrical stunt: walking from London to Italy and back. Coryate's journey, which lasted a little more than five months, took him on foot through France, Switzerland, Italy, Germany, and Holland. His eccentric travelogue of his walk through Europe, *Coryate's Crudities,* published in 1611, made him something of an odd-ball celebrity. Its title-page makes clear that he was a particularly histrionic traveler—its illustrations depict him carried by palanquin over the Swiss Alps, fleeing Venetian Jews with knives, pelted with fruit by angry courtesans, even vomited on by a figure representing Germany. And everywhere he walked, he delivered theatrical orations.

For his encore, Coryate chose in 1613 to walk to India. It is in Asia, confronted with the material remains of a diverse array of antique cultures, that he most displayed his archaeo-theatrical bent. Coryate's reference points throughout his wanderings were literary texts that provided him with occasions for performances next to antique matter. While visiting the ruins of Troy in Turkey, for example, he was inspired to dub his traveling companions, with a borrowed sword, as heroic knights—modern-day counterparts of Hector and Achilles.[15] (This apparently provoked the consternation of local bystanders, who thought he was about to behead his friends.) Coryate's Homeric inspiration sustained him for much of his journey: he saw himself as a type of Ulysses, wandering for many years through foreign climes before wending his way back home. Coryate's encounter with the ruins of Troy was, for all its histrionic excess and the consternation it provoked in its spectators, shaped by the same archaeo-theatrical impulse that we have seen in King James's and John Stow's responses to the antiquity of Ludgate: the Trojan ruins prompted in Coryate less archaeological knowledge of a cultural and temporal Other than theatrical performance of a typological relation between past and present.

Coryate theatrically channeled Ulysses in Troy. But throughout his Asian walk, he performed many theatrical scenes in a variety of tongues: in what is now Pakistan, he delivered an impromptu oration, in Italian, about the errors of the prophet Mohammed to a doubtless baffled Muslim mercenary who had once worked in Florence; in Agra, he climbed atop a mosque to deliver an updated version, in Arabic, of the muezzin's call to prayer. But he was arguably most inspired theatrically by Marlowe's stage despot Tamburlaine, the grand conqueror of Asia, a theatrical version of the fourteenth-century Turkic king Timur-e-Lang.

---

the County of Somerset, and Now Dispersed to the Nourishment of the Travelling Members of this Kingdom (London, 1611), 1:24.

15. For an excellent account of Coryate's Trojan adventure, see Efterpi Mitsi, *Greece in Early English Travel Writing* (London: Palgrave Macmillan, 2017), 142–46.

Coryate maintained this identification despite the fact that, unlike the Scythian shepherd-cum-emperor, he "conquered" Asia in a state of extreme poverty. Upon crossing the border between Ottoman Turkey and Persia, he was robbed of all his money; arriving in India almost penniless in 1615, he seems to have fed himself by begging in the streets of Ajmer in Rajasthan. Yet dreams of Tamburlaine kept him going. In 1616, he delivered another oration, this time in makeshift Persian, outside the Mughal emperor Jahangir's temporary palace in Ajmer. In the oration, he claimed that the purpose of his Asian journey was to find the ancient Samarkand grave of Tamburlaine the Great—a stage character whom he hoped not just to locate in "real" space and time but also to theatrically emulate by means of his pan-Asian march.[16] He begged Jahangir to grant him safe passage to his destination. Heaven knows what he hoped to do upon reaching Samarkand; but he clearly viewed Tamburlaine's grave as a typologically appropriate stage property for his own drama of Asian "conquest." The by now three-centuries-old grave would allow him to perform, archaeo-theatrically, the relation of a world-conquering Asian antiquity to the transcontinental peregrinations of a contemporary Englishman.

Coryate never made it to Samarkand, as he fell terminally sick en route. (He died of dysentery in Surat in 1616.) But his sense of drama did not desert him during this time. One of the highlights of Coryate's northbound itinerary from Ajmer was his visit to Delhi in 1616. Here Coryate saw a spectacular antique object, one that left a huge impression on him; more than twenty-five years later, his sometime traveling companion still remembered what Coryate had to say about it. As we will see, Coryate inducted it into yet another scene of archaeo-theatrics. This scene typified his unique histrionic eccentricity. But it also emerged from the same hermeneutics of typological reading that we have seen with John Stow.

The antique object in question was a 42-foot-high pillar. It is still standing in the ruins of Feroz Shah Kotla, a fort erected by the Mamluk Sultan Feroz Shah in the 1350s (figure 9.1). The site is in some ways highly theatrical even now, inasmuch as it is adjacent to an amphitheater: this is used not for the performance of plays, however, but for that most dramatic of Indian pastimes, cricket. But the pillar of Feroz Shah Kotla was not created by the Sultan. Feroz Shah had found it during a hunting expedition in Topra, to the east of Delhi.[17] Making inquiries among the local Brahmin pandits, he ascertained that the

---

16. I discuss Coryate's oration to Jehangir and its Tamburlainian connections in *First Firangis*, 200–204.

17. My information about Feroz Shah and the Ashoka pillar comes from Charles Allen, "The Golden Column of Firoz Shah," in *Ashoka: The Search for India's Lost Emperor* (New Delhi: Hachette, 2012), 6–27.

FIGURE 9.1. Pillar of Ashoka. © Jonathan Gil Harris.

pillar was a "walking stick of Bhim," the mythical colossus who was one of the five Pandava brothers whose story is the basis of the great Indian epic, the *Mahabharata*. Entranced by the pillar's polished red hue, Feroz Shah named it, in Persian, the *minar-e-zarin*, the pillar of gold. He resolved to remove it from Topra and install it in his newly built fort in Delhi, despite the fact that it weighed 25 tons. The means by which he transported it is almost as remarkable as the pillar itself. After gently felling it onto a bed of cotton, he had the pillar encased from top to bottom in reeds so that no damage could come to it; he conveyed it by carriage to the Yamuna river and then floated it down the river to Delhi on a flotilla of large boats lashed together.

What Feroz Shah believed to be an antique walking stick of a Hindu hero had, in fact, been created at the orders of the Buddhist Mauryan Emperor, Ashoka, who ruled much of India in the fourth century BCE. It was one of many such pillars that Ashoka had had erected throughout the subcontinent, inscribed with what have come to be known as the "Ashokan edicts," guides to ethical living.[18] Knowledge of Ashoka had vanished by Feroz Shah's time. But the inscriptions on the pillar are still clearly visible nearly 2,500 years after they were etched into its surface.

In 1610, five years before Coryate reached Delhi, the English traveler William Finch visited the remains of Feroz Shah Kotla. The fort had long been deserted and had gone to ruin; Finch believed it to be simply an old hunting house. He clearly wasn't able to get up close to the pillar. But he remarked that this "stone pillar, they say . . . hath inscriptions."[19] Even if he had seen them, Finch wouldn't have been able to decipher them, and neither would anyone else at this time, because they were written in the lost scripts of what were now dead languages—Prakrit, the official indigenous language of the Mauryan Empire, but also in Sanskrit and Pali. These multilingual characters give some indication of Ashoka's commitment to a pluralist ethos, an ethos most resonantly pronounced in the edicts he had engraved on a rock near Kandahar in Prakrit, and astonishingly, Aramaic, and Greek. Ashoka's stepgrandmother, after all, was most likely Greek. Not only the form but also the content of Ashoka's edicts signal his commitment to pluralism: As one of them says, "Contact [between religions] is good. One should listen to and respect the doctrines of others. King Piyadasi [i.e., Ashoka] desires that all his subjects should be well learned in the good doctrines of others."[20] Little did Ashoka know that his multilingual pillar would 2,000 years later become a theatrical scene for a multilingual performer from another continent.

Enter (again) Thomas Coryate. While embarked on his search for Tamburlaine in 1615, Coryate stopped briefly in Delhi and was clearly transfixed by the pillar: Feroz Shah Kotla is the one landmark in Delhi he seems to have cared to discuss. In a letter he wrote shortly afterward to his friend Laurence Whitaker—a letter which, miraculously, survived the journey from India to London—Coryate talks only about the pillar he saw in Delhi. His accounts of it must have been particularly vivid, as they were committed several years later to writing by Edmund Terry, a pastor who accompanied the English ambassador Thomas Roe on his famous journey to Ajmer and who became friendly with Coryate. Terry remarked, "I was told by Tom Coryat (who took special

---

18. See Nayanjot Lahiri, *Ashoka in Ancient India* (Cambridge, MA: Harvard University Press, 2015).

19. William Finch's travelogue is quoted in William Foster, *Early Travels in India, 1583–1619* (Oxford: Oxford University Press, 1911), 157.

20. The translated text of the Ashoka edict is taken from Stephen A. Smith, *Freedom of Religion: Foundational Documents and Historical Arguments* (Oxford: Oxbridge Research Associates, 2017), 5.

notice of this place) that he, being in the city of Dellee, observed a very great pillar of marble, with a Greek inscription upon it which Time hath almost quite worn out."²¹ As the current state of the pillar makes clear, Time in fact *hasn't* succeeded in erasing the inscriptions. So Terry's statement may be his own interpolation. It could also be due to Coryate's faulty assessment for the state of the pillar. If the latter, there may be a reason for his error. Coryate could, in fact, read Greek: the Prakrit characters, while bearing some superficial resemblance to Greek script, are also clearly different—perhaps different enough to suggest to one determined to see them as Greek letters that they must have been disfigured over time.

Why was Coryate adamant that the pillar was inscribed in Greek? We know that this was his own theory, and not Terry's. Coryate himself writes that Delhi is "where Alexander the Great joined battell with Porus, King of India, and conquered him; and in token of his victorie, erected a brass pillar"—not the marble that Terry had thought—"which remaineth there to this day."²² This explanation was repeated by Terry in 1655, some forty years after Coryate visited Delhi: the pillar, Terry reports Coryate saying, was "erected (as he supposed) there and then by great Alexander, to preserve the memory of that famous victory."²³

Coryate's theory was no doubt partly the surmise of a classically educated scholar, whose knowledge of India before his arrival was in large part confined to tales of its conquest—by Tamburlaine and, before him, by Alexander. But the pillar's Greek origin does not seem to be just the calculated guess of an educated tourist. I would hazard that it is also the consequence of an archaeo-theatrical response to the pillar. Coryate may have seen himself as Ulysses during his years away from home. But he also identified himself with Tamburlaine and Alexander. And he did so not just in some bizarre Karaoke bar of his own imagination, but more specifically in an archaeo-theatrical manner: he saw them as ancient types of himself—as eastward Asian travelers, taking possession of what they saw. One consequence of his archaeo-theatrical disposition is this: The past that the material remains of Asia evoked in Coryate was never a self-contained temporal event but, rather, part of a continuum that culminated in, and made sense of, his own journey.

Alexander would have been known to Coryate through a number of classical sources, including Pliny the Elder's natural history. The Macedonian was strangely absent from the Elizabethan stage, though Coryate may have seen

---

21. Edmund Terry's reminiscences of Coryate's remarks are quoted in Foster, *Early Travels in India*, 248.

22. Foster, *Early Travels in India*, 248.

23. Foster, *Early Travels in India*, 248.

the university play *Alexander and Campaspe* by John Lyly.[24] But Alexander still haunted the early modern European imagination as the exemplary conqueror. As Coryate's own remarks to Terry make clear, Alexander's victory over Porus in the Battle of Hydaspes loomed large in the European imagination. This is suggested, too, by an engraving by Johannes van den Avele of Alexander's victory over Porus.[25] The picture betrays a fascination with the idea that Alexander could defeat an oriental army possessed of ferocious animal power—the same animal power that Hannibal had used to invade the Italian peninsula. Indeed, the Alexander legend derived some of its force from the proposition that the Macedonian conqueror could overcome Indian elephants in such a way as to use them against his enemy: various sources claimed that many of Porus's troops were crushed to death by his own elephants after they were cornered by Alexander's battalions.[26] To gain mastery over the elephant, for a classically educated early modern European, is very much a fantasy derived from this legend.

It is in this respect that Coryate's self-image as an Asian traveler bears a telltale trace of the Alexander legend. In one of his letters back to England from Ajmer, when he was at his poorest, he dreams of being "pictured on an elephant."[27] On the one hand, this seems like the desire of any modern tourist visiting India. But the wish communicated itself with particular force to the man who published Coryate's letters, and who contracted a woodcutter to illustrate him atop of an elephant. The image is pure Coryate—theatrical and even faintly ridiculous—but its theatricality exceeds or departs from what we might attribute to it. This is an image of Coryate that taps into a collective early modern fantasy of Western mastery in Asia. And it functions in a way that recalls the typological logic of archaeo-theatricality that I have teased out here—presenting Coryate as a latter-day type of Alexander, a master of India.

One might speculate about how Coryate's archaeo-theatrical relation to the animals as well as the material ruins of Asia was implicated in a logic that

---

24. On Alexander's presence in the early modern British as well as Asian imaginations, see Su Fang Ng, "Global Renaissance: Alexander the Great and Early Modern Classicism from the British Isles to the Malay Archipelago," *Comparative Literature* 58 (2006): 293–312.

25. For Johannes van den Avele's 1685 picture of Alexander's victory over Hydaspes at Porus, see "Imaginative Interpretation of an Indian War Elephant in Action against Alexander's Troops by Johannes van den Avele, 1685," Alexanders tomb, accessed June 2, 2020, http://www.alexanderstomb.com/main/imageslibrary/ atgrelated/WarElephant1685.jpg.

26. On the elephant lore associated with Alexander, see Frank L. Holt, *Alexander the Great and the Mystery of the Elephant Medallions* (Berkeley: University of California Press, 2003).

27. Coryate's desire to be pictured riding an elephant was honoured by his publisher, who commissioned such a picture for the frontispiece of Coryate's posthumous publication, *Greetings from the Court of the Great Mughal* (London, 1618). See Foster, *Early Travels in India*, 237.

would later serve colonial ends. It is hard not to recoil from his narcissistic tendency to read signs of non-European cultures and times as types or even prophesies of his own supposedly heroic mission in Asia. Yet I would like to argue, too, that Coryate's archaeo-theatrical performance in Delhi, for all its ludicrousness, helpfully reminds us of something we often disavow about archaeology: namely, the central role played by storytelling to make sense of material remains, and how the past is always less simply found than it is artfully performed.

•

At this point, we might recall a scene that is in some ways, at least in Western drama, the ur-scene of archaeology. I am referring here to the graveyard scene in *Hamlet*.[28] The gravediggers unearth a skull that Hamlet immediately recognizes as that of the former court jester, Yorick. He claims the fruits of the dig for a kind of knowledge—"Alas, poor Yorick, I knew him"—but what we are given is less an illustration of a knowable past turned up by a dig than a story prompted by a surface.

Hamlet continues:

> A fellow of infinite jest, of most excellent fancy. He hath borne me on his back a thousand times, and now, how abhorred in my imagination it is! My gorge rises at it. Here hung those lips that I have kissed I know not how oft.—Where be your gibes now? Your gambols? Your songs? Your flashes of merriment that were wont to set the table on a roar? Not one now to mock your own grinning? Quite chapfallen? Now get you to my lady's chamber and tell her, let her paint an inch thick, to this favor she must come. (5.1.80–88)

What we get here is not history in an archaeological sense but something closer to what the French call *histoire,* history as story. How does Hamlet know the skull is Yorick's? He doesn't, he can't; but the ancient death's head he famously holds up for view—the *locus classicus* not just of the memento mori but also of the Shakespearean stage property—is a mnemonic that prompts an archaeo-theatrical performance. It is a performance that allows Hamlet not just to reflect on the inevitability of death and the vanity of what we value in life but also to continue railing against women as the exemplars of that vanity. And the performance's temporal reach is extensive: dead Yorick, from the

---

28. All references to *Hamlet* are to Barbara A. Mowat and Paul Werstine, eds., *Hamlet* (New York: Simon and Schuster, 2003).

past, evokes women, from the present, whose reproductive power (something Hamlet inveighs against repeatedly in his jeremiads about "breeding sinners") points to the future.

But what is particularly striking is how the skull triggers another series of reflections. Skull in hand, Hamlet's performance, like Coryate's, returns compulsively to the antiquity of Alexander. "Dost thou think," asks Hamlet, "Alexander looked o'this fashion in th'earth? . . . And smelt so? Pah! . . . Why may not imagination trace the noble dust of *Alexander*, till he find it stopping a *bung-hole?*" (5.1.170, 172, 175). This disgusted invocation of the remains of Alexander is a long way from Coryate's invocation of conquering Alexander in his encounter with the Ashoka pillar. But like Coryate, Hamlet is reading typologically here. He sees Alexander as a type for Yorick, and both Alexander and Yorick as types for himself: people in powerful places that must go the way of all flesh. Yet even as Hamlet, like Coryate, reads the supposed remains of Alexander typologically, he also reads in a way that makes him the anti-Coryate, the poor beggar who imagined himself a conquering king. Instead, Hamlet is the prince who imagines himself turned into dust, food for worms that will in turn "go a progress through the guts of a beggar." If Hamlet's archaeo-theatrical performance deploys the typological hermeneutic we have seen at work in King James's coronation procession, John Stow's description of Ludgate, and Thomas Coryate's encounter with the Ashoka pillar, it is not a typology of increasing perfection but of endless, pointless repetition that extends from the past into the future.

The metaphor of the "dig" presumes truth in depth; but as Hamlet makes clear to the gravediggers with his own tale of Alexander the Great stopping the bunghole of a barrel, the material relics of the past—whether unearthed or immediately visible—are equally stage props in dramas of our own making. What a theory of archaeo-theatrics can help us do, perhaps, is make us pay more attention to the ways in which we use the supposedly found objects of the past to narrate stories about ourselves in the present and the time to come. And as the differences between Coryate's and Hamlet's archaeo-theatrical Alexanders make clear, there can never be a singular story. Archaeo-theatrics differs from archaeology most in this regard: the archaeo-theatrical performance insists that the past is never absolute, self-contained, and complete. It is constantly being refashioned in the stories we tell about it and its objects.

CHAPTER 10

11 Ways of Looking at Renaissance Ruins

ANDREW HUI

1. As Object Lesson

The Renaissance was the *Ruin-naissance*: the ruin constituted a distinct category of cultural discourse that became an inspirational force in the poetic imagination, artistic expression, and historical inquiry of fifteenth- and sixteenth-century Europe. There was not a single way of looking at Roman ruins: they were material and metaphoric, architectural and allegorical, ever responsive to the dictates of the architectural needs, fashions, and exigencies of the moment. What marks a ruin's significance is its multiplicity: it is a palimpsest and a kaleidoscope.[1]

The revival of antiquity that began in full force in the mid-fourteenth century was concomitant with a new understanding of the ruins of Rome. Jacob Burckhardt already recognized this over a hundred years ago in his foundational—though today somewhat controversial—*The Civilization of the Renaissance in Italy* (1860): the dilapidated city "awakened not only archaeological zeal and patriotic enthusiasm, but an elegiac or sentimental melancholy."[2]

---

1. This essay incorporates some thoughts from my *The Poetics of Ruins in Renaissance Literature* (New York: Fordham University Press, 2016), especially ch. 2, "The Rebirth of Ruins."

2. Jacob Burckhardt, *The Civilization of the Renaissance in Italy*, 1860, trans. S. C. G. Middlemore (London: Phaidon, 1944), 113. Important source materials on Renaissance Rome are collected in Eugène Müntz, *Les arts à la cour des papes aux XVe et XVIe siècle*, 4 vols.

The broken monuments underscored with haunting pathos the vast gulf that was now assumed to exist between the time of humanism and antiquity, and made the humanists realize just how irretrievably lost the classical past was. In 1398, Pier Paolo Vergerio lamented, "Rome, once the center of the world, is now nothing but a name and a legend."³ Manuel Chrysoloras wrote to the Byzantine Emperor in 1411, "Even these ruins and heaps of stones show what great things once existed, and how enormous and beautiful were the original constructions. For what in Rome was not beautiful?"⁴ So, too, Alberto degli Alberti to Giovanni de' Medici in 1443: "The modern things here are in a very sorry state, the things that have fallen are Rome's beauty."⁵ In a manner almost unprecedented in the post-classical world, the ruins of antiquity were seen as beautiful, an aesthetic phenomenon, something deserving of wonder. But they were also raw material to be reused. Some two centuries later, Pope Urban VIII (reign 1623–44) ordered that the ancient bronze beams from the Pantheon's portico be removed so that he could have enough bronze for the baldachin of St Peter's Basilica. A popular tag went: "Quod non fecerunt barbari, fecerunt Barberini" [What the barbarians did not do, the Barberini did].

(Paris: Ernest Leroux, 1898); Roberto Valentini and Giuseppe Zucchetti, eds., *Codice topografico della città di Roma*, 4 vols. (Rome: Tipografia del senato, 1953); Cesare D'Onofrio, ed., *Visitiamo Roma nel Quattrocento: La città degli umanisti* (Rome: Romano società editrice, 1989). Important secondary works include: Salvatore Settis, ed., *Memoria dell'antico nell'arte italiana*, 3 vols. (Turin: Einaudi, 1984–86), especially vol. 1, *L'uso dei classici*; Leonard Barkan, *Unearthing the Past: Archaeology and Aesthetics in the Making of Renaissance Culture* (New Haven, CT: Yale University Press, 1999); Sabine Forero-Mendoza, *Le temps des ruines: Le goût des ruines et les formes de la conscience historique à la Renaissance* (Seyssel, FR: Champ Vallon, 2002); Nicole Dacos, *Roma quanta fuit, ou, l'invention du paysage de ruines* (Paris: Somogy, 2004); Kathleen Wren Christian, *Empire without End: Antiquities Collections in Renaissance Rome, c. 1350–1527* (New Haven, CT: Yale University Press, 2010); David Karmon, *The Ruin of the Eternal City: Antiquity and Preservation in Renaissance Rome* (Oxford: Oxford University Press, 2011); Nicole Dacos, *Voyage à Rome: Les artistes européens au XVIe siècle* (Brussels: Fonds Mercator, 2012); Jessica Maier, *Rome Measured and Imagined: Early Modern Maps of the Eternal City* (Chicago: University of Chicago Press, 2015); Susan Stewart, *The Ruins Lesson: Meaning and Material in Western Culture* (Chicago: University of Chicago Press, 2020).

3. "Roma, quondam orbis caput nunc nudum nomen et fabula" (Pier Paolo Vergerio, *Epistolario di Pier Paolo Vergerio*, ed. Leonard Smith, Fonti per la Storia d'Italia [Rome: Istituto Storico Italiano per il Medio Evo, 1934], 212), translated and discussed in Christian, *Empire without End*, 1.

4. A complete translation of the letter is in Christine Smith, *Architecture in the Culture of Early Humanism: Ethics, Aesthetics, and Eloquence, 1400–1470* (Oxford: Oxford University Press, 1992), 199–215, quote on 200. Her analysis is on 150–70.

5. Alberto degli Alberti, letter "ex urbe delacerata," March 14, 1443, in A. Fabroni, *Magni Cosmi Medici Vita* (Pisa, 1788), 2:165, quoted in Christof Thoenes, "St. Peter's as Ruins: On Some *vedute* by Heemskerck," in *Sixteenth-Century Italian Art*, ed. Michael W. Cole (London: Blackwell, 2006), 25.

FIGURE 10.1. Sebastiano Serlio, frontispiece of *Quinto libro d'architettura di Sebastiano Serlio Bolognese,* the fifth book of his *Tutte l'opere d'architettura,* originally published in 1547 (1584 edition). Universitätsbibliothek Heidelberg, https://digi.ub.uni-heidelberg.de/diglit/serlio1584/0445, accessed June 2, 2020.

The ruin functions as a privileged cipher or master *topos* that marks the rupture between the world of the humanists and the world of antiquity. The discourse of Roman ruins coincides with a renewed interest in the classical past: architects used ancient buildings as models for their own construction, antiquarians systematically collected their remains, philologists sought to understand the past through inscriptions on buildings and fragments of manuscripts, and artists illustrated the desolate urban views as exercises in spatial and historical perspective.

When the humanists saw ruins, what did they see? What did they want to see? The commonplace "Roma quanta fuit, ipsa ruina docet" [How Rome was, her ruins themselves teach] epitomizes their didactic value (figure 10.1).[6] Every word of this epigram carries weight. The contrasting tenses of "fuit" and "docet" underscore continuity and rupture between time past and time present. "Quanta" is about the magnitude, the distance between now and then. The pronoun "ipsa" as the intensifier stresses the evidentiary power of the ruin and the coextension between Rome as a totality and its materiality. In medieval thought, too, the ruin has the power to teach (docere), but primarily as a moral lesson on the vanity of all earthly things. For the early humanists, the ruin teaches because it has real empirical value. It demonstrates the achievements of a past age and embodies recoverable knowledge.

"The Golden Capitol decays. Every temple in Rome is covered with soot and cobwebs. . . . Even in Rome paganism languishes in solitude. Those who once were the gods of the gentiles remain under the lonely roofs with owls and the birds of the night," intones St. Jerome in the fourth century.[7] Though early Christian writers tended to blame pagan Rome herself for her ruin, Renaissance humanists recognized that the destruction of antiquity was often perpetuated by the Christians themselves. Giorgio Vasari in his *Lives of the Artists* basically constructs the idea of the Middle Ages as the "Dark Ages" when he writes:

> But what brought infinite harm and damage on the said professions, even more than all the aforesaid causes, was the burning zeal of the new Christian religion, which, after a long and bloody combat, with its wealth of miracles and with the sincerity of its works, had finally cast down and swept away the old faith of the heathens, and, devoting itself most ardently with all diligence to driving out and extirpating root and branch every least occasion whence error could arise, not only defaced or threw to the ground all the marvelous statues, sculptures, pictures, mosaics, and ornaments of the false gods of the heathens, but even the memorials and the honours of numberless men of

---

6. First recorded in Francesco Albertini's *Opusculum de mirabilibus novae et veteris urbis romae* (Rome: Mazochius, 1510).

7. "Auratum squalet Capitolum, fuligine et aranearum telis omnia Romae templa cooperta sunt . . . Solitudinem patitur et in urbe gentilitas. Dii quodam nationum cum bubonibus et noctuis in solis culminibus remanserunt" (Letter 107, "To Laeta," St. Jerome, *Selected Letters*, trans. F. A. Wright [Cambridge, MA: Harvard University Press, 1933], 340, 342, translation modified).

mark, to whom, for their excellent merits, the noble spirits of the ancients had set up statues and other memorials in public spaces.[8]

For Vasari, making monuments ruins was a symptom of the fervor of the early Christians, such as Pope Gregory. Granted, his polemic underscores his perception of living in a more enlightened age by exaggerating his predecessors' destructive zeal. Renaissance humanists would express their own fervor in the opposite manner—not ruining monuments, but monumentalizing ruins. In other words, monuments became ruins in the Middle Ages, ruins became monuments in the Renaissance.

From the fifteenth century onward, there were many treatises that treated the ruin as an object of study. Poggio Bracciolini's *De varietate fortunae* (1447) was one of the first. Later, "professional" architects such as Alberti, Serlio, and Palladio followed suit.[9] Departing from the touristic folktales and pious legends of the medieval *mirabilia* tradition, Poggio interrogated and scrutinized the remaining site of Rome with references to written sources and epigraphic evidence.[10] He regarded the material sites as objects of genuine empirical inquiry from which knowledge about the past could be extracted. This was supplemented by cross-references to the manuscripts of Lucretius, Quintilian, Vitruvius, Manilius, and Valerius Flaccus that he discovered in monastic libraries across Europe. These scattered texts, rescued from their obscurity, helped Poggio to decipher the silent markers of Rome's material remains. In turn, the inscriptions on the buildings helped Poggio determine the veracity of the texts he found.

2. As Corpse

Poggio recounts how he and his friend Antonio Loschi explored the deserted places of the city in their free time. Once, as they sit on the ruins of the Tar-

---

8. Giorgio Vasari, *Lives of the Painters, Sculptors, and Architects*, trans. Gaston du C. de Vere (New York: Modern Library, 1996), 1:36–37.

9. See Smith, *Architecture*; Alina Payne, *The Architectural Treatise in the Italian Renaissance* (Cambridge: Cambridge University Press, 1999).

10. Anthony Grafton, "The Ancient City Restored: Archaeology, Ecclesiastical History, and Egyptology," in *Rome Reborn: The Vatican Library and Renaissance Culture* (Washington, DC: Library of Congress; New Haven, CT: Yale University Press, 1993), 101. On the epigraphic studies that developed in this period, see in general Armando Petrucci, *Public Lettering: Script, Power, and Culture*, trans. Linda Lappin (Chicago: University of Chicago Press, 1993), 34–49; and in specific, William Stenhouse, *Reading Inscriptions and Writing Ancient History: Historical Scholarship in the Late Renaissance* (London: Institute of Classical Studies, 2005). See also Phyllis Walter Goodhart Gordon, trans. and ed., *Two Renaissance Book Hunters: The Letters of Poggius Bracciolini and Nicolaus de Niccolis* (New York: Columbia University Press, 1991).

peian Rock, Antonio quotes a verse from the *Aeneid*—"Aurea nunc, olim silvestribus horrida dumis" (8.348)—which he alters to "Aurea quondam, nunc squalida spinetis uepribusque referta." Absorbing the panorama of the city, they admire the greatness of Rome's past, deplore the wretched state of its present, and contemplate the evanescence of human affairs:

> What is most wonderful to tell and most sorrowful to see, is that the cruelty of fortune has to such an extent changed her aspect and beauty, that now deprived of all her glory, she lies prostrate like a gigantic putrescent corpse, eaten away on all sides: it is truly deplorable that this city which at one time teemed with illustrious men and leaders, was nurse to so many generals of war, so many excellent princes, and mother to so many and so great virtues, progenitor once to the ruler of the world, should now, through the iniquity of fortune which overthrows all things, be not only spoliated of her sovereignty and majesty, but condemned to vile servitude, disfigured, dishonored, so that only by ruin she reveals her past dignity and magnitude.[11]

The tone of this passage is similar to that of many other authors, from Petrarch to Castiglione to Montaigne. Stressing the gulf between Rome at her greatest when she was the progenitor of all values and her present state as *gigantei cadaveris corrupti*, its plangent emotion is evoked through a series of contrasting adjectives: *mirabile, acerbum, deflendum* serve to magnify the crumbling ancient buildings that disfigure Rome's present. The flow of Fortune is indicated in the present tense: "kingdoms are changed, empires succeed each other, nations crumble." By inventing the gigantic proportions of Rome, Poggio expresses the inseparability of its greatness and decadence.

Indeed, early modern cartographers and anatomists often made the analogy between the human body and geographical space. A clear conflation of anatomy and topography is shown in a woodcut by the Parisian professor of medicine Charles Estienne. His 1545 anatomical treatise *De dissectione partium corporis humani* contains an illustration in which a corpse is resting against a

---

11. "Quo magis dictu mirabile est & acerbum aspectu, adeo speciem formamque ipsius immutasse fortunae crudelitatem, ut nunc omni decore nudata prostrata jaceat instar gigantei cadaveris corrupti, atque undique exesi: deflendum quippe est hanc urbem tot quondam illustrium virorum atque imperatorum foetam, tot belli ducum, tot principum excellentissimorum altricem, tot tantarumque virtutum parentem, tot bonarum atrium procreatricem, ex qua rei militaris disciplina, morum sanctimonia & vitae, sanctiones legum, virtutum omnium exempla & bene vivendi ratio defluxerunt, quondam rerum dominam, nunc per fortunae monia vertentis iniquitatem, non solum imperio majestateque sua spoliatam, sed addictam vilissimae servituti, deformem, abjectam, sola ruina praeteritam, dignitatem ac magnitudinem ostentantem, Historiae de varietate fortunae" (Poggio Bracciolini, *Opera omnia* [Turin: Bottega d'Erasmo, 1966], 2:6–7).

ruined building, holding its chest open with the intent to instruct the viewer about the mechanism of the human body, in the same manner that ruined classical edifices provided architects with the skeletons and principles of construction (figure 10.2). This conflation of the dissection of the human body and the description of Rome makes us see the analogy between the discovery of the interior body now made exterior. Through the discourses of the humanists, the antiquity of Rome could now be seen "inside out," since in ruins the distinction between interior and exterior space collapses. As dissection—making parts out of a whole—gave early modern physicians a new account of the human body, gazing on ruins—seeing the parts from the whole—similarly gave early modern humanists a new account of the constitution of Rome. Artists and writers present Rome as the "body emblazoned,"[12] which is to say that there is a "blazon" of the historical body of a city, one that is embellished through art and poetry, hacked into pieces, so that the fragments of its historical decline are displayed as trophies.

Andrea Mantegna fuses the suffering of the human body with the collapse of pagan antiquity in his depictions of St. Sebastian (figure 10.3).[13] Mantegna's figure of the martyr parodies the Vitruvian man: for if the Roman architect described the human figure as the source of proportion in the classical orders of architecture, the Italian artist portrays the figure of a man that is literally bound by the elegant rectitude of the column. Mantegna draws from the legend of St. Sebastian in which the Emperor Diocletian commanded archers to shoot at the saint until he was as full of arrows as a hedgehog.[14] Yet his body, though punctured and writhing, remains whole. At his feet lie the fragments of classical sculptures, symbolizing the shattering of the pagan ideal forms, and the partial arch to which he is attached is disintegrating, symbolizing the collapse of Diocletian's empire. Mantegna treats the human body as a site of invincible ruination.

As I will argue later, Nativity scenes present the fullness of ruins as the expectant space that opens Christ's mission on earth. In Vittore Carpaccio's death scenes of Christ, ruins represent the evacuation of the divine, the aftermath when God fled the earth. In *The Meditation on the Passion* of 1510 (figure 10.4), the slouched sleeping Christ, seated on a crumbling throne, is flanked on his right by a gaunt, snowy-bearded St. Jerome and on his left by a leathery-skinned Job, a reversal of medieval images of the triumphant Christ enthroned

---

12. See Jonathan Sawday, *The Body Emblazoned: Dissection and the Human Body in Renaissance Culture* (London: Routledge, 1995).

13. See Jack M. Greenstein, *Temporality in Mantegna and Painting as Historical Narrative* (Chicago: University of Chicago Press, 1992), 71–86.

14. See Jacobus de Voragine, "Life of St. Sebastian," in *The Golden Legend: Readings on the Saints*, trans. William Granger Ryan (Princeton, NJ: Princeton University Press, 1995), 1:97–100.

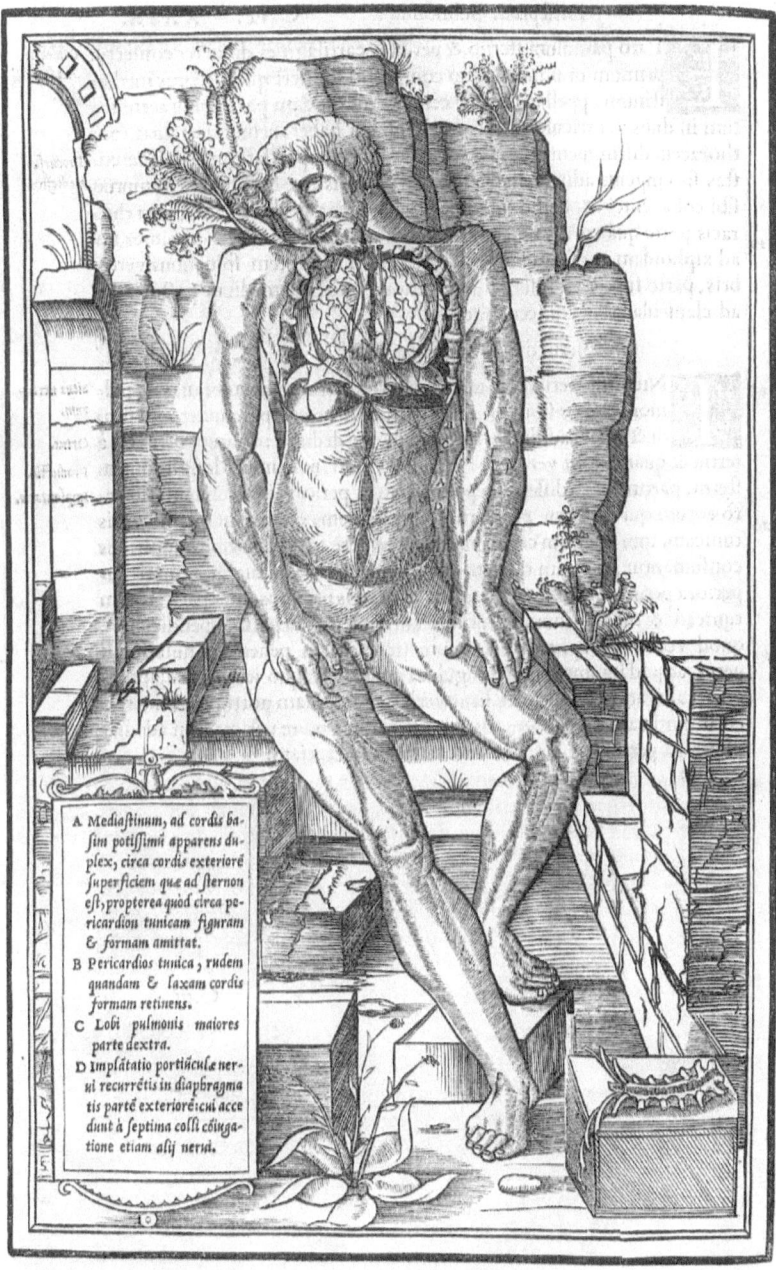

FIGURE 10.2. Woodcut from Charles Estienne, *De dissectione partium corporis humani*, 1545. US National Library of Medicine, Historical Anatomies on the Web, https://www.nlm.nih.gov/exhibition/historicalanatomies/estienne_home.html, accessed June 2, 2020.

FIGURE 10.3. Andrea Mantegna, *Martyrdom of St. Sebastian*, 1480, Louvre Museum, Paris. © bpk / RMN—Grand Palais / René-Gabriel Ojéda.

FIGURE 10.4. Vittore Carpaccio, *Meditation on the Passion*, 1510, Metropolitan Museum of Art, New York

in Heaven supported by his angelic hosts. In the background are two dramatically different scenes: on Jerome's side, beasts prowl treacherously on desolate high rocks. On the side of Job are pastoral rolling hills, delicate trees, a glassy flow of water, gentle deer, and a scarlet cardinal.

Carpaccio's 1520 *The Dead Christ* (figure 10.5) also contains a dualistic scene. In the larger part of the painting, the vegetation is desolate and the ambience a sickly jaundiced yellow. The dusty ground is littered with orphaned pediments, broken epitaphs, and bits of mummified bodies. Skulls lie underneath the head of Christ, tomb raiders hover like vultures by his tomb, Mother Mary and Mary Magdalene are forlorn, and a shriveled St. John rests against a withered tree. Yet there is a hint of bounteous life on the top left quadrant, as leaves flourish on the half of the tree on which the apostle leans, the emerald sea shimmers with dots of ships, and farmers harvest grain on yellow fields, arranging the sheaves in nicely organized stacks. Such vision of regeneration is part of the discourse on the salvific plan of Christ: in his death there is life; in ruins there is rebirth.

FIGURE 10.5. Vittore Carpaccio, *The Dead Christ*, 1520, Gemäldegalerie, Berlin. © bpk / Gemäldegalerie, SMB / Jörg P. Anders.

3. As the Converse of Utopia

In the anonymous painting *The Ideal City* (ca. 1480–84), now in the Walters Art Museum (Baltimore) and sometimes attributed to Fra Carnevale, there are no humans at all. The cityscape exemplifies the Renaissance ideal of urban planning in its most refined geometric purity (figure 10.6).[15] Visually, the work is first and foremost an exemplary exercise in single-point perspective. Philosophically, the work is a visual treatise on the art of utopia: the models of palazzo, the coliseum, triumphal arch, and baptistery correspond to the ideal paradigms of private residences, civic, military, and religious spaces. The aesthetic effect is one of an almost serene immobility, a pure equipoise between space and place, all in accordance with a set of rational principles. In the philosophy of humanism, utopian thinking aspired to an orderly, harmonious

---

15. See Hubert Damisch's poststructuralist reading in *The Origin of Perspective*, trans. John Goodman (Cambridge, MA: MIT Press, 1994).

FIGURE 10.6. Unknown, *Ideal City*, ca. 1480–84, Walters Art Museum, Baltimore. © The Walters Art Museum.

world based on the classical rules of antiquity. It depicts an ideal society in which humans, endowed with unlimited capacities and soaring intelligence, have the possibility of perfecting themselves. Ruins, as emblems of civil disorder, are then something to be conquered.

4. As Old Testament Dystopia

Consider the opposite case—ruins as dystopia. Botticelli's *The Punishment of Korah* (ca. 1480, figure 10.7), like the *Ideal City*, also contains the central features of civic architecture—the Arch of Constantine is flanked by a generic medieval edifice and the Septizonium (destroyed, incidentally, a century later in 1588 by Sixtus V)—but here they are all tattered. The painting throbs with turmoil. Depicting the rebellion of the Hebrew people in the desert and their subsequent punishment (Numbers 16:1–40), Botticelli foregrounds the writhing human subjects. Here, the architecture is a material reflection of the upheaval that is engulfing the Old Testament people: the broken columns of the Septizonium resemble spiny trees, and the *opus quadratum* on the Arch is precariously placed on top of the entablature without mortar. A wayward brick in the center is inclined at the same angle as the man that Moses is striking. And the mural's position in the south wall of the Sistine Chapel makes clear in no uncertain terms the fates of those who would disobey the pope.

5. As Protestant/Catholic Typology

Even more ghastly is Antoine Caron's *Massacres of the Triumvirate* (1566, figure 10.8). Like the *The Punishment of Korah* and the Baltimore panel, the com-

FIGURE 10.7. Sandro Botticelli, *The Punishment of Korah*, ca. 1480, Sistine Chapel, Vatican. © bpk / Scala.

FIGURE 10.8. Antoine Caron, *Massacres of the Triumvirate*, 1566, Louvre Museum, Paris. © bpk / RMN—Grand Palais / Gérard Blot.

position is perfectly symmetrical, centered on a cross-section of the Coliseum and the Pantheon behind it. But whereas Botticelli references the authority of Moses and the Popes, Caron surreally depicts the massacres wrought by the triumvirs Mark Antony, Octavius, and Lepidus in 43 BCE. Caron's historical choice of subject is a code to a more recent event: the murders of Protestants in 1561 by the Catholic "triumvirate" of the Constable of Montmorency, Jacques d'Albon de Saint-André, and the Duc de Guise. Caron had never been to Rome, his models were from Lafréry's prints. And though the architecture is not strictly speaking in ruins, the people are. Caron paints a veritable theater of slaughter: a row of decapitated heads line the elevated stage in the foreground; the vermilion sky resembles the blood-stained ground; exquisitely detailed tourist attractions hover in the backdrop; a multitude of costumed soldiers hack women and old men into pieces. Civic tumult, dissension, and sedition occur in the full light of synchronic monuments: the Arch of Constantine, Michelangelo's Capitoline Square, the equestrian statue of Marcus Aurelius, the triumphal arch of Septimius Severus, Trajan's Column, the statues of Hercules and the Apollo Belvedere. The distant Roman civil war, the recent wars of religion, and the Roman "postcard" sites all contribute to the fantasy of a transhistorical impulse of violence.

As such, Caron's painting is representative of a genre of history that makes a correspondence between pagan and ecclesiastical history: the religious wars between two sects of Christianity mapped onto Roman civil war. Through the architecture of types, they lucidly capture the tension of civil humanism: on the one hand, a society that is noetic, rational, balanced; on the other, the roiling discord of politics.

6. As Messianic Birth

In the second half of the fifteenth century, pictorial representations of the birth of Christ began to change: ruins started to appear in the background.[16] In the *Nativity* of Francesco di Giorgio Martini (Siena, San Domenico, 1490s), the humbling of antiquity and its redemption are again expressed through the image of a ruin (figure 10.9). The wooden manger has disappeared; an enormous arch of triumph, resembling a pristine Arch of Constantine, now serves as a shelter for the Christ child. The clean, unblemished coloration of the façade could be a reference to Jesus's denunciation of deceiving appear-

---

16. For a more elaborated discussion and bibliography, see my "The Birth of Ruins in Quattrocento Adoration Paintings," *I Tatti Studies in the Italian Renaissance* 18, no. 2 (2015): 319–48.

FIGURE 10.9. Francesco di Giorgio Martini, *Nativity*, 1490s, San Domenico, Siena. © bpk / Scala.

ances: "Woe to you, scribes and Pharisees, hypocrites! For you are like whitewashed tombs, which on the outside look beautiful, but inside they are full of the bones of the dead and of all kinds of filth" (Matthew 23:27).

The integration of the classical ruin into late-quattrocento Nativity and Adoration paintings is a symbolic gesture imbued with theological meaning and historical self-awareness. The appearance of the ruin at the birth scene of the Messiah not only underscores broken architecture's potent force in the realm of Christian imagination but also stands as a testament to the ruin's evocative powers as a sign of an ancient achievement that had been, as the Renaissance humanists saw it, ignored until their own epoch.

By claiming to be rescuing classical architecture from its supposed medieval oblivion, the Renaissance artists signaled that the ruin had both evocative and epistemological value—it signaled their interest for antiquity as well as the belief that these broken buildings could be object lessons to be studied and emulated. Yet by rendering them in ruins, the artists indicated their ultimate mastery and absorption of antiquity into their own discursive program. The ruin thus became double-faced—it marked not only the triumph of Christianity, something that the medieval worldview had always held (and has been repeated in the received art-historical scholarship), but suggested a more humanist, nostalgic attitude that recognized what had been lost. Renaissance artists conflated the birth and life of the Christ story with the period's own conception of itself as one of rebirth.

By depicting ancient temples in ruins, Christian interpreters gathered the broken remnants of the past into an intelligible structure. But the move of depicting classical culture in fragments paradoxically also means that one reanimates and monumentalizes them. Moreover, Renaissance artists seem to suggest that it was only their unique knowledge of antiquity that made it possible for them to recognize ruins *as* ruins. In this system of visual allegory, the birthplace of Christ became the imagined birthplace of classical ruins.

7. As the Unfinished

Since a ruin and an unfinished work inhabit the opposite ends of the spectrum, we can use this ambiguous perspective to meditate on the process of the work of art. Consider Leonardo's early abandoned *Adoration of the Magi* and its preparatory sketch (both 1481, figures 10.10 and 10.11). From the perspective study to the unfinished painting, the double staircase in perfect linear perspective is the constant visual anchor. The painting as a whole impresses us

FIGURE 10.10. Leonardo, *Adoration of the Magi*, unfinished, 1481. © bpk / Scala—courtesy of the Ministero per i Beni e le Attività Culturali e per il Turismo.

FIGURE 10.11. Leonardo, sketch for *Adoration of the Magi*, unfinished, 1481. © bpk / Scala—courtesy of the Ministero per i Beni e le Attività Culturali e per il Turismo.

not only in the precise clarity of its metrics but also in how it is suffused with the haze of evocation through the techniques of *sfumato* and *chiaroscuro*.[17]

Recently, Francesca Fiorani raised the question of why Leonardo left the painting incomplete. The painting was commissioned in Florence by the Augustinian friars, but Leonardo departed to Milan before finishing it.[18] Her answer is that the painter's idea was greater than his skill to execute it:

> He realized that his grand plan to have kings and shepherds side by side was brilliant, as was the idea to make the miraculous light of the Biblical story the protagonist of his painting. Not only this: He had even come up with the idea that the light of the divine manifestation at the climax of the event would coincide with the physical light of the entire painted scene. But as brilliant as the scheme was, it was also too complex to pull it off with the sophistication and scientific rigor that he demanded from himself.[19]

Thus, the painting is unfinished, a failure not of the imagination but of execution. Fiorani's explanation, then, rests on the incommensurability between *noesis* and *techne*—the central *agon* from antiquity to the Renaissance, between the ideal and the real. In many ways her suggestion is itself brilliant. But I wish to offer a more theological explanation, even if it might have been beyond the intention of the artist himself.

There are two states of incompletion in Leonardo's *Adoration*: the painting itself, and the architectural background in the painting. In the preparatory drawing, there is no ruin yet. But in the painting, the arches are unmistakably ruined, its top a gaping hole. The very nature of the architecture in the background is deeply ambiguous: are they ruins or are they merely incomplete? To put it differently: the painting displays objects that are obviously meant to be ruined and others that resemble ruins in their lack of completeness, but that may simply be incomplete as representations and would almost certainly have been completed had Leonardo not abandoned this project.

---

17. For a discussion of this technique, see John Shearman, "Leonardo's Colour and Chiaroscuro," in *Sixteenth-Century Italian Art*, ed. Michael W. Cole (Oxford: Blackwell, 2006), 408–40, originally published in *Zeitschrift für Kunstgeschichte* 25, no. 1 (1962): 13–47. See E. H. Gombrich, "Leonardo's Method for Working Out Compositions," in *The Essential Gombrich*, ed. Richard Woodfield (London: Phaidon Press, 1996), 211–21, for the ways in which the artist incorporated the role of chance and accident in his method.

18. See the bibliography in Frank Zöllner, *Leonardo da Vinci: The Complete Paintings and Drawings* (Cologne: Taschen, 2003), 1:50–60.

19. Francesca Fiorani, "Why Did Leonardo Not Finish the Adoration of the Magi?," in *Illuminating Leonardo: A Festschrift for Carlo Pedretti Celebrating His 70 Years of Scholarship (1944–2014)*, ed. Constance Moffatt and Sara Taglialagamba (Leiden: Brill, 2016), 128.

My interpretation is that Leonardo's architecture is allegorical: it is about the entire project of Christianity. In art history, the term *pentimento* means "a sign or trace of an alteration in a literary or artistic work; a visible trace of a mistake or an earlier composition seen through later layers of paint on a canvas" (*OED*). The word is from the Italian *pentirsi*, "to repent." I want to suggest that *pentimento* in the *Adoration* is both aesthetic and theological, especially in this sacred scene that depicts Christ's entrance into the world. What I mean is that the painting's unfinished state, bearing the traces of the creator's experiments and trials, is a manifestation of his *metanoia* [(Gr.) "conversion"], literally his "change of mind."

It is as if once the work exits the atemporal world of the perspective, materials start disintegrating. In Christian allegory, what was shadowy in the Old Testament (*umbra*), and became an image (*imago*) in the New, will be completed in the future, in truth (*veritas*), upon Christ's return.[20] Likewise, the preparatory drawing and the painting with the shadows and smokes of the saints' faces also have a typological relationship: one is supposed to fulfill what was inchoate and latent in the other. At the scene of his birth, the full presence of Christ resolves the absence of the classical ruins. At the scene of its representation, the ruin's present absence in the viewer's spiritual imagination guides the viewer toward an interpretation, a movement of the soul to fill the absence of Christ with the presence of the artwork.[21]

Like Michelangelo's late *Slaves*, the aesthetic power in Leonardo's *Adoration* is in its very state of the *non finito*. Its pathos is precisely in what it is *not*; in Pliny's sense, "unfinished paintings are more admired than the finished because the artist's thoughts are left visible."[22] And to furnish a scriptural dimension: Paul, a contemporary of Pliny, writes in the First Letter to the Corinthians, "For we know only in part, and we prophesy only in part; but when the complete comes, the partial will come to an end" (13:9). As a partial record of the artist's procedure, full of aesthetic contrition, Leonardo's exercise allows us to trace the visual thinking that comes before full knowing. The unfinished ruin's empty space creates an opening, an aperture, toward the hermeneutic creation of commemorating the birth of Christ in the fullness of the here and now.

---

20. See Henri de Lubac, *Medieval Exegesis: The Four Senses of Scripture*, trans. Mark Sebanc (Grand Rapids, MI: Wm. B. Eerdmans, 1996), 1:225–67.

21. Cf. Matt. 5:16, "non veni solvere sed adimplete" [I am not come to abolish but to fulfill].

22. Pliny, *Natural History* 35.145, trans. H. Rackham (Cambridge, MA: Harvard University Press, 1968), 367. Translation modified.

8. As Fantastic Nocturne

The little-known François de Nomé (pseudonym Monsù Desiderio, ca. 1593–1623), a French artist working in Naples, anticipating the dark imaginings of Piranesi, painted hundreds of ashen, postapocalyptic nocturnal scenes with delicate toppled structures in Greco-esque tonality. Instead of following the tradition of the *veduta,* realistic representations of the country or the city, his works are more like *capricci,* imaginative scenes that are fictive or fantastic. In his 1623 *Ruins with Augustine and the Child* (figure 10.12), the fallen Gothic architecture appears menacing, fragments of statues strewn, and a half-entombed ship wrecked on the dry ground. Instead of the calm and serenity of a Lorrain or Poussin ruin, there is a mood of devastation underneath the black sky. In the foreground, de Nomé represents the vision of St. Augustine seeing a child trying to empty the sea into a hole dug in the sand; when Augustine told him that this was impossible, the child replied that Augustine was engaged in the equally impossible task of explaining the Trinity.

9. As Catastrophic Play

Rose Macaulay writes that love of ruins is "part of the general *Weltschmerz, Sehnsucht,* malaise, nostalgia, angst, frustration, sickness, passion of the human soul," which representations of ruins also invoke. Indeed, other artists display ruins in scenes that are even more playful, pleasurable, and domestic, in tune with Serlio's categories of the comic and pastoral.[23] The most ludic of all ruins, of course, is the artificial ruin, a structure designed purely for the gratification of the present. Through the mastery of illusion, artists command brute mass to obey the force of their ludic will. The first documented artificial ruin occurs sometime in the 1530s, when Girolamo Genga constructed a hermitage in the garden of the Duke of Urbino's villa in Pesaro, which Vasari reported to be "molto bella." Certainly one of the most virtuosic is Giulio Romano's *Sala dei giganti* at the Palazzo del Te in Mantua (1524–34). Depicting the mythical Fall of Giants, Romano combines multiple visual elements—the giants' grotesque physiognomy and contorted expressions, the billowing clouds and smoke, the bellowing horns of the wind gods, the toppled columns and a cluster of painted bricks that resemble real ones on the top of the entrance, a working fireplace—to create an illusion of imminent collapse (figure 10.13). Vasari admired the room enormously, praising it at great length:

---

23. Rose Macaulay, *The Pleasure of Ruins* (London: Thames and Hudson, 1953), 23.

FIGURE 10.12. François de Nomé, *Ruins with Augustine and the Child*, 1623, National Gallery, London. © The National Gallery, London. Presented by Sir Philip Sassoon Bt, GBE, through the Art Fund, 1923.

FIGURE 10.13. Giulio Romano, fresco on the north wall of the *Sala dei giganti*, Palazzo del Te, Mantua (1524–34, detail). © bpk | Scala.

No more terrible work of the brush exists, and anyone entering the room and seeing the windows, doors and other things so twisted that they appear about to fall, and the tumbling mountains and ruins, will fear that all is about to come about his ears, especially as he sees the gods fleeing hither and thither. A marvelous feature is that the painting has neither beginning nor end, and is not interrupted in any way.[24]

Modern scholars have observed that the room also functions as a whispering gallery, in which the slightest noise ricochets off the walls.[25] Even the floor (laid later) has a disorienting effect: the center of the design is a wheel that radiates concentric circles of triangular petals, like a vortex. Romano's conception anticipates the baroque's fascination with folly houses and pleasure gardens.[26] The booming acoustics, the fractured whirling floor, the fireplace all conspire together with the stunning visuals to make this horror chamber a delightful scene of cosmic catastrophe.

In the drawings of Jean Cousin (1540–70), the immense ruins become a children's playground of frivolity.[27] Cute putti—one of them peeing, a couple horsing around on piggybacks—frolic amongst a delicately ornamented Trajan's column and folly-garden arcades (figure 10.14). Whether in combination with giants or cherubs, Romano and Cousin show ruins in their comic mode by the virtue of their extreme proportions. Artificial ruins thus ironized the sublimity and terror of ancient ones: lacking any dignity of their own, they possessed a thematic and stylistic flexibility that embodies their extravagant age.

German artists were not so much interested in the historical dimension of ruins than their odd, tortured appearances, manifesting themselves in what James Elkins calls "an almost obsessive *intarsia* mania."[28] Lorenz Stoer's *Geo-*

---

24. "Onde non si pensi alcuno vedere mai opera di pennello più orribile e spaventosa, nè più naturale di questa; e chi entra in quella stanza, vedendo le finestre, le porte, ed altre così fatte cose torcersi, e quasi per rovinare, ed i monti e gli edifizi cadere, non può non temere che ogni cosa non gli rovini addosso, vedendo massimamente in quel cielo tutti gli Dei andare chi qua e chi là fuggendo: e quello che è in questa opera maraviglioso, è il veder tutta quella pittura non avere principio nè fine, ed attaccata tutta e tanto bene continuata insieme, senza termine o tramezzo di ornamento" (Gaetano Milanesi, ed., *Le opere di Giorgio Vasari* [Florence: Sansoni, 1906], 5:543, in English, Giorgio Vasari, *The Lives of the Painters, Sculptors, and Architects*, trans. A. B. Hings [London: Dent, 1963], 3:106).

25. Frederick Hartt, *Giulio Romano* (New Haven, CT: Yale University Press, 1958), 1:154–55. See also Barbara Furlotti and Guido Rebecchini, *The Art of Mantua: Power and Patronage in the Renaissance*, trans. A. Lawrence Jenkens (Los Angeles: Getty, 2008).

26. See George Mott and Sally Sample Aall, *Follies and Pleasure Pavilions* (New York: H. M. Abrams, 1989).

27. See Margaret M. McGowan's analysis in *The Vision of Rome in Late Renaissance France* (New Haven, CT: Yale University Press, 2000), 151.

28. See James Elkins, *The Poetics of Perspective* (Ithaca, NY: Cornell University Press, 1994), 159–66.

FIGURE 10.14. Jean Cousin, *Enfants nus jouant dans des ruines*, Louvre Museum, Paris. © bpk / RMN—

Grand Palais / Jean-Gilles Berizzi.

FIGURE 10.15. Lorenz Stoer, *Geometria et perspectiva*, 1567. © Universitätsbibliothek Salzburg, Grafiksammlung, G 363 II/9.

metria et perspectiva (1567) juxtaposes ruins with polyhedral solids, depicting the oddly curved scrolls (called *Rollkörper*) formed by half-destroyed columns and arcades within abandoned courtyards and overgrown gardens (figure 10.15).[29] Ruins here finally become mere ornament, another element amongst the assorted spiky globes, dissected spheres, and labyrinthine configurations.

---

29. See Christopher S. Wood, "The Perspective Treatise in Ruins: Lorenz Stoer, *Geometria et perspectiva*, 1567," in *The Treatise in Perspective: Published and Unpublished*, ed. Lyle Massey (Washington, DC: National Gallery of Art, 2003), 235–57.

Completely evacuated from the ambience of Rome, the ruins are reduced to another mathematical puzzle.

10. As the Sublime

Georg Simmel in his brief but elegant essay, "The Ruin," writes that "architecture is the only art in which the great struggle between the will of the spirit and the necessity of nature issues into real peace, in which the soul in its upward striving and nature in its gravity are held in balance."[30] For Simmel, the ruin becomes a "cosmic tragedy," in which "the balance between nature and spirit, which the building manifested, shifts in favor of nature . . . the decay appears as nature's revenge for the spirit's having violated it by making a form in its own image."[31] What remains is suspended between the "downward" thrust of *Natur* and the "upward" thrust of *Geist*.

In the landscapes of Nicolas Poussin, the ruin has perfectly merged with nature. His *Landscape with St. John of Patmos* (1640, figure 10.16) takes the familiar trope of a figure composing in a field of ruins. Whereas in other paintings the figure is inspired to compose because of the ruins, St. John seems to be composing *in spite* of them. Nature is elevated to an ideal state as the elements of rocks and trees mingle with rounded Doric columns and rough-hewn stones. In the Revelation, St. John prophesied the fall of empires and the conflagration of cities in the end of days; in Poussin's interpretation, he appears as if the cataclysmic violence of the eschaton has already happened. Surviving the aftermath, he writes on the day after tomorrow in a classical landscape of lush trees and clear skies.

Poussin's career, according to Louis Marin, plots the generic shift from the painting of history—recording the former existence of one who had lived in Arcadia—to that of allegorical fable—mythologizing the past in the present and in future experience.[32] The layer-by-layer and plane-by-plane composition of his late works is an exercise in luminous depth. As Nicolas Boileau defines it, "The sublime is that indefinable element [*je ne sais quoi*] that charms and delights us, without which Beauty would have neither grace nor beauty."[33] Poussin summons the sublime by way of the pathos of the ruin, for the ruin is precisely the *je ne sais quoi* of materiality. Marin explains that the sublime

---

30. Georg Simmel, "The Ruin," in *Essays on Sociology, Philosophy, and Aesthetics*, ed. Kurt H. Wolff (New York: Harper and Row, 1965), 259.

31. Simmel, "Ruin," 259.

32. Louis Marin, *Sublime Poussin*, trans. Catherine Porter (Stanford, CA: Stanford University Press, 1999), 143.

33. Marin, *Sublime Poussin*, 120.

FIGURE 10.16. Nicolas Poussin, *Landscape with St. John of Patmos*, 1640, Art Institute of Chicago

is "added to beauty as a supplement, a surplus, a plenitude enriching a plenitude, but it compensates (*supplée*), it names that without which beauty would not be beautiful."[34] The sublime fills (*comblé*) the void. But paradoxically, the ruin is precisely both the void and the filling of the void. Thus both ruins and the sublime grasp at the inexplicable and the indefinite.

11. As Perspective

Once you start looking for ruins in the Renaissance, they appear everywhere. The eleven ways of looking at ruins are, of course, not exhaustive. There are many more examples we can discuss. And after the Renaissance, the aesthetics of ruins continues undiminished, and even accelerates. Consider only the works of Piranesi, Pannini, Canaletto, Hubert Robert, and Caspar David Friedrich, amongst others. At the end of this essay, we might feel overwhelmed

---

34. Nicolas Boileau's translation of Longinus, *Traité du Sublime* (1674), cited in Nicholas Cronk, *The Classical Sublime: French Neoclassicism and the Languages of Literature*, EMF Critiques (Charlottesville, VA: Rockwood Press, 2002), 78.

FIGURE 10.17. Henri Fuseli, *The Artist Moved by the Grandeur of Antique Fragments,* ca. 1778, Kunsthaus Zürich. © Kunsthaus Zürich, Department of Prints and Drawings, 1940.

and exhausted by such a ubiquitous phenomenon, like Henri Fuseli's *The Artist Moved by the Grandeur of Antique Fragments* (ca. 1778, figure 10.17).[35] But perhaps what unites this proliferation of images and gives us a measure of hope is that they are represented by means of *the* great artistic innovation of the period—perspective.

The rise of perspective is concomitant with the invention of the ruin—they both afford us new ways of seeing. Vision, of course, is historically constructed—what we see depends on what we want to see, in accordance with our mood, ideology, or epistemology.[36] And it is not for nothing that so many

---

35. See the readings of Leonard Barkan in *Unearthing the Past,* and Linda Nochlin in *The Body in Pieces: The Fragment as a Metaphor of Modernity* (London: Thames and Hudson, 2001).
36. Work on early modern perspective is enormous. Besides Erwin Panofsky's *Perspective as Symbolic Form* ([1927], trans. Christopher S. Wood [New York: Zone Books, 1991]), see Samuel Y. Edgerton, *The Renaissance Rediscovery of Linear Perspective* (New York: Icon, 1975); John White, *The Birth and Rebirth of Pictorial Space* (Cambridge, MA: Harvard University Press, 1987); Elkins, *Poetics of Perspective*; Damisch, *Origin of Perspective.*

impressions of Rome carry the title *vedute*; others are *prospectiva*. Like the technique of perspective, ruins provide the rules, measurements, and bases for viewing, furnishing the illusion of depth and space. Perspective, after all, is literally invisible without the presence of physical objects.

The absence of perspective in the Middle Ages, as Erwin Panofsky argued in his highly influential and characteristically teleological *Perspective as Symbolic Form*, was not due to any technical ignorance, but to the artist's attempt to paint from "God's eye"—objective, omniscient, and omnipresent.[37] A more nuanced view of the rise of perspective, describing the origins of perspective in the medieval reception of Arab science, has recently been put forward by Hans Belting.[38]

Starting in the fifteenth century, understanding and sight became increasingly contingent upon the individual as marked by the relative distance between the viewer and the object, a "point of view." In 1537, Sebastiano Serlio in *I sette libri dell'architettura* pronounced that "perspective would be nothing without architecture and the architect nothing without perspective."[39] That said, Renaissance architecture would be nothing without the study of ruins, and the study of ruins would be nothing without Renaissance architecture. After all, in Serlio's *Sette libri*, the study of antiquities in Book III follows the study of perspective in Book II.

The monument as a ruin and the ruin as monument are proleptic and analeptic—the loci in which memory, retrieval, reconstruction, return, repetition, and reimagining occur. It is the retaken to the nth degree. But ruins are not representation in the mimetic sense of a different object substituting for another. It is the thing itself standing in place of its former self. Nor does the ruin seem to be a simulacrum either, in the way semiotics talks about a copy of a copy, which has been so dissipated in its relation to the original that it can no longer be a copy, because the ruin is the non-mimetic itself.

In this sense, the ruin *is* Alberti's open window—not so much into the landscape of nature, but into the memory palace of history. As such, it is both a metaphor and a rule.[40] Renaissance perspective operated with the theorem that one paints not just an object, but one's mental image of it. Indeed, when we look at a ruin, not only do we see what is in front of our eyes, it also activates the storehouse of texts and images within our minds. But unlike

---

37. Panofsky, *Perspective*.

38. Hans Belting, *Florence and Baghdad: Renaissance Art and Arab Science*, trans. Deborah Lucas Schneider (Cambridge, MA: Belknap Press of Harvard University Press, 2011).

39. Sebastiano Serlio, *Sebastiano Serlio on Architecture*, trans. Vaughan Hart and Peter Hicks (New Haven, CT: Yale University Press, 1996), 37.

40. See Elkins, *Poetics of Perspective*, especially 1–45.

perspective, the ruin attends to nonquantifiable features of the human experience that cannot be captured by mathematics: chaos, historicity, ambiguity, and subjectivity. "With perspectives it would be impossible—or at least exceedingly difficult—to resolve things to their original form," Raphael and Castiglione write at the end of their famous letter to Leo X.[41] If perspective is a mastery of space outside of time, then the art of the ruin is the mastery of materiality within time. And if the vanishing point creates a self-enclosed abstract world, ruins puncture this space and bring it back into the embodied world. Ultimately residing at the convergence of materiality and temporality, the ruin vanishes and appears at once and for all time.

---

41. "The Letter to Leo X by Raphael and Baldassare Castiglione (c. 1519)," in *Palladio's Rome: A Translation of Andrea Palladio's Two Guidebooks to Rome*, trans. and ed. Vaughan Hart and Peter Hicks (New Haven, CT: Yale University Press, 2006), 191.

CHAPTER 11

But men seyn, "What may ever laste?"

Chaucer's House of Fame as a Medieval Museum

JOHN HINES

A welcome development in literary studies of the last decade or so has been the emergence of a serious and extensive engagement not only with the history but also with the archaeological materiality of the past in relation to literature—the "past" comprising not only the contexts from which works of literature are originally derived but also the multitudinous pasts through which they have been transmitted. There is, however, still a great deal to be explored and discussed in terms both of what we can and what we should try to do under the aegis of "Literature and Archaeology," and, consequently, how we may go about that. It is precisely in that light that I offer a contribution to this volume, which involves some questioning and even problematizing of key ideas implicit in its theme, yet still makes a constructive reading of one of the most enigmatic poems of the master of Middle English writing, Geoffrey Chaucer.

Engagement with the material past was necessarily a feature of medieval English literature, just as it was of the cultural life of medieval Britain and Europe generally. Indeed, engagement with the material past can be counted practically a cultural universal: no human population can escape a material heritage in the context of which it lives any more than its members can live entirely immaterial lives. How salient a society's interaction with the material past is in its cultural life, and how that interaction takes shape: those are phenomena that can vary hugely, and so are themselves culturally specific.

Each and every period of human history is therefore characterized in some measure by its relationship with its own past, historically (i.e., textually and discursively) recorded and remembered, and materially (i.e., archaeologically) curated and still present.

This also means that, in practice, Archaeology itself—meaning the curation, interpretation, and active use of material remains—is a near-constant feature of the activities of the peoples, places, and cultures archaeologists study archaeologically, however remote in time. The guise of an academic and scientific discipline is Archaeology's contemporary, culturally specific form. We can further postulate that the later Middle Ages in Western Europe was a phase in which a fundamental change in the cognitive status of the material world occurred that proved essential to the transition from the medieval world to the early modern. This transformation necessarily enveloped and constrained the relationship with the material past in a way that could provide fertile opportunities for creative artistic exploration across this period of change while it was taking place.

The hypothesis thus ambitiously proposed is something akin to the famous "dissociation of sensibility" that T. S. Eliot argued could be discerned in seventeenth-century English literature, effectively between Donne and Herbert on the one hand, and Milton and Dryden on the other: a fundamental separation of thought and emotion.[1] One may indeed argue that that aspect of change in dominant habits of perception and understanding was historically secondary to a preceding "dissociation of realities." By that, I mean a growing and ultimately dominant sense of a fundamental division and opposition between an abstract universe of thought, spirit, truth, and not least The Word, and a material substrate of matter and physical properties to which The Flesh belongs. Both versions of dissociation in fact contrast the intellectual world of abstraction and rationality with a realm of experience based upon the senses and feelings; within what is suggested here to be the prior divergency, however, spirituality could continue to be highly emotional even if thought and ratiocination were ideally or supposedly becoming less so. To generalize very broadly, there had formerly been a distinctly medieval state of cognition that readily recognized an intrinsic meaningfulness of material objects and thus could deploy the elements of material culture discursively in essentially the same way as the resources of a natural language. It is not least through the texts of Lollard and subsequently Protestant reformers that we can see the growth of a revulsion from this position, which could appear

---

1. T. S. Eliot, *The Metaphysical Poets* (1921), reprinted in *Selected Essays*, 3rd ed. (London: Faber & Faber, 1951).

to place material artifacts idolatrously on a par with Scripture and Creed.[2] Enlightenment science was a subsequent elaboration of the literal "objectification" of the material world.

While this postulated historical transformation needs to be introduced in clear and direct terms, even when advocating it as a serious interpretative perspective it is simultaneously to be insisted that the historical relationship between the medieval and the modern in these terms could never possibly have been a matter of some absolute opposition and polar contrast between two cultural ages. Between, say, 1350 at one end and 1650 at the other, the material world and material objects did not lose meaning entirely—or, to use a word much beloved by archaeologists in recent years, they did not diminish in their own significant "agency." In brief, the direct agency of the material world can be understood as the power of material objects and circumstances to constrain or even stimulate specific aspects of human behavior, so that determinative agency does not lie solely with autonomous human subjects using material culture in a purely instrumental way. This way of looking at material culture has been derived from agency theories of economics and psychology, which explore how multiple and overarching interests and governing factors are operative within and can influence human transactions and interactions.[3] The intensity of mass production and marketing, rapid obsolescence and consumerism, and the consequent levels of waste and pollution of the contemporary world can be cited as an extreme example of an overwhelming context of material culture that may appear terrifyingly out of control. Between the High Middle Ages and the High Renaissance, however, what became the major problem was to recognize, to express, or to accept the semiotics of the material world. As images became a source of embarrassment or even hostility, emblemism, associating symbolic significations with natural and physico-chemical properties of objects and elements, grew in prominence.[4] Pictures could still teach or exhort, of course, but as the mate-

---

2. John Hines, *Voices in the Past: English Literature and Archaeology* (Cambridge: D. S. Brewer, 2004), 105–16.

3. The foundations of modern Agency Theory lay in the psychological experiments of Stanley Milgram, *Obedience to Authority: An Experimental View* (New York: Harper & Row, 1964). See also Marcia-Anne Dobres and John Ernest Robb, "Agency in Archaeology: Paradigm or Platitude?," in *Agency in Archaeology*, ed. Marcia-Anne Dobres and John Ernest Robb (London: Routledge, 2000), 12.

4. John Manning, *The Emblem* (London: Reaktion, 2002); Michael Bath, *Speaking Pictures: English Emblem Books and Renaissance Culture* (Harlow, UK: Longman, 1994). It is salient to note that modern emblem scholarship is focused particularly on baroque artistic elaborations of emblematic images and relations. There is room, indeed an urgent need, for a robust and thorough, archaeologically informed investigation of the emblematic interpretation and deployment of materials and everyday objects.

rial world came to be seen as, for the most part, an inert palimpsest, pious pictures, such as those used as woodcuts to illustrate Lutheran Bibles, could be reproduced anywhere—even, for instance, as stove tiles.

I put this interpretation forward first in *Voices in the Past: English Literature and Archaeology*, a book published in 2004. My particular objective in that study was not to explore Archaeology as a theme within medieval or more modern English literature but rather to explore and to demonstrate what I saw as the core critical benefits of reading literature in its material contexts. There are several facets of that relationship one might summarize, but it is not appropriate to talk about every one here. If there is one set of connected ideas I would seek to highlight before proceeding to my case study, it is that which starts with the demonstration that there can be a form of "material semantics" operating in literature. Structurally, this in fact has a great deal in common with the semantics of Saussurean or Chomskyan linguistics; yet, at the same time, it is diametrically opposed to their concept of language as a totally autonomous and hermetically self-sufficient system. From a different basis, but of related significance, comes the observation of how material circumstances can profoundly interact with texts as contexts of performance and reception; in this respect, elements of linguistic pragmatics and speech-act theory become very productive. What one can recognize as a consequence, when such perspectives are applied in tandem, is that "material historicism" as a mode of critical reading becomes most effective—or rather has most to do—when what the literature is really concerned with is literally *implicit* rather than *explicit*.[5] To put this succinctly, material allusions may have little to contribute to the interpretation of, for instance, a simple and direct work of hagiography or a sermon. The more directly and explicitly a text addresses its readers, the less it will need or wish to invoke recognizable and significant extrinsic references, material or otherwise. The valorization of physical and material relics in medieval culture, and the consequent multiplication of narratives involving relics, is in fact nothing other than a significant corollary of this position. In relation to the hagiography, such relics are external counterparts to a story that is already told, and in their actual form and of themselves they tell no story of their own. Their objective semantic value is thus null.

For our present purposes, an interesting corollary of this principle is that if, in medieval cognition, material objects could themselves be used discursively in a relatively direct manner, they may concurrently be deployed less in the implicit discourses of creative literature. This proves indeed to be the case to a significant degree in respect of later medieval, Middle English literature.

---

5. Hines, *Voices*, 12–13, 35, 70, 97–104, 144–58, 206–7.

It may therefore be much more than a product of random selection that the present chapter on a work by Chaucer is the sole paper in this whole volume that is focused primarily in this context. But if, with this understanding, we identify a period and body of literary culture in relation to which "reading the past through archaeological objects" is not only quantitatively uncharacteristic, but is so in a systematically explicable way, it makes the interpretation of the relevant evidence that we have all the more "meaningful." Chaucer's poem *The Hous of Fame* can in fact be read as embodying the pressures and currents that were operative in the embryonic stages of the Renaissance particularly well.

The Hous of Fame

The Hous of Fame is an incomplete composition, and indeed when and where it breaks off after 2,158 lines, it is still—or rather it has increasingly become— far from clear where it might be heading. It is also a relatively early work in the Chaucer canon.[6] It is in eight-syllable couplets, like Chaucer's translation from *The Romance of the Rose* and *The Book of the Duchess*. It is referred to, under the title *The Hous of Fame*, in the prologue to *The Legend of Good Women*, where it is linked with *The Book of the Duchess*, *The Parliament of Fowls*, and some version of the story that became the Knight's Tale of Palamon and Arcite, as works which serve and praise Cupid and his mother Venus, the goddess of love.[7] There is a case for regarding *The Hous of Fame* as a failed experiment, abandoned for a better focused and structured (although still never completed) work in *The Legend of Good Women*.[8]

Evaluatively, though, *The Hous of Fame* does not deserve to be regarded dismissively. There are several purely literary or aesthetic reasons to appreciate it as interesting and valuable literary art; these, however, involve appreciating it as a large sample of the Chaucerian poetic medium rather than looking into it to find structure and focused argument. Not least because of the way the work is referred to in the prologue to *The Legend of Good Women*, where Alceste the Queen of the God of Love, Cupid, names it first amongst compositions made "to serve yow [Cupid], in preysinge of your name," the dream

---

6. Larry D. Benson, *The Riverside Chaucer*, 3rd ed. (Oxford: Oxford University Press, 1988), 347–73; Geoffrey Chaucer, *The House of Fame*, ed. Nick Havely, 2nd ed., Durham Medieval and Renaissance Texts 3 (Turnhout: Brepols, 2013). Quotations are from Havely's edition.

7. *Legend of Good Women*, version F line 417, version G line 405.

8. A. J. Minnis, V. J. Scattergood, and J. J. Smith, *Oxford Guides to Chaucer: The Shorter Poems* (Oxford: Clarendon Press, 1995), especially 244–51, 387–88.

vision that constitutes *The Hous of Fame* is usually discussed as having been intended to be a "love vision": a work that explores and recognizes the power of sexual love in human life, and its often ennobling if comparably often tragic effect. That is clearly implied when the Eagle tells the narrator that Jupiter has sent him to lift him into the visionary state because "thou hast no tydynges / Of Loves folke" (*Hous of Fame*, lines 644–45),[9] and indeed, the very final scene of the poem is of the cacophony in a corner of the hall, "Ther men of love-tydynges tolde" (line 2143), in the midst of which a "man of grete auctorite" is discovered (line 2158).

The categorization of *The Hous of Fame* as love vision does not, however, really fit or work as a description of what we actually have. Far more strongly foregrounded in the opening sections is the theme of the interpretability and authority of dreams. The dream that the narrator, named as "Geffrey" (line 729), reportedly experiences is divided into four quite distinct, sequential episodes across three books of the poem. It may be particularly because we do *not* have a conclusion that imposes some overall structure and significance upon these episodes that they achieve quite a powerful impact as a surreal series of imaginary experiences.[10] The reader can stop worrying about the logic, practicality, or meaning of what is narrated and can focus instead on an interplay of insight and experience that is conveyed through skillful versification.

The four completed episodes of the extant text—there is no evidence that any more was ever written and has since been lost—are more or less of equal length, occupying about 500 lines each. Indeed, the poem breaks off at the introduction of a new character who "semed for to be / A man of grete auctorite" (*Hous of Fame*, lines 2157–58). It is entirely plausible that even Chaucer did not know how he, through this character, was going to bring the work to a conclusion. The work opens with a Proem on the subject of dreams, followed by an Invocation to the God of Sleep before the story begins, set on the night of the tenth of December (then the longest night of the year, and thus potentially an optimistic turning point), when the narrator duly falls asleep and dreams. In the first section of the dream, he finds himself in a Temple of Venus, where he sees depicted and summarily relates the story of Virgil's *Aeneid*, with particular attention to the tragic lover figure of Dido, a depiction strongly influenced by the Ovidian tradition. In the second section, the dreamer is snatched up by the Eagle and taken up through the sky to the House of Fame, Fame being a personified entity. This section combines a cos-

---

9. See also the remainder of this speech, down to line 699.
10. See, for instance, Ruth Evans, "Chaucer in Cyberspace: Medieval Technologies of Memory and *The House of Fame*," *Studies in the Age of Chaucer* 23 (2001): 43–69.

mographical vision with a scientific exposition from the Eagle of how the House of Fame comes to be a necessary part of the physical universe.[11]

The next section, inside the House, is where the dreamer recounts what he sees portrayed there; comparable with the first part of the dream in the Temple of Venus, this section is dominated by references to authors and stories: specifically historical or legendary *gestes*.[12] The fourth part is a pageant-like drama in which groups of petitioners approach the goddess Fame with requests concerning how they themselves should be known and famed—requests which are summarily and arbitrarily rejected or granted, with immediate instructions to Eolus, the wind god, with his trumpet, to put what Fame wills directly into effect.

A fifth episode has just been introduced and a new scene set when the text comes to its premature end. The dreamer and dream relocate to the house of Daedalus, "domus Dedaly," close by the House of Fame, where the dreamer is promised he will be rewarded with "tydynges," specifically tidings "of love," to compensate in some way for his own failure to experience the joy of love. The house of Daedalus is neither an obvious nor a familiar symbol of information and enlightenment. The motif is associable with Book VIII of Ovid's *Metamorphoses*, which tells the tale of how Daedalus designed and constructed a house as a labyrinthine hiding place where the monstrous Minotaur, half-human, half-bull son of Minos of Crete, could be concealed (lines 157–68).[13] Although medieval readings of the classical myths could emphasize virtues in the figure of Daedalus—for instance, his constructive skill and the moderation he exhorts in Icarus—the construction of the labyrinth embodies deceit: "lumina flexu / duxit in errorem" [by twisting it deceived the eyes].[14] Clearly, then, we might expect the dreamer to be misled, not to be informed, here. The story of Daedalus and his son Icarus is also prominent in the medieval moralized reading of Ovid as an example of worldliness and the self-destructive peril of high-flying pride—remember that the dreamer-narrator, Geffrey, has flown up to the House of Fame in the Eagle's grasp.[15] The thematic congruency of this

---

11. See particularly lines 699–710.

12. *Hous of Fame*, lines 1434, 1515, 1518.

13. Ovid, *Metamorphoses*, ed. R. J. Tarrant, Oxford Classical Texts (Oxford: Oxford University Press, 2004); Christiania Whitehead, *Castles of the Mind: A Study of Medieval Architectural Allegory* (Cardiff: University of Wales Press, 2003), 182–83.

14. Ovid, *Metamorphoses*, bk. 8, lines 160–61; cf. Sheila Delany, ed., *Chaucer's "House of Fame": The Poetics of Skeptical Fideism* (Gainesville: University Press of Florida, 1994), especially 108, with an oft-quoted characterization of the work as "a literary statement about the unreliability of literary statements."

15. Pierre Bersuire interprets the story of Daedalus literally as a warning against the designing of labyrinthine mazes; morally as a warning against becoming ensnared in the "lab-

dramatization of the fickle nature of Fame in practice and the early focus on the uncertain reliability of dreams is obvious. But how all that may have been planned for explication and resolution in this poem, we cannot know.

In reflecting constructively on what we can make of *The Hous of Fame* as a literary work, it is important to give due weight to the structuration, contents, and emphases that Chaucer wrote into the work, and not to be tempted to complete it imaginatively ourselves by following seductive hints and assuming teleologically that the unwritten, "missing" conclusion should have conformed to what Chaucer subsequently wrote in other works. The dream vision framework is itself a thematically vital element, not least because Chaucer as author appears from the outset to be more engrossed by the opposition between truth and falsehood in dream than with the theme of love. As the opening passage concludes: "Why this a Fantome, why these oracles, / I not" (*Hous of Fame*, lines 11–12). In the contexts both of the narration of history, such as the tale of Aeneas's flight from Troy to Carthage and Italy, and of the telling of tidings, the analogousness of the dichotomies between fantasy and revelation in dreams on the one hand, and between historical truth and fictional falsehood on the other, is abundantly clear. In the context of a special interest in the literary engagement with the material *past* in medieval literature, however, it is highly pertinent to appreciate that Chaucer actually engages with the problem of the truth of dreams primarily as a relationship between present and future. Do dreams reveal what *will* happen? That question, however, cannot be separated from the massive influence of the past. The story of the past is not only inescapable, but it is also insistent and authoritative precisely in respect of this essential question. The bereft state of the subject detached from history is encapsulated by the state of the dreamer after he has left the Temple of Venus and its portrayal of the story of Aeneas: he finds himself in a desert; he sees nothing; he prays: "'O Criste' thoughte I 'that art in blysse, / Fro Fantoume and illusion / Me save!'" (*Hous of Fame*, lines 492–94).

A truly vital issue, consequently, is *how* the stories of the past are encountered. It is no distortion to reformulate that indirect question as the issue of how the past was embodied, and, therefore, how the past was present for a sensitive and reflective, later fourteenth-century individual such as Chaucer. He does not simply refer to the past in terms of "olde bookes"—although of

---

yrinth" of worldly business and worldly good things; allegorically as an *exemplum* "against disobedient and presumptuous sons"; yet anagogically it is read as figuring God as the architect of the framework and machinery of this world and the Christian as his son (Peter Berchorius, *Reductorium morale, Liber 15: Ovidius Moralizatus*, ed. Joseph Engels and Erwin Panofsky, Werkmateriel uitgegeven door het Instituut voor Laat Latijn der Rijksuniversiteit Utrecht 2-3 [Utrecht: Academia Rheno-Trajectina, 1962–66]).

course the material reality of those books is not to be waved away as archaeologically irrelevant—but rather, in this case, he refers to it in the form of "olde werk":

> But, as I slept, me mette I was
> Withyn a temple y-made of glas,
> In which ther were moo ymages
> Of golde, stondynge in sondry stages,
> And moo ryche tabernacles
> And, with perré, moo pynacles
> And moo curiouse portreytures
> And queynt maner of figures
> Of olde werk then I sawgh ever.
> (*Hous of Fame*, lines 119–27)

In the extended paraphrase and the epitome of the story of Aeneas,[16] it is quite insistently and prominently emphasized that the dreamer is somehow "seeing" the story: this verb is repeated sixteen times within the 326 lines, generally at regular intervals, albeit with one significant exception, which is discussed in more detail shortly. On six of these occasions, the verb "to see" is embedded quite formulaically in a phrase like "ther sawgh I grave" (e.g., line 193), and there are no fewer than six further explicit statements that the story was somehow engraved.[17] There is also one point where painting is referred to—"Ther saugh I such tempeste aryse / That euery herte myght agryse / To se hyt peynted on the walle" (*Hous of Fame*, lines 209–11)—although strictly speaking, those lines do not declare that the representation imagined in the Temple of Venus was painted. The significant contrast comes at the very beginning, where the imagined encounter with the *Aeneid* starts with the text itself:

> But as I romed up and doune
> I fonde that on a walle ther was
> Thus writen on a table of bras:
> "I wol now say, yif I kan,
> The armes and also the man."
> (*Hous of Fame*, lines 140–44)

---

16. *Hous of Fame*, lines 140–465.
17. *Hous of Fame*, lines 212, 253, 256, 423, 451, 473.

The terminology used by Chaucer is precisely what one would expect of metalworking, and not least of monumental brasses. The Middle English Dictionary records the regular use of the verb *graven* for the carving or engraving of metal or stone. There are also regular instances of the verb used for textual inscriptions, but typically then with a clear adverbial phrase appended to specify that lettering is involved, as in Lydgate's *Troy Book*: "She toke an appil rounde of purid gold / With greke lettris graven up and doun."[18] The story of Aeneas is unmistakably presented in the first book of *The Hous of Fame* as if Chaucer imagined it in an extensive series of engraved brass panels, comparable with, although by no means closely paralleled by, extant brass monuments. The formal repertoire of the fourteenth-century English monumental brass makers was actually quite limited. England, it should be noted, was the country in which this form of monument was most profusely produced in the Middle Ages; the other European centers were just across the Channel, in northern France and in Flanders.[19] The brasses are overwhelmingly figural and stylized, with little creativity in composition before the sixteenth century. Nonetheless, one of the most unusual brasses of the late fourteenth century does reflect Chaucer's idea of a narrative use. The monument of Bishop Robert de Wyvill of Salisbury, who died in 1375, has been described as "by far the most original" of medieval monumental brasses.[20] It portrays the tale of how Bishop Wyvill recovered the castle of Sherborne, by issuing a writ against the Earl of Salisbury, who chose to settle the matter—or, one presumes, to assert his possession—by trial by combat. The bishop had to agree to this proceeding, but the king intervened at the last minute to forbid this procedure, and the bishop paid a considerable sum to redeem the castle. In fact, the portrayal of the bishop inside the castle, while his champion stands unopposed outside to assert his right, along with animals in the park, is similar in significant respects to contemporary romance illustrations of a beleaguered lady in her castle (figure 11.1).

---

18. John Lydgate, *Lydgate's Troy Book A. D. 1412–20*, ed. Henry Bergen, EETS e.s. 99, 103, 106, 126 (London: Oxford University Press, 1906–35), bk. 2, lines 2648–49. Of considerable interest in respect of the theme of the current volume is the account in the same text of how Pyrrhus performs the *funeralia* of Ajax, the ashes of whose cremated body are interred in a golden urn, "coriously y-grave" with an image of his arms, to protect the venerated contents (*Lydgate's Troy Book*, bk. 5, lines 306–22). Cf. also *Middle English Dictionary*, s.v. "graven," 3 (a) and (d).

19. Herbert Walter Mackin, *The Brasses of England* (London: Methuen, 1907); M. W. Norris, *Monumental Brasses: The Portfolio Plates of the Monumental Brass Society* (Woodbridge, UK: Boydell Press, 1988); Nigel Saul, *English Church Monuments in the Middle Ages: History and Representation* (Oxford: Oxford University Press, 2009), 76–82.

20. Norris, *Monumental Brasses*, 78, figure 62.

FIGURE 11.1. From the monumental brass of Bishop Robert de Wyvill, ca. 1375, in Salisbury Cathedral. Length of area shown 2.28 metres. Illustration published by John G. Waller and A. B. Waller, *A Series of Monumental Brasses from the Thirteenth to the Sixteenth Century* (London: J. B. Nichols and Sons, 1864). By kind permission of the Society of Antiquaries of London.

The point to be emphasized, then, is the ability of the story of the past to rematerialize in diverse forms in the later fourteenth-century world. All the components of Chaucer's imagined Temple of Venus can be described as realistic in contemporary terms, but the way they are creatively composed takes material culture far beyond the reality.[21] Nobody, anywhere, produced brasswork quite like this, although we do have a few glimpses of famous stories having been turned into pictorial decoration: for instance the set of ceramic floor tiles dated to the thirteenth century from Chertsey Abbey, Surrey, showing images from the romance of Tristram and Isolde, now in the British Museum, and the front panel of an early fifteenth-century wooden chest with a scene from Chaucer's *Pardoner's Tale* in the Museum of London.[22] Perhaps even more pertinently comparable are the painted murals of the tales of Neidhart Fuchs found in Vienna of around the year 1400.[23]

Returning to the epitome of the *Aeneid* in *The Hous of Fame*, there is a section from line 256 to line 432 that stands apart as one within which references to how the dreamer "saw" the tale "engraved" cease. These lines contain the core story of Dido's betrayal by Aeneas, followed by summary tales of other "good women" betrayed by faithless men. The tale itself appears to have taken over in this passage; the verses become occupied by a story that is, as it were, telling itself. This episode is nonetheless solidly enclosed within its own framing narrative, which unambiguously presents a situation in which the whole of the history of Aeneas's destiny has been made material, and is encountered as a thing seen, not a text that is read. It is indeed precisely on that basis that the most intense episode, that of Dido's betrayal and suicide, is not merely a point where the story is of such interest that the frame narrative is temporarily forgotten but rather a focal point where the study starts to enact itself (in literary terms): it is really here alone that characters within the *Aeneid* story use direct speech extensively.

---

21. See, e.g., Mary Flowers Braswell, "Architectural Portraiture in Chaucer's *House of Fame*," *Journal of Medieval and Renaissance Studies* 11 (1981): 101–12; A. J. Minnis, "'Figures of olde werk': Chaucer's Poetic Sculptures," in *Secular Sculpture 1300–1550*, ed. Phillip Lindley and Thomas Frangenberg (Stamford, CT: Shaun Tyas, 2000), 124–43; discussed further below.

22. Elizabeth Eames, *Medieval Tiles: A Handbook* (London: British Museum, 1968), 7–10; Muriel A. Whitaker, "The Chaucer Chest and the *Pardoner's Tale*: Didacticism in Narrative Art," *Chaucer Review* 34 (1999): 174–89.

23. Eva-Marie Höhle, Oskar Pausch, and Richard Perger, "Die Neidhard-Fresken im Haus Tuchlauben 19 in Wien: Zum Funde profaner Wandmalereien der Zeit um 1400," *Österreichische Zeitschrift für Kunst und Denkmalpflege* 36 (1982): 110–44.

The Redeployment of Material and Narrative in *The Hous of Fame*

The idea that we can regard this representation of an encounter with a transmitted and meaningful past, the story of Troy, as closely akin to a medieval version of the museum becomes all the more clear in Book III, when we enter the House of Fame itself.[24] There is much about the description of this building that echoes the Temple of Venus closely: the pinnacles, imagery, tabernacles, and so on that are viewed.[25] The house is made of beryl, a stone with lapidary associations with clarity, magnification, and virtuous love.[26] A particularly significant transition, however, is that in lines 1341–55, where the text comes to the very threshold of an extended discussion of the palace in lapidary terms, but it is abruptly curtailed, and the text swerves away: "But hit were alle to longe to rede / The names, and therfore I pace" (*Hous of Fame*, lines 1354–55). What gains a more careful description instead is a gallery of pillars within a hall on which authors, particularly of history and legend, are represented: the pillars themselves are symbolic, or even emblematic, in material, although not very diverse. There is Josephus on a pillar of lead, associated with Saturn, and iron, associated with Mars; Statius on a pillar painted with Tiger's blood; Homer and other poets of the story of Troy on an iron pillar; Virgil on a tinned iron pillar, tin being associated with Jupiter; Lucan on yet another iron pillar. Ovid, the poet of love closely associated with Venus, is more appropriately placed on a copper pillar, while Claudian, the poet who told of the underworld in *De raptu Proserpinae*, is symbolically just as significantly but much less realistically found on a pillar of sulphur. In a significant way, too, we have been prepared for this by the Eagle, who, while bringing the dreamer to the House in Book II, explains in "scientific" terms *how* all the talk in the world—and all the talk there ever has been—can physically make its way to this collecting point in the heavens. In this flight of the medieval imagination, discourse rematerializes in the physical form of its original source.

"Whan eny spech y-comen ys
Up to the paleys, anon-ryght

---

24. Martine Yvernault, "The *House of Fame*: Unfamous Fame; La maison de papier, une entreprise de (dé)construction," in *L'articulation langue-littérature dans les textes médiévaux anglais*, ed. Collette Stévanovitch, Collection GRENDEL 5 (Nancy: Publications de l'AMAES, 2005), 232–33.

25. Braswell, "Architectural Portraiture"; J. A. W. Bennett, *Chaucer's Book of Fame: An Exposition of "The House of Fame"* (Oxford: Oxford University Press, 1968), 11–13.

26. Howard R. Patch, "Precious Stones in *The House of Fame*," *Modern Language Notes* 50 (1935): 312–27; Whitehead, *Castles of the Mind*, 178.

Hyt wexeth lyke the same wight
Which that the worde in erthe spake."
(*Hous of Fame*, lines 1074–77)

Chaucer's presentation of the buildings of the Temple of Venus and the House of Fame, and of their ornamentation, makes it perfectly clear that this was an author with both a sharp perception and a thorough understanding of their materiality. That is not the limit of his literary reapplication of familiarity with and interest in material processes. Most of the references to specific materials are clearly emblematic, although, as just noted, that was not a mode of symbolism and interpretation that Chaucer was willing to dwell or expand upon in this work. Both a concerned and a critical eye is cast on the entrance to the House of Fame itself: "The castel yate on my ryght honde, / Which that so wel corven was / That never suche another nas" (*Hous of Fame*, lines 1294–96)—straightforward praise enough, but then expanded with the thought-provoking qualification—"and yit it was by aventure / I-wrought as often as be cure" (*Hous of Fame*, lines 1297–98). In reading the materiality of architecture, Chaucer does not fall into an "intentionalist fallacy." The story that an object like this building tells may be far more than what its designer had ever thought of.

A significant way in which we may characterize Chaucer's understanding of the *agency* of the material world resides therefore in the temporally significant form of a sense of material forces as *process*. Nearly all of the similes and emblems through which this is expressed are unsurprising: at a distance, the noise of the House of Fame resembles a storm at sea, waves beating on the rocks; the melting of the ice either side of the House differentiates preservation from loss; the noise of the House of Daedalus is that of a rolling stone.[27] The one exception in terms of conventionality is the description of how Eolus blows out slander like the firing of a gun—one of the earliest recorded instances of this noun in English—and like the foul smoke produced when lead is melted, swelling like a river as it flows onward.[28] Both of these would be very familiar as real experiences to a man in Chaucer's position, although quite distinctly the latter, leadworking, was a common sight in his world, while the former, artillery, was a less common one. Both testify to the grounding of *The Hous of Fame* in a real and material medieval world rather than an exclusively literary one.

---

27. *Hous of Fame*, lines 1033–41, 1110–64, 1927–34.
28. *Hous of Fame*, lines 1645–49; OED, s.v. "*gun*."

Tantalizingly different, meanwhile, is the portrayal of Venus, seen upon entering her temple: "In portreytoure / I sawgh anoon-ryght hir figure, / Naked, fletynge in a see" (*Hous of Fame*, lines 131–33). Naked figures were familiar in medieval pictorial art, but really only in the characters of Adam and Eve. The classical tradition of nude portraiture, particularly for beautiful goddesses, was known to educated medieval people. However, the image here is one that specifically evokes the art of the classical past, and nothing contemporary. A direct source could well have been Benvenuto Rambaldi da Imola's *Comentum super Dantis Aldighierij comœdiam,* attributed to the 1370s, where an account of a nude Venus Benvenuto himself had seen in Florence is appended to commentary on Dante's reference to the classical sculptor Polycletus in *Purgatorio* (canto 10, lines 28–33).[29] In terms of its direct source, Chaucer's usage here may therefore be explained intertextually. Behind that, however, the Italian authors were both directly reading the past through firsthand experience of "archaeological objects."

There are two distinct facets to Archaeology, both equally significant. Archaeology can be the use of material culture to reconstruct the past—forensically analyzing and interpreting material clues to write more history. However, Archaeology is also concerned with understanding the fullness of our human relationship with material culture, context by context and universally. In a parallel manner, the (archaeological) museum is now conceptualized in two quite different lights. One is as the formal repository of relics of the past, preserved, ordered, and displayed (the "didactic" museum). However, alongside this, for at least thirty years now, interactivity, with the visitor as participant stakeholder rather than humble and passive viewer, has been a staple of museum studies and theory (the "engaged" museum). In this respect, the archaeological museum and the art gallery have been assimilated in the modern world to the museum of science and technology, as places of experiential and experimental learning.[30] Not only in this respect, but perhaps even more in relation to the contemporary emphasis on the role of the museum

---

29. Dante Alighieri, *The Divine Comedy of Dante Alighieri,* vol. 2, *Purgatorio,* trans. and ed. John D. Sinclair (Oxford: Oxford University Press, 1939); William Warren Vernon and J. P. Lacaita, eds., *Benevenuti de Rambaldis de Imola Comentum super Dantis Aldigherij Comoediam* (Florence: G. Barbèra, 1887); 3:279–80. Cf. Minnis, "Figures of olde werk," 134; and Meg Twycross, *The Medieval Anadyomene: A Study in Chaucer's Mythography,* Medium Ævum Monographs New Series 1 (Oxford: Blackwell, 1972), especially 70–96.

30. Janet Marstine, ed., *New Museum Theory and Practice: An Introduction* (Oxford: Wiley, 2005), 4–7; Marguerite Barry, "Please Do Touch: Discourses on Aesthetic Interactivity in the Exhibition Space," *Participations: Journal of Audience & Reception Studies* 11 (2014): 216–36. I am most grateful to Penelope Hines (National Trust; formerly of the Victoria & Albert Museum) for advice on this subject.

sector as a forum for cross-cultural exchange, we can appreciate Chaucer's Temple of Venus and the House of Fame as strikingly more akin in essence to the contemporary museum ideal than to the traditional, historical museum. "Cross-cultural," indeed, may emphatically be understood as "intra-cultural," combining the literary and material worlds.[31]

The past that Chaucer engaged with and represents in his writing was indeed a past constituted predominantly of stories—of texts and of authors. There was also a material past, of which he was well aware, but it was not one that pressed heavily on his consciousness or on his literary imagination. Chaucer's present was also constituted meaningfully of stories, texts, authors, and material forces and practices—and it may, as already suggested, be precisely because of the richer status of the material as a discursive medium in medieval cognition that the direction of relationship in *The Hous of Fame* shows the literary becoming material rather than "archaeological objects" providing material for literature. "Old Books Brought to Life in Dreams" is the title of an essay by Piero Boitani on Chaucer's early dream poetry.[32] His title perfectly encapsulates the purely literary critical view of these texts: old books are the source material; the dramatic but evanescent fantasies of the dream are credited with bringing them to life. The extraordinarily concrete materialization of the imagery and the similes, which is equally fundamental to *The Book of the Duchess* in fact, is marginalized, or rather relegated to that same inert status that the Reformers were to insist upon.

Both the degree of material realism in *The Hous of Fame* and its interpretative significance have proved to be a key dividing line in critical readings of the poem. A minority opinion is that of Mary Flowers Braswell, who reviewed parallels between Chaucer's descriptions and contemporary Gothic architecture, and especially the form of reliquary shrines and chapels, to speak of "Chaucer's stubborn adherence to material reality."[33] The opposing view is most effectively enunciated by Alastair Minnis, in an article emphasizing Chaucer's *poetic* sculptures, where he refers to certain concrete parallels (or, rather, to descriptive textual accounts of the material) as "too general and vague to be significant," and concludes conversely that "Chaucer was con-

---

31. Andreas Huyssen, *Twilight Memories: Marking Time in a Culture of Amnesia* (London: Psychology Press, 1995) has explored the attraction of encountering real objects in the museum in the context of a fast-paced, digitally saturated contemporary world.

32. Piero Boitani, "Old Books Brought to Life in Dreams: The *Book of the Duchess*, the *House of Fame*, the *Parliament of Fowls*," in *The Cambridge Companion to Chaucer*, ed. Piero Boitani and Jill Mann (Cambridge: Cambridge University Press, 2003), 58–77.

33. Braswell, "Architectural Portraiture," 101–2; cf. also Michael Hagiioannu, "Giotto Bardi's Chapel Frescoes and Chaucer's *House of Fame*: Influence, Evidence and Interpretations," *Chaucer Review* 36 (2001): 28–47.

cerned to create images of an utterly fictional, physically impossible kind rather than offering eyewitness testimony of actual structures and artifacts which existed in his own world" and that "Chaucer's project is heavily text-based."[34] In so doing, he refines and crystallizes a protextual and antimaterial bias in reading already evident in J. A. W. Bennett's monograph study of the poem, which had similarly noted parallels in architecture and material art but passed swiftly into literary sources and analogues.[35]

Of course, a self-consciously and deliberately archaeologically influenced reading will demur at such a position and align itself more closely with the positive implications of the sorts of parallels noted by Braswell and within this paper above. Indeed, Minnis fairly finds himself acknowledging and yet determined to play down the "interest" of the material parallels that can be cited.[36] There is a rational and productive middle way here: we do not have to claim to identify specific extant models of what Chaucer portrays to be able to incorporate a substantive appreciation of the importance of material culture, and not least what was being constructively done with contemporary material culture, into a comprehensive and balanced interpretation and evaluation of the poem. It is far more than just a matter of curiosity that "olde stories" were being realized in Chaucer's time and surroundings in material ways. Minnis indeed comes to this point, too, using Kolve's excellent analysis of the pictorial evidence in the context of the *Canterbury Tales* to emphasize how the ear and the eye were the doors to memory and so to the contemplative mind.[37] Minnis justifies his position (which in effect predetermines his conclusions), however, by averring that these perspectives are relevant in respect of a text that would be experienced read aloud. By doing so, however, he has invoked the text as actual performance, and (as noted above) an actual performance requires a real spatial setting. Within that setting, what is read invites readers and listeners alike to recall or even imaginatively design other settings. The generative power and positive critical potential of these relationships between author, performer, listeners/readers, and physical context is exceptionally well exemplified in a discussion by Martine Yvernault, who marks the ambiguity and ambivalence of a process of critical *(dé)construction* of material references being concurrent with *construction* or even *reconstruction* into a version on

---

34. Minnis, "Figures of olde werk," quotations from 127, 136, 140.
35. Bennett, *Chaucer's Book of Fame*, especially 11–15; cf. also Whitehead, *Castles of the Mind*, 174–84, and particularly 179: "The house is *nothing* other than an ambitious spatial representation of the entire literary canon" (my emphasis).
36. Minnis, "Figures of olde werk," 127.
37. Minnis, "Figures of olde werk," 138–39; V. A. Kolve, *Chaucer and the Imagery of Narrative: The First Five Canterbury Tales* (London: Edwin Arnold, 1984), 41–42.

paper by bracketing and confining the negative prefix.[38] The modern critic may well wish or even need to emphasize how far the experience provided by the poem can be effective and rich in purely bookish terms. But there is no need to present intertextual and archaeological approaches in terms of a necessary choice of one or the other.

Materiality was not merely a subsidiary or superficial layer of "style" or "imagery." It was a mode of experience and cognition essential to the context in which Chaucer wrote *The Hous of Fame,* which is thus, according to this reading, essentially medieval in the unfolding of its dreamy, imagined visions. Yet, as F. N. Robinson declared, the poem itself "has been said to mark the transition from the Middle Ages to the Renaissance."[39] It does indeed bear the marks of incipient Classicism and Humanism, which were to supplant the Medievalism of the Middle Ages themselves. I am usually one of the first to take a skeptical and dismissive attitude toward deliberately elegant formulations of the kind, but in this case one can justifiably suggest that Chaucer's *The Hous of Fame* remained unfinished, not just because Chaucer never managed to write the last few hundred lines to complete it (in some scholars' view, maybe just a few dozen were needed) but because the processes of reconceptualizing both the classical heritage (which was primarily literary) and the material present had only just begun in the context in which it was composed. Chaucer could start *The Hous of Fame* and could travel a long way within this artistic exercise, but he did not know where or how to direct it to an end. The museum in its modern sense (ultimately from Greek μουσεῖον [the seat of the Muses]) was in fact still in the process of being invented. To deconstruct the poem in these thoroughly archaeological terms suggests deep insights into Chaucer as representative of a late medieval English, and indeed European, context and culture, and the range of those insights goes far beyond purely literary relevance. They revealingly illustrate the real interdependency of the physical world and the mental world in the late fourteenth century.

---

38. Yvernault, *"House of Fame."* Unfortunately, this excellent paper is not easy to obtain; the UK university interlibrary loan system could not supply a copy, and I am most grateful to Professor Yvernault herself for sending me one.

39. F. N. Robinson, ed., *The Works of Geoffrey Chaucer,* 2nd ed. (Cambridge, MA: Riverside Press, 1957), 281.

BIBLIOGRAPHY

Abram, Christopher. "Kennings and Things: Towards an Object-Oriented Skaldic Poetics." In *The Shape of Early English Poetry: Style, Form, History*, edited by Irina Dumitrescu and Eric Weiskott, 161–88. Kalamazoo, MI: Medieval Institute Publications, 2019.

Abu El-Haj, Nadia. *Facts on the Ground: Archaeological Practice and Territorial Self-Fashioning in Israeli Society*. Chicago: University of Chicago Press, 2001.

Adams, Matt. "St Albans Cathedral Archaeological Dig Uncovers the Lost Grave of Abbot Wheathampstead." *Herts Advertiser*, December 7, 2017. Accessed June 2, 2020. http://www.hertsad.co.uk/news/st-albans-cathedral-archaeological-dig-uncovers-the-lost-grave-of-abbot-wheathampstead-1-5312692.

Ælfric of Eynsham. *Ælfric's Catholic Homilies: The Second Series Text*. Edited by Malcolm Godden. EETS s.s. 5. London: Oxford University Press, 1979.

Albertini, Francesco. *Opusculum de mirabilibus novae et veteris urbis romae*. Rome: Mazochius, 1510.

Alcuin. "Epistola 81." In *Monumenta Alcuiniana*, edited by W. Wattenbach and Ernst Dümmler, 353–58. Bibliotheca rerum Germanicarum 6. Berlin: Weidmann, 1873.

Allen, Charles. "The Golden Column of Firoz Shah." In *Ashoka: The Search for India's Lost Emperor*, 6–27. New Delhi: Hachette, 2012.

Allgeier, Arthur. "Untersuchungen zur syrischen Überlieferung der Siebenschläferlegende." *Oriens Christianus* n.s. 4–8. 1915–18.

Amodio, Mark C. *Writing the Oral Tradition: Oral Poetics and Literate Culture in Medieval England*. Notre Dame, IN: University of Notre Dame Press, 2004.

Andrew, Malcolm, Ronald Waldron, and Clifford Peterson, eds. *Saint Erkenwald*. In *The Complete Works of the Pearl Poet*. Translated with an Introduction by Casey Finch, 323–40. Berkeley: University of California Press, 1993.

Appadurai, Arjun. "Introduction: Commodities and the Politics of Value." In *The Social Life of Things: Commodities in Cultural Perspective*, 3–63. Cambridge: Cambridge University Press, 1986.

Appleby, Jo, Piers D. Mitchell, Claire Robinson, Alison Brough, Guy Rutty, Russell A. Harris, David Thompson, and Bruno Morgan. "The Scoliosis of Richard III, Last Plantagenet King of England: Diagnosis and Clinical Significance." *Lancet* 383, no. 9932 (2014): 1944.

Arnold, Bettina, and Henning Hassmann. "Archaeology in Nazi Germany: The Legacy of the Faustian Bargain." In *Nationalism, Politics, and the Pracitice of Archaeology*, edited by Philip L. Kohl and Clare Fawcett, 70–81. Cambridge: Cambridge University Press, 1996.

Arnovick, Leslie K. *Written Reliquaries: The Resonance of Orality in Medieval English Texts*. Amsterdam: John Benjamins Publishing, 2006.

Audelay, John. "Three Dead Kings." In *Poems and Carols (Oxford, Bodleian Library MS Douce 302)*, edited by Susanna Fein. TEAMS Middle English Texts Series. Kalamazoo, MI: Medieval Institute Publications, 2009. Online edition. Accessed June 2, 2020. http://d.lib.rochester.edu/teams/text/fein-audelay-poems-and-carols-meditative-close#3dk.

Auerbach, Erich. "Figura." Translated by Ralph Manheim. In *Scenes from the Drama of European Literature: Six Essays by Erich Auerbach*, 11–76. New York: Meridian, 1959.

Bailey, Ann E. "Anthropology, the Medievalist . . . and Richard III." *Reading Medieval Studies* 41 (2015): 27–51.

——. "Richard III: A Medieval Relic?" *History Today* 65, no. 8 (2015): 11–17.

Baker, Peter S. *Honour, Exchange and Violence in "Beowulf."* Anglo-Saxon Studies 20. Cambridge: D. S. Brewer, 2013.

Bale, Anthony. "Stow's Medievalism and Antique Judaism in Early Modern London." In *John Stow (1525–1605) and the Making of the English Past: Studies in Early Modern Culture and the History of the Book*, edited by Ian Gadd and Alexandra Gillespie, 69–80. London: British Library, 2004.

Barad, Karen. *Meeting the Universe Halfway: Quantum Physics and the Entanglement of Matter and Meaning*. Durham, NC: Duke University Press, 2007.

Barber, Richard. "Was Mordred Buried at Glastonbury?" In *Glastonbury Abbey and the Arthurian Tradition*, edited by James P. Carley, 145–59; 617–28 [Appendix]. Cambridge: D. S. Brewer, 2001.

Barkan, Leonard. *Unearthing the Past: Archaeology and Aesthetics in the Making of Renaissance Culture*. New Haven, CT: Yale University Press, 1999.

Barry, Marguerite. "Please Do Touch: Discourses on Aesthetic Interactivity in the Exhibition Space." *Participations: Journal of Audience & Reception Studies* 11 (2014): 216–36.

Bartlett, Robert. *Why Can the Dead Do Such Great Things: Saints and Worshippers from the Martyrs to the Reformation*. Princeton, NJ: Princeton University Press, 2013.

Bath, Michael. *Speaking Pictures: English Emblem Books and Renaissance Culture*. Harlow, UK: Longman, 1994.

Bauer, Ralph. "A New World of Secrets: Occult Philosophy and the Sixteenth-Century Atlantic." In *Science and Empire in the Atlantic Worlds*, edited by James Delbourgo and Nicholas Dew, 99–126. New York: Routledge, 2008.

Bauer, Thomas. *Warum es kein islamisches Mittelalter gab: Das Erbe der Antike und der Orient*. Munich: C. H. Beck, 2018.

Bede. *The Ecclesiastical History of the English People, The Greater Chronicle, Bede's Letter to Egbert*. Edited by Judith McClure and Roger Collins. Oxford: Oxford University Press, 1994.

Belting, Hans. *Florence and Baghdad: Renaissance Art and Arab Science.* Translated by Deborah Lucas Schneider. Cambridge, MA: Belknap Press of Harvard University Press, 2011.

Benjamin, Walter. "Theses on the Philosophy of History." In *Illuminations.* Translated by Harry Zorn. Edited by Hannah Arendt, 245–55. London: Pimlico, 1999.

Bennett, J. A. W. *Chaucer's Book of Fame: An Exposition of "The House of Fame."* Oxford: Oxford University Press, 1968.

Benson, Larry D., ed. *The Riverside Chaucer.* 3rd ed. Oxford: Oxford University Press, 1988.

Berchorius, Peter. *Reductorium morale, Liber 15: Ovidius Moralizatus.* Edited by Joseph Engels and Erwin Panofsky. Werkmateriel uitgegeven door het Instituut voor Laat Latijn der Rijksuniversiteit Utrecht 2–3. Utrecht: Academia Rheno-Trajectina, 1962–66.

Biddick, Kathleen. *The Typological Imaginary: Circumcision, Technology, History.* Philadelphia: University of Pennsylvania Press, 2003.

Bjork, Robert E., trans. and ed. *Old English Shorter Poems.* Dumbarton Oaks Medieval Library 32. 2 vols. Cambridge, MA: Harvard University Press, 2014.

Blackwell, Mark. *The Secret Life of Things: Animals, Objects, and It-Narratives in Eighteenth-Century England.* Lewisburg, PA: Bucknell University Press, 2007.

Bliss, Alan J. "Single Half-Lines in Old English Poetry." *Notes and Queries* 18 (1971): 442–49.

Boitani, Piero. "Old Books Brought to Life in Dreams: The *Book of the Duchess*, the *House of Fame*, the *Parliament of Fowls*." In *The Cambridge Companion to Chaucer*, edited by Piero Boitani and Jill Mann, 58–77. Cambridge: Cambridge University Press, 2003.

Bokenham, Osbern. *Legendys of Hooly Wummen.* Edited by Mary S. Serjeantson. EETS o.s. 206. London: Oxford University Press, 1938.

Bolton, Brenda. "St Albans' Loyal Son." In *Adrian IV, The English Pope (1154–1159): Studies and Texts*, edited by Brenda Bolton and Anne J. Duggan, 75–104. Abington, UK: Routledge, 2016.

Bracciolini, Poggio. *Opera omnia.* 4 vols. Turin: Bottega d'Erasmo, 1966.

Bradford, Charles Angell. *Heart Burial.* London: Allen and Unwin, 1933.

Bradley, S. A. J., trans. and ed. *Anglo-Saxon Poetry.* London: Dent, 1982.

Bragg, Lois. "The Modes of the Old English Metrical Charms." *Comparatist* 16 (1992): 3–23.

Brandl, Alois. "Die angelsächsische Literatur." In *Grundriss der germanischen Philologie*, edited by Hermann Paul, 2:941–1134. 2nd ed. Strassburg: Karl J. Trübner, 1901–9.

Braswell, Mary Flowers. "Architectural Portraiture in Chaucer's *House of Fame*." *Journal of Medieval and Renaissance Studies* 11 (1981): 101–12.

Brilliant, Richard. *My Laocoön: Alternative Claims in the Interpretation of Artworks.* Berkeley: University of California Press, 2000.

Brooks, N. P. "Arms and Armour." In *The Blackwell Encyclopedia of Anglo-Saxon England*, edited by Michael Lapidge, John Blair, Simon Keynes, and Donald Scragg, 45–47. Oxford: Blackwell, 1999.

———. "Weapons and Armour." In *The Battle of Maldon, A. D. 991*, edited by Donald Scragg, 208–19. Oxford: Blackwell, 1991.

Browne, Thomas. *Hydrotaphia, Urne-buriall, or, a Discourse of the Sepulchral Urnes Lately Found in Norfolk.* London: Brome, 1658.

Buckley, Richard, Matthew Morris, Jo Appleby, Turi King, Deirdre O'Sullivan, and Lin Foxhall. "'The King in the Car Park': New Light on the Death and Burial of Richard III in the Grey Friars Church, Leicester, in 1485." *Antiquity* 87 (2013): 519–38.

Burckhardt, Jacob. *The Civilization of the Renaissance in Italy.* 1860. Translated by S. C. G. Middlemore. London: Phaidon, 1944.

Bynum, Caroline Walker. *The Resurrection of the Body in Western Christianity, 200–1336.* New York: Columbia University Press, 1995.

Cameron, M. L. *Anglo-Saxon Medicine.* Cambridge: Cambridge University Press, 1993.

Camp, Cynthia Turner. "Spatial Memory, Historiographic Fantasy and the Place of the Past in *St. Erkenwald.*" *New Literary History* 44, no. 3 (2013): 472–91.

Carley, James P., ed. *The Chronicle of Glastonbury Abbey: An Edition, Translation and Study of John of Glastonbury's "Cronica sive antiquitates Glastoniensis ecclesie."* Woodbridge, UK: Boydell Press, 1978.

———, ed. *Glastonbury Abbey and the Arthurian Tradition.* Cambridge: D. S. Brewer, 2001.

Carroll, Lewis. *Through the Looking-Glass, and What Alice Found There.* London: Macmillan, 1871.

Carruthers, Mary J. *The Book of Memory: A Study of Memory in Medieval Culture.* Cambridge: Cambridge University Press, 1990.

Carson, A. J., ed. *Finding Richard III: The Official Account of Research by the Retrieval and Reburial Project.* Horstead, UK: Imprimis Imprimatur, 2015.

Cartlidge, Neil, trans. and ed. *The Works of Chardri: Three Poems in the French of Thirteenth-Century England; "The Little Debate," "The Life of the Seven Sleepers," and "The Life of St Josaphaz."* Tempe: Arizona Center for Medieval and Renaissance Studies, 2015.

Cassidy, Brendan. "The Later Life of the Ruthwell Cross: From the Seventeenth Century to the Present." In *The Ruthwell Cross: Papers from the Colloquium Sponsored by the Index of Christian Art, Princeton University, 8 December 1989,* edited by Brendan Cassidy, 3–34. Index of Christian Art, Occasional Papers 1. Princeton, NJ: Index of Christian Art, Department of Art and Archaeology, Princeton University, 1992.

———, ed. *The Ruthwell Cross: Papers from the Colloquium Sponsored by the Index of Christian Art, Princeton University, 8 December 1989.* Index of Christian Art, Occasional Papers 1. Princeton, NJ: Index of Christian Art, Department of Art and Archaeology, Princeton University, 1992.

Catlos, Brian A. *Muslims of Medieval Latin Christendom, c. 1050–1614.* Cambridge: Cambridge University Press, 2014.

Caxton, William. "Appendix: Caxton's Prefix." In *Le Morte Darthur: The Winchester Manuscript,* by Sir Thomas Malory. Edited by Helen Cooper, 528–30. Oxford: Oxford University Press, 1998.

Chaganti, Seeta. *The Medieval Poetics of the Reliquary: Enshrinement, Inscription, Performance.* The New Middle Ages. New York: Palgrave Macmillan, 2008.

———. "Vestigial Signs: Inscription, Performance, and *The Dream of the Rood.*" *PMLA* 125 (2010): 48–72.

Chapman, Robert, and Alison Wylie. *Evidential Reasoning in Archaeology.* London: Bloomsbury, 2016.

Chaucer, Geoffrey. *The House of Fame.* Edited by Nick Havely. 2nd ed. Durham Medieval and Renaissance Texts 3. Turnhout: Brepols, 2013.

Chickering, Howell. "The Literary Magic of *Wið Færstice.*" *Viator* 2 (1972): 83–104.

Christian, Kathleen Wren. *Empire without End: Antiquities Collections in Renaissance Rome, c. 1350–1527.* New Haven, CT: Yale University Press, 2010.

Clare, Eli. *Brilliant Imperfection: Grappling with Cure.* Durham, NC: Duke University Press, 2017.

Clark, Elizabeth A. *The Origenist Controversy: The Cultural Construction of an Early Christian Debate*. Princeton, NJ: Princeton University Press, 1992.

Clark, John. "London Stone: Stone of Brutus or Fetish Stone—Making the Myth." *Folklore* 121, no. 1 (2010): 38–60.

Cleaver, Laura. *Illuminated History Books in the Anglo-Norman World, 1066–1272*. Oxford: Oxford University Press, 2018.

Clifford, James. *Routes: Travel and Translation in the Late Twentieth Century*. Cambridge, MA: Harvard University Press, 1997.

Cockayne, Oswald, ed. *Leechdoms, Wortcunning, and Starcraft of Early English*. 3 vols. 1857. Reprint, Wiesbaden: Kraus, 1965.

Cohen, Jeffrey Jerome. *Stone: An Ecology of the Inhuman*. Minneapolis: University of Minnesota Press, 2015.

———. "Stories of Stone." *Postmedieval: A Journal of Medieval Cultural Studies* 1 (2010): 56–63.

Colgrave, Bertram. "Sir Gawayne's Green Chapel." *Antiquity* 12, no. 47 (1938): 351–53.

Collier, Michael. "Against a Sudden Stitch." In *The Word Exchange: Anglo-Saxon Poems in Translation*, edited by Greg Delanty and Michael Matto, 483–34. New York: W. W. Norton & Company, 2012.

Conner, Patrick W. "The Ruthwell Monument Runic Poem in a Tenth-Century Context." *Review of English Studies* n.s. 59, no. 238 (2008): 25–51.

Connolly, Daniel K. *The Maps of Matthew Paris: Medieval Journeys Through Space, Time and Liturgy*. Woodbridge, UK: Boydell Press, 2009.

Conrad, Sebastian. *What Is Global History?* Princeton, NJ: Princeton University Press, 2016.

Corpus Iuris Civilis: Editio stereotypa. Vol. 1, *Institutiones*, ed. Paulus Krueger; *Digesta*, ed. Theodorus Mommsen, rev. Paulus Krueger. 13th ed. Berlin: Weidmann, 1920.

Coryate, Thomas. *Coryats Crudities Hastily Gobbled up in Five Months Travels in France, Savoy, Italy, Rhetia Commonly Called the Orison's Country, Helvetia Alias Switzerland, Some Parts of High Germany and the Netherlands, Newly Digested in the Hungry Air of Odcombe in the County of Somerset, and Now Dispersed to the Nourishment of the Travelling Members of this Kingdom*. 2 vols. London, 1611.

———. *Greetings from the Court of the Great Mughal*. London, 1618.

Cramp, Rosemary. "*Beowulf* and Archaeology." *Medieval Archaeology* 1 (1957): 57–77.

Crane, Mary Thomas. "Surface, Depth, and the Spatial Imaginary: A Cognitive Reading of *The Political Unconscious*." *Representations* 108 (2009): 76–97.

Crick, Julia. "Offa, Aelfric and the Refoundation of St Albans." In *Alban and St Albans: Roman and Medieval Architecture, Art and Archaeology*, edited by Martin Henig and Phillip Lindley, 78–84. Leeds: British Archaeological Association, 2001.

Cronan, Dennis. "The Origin of Ancient Strife in *Beowulf*." *North-Western European Language Evolution* 31–32 (1997): 57–68.

Cronk, Nicholas. *The Classical Sublime: French Neoclassicism and the Languages of Literature*. EMF Critiques. Charlottesville, VA: Rockwood Press, 2002.

Cubitt, Catherine R. E. "'As the Lawbook Teaches': Reeves, Lawbooks and Urban Life in the Anonymous Old English Legend of the Seven Sleepers." *English Historical Review* 124 (2009): 1021–49.

Curran, John E., Jr. *Roman Invasions: British History, Protestant Anti-Romanism, and the Historical Imagination in England, 1530–1660*. Newark, NJ: University of Delaware Press, 2002.

Dacos, Nicole. *Roma quanta fuit, ou, l'invention du paysage de ruines*. Paris: Somogy, 2004.

———. *Voyage à Rome: Les artistes européens au XVIe siècle*. Brussels: Fonds Mercator, 2012.

Damisch, Hubert. *The Origin of Perspective*. Translated by John Goodman. Cambridge, MA: MIT Press, 1994.

Dante Alighieri. *The Divine Comedy of Dante Alighieri*. Vol. 2, *Purgatorio*. Translated and edited by John D. Sinclair. Oxford: Oxford University Press, 1939.

D'Aronco, Maria Amalia. "Anglo-Saxon Plant Pharmacy and the Latin Medical Tradition." In *From Earth to Art: The Many Aspects of the Plant World in Anglo-Saxon England*, edited by C. P. Biggam, 133–51. Costerus New Series 148. Amsterdam: Rodopi, 2003.

Daston, Lorraine. *Things That Talk*. New York: Zone Books, 2008.

Davidson, Hilda Roderick Ellis. *The Sword in Anglo-Saxon England*. Oxford: Clarendon Press, 1962.

Davies, Glyn. "New Light on the Luck of Edenhall." *Burlington Magazine* 152 (2010): 4–7.

Dekker, Thomas. *The Royal Entertainment*. London, 1603.

Delany, Sheila, ed. *Chaucer's "House of Fame": The Poetics of Skeptical Fideism*. Gainesville: University Press of Florida, 1994.

De Lubac, Henri. *Medieval Exegesis: The Four Senses of Scripture*. Translated by Mark Sebanc. 3 vols. Grand Rapids, MI: Wm. B. Eerdmans, 1996.

Derolez, René. "Epigraphical versus Manuscript English Runes: One or Two Worlds?" *Academiae Analecta. Mededelingen van de Koninklijke Academie voor Wetenschappen, Letteren en Schone Künsten van België, Klasse der Letteren* 45 (1983): 70–93.

Derrida, Jacques. *Apprendre à vivre enfin: Entretien avec Jean Birnbaum*. Paris: Galilée / Le monde, 2005.

De Vriend, Hubert Jan, ed. *The Old English Herbarium and Medicina de quadrupedibus*. Oxford: Oxford University Press, 1984.

De Vries, Jan. *Altnordisches etymologisches Wörterbuch*. 2nd rev. ed. Leiden: Brill, 1962.

Dickins, Bruce, and Alan S. C. Ross, eds. *The Dream of the Rood*. London: Methuen, 1963.

Dietler, Michael. "A Tale of Three Sites: The Monumentalization of Celtic Oppida and the Politics of Collective Memory and Identity." *World Archaeology* 30, no. 1 (1998): 72–89.

Dinshaw, Carolyn. "Temporalities." In *Middle English*, edited by Paul Strohm, 107–23. Oxford Twenty-First Century Approaches to Literature. Oxford: Oxford University Press, 2007.

Doane, A. N. "Editing Old English Oral/Written Texts: Problems of Method (With an Illustrated Edition of Charm 4, *Wiþ Færstice*)." In *The Editing of Old English: Papers from the 1990 Manchester Conference*, edited by Donald G. Scragg and Paul E. Szarmach, 125–46. Woodbridge, UK: D. S. Brewer, 1994.

Dobbie, Elliott Van Kirk, ed. *The Anglo-Saxon Minor Poems*. Anglo-Saxon Poetic Records 6. New York: Columbia University Press, 1942.

Dobres, Marcia-Anne, and John Ernest Robb. "Agency in Archaeology: Paradigm or Platitude?" In *Agency in Archaeology*, edited by Marcia-Anne Dobres and John Ernest Robb, 3–17. London: Routledge, 2000.

Dodwell, Charles R. *Anglo-Saxon Art: A New Perspective*. Manchester: Manchester University Press, 1982.

Dolezalek, Isabelle. *Arabic Script on Christian Kings: Textile Inscriptions on Royal Garments from Norman Sicily*. Das Mittelalter. Perspektiven mediävistischer Forschung. Beihefte 5. Berlin: de Gruyter, 2017.

Donaldson, E. Talbot. *Beowulf: A Prose Translation*. Edited by Nicholas Howe. Norton Critical Edition. 2nd ed. New York: W. W. Norton and Company, 2002.

D'Onofrio, Cesare, ed. *Visitiamo Roma nel Quattrocento: La città degli umanisti*. Rome: Romano società editrice, 1989.

Doskow, Minna. "Poetic Structure and the Problem of the Smiths in *Wið Færstice*." *Papers on Language and Literature* 12 (1979): 321–26.

Eames, Elizabeth. *Medieval Tiles: A Handbook*. London: British Museum, 1968.

Echard, Siân. "Boom: Seeing *Beowulf* in Pictures and Print." In *Anglo-Saxon Culture and the Modern Imagination*, edited by David Clark and Nicholas Perkins, 129–45. Cambridge: D. S. Brewer, 2010.

Edgerton, Samuel Y. *The Renaissance Rediscovery of Linear Perspective*. New York: Icon, 1975.

Effros, Bonnie. *Merovingian Mortuary Archaeology and the Making of the Early Middle Ages*. Berkeley: University of California Press, 2003.

Eliot, George. *Middlemarch: A Story of Provincial Life*. London: Blackwood & Sons, 1871.

Eliot, T. S. *The Metaphysical Poets*. 1921. Reprinted in *Selected Essays*. 3rd ed. London: Faber & Faber, 1951.

Elkins, James. *The Poetics of Perspective*. Ithaca, NY: Cornell University Press, 1994.

Elliott, Alison Goddard. *Roads to Paradise: Reading the Lives of the Early Saints*. Hanover, NH: Brown University Press / University Press of New England, 1987.

Ellis, David H. "Development of Behaviour in the Golden Eagle." *Wildlife Monographs* 70 (1979): 3–94.

Emden, Cecil S. "The Law of Treasure-Trove, Past and Present." *Numismatic Chronicle and Journal of the Royal Numismatic Society* 9 (1929): 85–105.

Eusebius. *Life of Constantine*. Edited by Averil Cameron and Stuart G. Hall. Oxford: Clarendon Press, 1999.

Evans, Ruth. "Chaucer in Cyberspace: Medieval Technologies of Memory and *The House of Fame*." *Studies in the Age of Chaucer* 23 (2001): 43–69.

Fabroni, A. *Magni Cosmi Medici Vita*. Vol. 2, *Adnotationes et monumenta*. Pisa, 1788.

Fabyan, Robert. *The New Chronicles of England and France*. London, 1516.

Farrell, Robert T. "The Construction, Deconstruction, and Reconstruction of the Ruthwell Cross: Some Caveats." In *The Ruthwell Cross: Papers from the Colloquium Sponsored by the Index of Christian Art, Princeton University, 8 December 1989*, edited by Brendan Cassidy, 35–47. Index of Christian Art, Occasional Papers 1. Princeton, NJ: Index of Christian Art, Department of Art and Archaeology, Princeton University, 1992.

Fell, Christine E. "Runes and Semantics." In *Old English Runes and Their Continental Background*, edited by Alfred Bammesberger, 195–229. Anglistische Forschungen 217. Heidelberg: Carl Winter Universitätsverlag, 1991.

Felski, Rita. "Context Stinks!" *New Literary History* 42, no. 4 (2011): 573–91.

Ferhatović, Denis. *Borrowed Objects and the Art of Poetry: Spolia in Old English Verse*. Manchester: Manchester University Press, 2019.

Fiorani, Francesca. "Why Did Leonardo Not Finish the Adoration of the Magi?" In *Illuminating Leonardo: A Festschrift for Carlo Pedretti Celebrating His 70 Years of Scholarship (1944–2014)*, edited by Constance Moffatt and Sara Taglialagamba, 117–30. Leiden: Brill, 2016.

Flood, Finbarr Barry. *Objects of Translation: Material Culture and Medieval "Hindu-Muslim" Encounter*. Princeton, NJ: Princeton University Press, 2009.

Foley, John Miles. "How Genres Leak in Traditional Verse." In *Unlocking the Wordhord: Anglo-Saxon Studies in Memory of Edward B. Irving, Jr.*, edited by Mark C. Amodio and Katherine O'Brien O'Keeffe, 76–108. Toronto: University of Toronto Press, 2003.

———. "Hybrid Prosody: Single Half-lines in Old English and Serbo-Croatian Poetry." *Neophilologus* 64 (1980): 284–89.

———. *Immanent Art: From Structure to Meaning in Traditional Oral Epic*. Bloomington: Indiana University Press, 1991.

Folsach, K. von. "What the Basket Contained: Some Dateable Glass Bottles from the Eastern Islamic World." In *Facts and Artefacts: Art in the Islamic World; Festschrift for Jens Kröger on his 65th Birthday*, edited by A. Hagedorn and A. Shalem, 3–11. Leiden: Brill, 2007.

Forero-Mendoza, Sabine. *Le temps des ruines: Le goût des ruines et les formes de la conscience historique à la Renaissance*. Seyssel, FR: Champ Vallon, 2002.

Foster, William. *Early Travels in India, 1583–1619*. Oxford: Oxford University Press, 1911.

Foucault, Michel. *Archéologie du savoir*. Paris: Gallimard, 1969.

Foxe, John. *Actes and Monuments*. London, 1583.

Frank, Roberta. "*Beowulf* and Sutton Hoo: The Odd Couple." In *Voyage to the Other World: The Legacy of Sutton Hoo*, edited by Calvin B. Kendall and Peter S. Wells, 47–64. Minneapolis: University of Minnesota Press, 1992.

———. "Germanic Legend in Old English Literature." In *The Cambridge Companion to Old English Literature*, edited by Malcolm Godden and Michael Lapidge, 82–100. 2nd ed. Cambridge: Cambridge University Press, 2013.

———. "Old English *Orc* 'Cup, Goblet': A Latin Loanword with Attitude." In *Alfred the Wise: Studies in Honour of Janet Bately*, edited by Jane Roberts and Janet L. Nelson, 15–24. Woodbridge, UK: Boydell & Brewer, 1997.

———. "Onomastic Play in Kormákr's Verse: The Name Steingerðr." *Mediaeval Scandinavia* 3 (1970): 7–30.

———. "Three 'Cups' and a Funeral in *Beowulf*." In *Latin Learning and English Lore: Studies in Anglo-Saxon Literature for Michael Lapidge*, edited by Katherine O'Brien O'Keeffe and Andy Orchard, 1:407–20. Toronto: University of Toronto Press, 2005.

Frantzen, Allen J. *The Desire for Origins: New Language, Old English, and Teaching the Tradition*. New Brunswick: Rutgers University Press, 1990.

Fulk, R. D., Robert E. Bjork, and John D. Niles, eds. *Klaeber's "Beowulf" and "The Fight at Finnsburg."* 4th ed. Toronto: University of Toronto Press, 2008.

Furlotti, Barbara, and Guido Rebecchini. *The Art of Mantua: Power and Patronage in the Renaissance*. Translated by A. Lawrence Jenkens. Los Angeles: Getty, 2008.

Gade, Kari Ellen, ed. *Poetry from Treatises on Poetics*. Skaldic Poetry of the Scandinavian Middle Ages 3. Turnhout: Brepols, 2017.

Gaiman, Neil. *The Graveyard Book*. HarperCollins e-books, 2008.

Gale, David. "The Seax." In *Weapons and Warfare in Anglo-Saxon England*, edited by Sonia Chadwick Hawkes, 71–84. Oxford: Oxford University Committee for Archaeology, 1989.

Garner, Lori Ann. "Anglo-Saxon Charms in Performance." *Oral Tradition* 19 (2004): 20–42.

———. *Structuring Spaces: Oral Poetics and Architecture in Early Medieval England*. Notre Dame, IN: University of Notre Dame Press, 2011.

Garner, Lori Ann, and Kayla M. Miller. "'A Swarm in July': Beekeeping Perspectives on the Old English *Wið Ymbe* Charm." *Oral Tradition* 26, no. 2 (2011): 355–76.

Garrison, Mary. "Quid Hinieldus cum Christo?" In *Latin Learning and English Lore: Studies in Anglo-Saxon Literature for Michael Lapidge*, edited by Katherine O'Brien O'Keeffe and Andy Orchard, 2:237–59. Toronto: University of Toronto Press, 2005.

Geary, Patrick. *Furta Sacra: Thefts of Relics in the Central Middle Ages*. Rev. ed. Princeton, NJ: Princeton University Press, 1990.

Geoffrey of Monmouth. *The History of the Kings of Britain*. Translated by Lewis Thorpe. London: Penguin, 1966.

George, Jodi-Anne. *"Beowulf": A Reader's Guide to Essential Criticism*. Houndmills, UK: Palgrave Macmillan, 2010.

Gerald of Wales. *The Journey Through Wales / The Description of Wales*. Translated by Lewis Thorpe. Edited by Betty Radice. London: Penguin, 1978.

———. *Liber de Principis Instructione*. Cited from "The Tomb of King Arthur," translated by John William Sutton. The Camelot Project. Rochester, NY: Robbins Library, University of Rochester, 2001. Accessed June 2, 2020. http://d.lib.rochester.edu/camelot/text/gerald-of-wales-arthurs-tomb.

———. *Speculum Ecclesiae*. Cited from "The Tomb of King Arthur," translated by John William Sutton. The Camelot Project. Rochester, NY: Robbins Library, University of Rochester, 2001. Accessed June 2, 2020. http://d.lib.rochester.edu/camelot/text/gerald-of-wales-arthurs-tomb.

Gibson, Gail McMurray. *Theater of Devotion: East Anglian Drama and Society in the Late Middle Ages*. Chicago: University of Chicago Press, 1989.

Gilchrist, Roberta. "The Materiality of Medieval Heirlooms: From Sacred to Biographical Objects." In *Mobility, Meaning and the Transformations of Things: Shifting Contexts of Material Culture through Time and Space*, edited by Hans Peter Hahn and Hadas Weiss, 170–82. Oxford: Oxbow, 2013.

Ginzburg, Carlo. *Ecstasies: Deciphering the Witches' Sabbath*. Translated by Raymond Rosenthal. London: Penguin, 1991.

Glosecki, Stephen. *Shamanism and Old English Poetry*. Albert Bates Lord Studies in Oral Tradition. 2 vols. New York: Garland Publishing, 1989.

Gombrich, E. H. "Leonardo's Method for Working Out Compositions." In *The Essential Gombrich*, edited by Richard Woodfield, 211–21. London: Phaidon Press, 1996.

Gordon, Phyllis Walter Goodhart, trans. and ed. *Two Renaissance Book Hunters: The Letters of Poggius Bracciolini and Nicolaus de Niccolis*. New York: Columbia University Press, 1991.

Gordon, Robert K., trans. and ed. *Anglo-Saxon Poetry*. London: Dent, 1954.

Gordon-Taylor, Benjamin Nicholas. "The Hagiography of St Alban and St Amphibalus in the Twelfth Century." Master's thesis, Durham University, 1991.

Gould, Stephen Jay. *Wonderful Life: The Burgess Shale and the Nature of History*. New York: W. W. Norton, 1989.

Grabar, Oleg. "About a Bronze Bird." In *Reading Medieval Images: The Art Historian and the Object*, edited by Elizabeth Sears, Thelma K. Thomas, and Ilene H. Forsyth, 117–25. Ann Arbor: University of Michigan Press, 2002.

———. "The Crusades and the Development of Islamic Art." In *The Crusades from the Perspective of Byzantium and the Muslim World*, edited by Angeliki E. Laiou and Roy Parviz Mottahedeh, 235–45. Washington, DC: Dumbarton Oaks, 2001.

Grafton, Anthony. "The Ancient City Restored: Archaeology, Ecclesiastical History, and Egyptology." In *Rome Reborn: The Vatican Library and Renaissance Culture*. Washington, DC: Library of Congress; New Haven, CT: Yale University Press, 1993.

Granger-Taylor, Hero. "The Inscription on the Nature Goddess Silk." In *St. Cuthbert, His Cult and His Community to AD 1200*, edited by Gerald Bonner, David W. Rollason, and Clare Stancliffe, 339–42. Woodbridge, UK: Boydell Press, 1989.

Gransden, Antonia. "The Growth of Glastonbury Traditions and Legends in the Twelfth Century." In *Glastonbury Abbey and the Arthurian Tradition,* edited by James P. Carley, 29–53. Cambridge: D. S. Brewer, 2001.

Green, Bernard. *Christianity in Ancient Rome: The First Three Centuries.* London: A&C Black / T&T Clark, 2010.

Greene, Thomas M. "Anti-Hermeneutics: The Case of Shakespeare's Sonnet 129." In *Poetic Traditions of the English Renaissance,* edited by Maynard Mack and George de Forest Lord, 143–62. New Haven, CT: Yale University Press, 1982.

Greenstein, Jack M. *Temporality in Mantegna and Painting as Historical Narrative.* Chicago: University of Chicago Press, 1992.

Grendon, Felix. "The Anglo-Saxon Charms." *Journal of American Folklore* 22 (1909): 105–237.

Greyfriars Research Team. *The Bones of a King: Richard III Rediscovered.* With Maev Kennedy and Lin Foxhall. Chichester: John Wiley & Sons, 2015.

Griffith, Mark. "Old English Poetic Diction Not in Old English Verse or Prose—and the Curious Case of Aldhelm's Five Athletes." *Anglo-Saxon England* 43 (2014): 99–132.

Grímur Jónsson Thorkelin, ed. *De Danorum rebus gestis secul[i] III & IV: Poëma danicum dialecto anglosaxonica.* Copenhagen: T. E. Rangel, 1815.

Gumbrecht, Hans Ulrich. *Our Broad Present: Time and Contemporary Culture.* New York: Columbia University Press, 2014.

Hagiioannu, Michael. "Giotto Bardi's Chapel Frescoes and Chaucer's *House of Fame*: Influence, Evidence and Interpretations." *Chaucer Review* 36 (2001): 28–47.

Hall, Alaric. *Elves in Anglo-Saxon England: Matters of Belief, Health, Gender and Identity.* Woodbridge, UK: Boydell Press, 2007.

Härke, Heinrich. "The Circulation of Weapons in Anglo-Saxon Society." In *Rituals of Power from Late Antiquity to the Middle Ages,* edited by Frans Theuws and Janet L. Nelson, 377–400. Leiden: Brill, 2000.

———. "Early Saxon Weapon Burials: Frequencies, Distributions and Weapon Combinations." In *Weapons and Warfare in Anglo-Saxon England,* edited by Sonia Chadwick Hawkes, 49–61. Oxford: Oxford University Committee for Archaeology, 1989.

———. "'Warrior graves'? The Background of the Anglo-Saxon Weapon Burial Rite." *Past & Present* 126 (1990): 22–43.

Harman, Graham. "The Well-Wrought Broken Hammer: Object-Oriented Literary Criticism." *New Literary History* 43 (2012): 183–203.

Harris, Jonathan Gil. *The First Firangis: Remarkable Stories of Heroes, Healers, Charlatans, Courtesans, and Other Foreigners Who Became Indian.* New Delhi: Aleph Books, 2015.

———. "Ludgate Time: Simon Eyre's Oath and the Temporal Economies of *The Shoemaker's Holiday.*" *Huntington Library Quarterly* 71, no. 1 (2008): 11–32.

———. *Untimely Matter in the Time of Shakespeare.* Philadelphia: University of Pennsylvania Press, 2008.

Harris, Joseph. "*Beowulf* in Literary History." *Pacific Coast Philology* 17 (1982): 16–23.

Hart, Vaughan, and Peter Hicks, eds. and trans. "The Letter to Leo X by Raphael and Baldassare Castiglione (c. 1519)." In *Palladio's Rome: A Translation of Andrea Palladio's Two Guidebooks to Rome,* 177–92. New Haven, CT: Yale University Press, 2006.

Hartshorne, Emily Sophia. *Enshrined Hearts of Warriors and Illustrious People.* London: Robert Hardwicke, 1861.

Hartt, Frederick. *Giulio Romano.* 2 vols. New Haven, CT: Yale University Press, 1958.

Hawkes, Sonia Chadwick, and R. I. Page. "Swords and Runes in South-East England." *Antiquaries Journal* 47 (1967): 1–26.

Heaney, Seamus, trans. *Beowulf: A New Verse Translation*. New York: Farrar, Straus and Giroux, 2000.

Heffernan, James A. W. *Museum of Words: The Poetics of Ekphrasis from Homer to Ashbery*. Chicago: University of Chicago Press, 1993.

Heinzelmann, Martin. *Translationsberichte und andere Quellen des Reliquienkultes*. Turnhout: Brepols, 1979.

Henig, Martin. "The Re-use and Copying of Ancient Intaglios Set in Medieval Personal Seals Mainly Found in England: An Aspect of the Renaissance of the 12th Century." In *Good Impressions: Image and Authority in Medieval Seals*, edited by Noel Adams, John Cherry, and James Robinson, 25–34. British Museum Research Publication 168. London: British Museum, 2008.

Hermann, John P. *Allegories of War: Language and Violence in Old English Poetry*. Ann Arbor: University of Michigan Press, 1989.

Hicks, Dan, and Mary C. Beaudry. "Introduction: The Place of Historical Archaeology." In *The Cambridge Companion to Historical Archaeology*, 1–10. Cambridge: Cambridge University Press, 2006.

Higgins, Clare. "Some New Thoughts on the Nature Goddess Silk." In *St. Cuthbert, His Cult and His Community to AD 1200*, edited by Gerald Bonner, David W. Rollason, and Clare Stancliffe, 329–38. Woodbridge, UK: Boydell Press, 1989.

Hill, Carole. "'Leave my Virginity Alone!': The Cult of St Margaret of Antioch in Norwich; In Pursuit of a Pragmatic Piety." In *Medieval East Anglia*, edited by Christopher Harper-Bill, 225–45. Woodbridge, UK: Boydell Press, 2005.

Hill, George Francis. *Treasure Trove in Law and Practice, from the Earliest Time to the Present Day*. Oxford: Clarendon, 1936.

Hill, John M. *The Cultural World in "Beowulf."* Toronto: University of Toronto Press, 1995.

Hill, Thomas D. "The Rod of Protection and the Witches' Ride: Christian and Germanic Syncretism in Two Old English Metrical Charms." *Journal of English and Germanic Philology* 111 (2012): 145–68.

Hills, Catherine M. "*Beowulf* and Archaeology." In *A "Beowulf" Handbook*, edited by Robert E. Bjork and John D. Niles, 291–310. Lincoln: University of Nebraska Press, 1997.

Hinds, Gareth. *Beowulf*. Cambridge, MA: Candlewick Press, 1999.

Hines, John. "*Beowulf* and Archaeology—Revisited." In *Aedificia Nova: Studies in Honor of Rosemary Cramp*, edited by Catherine E. Karkov and Helen Damico, 89–105. Kalamazoo, MI: Medieval Institute Publications, 2008.

———. "The Military Context of the *Adventus Saxonum*: Some Continental Evidence." In *Weapons and Warfare in Anglo-Saxon England*, edited by Sonia Chadwick Hawkes, 25–48. Oxford: Oxford University Committee for Archaeology, 1989.

———. "The Ruthwell Cross, the Brussels Cross, and *The Dream of the Rood*." In *Transitional States: Change, Tradition, and Memory in Medieval Literature and Culture*, edited by Graham D. Caie and Michael D. C. Drout, 175–92. Medieval and Renaissance Texts and Studies 530. Tempe: Arizona Center for Medieval and Renaissance Studies, 2018.

———. *Voices in the Past: English Literature and Archaeology*. Cambridge: D. S. Brewer, 2004.

Hodder, Ian. *Entangled: An Archaeology of the Relationships between Humans and Things*. Chichester: Wiley-Blackwell, 2012.

Höhle, Eva-Marie, Oskar Pausch, and Richard Perger. "Die Neidhart-Fresken im Haus Tuchlauben 19 in Wien: Zum Funde profaner Wandmalereien der Zeit um 1400." *Österreichische Zeitschrift für Kunst und Denkmalpflege* 36 (1982): 110–44.

Holdsworth, Carolyn. "Frames: Time Level and Variation in *The Dream of the Rood*." *Neophilologus* 66 (1982): 622–28.

Holt, Frank L. *Alexander the Great and the Mystery of the Elephant Medallions*. Berkeley: University of California Press, 2003.

Holthausen, Ferdinand. *Altenglisches etymologisches Wörterbuch*. Heidelberg: Carl Winter Universitätsverlag, 1934.

———. "Zu altenglischen Dichtungen." In *Beiblatt zur Anglia XXXI* (1920): 346–56.

Holtorf, Cornelius. *From Stonehenge to Las Vegas: Archaeology as Popular Culture*. Lanham, MD: AltaMira, 2005.

Honigmann, Ernest. "Stephen of Ephesus (April 15, 448–Oct. 29, 451) and the Legend of the Seven Sleepers." In *Patristic Studies*, 125–68. Studi e testi 173. Vatican City: Biblioteca Apostolica Vaticana, 1953.

Horstmann, Carl. "Mappula Angliae, von Osbern Bokenham." *Englische Studien* 10 (1886): 1–34.

Howlett, David. "Inscriptions and Design of the Ruthwell Cross." In *The Ruthwell Cross: Papers from the Colloquium Sponsored by the Index of Christian Art, Princeton University, 8 December 1989*, edited by Brendan Cassidy, 71–93. Index of Christian Art, Occasional Papers 1. Princeton, NJ: Index of Christian Art, Department of Art and Archaeology, Princeton University, 1992.

Huber, Michael, ed. *Beitrag zur Visionsliteratur und Siebenschläferlegende des Mittelalters: Eine literaturgeschichtliche Untersuchung; I. Teil: Texte*. Beilage zum Jahresbericht des humanistischen Gymnasiums Metten (1902–3): 39–78.

———. *Die Wanderlegende von den Siebenschläfern: Eine literaturgeschichtliche Untersuchung*. Leipzig: Harrassowitz, 1910.

Hui, Andrew. "The Birth of Ruins in Quattrocento Adoration Paintings." *I Tatti Studies in the Italian Renaissance* 18, no. 2 (2015): 319–48.

———. *The Poetics of Ruins in Renaissance Literature*. New York: Fordham University Press, 2016.

Hunter, Michael. "Germanic and Roman Antiquity and the Sense of the Past in Anglo-Saxon England." *Anglo-Saxon England* 3 (1974): 29–50.

Huyssen, Andreas. *Twilight Memories: Marking Time in a Culture of Amnesia*. London: Psychology Press, 1995.

Ingham, Patricia Clare. "Little Nothings: *The Squire's Tale* and the Ambition of Gadgets." *Studies in the Age of Chaucer* 31 (2009): 53–80.

Irving, Edward B., Jr. *Rereading "Beowulf*." Philadelphia: University of Pennsylvania Press, 1989.

Jacobus de Voragine. "Life of St. Sebastian." In *The Golden Legend: Readings on the Saints*, translated by William Granger Ryan, 1:97–100. Princeton, NJ: Princeton University Press, 1995.

James, M. R. "The Drawings of Matthew Paris." *Volume of the Walpole Society* 14 (1925–26): 1–26.

Jennings, Margaret. "Rood and Ruthwell: The Power of Paradox." *English Language Notes* 31 (1994): 6–11.

Jerome. *Selected Letters*. Translated by F. A. Wright. Cambridge, MA: Harvard University Press, 1933.

John Amundesham. *Account of the Altars, Monuments, and Tombs, Existing A. D. 1428 in Saint Alban's Abbey*. Translated by Ridgway Lloyd. Saint Albans: Langley, 1873.

———. *Annales monasterii S. Albani, a Johanne Amundesham, monacho ut videtur, conscripti (AD 1421–1440)*. Edited by Henry Thomas Riley. Rolls Series 28. Part 5. 2 vols. London: Longmans, Green, and Co., 1870–71.

Johnston, Andrew James. "*Beowulf* and the Remains of Imperial Rome: Archaeology, Legendary History and the Problems of Periodisation." In *Anglistentag 2008 Tübingen: Proceedings*, edited by Lars Eckstein and Christoph Reinfandt, 127–36. Proceedings of the Conference of the German Association of University Teachers of English 30. Trier: Wissenschaftlicher Verlag Trier, 2009.

———. "*Beowulf* as Anti-Virgilian World Literature: Archaeology, Ekphrasis, and Epic." In *The Shapes of Early English Poetry: Style, Form, History*, edited by Irina Dumitrescu and Eric Weiskott, 37–58. Kalamazoo, MI: Medieval Institute Publications, Western Michigan University, 2019.

———. "Medialität in *Beowulf*." *Germanisch-Romanische Monatsschrift* 59, no. 1 (2009): 129–47.

———. "The Riddle of *Deor* and the Performance of Fiction." In *Language and Text: Current Perspectives on English and Germanic Historical Linguistics and Philology*, edited by Andrew James Johnston, Ferdinand von Mengden, and Stefan Thim, 133–50. Heidelberg: Carl Winter Universitätsverlag, 2006.

Jolly, Karen. *Popular Religion in Late Saxon England: Elf Charms in Context*. Chapel Hill: University of North Carolina Press, 1996.

Karkov, Catherine E. "Naming and Renaming: The Inscription of Gender in Anglo-Saxon Sculpture." In *Theorizing Anglo-Saxon Stone Sculpture*, edited by Catherine E. Karkov and Fred Orton, 31–64. Morgantown: West Virginia University Press, 2003.

Karmon, David. *The Ruin of the Eternal City: Antiquity and Preservation in Renaissance Rome*. Oxford: Oxford University Press, 2011.

Kaye, Joel. "Monetary and Market Consciousness in Thirteenth and Fourteenth Century Europe." In *Ancient and Medieval Economic Ideas and Concepts of Social Justice*, edited by S. Todd Lowry and Barry Gordan, 371–404. Leiden: Brill, 1998.

Kelsall, Jane. "The Chantry of Humphrey Duke of Gloucester (1391–1447) at the Cathedral and Abbey Church of St Alban." Church Monuments Society: Monument of the Month, May 2010. Accessed June 2, 2020. https://churchmonumentssociety.org/monument-of-the-month/the-chantry-of-humphrey-duke-of-gloucester-1391-1447-at-the-cathedral-and-abbey-church-of-st-alban.

Kelton, Arthur. *A Commendacyon of Welshmen*. London, 1546.

Kiening, Christian. Introduction to *Figura*, edited by Christian Kiening and Katharina Mertens Fleury, 7–20. Philologie der Kultur 8. Würzburg: Königshausen & Neumann, 2013.

Kinoshita, Sharon. *Medieval Boundaries: Rethinking Difference in Old French Literature*. Philadelphia: University of Pennsylvania Press, 2006.

Klaeber, Frederick, ed. *"Beowulf" and "The Fight at Finnsburg."* Boston: D. C. Heath and Co., 1922.

———, ed. *"Beowulf" and "The Fight at Finnsburg."* 3rd ed. Boston: D. C. Heath and Co., 1950.

Klinck, Anne, ed. *The Old English Elegies: A Critical Edition and Genre Study*. Montreal: McGill-Queen's University Press, 1992.

Knight, Barry. "The Heart Case of Abbot Roger de Norton from St Albans Abbey: An Islamic Object in a Medieval English Context." *Muqarnas* 36, no. 1 (2019): 221–28.

Köberl, Johann. "The Magic Sword in *Beowulf*." *Neophilologus* 71 (1987): 120–28.

Koch, John, ed. *Chardry's Josaphaz, Set Dormanz und Petit Plet: Dichtungen in der Anglo-Normannischen Mundart des XIII. Jahrhunderts*. Heilbronn: Henninger, 1879.

———. *Die Siebenschläferlegende, ihr Ursprung und ihre Verbreitung: Eine mythologisch-literaturgeschichtliche Studie.* Leipzig: Reissner, 1883.

Kolve, V. A. *Chaucer and the Imagery of Narrative: The First Five Canterbury Tales.* London: Edwin Arnold, 1984.

Krapp, George Philip, and Elliott Van Kirk Dobbie, eds. *The Exeter Book.* Anglo-Saxon Poetic Records 3. New York: Columbia University Press, 1936.

Krochalis, Jeanne. "*Magna Tabula*: The Glastonbury Tablets." Pts. 1 and 2. *Arthurian Literature* 15 (1997): 93–183; 16 (1998): 41–82. Reprinted together in *Glastonbury Abbey and the Arthurian Tradition,* edited by James P. Carley. Cambridge: D. S. Brewer, 2001.

Lahiri, Nayanjot. *Ashoka in Ancient India.* Cambridge, MA: Harvard University Press, 2015.

Lakoff, George, and Mark Johnson. *Metaphors We Live By.* 2nd ed. Chicago: University of Chicago Press, 2003.

Lane, H. M. M. "Queen Eleanor of Castile." *Transactions of the St Albans and Hertfordshire Architectural and Archaeological Society* (1928–30): 255–73.

Langley, Philippa, and Michael Jones. *The King's Grave: The Search for Richard III.* London: John Murray, 2013.

Laqueur, Thomas W. *The Work of the Dead: A Cultural History of Mortal Remains.* Princeton, NJ: Princeton University Press, 2015.

Latour, Bruno. *Reassembling the Social: An Introduction to Actor-Network Theory.* Oxford: Oxford University Press, 2005.

———. *We Have Never Been Modern.* Translated by Catherine Porter. Cambridge, MA: Harvard University Press, 1993.

Lavezzo, Kathy. *The Accommodated Jew: English Antisemitism from Bede to Milton.* Ithaca, NY: Cornell University Press, 2016.

Leahy, Kevin, and Roger Bland. *The Staffordshire Hoard.* 2nd ed. London: British Museum, 2014.

Leland, John, and John Bale. *The Laboryouse Journey and Serche of Johan Leylande.* 1549.

Lerer, Seth. *Literacy and Power in Anglo-Saxon Literature.* Lincoln: University of Nebraska Press, 1991.

———. "'On fagne flor': The Postcolonial *Beowulf.*" In *Postcolonial Approaches to the European Middle Ages,* edited by Ananya Jahanara Kabir and Deanne Williams, 77–102. Cambridge: Cambridge University Press, 2005.

Leslie, R. F., ed. *The Wanderer.* Manchester: Manchester University Press, 1966.

Levy, F. J. *Tudor Historical Thought.* San Marino, CA: Huntington Library, 1967.

Leyerle, John. "The Interlace Structure of *Beowulf.*" In *Interpretations of "Beowulf": A Critical Anthology,* edited by R. D. Fulk, 146–58. Bloomington: Indiana University Press, 1991.

Linde, Nancy, dir. "Cancer Warrior." *Nova.* Aired February 27, 2001, on PBS. Television.

Liu, Xinru. *Silk and Religion: An Exploration of Material Life and the Thought of People.* New Delhi: Oxford University Press, 1996.

Liuzza, Roy M. "*Beowulf*: Monuments, Memory, History." In *Readings in Medieval Texts: Interpreting Old and Middle English Literature,* edited by David F. Johnson and Elaine Treharne, 91–108. Oxford: Oxford University Press, 2005.

———, trans. and ed. *Beowulf: A New Verse Translation.* Peterborough, ON: Broadview Press, 2000.

———, trans. and ed. *Beowulf: Second Edition.* Peterborough, ON: Broadview Press, 2013.

Luckhurst, Roger. *The Mummy's Curse: The True History of a Dark Fantasy.* Oxford: Oxford University Press, 2012.

Ludden, David. "History Outside Civilisation and the Mobility of South Asia." *South Asia: Journal of South Asian Studies* 17 (1994): 1–23.

Lydgate, John. *Lydgate's Troy Book A. D. 1412–20*. Edited by Henry Bergen. 4 vols. EETS extra series 99, 103, 106, 126. London: Oxford University Press, 1906–35.

Macaulay, Rose. *The Pleasure of Ruins*. London: Thames and Hudson, 1953.

Mackin, Herbert Walter. *The Brasses of England*. London: Methuen, 1907.

Magennis, Hugh, ed. *The Anonymous Old English Legend of the Seven Sleepers*. Durham Medieval Texts 7. Durham, NC: Department of English Studies, 1994.

———. "Crowd Control? Depictions of the Many in Anglo-Saxon Literature, with Particular Reference to the Old English Legend of the Seven Sleepers." *English Studies* 93 (2012): 119–37.

———. "Style and Method in the Old English Version of the Legend of the Seven Sleepers." *English Studies* 66 (1985): 285–95.

Maidstone, Richard. *Concordia: The Reconciliation of Richard II with London*. Translated by A. G. Rigg. Edited by David R. Carlson. TEAMS Middle English Texts Series. Kalamazoo, MI: Medieval Institute Publications, 2003. Online edition. Accessed June 2, 2020. http://d.lib.rochester.edu/teams/text/rigg-and-carlson-maidstone-concordia.

Maier, Jessica. *Rome Measured and Imagined: Early Modern Maps of the Eternal City*. Chicago: University of Chicago Press, 2015.

Malory, Thomas. *Works*. Edited by Eugène Vinaver. Oxford: Oxford University Press, 1971.

Mandeville, John. *The Book of Marvels and Travels*. Edited and translated by Anthony Bale. Oxford: Oxford University Press, 2012.

Manley, John. "The Archer and the Army in the Late Saxon Period." *Anglo-Saxon Studies in History and Archaeology* 4 (1985): 223–35.

Manley, Lawrence. *Literature and Culture in Early Modern London*. Cambridge: Cambridge University Press, 1997.

Manning, John. *The Emblem*. London: Reaktion, 2002.

Marin, Louis. *Sublime Poussin*. Translated by Catherine Porter. Stanford, CA: Stanford University Press, 1999.

Márquez, Gabriel García. *One Hundred Years of Solitude*. Translated by Gregory Rabassa. London: Penguin Books, 2014.

Marsden, Richard. "Biblical Literature: The New Testament." In *The Cambridge Companion to Old English Literature*, edited by Malcolm Godden and Michael Lapidge, 234–50. 2nd ed. Cambridge: Cambridge University Press, 2013.

Marstine, Janet, ed. *New Museum Theory and Practice: An Introduction*. Oxford: Wiley, 2005.

Mason, Fred B. *Gibbs' Illustrated Handbook to St Albans: Containing a Sketch of Its History, and a Description of Its Abbey, Its Antiquities, and Other Objects of Interest*. St. Albans: Gibbs and Bamforth, 1884.

Massignon, Louis. "Le culte liturgique et populaire des VII dormants martyrs d'Ephèse (Ahl Al-Kahf): Trait d'union Orient-Occident entre l'Islam et la Chrétienté." In *Opera Minora*, edited by Y. Moubarac, 3:119–80. Beirut: Dar Al-Maaref, 1963.

Matthew Paris. *Chronica Majora*. Edited by H. R. Luard. 7 vols. London: Longman, 1872–83.

———. *The Life of Saint Alban*. Translated and edited by Jocelyn Wogan-Browne and Thelma S. Fenster. Tempe: Arizona Center for Medieval and Renaissance Studies, 2010.

———. *"Vie de Seint Auban": A Poem in Old French*. Edited by Robert Atkinson. London: John Murray, 1876.

Mayor, Adrienne. *The First Fossil Hunters: Paleontology in Greek and Roman Times*. Princeton, NJ: Princeton University Press, 2000.

McGillvray, Murray, ed. *Old English Reader*. Peterborough, ON: Broadview Press, 2011.

McGowan, Margaret M. *The Vision of Rome in Late Renaissance France*. New Haven, CT: Yale University Press, 2000.

Mély, Fernand de. *Du rôle des pierres gravées au Moyen Âge*. Lille: Desclée & De Brouwer, 1893.

Merrigan, Terrence. "Revelation." In *The Cambridge Companion to John Henry Newman*, edited by Ian Ker and Terrence Merrigan, 47–72. Cambridge: Cambridge University Press, 2009.

Merrilees, Brian S., ed. *La vie des set dormanz by Chardri*. Anglo-Norman Text Society 35. London: Westfield College / Anglo-Norman Text Society, 1977.

Meyvaert, Paul. "An Apocalypse Panel on the Ruthwell Cross." In *Medieval and Renaissance Studies: Proceedings of the Southeastern Institute of Medieval and Renaissance Studies, Summer 1978*, edited by Frank Tirro, 3–32. Durham, NC: Duke University Press, 1982.

———. "Necessity Mother of Invention: A Fresh Look at the Rune Verses on the Ruthwell Cross." *Anglo-Saxon England* 41 (2012): 407–16.

———. "A New Perspective on the Ruthwell Cross: Ecclesia and Vita Monastica." In *The Ruthwell Cross: Papers from the Colloquium Sponsored by the Index of Christian Art, Princeton University, 8 December 1989*, edited by Brendan Cassidy, 95–166. Index of Christian Art, Occasional Papers 1. Princeton, NJ: Index of Christian Art, Department of Art and Archaeology, Princeton University, 1992.

Milanesi, Gaetano, ed. *Le opere di Giorgio Vasari*. 9 vols. Florence: Sansoni, 1906.

Milgram, Stanley. *Obedience to Authority: An Experimental View*. New York: Harper & Row, 1964.

Minnis, A. J. "'Figures of olde werk': Chaucer's Poetic Sculptures." In *Secular Sculpture 1300–1550*, edited by Phillip Lindley and Thomas Frangenberg, 124–43. Stamford, CT: Shaun Tyas, 2000.

Minnis, A. J., V. J. Scattergood, and J. J. Smith. *Oxford Guides to Chaucer: The Shorter Poems*. Oxford: Clarendon Press, 1995.

Mitchell, W. J. T. *Picture Theory: Essays on Verbal and Visual Representation*. Chicago: University of Chicago Press, 1994.

Mitsi, Efterpi. *Greece in Early English Travel Writing*. London: Palgrave Macmillan, 2017.

Mone, Franz Joseph. "Zur Kritik des Gedichts vom Beowulf." In *Untersuchungen zur Geschichte der teutschen Heldensage*. 2nd series of the Bibliothek der gesammten deutschen National-Literatur, 1:129–36. Quedlinburg, 1836.

Moraes, Dom, and Sarayu Srivatsa. *The Long Strider: How Thomas Coryate Walked from England to India in the Year 1613*. Delhi: Penguin India, 2003.

Mott, George, and Sally Sample Aall. *Follies and Pleasure Pavilions*. New York: H. M. Abrams, 1989.

Mowat, Barbara A., and Paul Werstine, eds. *Hamlet*. New York: Simon and Schuster, 2003.

Mullally, Erin. "The Cross-Gendered Gift: Weaponry in the Old English *Judith*." *Exemplaria* 17 (2013): 255–84.

Mullaney, Steven. *The Place of the Stage: Licence, Play, and Power in Renaissance England*. Chicago: Chicago University Press, 1988.

Müntz, Eugène. *Les arts à la cour des papes aux XVe et XVIe siècle*. 4 vols. Paris: Ernest Leroux, 1898.

Muthesius, Anna. "Silks and Saints: The Rider and Peacock Silks from the Relics of St. Cuthbert." In *St. Cuthbert, His Cult and His Community to AD 1200*, edited by Gerald Bonner, David W. Rollason, and Clare Stancliffe, 343–66. Woodbridge, UK: Boydell Press, 1989.

Nagel, Alexander, and Christopher S. Wood. *Anachronic Renaissance*. New York: Zone Books, 2010.

Ng, Su Fang. "Global Renaissance: Alexander the Great and Early Modern Classicism from the British Isles to the Malay Archipelago." *Comparative Literature* 58 (2006): 293–312.

Nice, Jason. *Sacred History and National Identity: Comparisons Between Early Modern Wales and Brittany*. Abingdon: Routledge, 2016.

Niles, John D., ed. *"Beowulf" and Lejre*. Tempe: Arizona Center for Medieval and Renaissance Studies, 2007.

———, ed. *Beowulf: Translated by Seamus Heaney; An Illustrated Edition*. New York: Norton, 2008.

———. *Old English Enigmatic Poems and the Play of the Texts*. Studies in the Early Middle Ages 13. Turnhout: Brepols, 2006.

———. *Old English Literature: A Guide to Criticism with Selected Readings*. Blackwell Guides to Criticism. Chichester: Wiley-Blackwell, 2016.

———. "Orality." In *The Cambridge Companion to Textual Scholarship*, edited by Neil Fraistat and Julia Flanders, 205–23. Cambridge: Cambridge University Press, 2013.

Nochlin, Linda. *The Body in Pieces: The Fragment as a Metaphor of Modernity*. London: Thames and Hudson, 2001.

Nora, Pierre. "General Introduction: Between Memory and History." In *Realms of Memory: Rethinking the French Past*. Translated by Arthur Goldhammer. Edited by Lawrence D. Kritzman, 1:1–20. New York: Columbia University Press, 1996–98.

Norris, M. W. *Monumental Brasses: The Portfolio Plates of the Monumental Brass Society*. Woodbridge, UK: Boydell Press, 1988.

Ó Carragáin, Éamonn. *Ritual and the Rood: Liturgical Images and the Old English Poems of the "Dream of the Rood" Tradition*. British Library Studies in Medieval Culture. London: British Library / University of Toronto Press, 2005.

Olrik, Axel. *Danmarks heltedigtning: En oldtidsstudie*. Vol. 1, *Rolf Krake og den ældre Skjoldungrække*. Copenhagen: G. E. C. Gad, 1903–19.

———. *The Heroic Legends of Denmark*. Translated and revised by Lee M. Hollander. New York: American-Scandinavian Foundation, 1919.

Olsan, Lea. "The Inscriptions of Charms in Anglo-Saxon Manuscripts." *Oral Tradition* 24 (1999): 401–19.

———. "Latin Charms of Medieval England: Verbal Healing in a Christian Oral Tradition." *Oral Tradition* 7 (1992): 116–42.

———. "The Marginality of Charms in Medieval England." In *The Power of Words: Studies on Charms and Charming in Europe*, edited by James Kapaló, Eva Pócs, and William Ryan, 135–64. Budapest: Central European University Press, 2013.

Orchard, Andy. *Pride and Prodigies: Studies in the Monsters of the "Beowulf"-Manuscript*. Toronto: University of Toronto Press, 2003.

Orel, Vladimir. *Handbook of Germanic Etymology*. Leiden: Brill, 2003.

Orton, Fred. "Rethinking the Ruthwell Monument: Fragments and Critique; Tradition and History; Tongues and Sockets." *Art History* 21 (1998): 65–106.

Orton, Fred, and Ian Wood. *Fragments of History: Rethinking the Ruthwell and Bewcastle Monuments*. With Clare A. Lees. Manchester: Manchester University Press, 2007.

Orton, Peter. "The Technique of Object Personification in *The Dream of the Rood* and a Comparison with the Old English *Riddles*." *Leeds Studies in English* 11 (1979): 1–18.

Osborn, Marijane. *Beowulf: A Verse Translation with Treasures of the Ancient North.* Berkeley: University of California Press, 1983.

———. "Legends of Lejre, Home of Kings." In *"Beowulf" and Lejre,* edited by John D. Niles, 235–54. Tempe: Arizona Center of Medieval and Renaissance Studies, 2007.

———. "Translations, Versions, Illustrations." In *A "Beowulf" Handbook,* edited by Robert E. Bjork and John D. Niles, 341–72. Lincoln: University of Nebraska Press, 1997.

Otter, Monika. *Inventiones: Fiction and Referentiality in Twelfth-Century English Historical Writing.* Chapel Hill: University of North Carolina Press, 1996.

———. "'New Werke': St. Erkenwald, St. Albans, and the Medieval Sense of the Past." *Journal of Medieval and Renaissance Studies* 24 (1994): 387–414.

Overing, Gillian R. "*Beowulf:* A Poem in Our Time." In *The Cambridge History of Early Medieval English Literature,* edited by Clare A. Lees, 309–31. Cambridge: Cambridge University Press, 2013.

———. *Language, Sign, and Gender in "Beowulf."* Carbondale and Edwardsville: Southern Illinois University Press, 1990.

Ovid. *Metamorphoses.* Edited by R. J. Tarrant. Oxford Classical Texts. Oxford: Oxford University Press, 2004.

Owen-Crocker, Gale R. "Dress and Identity." In *The Oxford Handbook of Anglo-Saxon Archaeology,* edited by Helena Hamerow, David A. Hinton, and Sally Crawford, 91–118. Oxford: Oxford University Press, 2011.

———. *The Four Funerals in "Beowulf" and the Structure of the Poem.* Manchester: Manchester University Press, 2009.

———. "Weapons and Armour." In *The Material Culture of Daily Living in the Anglo-Saxon World,* edited by Maren Clegg Hyer and Gale R. Owen-Crocker, 201–30. Liverpool: Liverpool University Press, 2011.

Padel, O. J. *Arthur in Medieval Welsh Literature.* Cardiff: University of Wales Press, 2013.

Page, R. I. *An Introduction to English Runes.* London: Methuen, 1973.

———. "Runic Writing, Roman Script and the Scriptorium." In *Runor och ABC: Elva föreläsningar från ett symposium i Stockholm, våren 1995,* edited by Staffan Nyström, 119–35. Stockholm: Sällskapet Runica et Mediævalia, Riksantikvarieämbetet, Stockholms Medeltidsmuseum, 1997.

Page, William. "Notes on the Heart-Case of Roger Norton." *Proceedings of the Society of Antiquaries* 22, 2nd series (1909): 253–54.

Panofsky, Erwin. *Perspective as Symbolic Form.* 1927. Translated by Christopher S. Wood. New York: Zone Books, 1991.

Park, Julie. *The Self and It: Novel Objects and Mimetic Subjects in Eighteenth-Century England.* Stanford, CA: Stanford University Press, 2009.

Parsons, David. "Anglo-Saxon Runes in Continental Manuscripts." In *Runische Schriftkultur in kontinental-skandinavischer und -angelsächsischer Wechselbeziehung,* edited by Klaus Düwel, 195–220. Ergänzungsbände zum Reallexikon der germanischen Altertumskunde 10. Berlin: de Gruyter, 1994.

Patch, Howard R. "Precious Stones in *The House of Fame.*" *Modern Language Notes* 50 (1935): 312–27.

Payne, Alina. *The Architectural Treatise in the Italian Renaissance.* Cambridge: Cambridge University Press, 1999.

Paz, James. *Nonhuman Voices in Anglo-Saxon Literature and Culture.* Manchester: Manchester University Press, 2017.

Peeters, Paul. "Le texte original de la Passion des Sept Dormants." *Analecta Bollandiana* 41 (1923): 369–85.

Pennant, Thomas. *A Tour in Scotland, and Voyage to the Hebrides; MDCCLXXII.* Chester: John Monk, 1774.

Perugi, Maurizio, ed. *La vie de Saint Alexis.* Geneva: Droz, 2000.

Petrucci, Armando. *Public Lettering: Script, Power, and Culture.* Translated by Linda Lappin. Chicago: University of Chicago Press, 1993.

Pettit, Edward, ed. *Anglo-Saxon Remedies, Charms, and Prayers from British Library MS Harley 585: The Lacnunga.* 2 vols. Lewiston, NY: Edwin Mellen Press, 2001.

Pliny. *Natural History.* Translated by H. Rackham. Cambridge, MA: Harvard University Press, 1968.

Pokorny, Julius. *Indogermanisches etymologisches Wörterbuch.* 2 vols. Bern: Francke, 1948–69.

Pollington, Stephen. *Leechcraft: Early English Charms, Plantlore, and Healing.* Hockwold-cum-Wilton, UK: Anglo-Saxon Books, 2000.

Poole, Russell. "Some Southern Perspectives on Starcatherus." *Viking and Medieval Scandinavia* 2 (2006): 141–66.

Prise, John. *Historiae Britannicae defensio / A Defence of the British History.* Edited by Ceri Davies. Toronto: PIMS, 2015.

Pritchard, R. E. *Odd Tom Coryate: The English Marco Polo.* Stroud: Sutton Publishing, 2004.

Rehm, Ulrich. "Diachrone Dialoge: Zur Interpretation antiker Gemmen mit mythologischen Motiven im Mittelalter." In *Dialog—Transfer—Konflikt: Künstlerische Wechselbeziehungen im Mittelalter und in der Frühen Neuzeit,* edited by Wolfgang Augustyn and Ulrich Söding, 71–88. Passau: Dietmar Klinger Verlag, 2014.

Roache, Joel. "Treasure Trove in *The Pardoner's Tale.*" *Journal of English and Germanic Philology* 64 (1965): 1–6.

Roberts, Eileen. *The Hill of the Martyr: An Architectural History of St. Albans Abbey.* Dunstable, UK: Book Castle, 1993.

Robertson, D. W. *A Preface to Chaucer: Studies in Medieval Perspectives.* Princeton, NJ: Princeton University Press, 1963.

Robinson, F. N., ed. *The Works of Geoffrey Chaucer.* 2nd ed. Cambridge, MA: Riverside Press, 1957.

Robinson, Fred C. "The Afterlife of Old English: A Brief History of Composition in Old English after the Close of the Anglo-Saxon Period." In *The Tomb of Beowulf and Other Essays on Old English,* 275–303. Oxford: Blackwell, 1993.

Rodrigues, Louis J., trans. and ed. *Anglo-Saxon Verse Charms, Maxims and Heroic Legends.* Pinner, UK: Anglo-Saxon Books, 1994.

Ross, Margaret Clunies. "Haustlöng 9." In *Poetry from Treatises on Poetics,* edited by Kari Ellen Gade and Edith Marold, 444–45. Skaldic Poetry of the Scandinavian Middle Ages 3. Turnhout: Brepols, 2017.

Rouse, Robert Allen, and Cory James Rushton. "Arthurian Geography." In *The Cambridge Companion to the Arthurian Legend,* edited by Elizabeth Archibald and Ad Putter, 218–34. Cambridge: Cambridge University Press, 2010.

Rupp, Katrin. "The Anxiety of Writing: A Reading of the Old English Journey Charm." *Oral Tradition* 23 (2008): 255–66.

Sauer, Hans, and Elisabeth Kubaschewski. *Planting the Seeds of Knowledge: An Inventory of Old English Plant Names.* Munich: Herbert Utz Verlag, 2018.

Saul, Nigel. *English Church Monuments in the Middle Ages: History and Representation*. Oxford: Oxford University Press, 2009.

Sawday, Jonathan. *The Body Emblazoned: Dissection and the Human Body in Renaissance Culture*. London: Routledge, 1995.

Scattergood, John. *The Lost Tradition: Essays on Middle English Alliterative Poetry*. Dublin: Four Courts Press, 2000.

Schlauch, Margaret. "The *Dream of the Rood* as Prosopopoeia." In *Essential Articles for the Study of Old English Poetry*, edited by Jess B. Bessinger Jr. and Stanley J. Kahrl, 428–41. Hamden, CT: Archon Books, 1968.

Schlie, Heike. "Der Klosterneuburger Ambo des Nikolaus von Verdun: Das Kunstwerk als *figura* zwischen Inkarnation und Wiederkunft des Logos." In *Figura*, edited by Christian Kiening and Katharina Mertens Fleury, 205–47. Philologie der Kultur 8. Würzburg: Königshausen & Neumann, 2013.

Schrader, Richard J. "The Language on the Giant's Sword Hilt in *Beowulf*." *Neuphilologische Mitteilungen* 94 (1993): 141–47.

Schwyzer, Philip. *Archaeologies of English Renaissance Literature*. Oxford: Oxford University Press, 2007.

———. "British History and 'The British History': The Same Old Story?" In *British Identities and English Renaissance Literature*, edited by David J. Baker and Willy Maley, 11–23. Cambridge: Cambridge University Press, 2002.

———. "Exhumation and Ethnic Conflict: From *St. Erkenwald* to Spenser in Ireland." *Representations* 95, no. 1 (2006): 1–26.

———. *Shakespeare and the Remains of Richard III*. Oxford: Oxford University Press, 2013.

Scott, G. G. "Notes upon the Burial of the Body and Heart of Abbot Roger de Norton in St Albans Abbey." *Archaeological Journal* 31 (1874): 293–95.

Scudder, Bernard, trans. *Egil's Saga*. New York: Penguin, 1997.

Sedgwick, Eve Kosofsky. *Touching Feeling: Affect, Pedagogy, Performance*. Raleigh, NC: Duke University Press, 2003.

Semple, Sarah. *Perceptions of the Prehistoric in Anglo-Saxon England: Religion, Ritual, and Rulership in the Landscape*. Oxford: Oxford University Press, 2013.

Serlio, Sebastiano. *Sebastiano Serlio on Architecture*. Translated by Vaughan Hart and Peter Hicks. New Haven, CT: Yale University Press, 1996.

Settis, Salvatore, ed. *Memoria dell'antico nell'arte italiana*. 3 vols. Turin: Einaudi, 1984–86.

Shalem, Avinoam. *Islam Christianized: Islamic Portable Objects in the Medieval Church Treasuries of the Latin West*. Bern: Peter Lang, 1998.

Shearman, John. "Leonardo's Colour and Chiaroscuro." In *Sixteenth-Century Italian Art*, edited by Michael W. Cole, 408–40. Oxford: Blackwell, 2006. Originally published in *Zeitschrift für Kunstgeschichte* 25, no. 1 (1962): 13–47.

Shippey, Tom. "Structure and Unity." In *A "Beowulf" Handbook*, edited by Robert E. Bjork and John D. Niles, 149–74. Lincoln: University of Nebraska Press, 1997.

Simmel, Georg. "The Ruin." In *Essays on Sociology, Philosophy, and Aesthetics*, edited by Kurt H. Wolff, 259–66. New York: Harper and Row, 1965.

Simpson, James. *Reform and Cultural Revolution*. Oxford English Literary History 2, 1350–1547. Oxford: Oxford University Press, 2002.

Sims-Williams, Patrick. "The Early Welsh Arthurian Poems." In *The Arthur of the Welsh*, edited by Rachel Bromwich, A. O. H. Jarman, and Brynley F. Roberts, 33–71. Cardiff: University of Wales Press, 1991.

Sirr, Peter. "Charm for a Journey." In *The Word Exchange: Anglo-Saxon Poems in Translation*, edited by Greg Delanty and Michael Matto, 495–98. New York: W. W. Norton & Company, 2012.

Skeat, W. W., ed. *Ælfric's Lives of Saints*. 2 vols. 1881. Reprint, London: Oxford University Press, 1966.

Smith, Christine. *Architecture in the Culture of Early Humanism: Ethics, Aesthetics, and Eloquence, 1400–1470*. Oxford: Oxford University Press, 1992.

Smith, James L. "Medievalisms of Moral Panic: Borrowing the Past to Frame Fear in the Present." *Studies in Medievalism* 25 (2016): 157–72.

Smith, Stephen A. *Freedom of Religion: Foundational Documents and Historical Arguments*. Oxford: Oxbridge Research Associates, 2017.

Smith, Terence Paul. "Early Recycling: The Anglo-Saxon and Norman Re-Use of Roman Bricks with Special Reference to Hertfordshire." In *Alban and St Albans: Roman and Medieval Architecture, Art and Archaeology*, edited by Martin Henig and Phillip Lindley, 111–17. Leeds: British Archaeological Association, 2001.

Snyder, Janet E. *Early Gothic Column-Figure Sculpture in France: Appearance, Materials, Significance*. Farnham, UK: Ashgate, 2011.

Speed, John. *The History of Great Britaine*. London, 1611.

Spivak, Gayatri Chakravorty. "Translator's Preface." In *Of Grammatology*, by Jacques Derrida. Translated by Gayatri Chakravorty Spivak, ix–lxxxvii. Baltimore: Johns Hopkins University Press, 1998.

Starzmann, Maria Theresia. "Der 'Orient' als Grenzraum: Die koloniale Dimension wissenschaftlicher Narrative zum Nahen Osten." *Forum Kritische Archäologie* 7 (2018): 1–17.

Stenhouse, William. *Reading Inscriptions and Writing Ancient History: Historical Scholarship in the Late Renaissance*. London: Institute of Classical Studies, 2005.

Stevenson, Robert B. K. "Further Thoughts on Some Well Known Problems." In *The Age of Migrating Ideas: Early Medieval Art in Northern Britain and Ireland*, edited by Michael Spearman and John Higgitt, 16–26. Edinburgh and Stroud: National Museums of Scotland and Alan Sutton, 1993.

Stewart, Susan. *The Ruins Lesson: Meaning and Material in Western Culture*. Chicago: University of Chicago Press, 2020.

Stjerna, Knut. *Essays on Questions Connected with the Old English Poem of Beowulf*. Edited and translated by John R. Clark Hall. Coventry: Curtis & Beamish, 1912.

Storms, Godfrid. *Anglo-Saxon Magic*. The Hague: Martinus Nijhoff, 1948.

Stow, John. *A Survey of London, by John Stow*. 2 vols. London, 1598.

Stuart, Heather. "'Ic me on þisse gyrde beluce': The Structure and Meaning of the Old English Journey Charm." *Medium Ævum* 50 (1981): 259–73.

Summit, Jennifer. *Memory's Library: Medieval Books in Early Modern England*. Chicago: University of Chicago Press, 2008.

Sussman, Rachel. *The Oldest Living Things in the World*. Chicago: University of Chicago Press, 2014.

Swanton, Michael J. *The Spearheads of the Anglo-Saxon Settlements*. London: Royal Archaeological Institute, 1973.

Swearer, Randolph, Raymond Oliver, and Marijane Osborn. *"Beowulf": A Likeness*. New Haven, CT: Yale University Press, 1990.

Sweetser, Eve. *From Etymology to Pragmatics: Metaphorical and Cultural Aspects of Semantic Structure*. Cambridge: Cambridge University Press, 1990.

Swift, Jonathan. *Gulliver's Travels,* edited by Colin McKelvie. Belfast: Appletree Press Limited, 1976.

Symons, Victoria. "*Wreopenhilt ond wyrmfah*: Confronting Serpents in *Beowulf* and Beyond." In *Representing Beasts in Early Medieval England and Scandinavia,* edited by Michael D. J. Bintley and Thomas J. T. Williams, 73–93. Woodbridge, UK: Boydell Press, 2015.

Tate, George S. "Chiasmus as Metaphor: The 'Figura Crucis' Tradition and *The Dream of the Rood.*" *Neuphilologische Mitteilungen* 79, no. 2 (1978): 114–25.

Thoenes, Christof. "St. Peter's as Ruins: On Some *vedute* by Heemskerck." In *Sixteenth-Century Italian Art,* edited by Michael W. Cole, 25–39. London: Blackwell, 2006.

Thormann, Janet. "Enjoyment of Violence and Desire for History in *Beowulf.*" In *The Postmodern "Beowulf": A Critical Casebook,* edited by Eileen A. Joy and Mary K. Ramsey, 287–318. Morgantown: West Virginia University Press, 2006.

Thornbury, Emily V. "*Eald enta geweorc* and the Relics of Empire: Revisiting the Dragon's Lair in *Beowulf.*" *Quaestio* 1 (2000): 82–92.

Tolan, John, Henry Laurens, and Gilles Veinstein. *Europe and the Islamic World: A History.* Princeton, NJ: Princeton University Press, 2013.

Tolkien, J. R. R. "The Monsters and the Critics." In *The Monsters and the Critics and Other Essays,* edited by Christopher Tolkien, 5–48. London: Harper Collins, 1997.

Tomaini, Thea. *The Corpse as Text: Disinterment and Antiquarian Enquiry, 1700–1900.* Woodbridge, UK: Boydell Press, 2017.

Toon, Richard, and Laurie Stone. "Game of Thrones: Richard III and the Creation of Cultural Heritage." In *Studies in Forensic Biohistory: Anthropological Perspectives,* edited by Christopher M. Stojanowski and William N. Duncan, 43–66. Cambridge: Cambridge University Press, 2016.

Trigger, Bruce G. *A History of Archaeological Thought.* 2nd ed. Cambridge: Cambridge University Press, 2006.

Tupper, Frederick. "Notes on Old English Poems." *Journal of English and Germanic Philology* 11 (1912): 82–103.

Twycross, Meg. *The Medieval Anadyomene: A Study in Chaucer's Mythography.* Medium Ævum Monographs New Series 1. Oxford: Blackwell, 1972.

Underwood, Richard. *Anglo-Saxon Weapons and Warfare.* Stroud: Tempus Publishing, 1999.

Valentini, Roberto, and Guiseppe Zucchetti, eds. *Codice topografico della città di Roma.* 4 vols. Rome: Tipografia del senato, 1953.

Van der Horst, Pieter W. "Pious Long-Sleepers in Greek, Jewish, and Christian Antiquity." In *Tradition, Transmission, and Transformation from Second Temple Literature through Judaism and Christianity in Late Antiquity: Proceedings of the Thirteenth International Symposium of the Orion Center for the Study of the Dead Sea Scrolls and Associated Literature, Jointly Sponsored by the Hebrew University Center for the Study of Christianity, 22–24 February, 2011,* edited by Menahem Kister, Hillel Newman, Michael Segal, and Ruth Clements, 93–111. Leiden: Brill, 2015.

Van Dussen, Michael. "Tourists and *Tabulae* in Late-Medieval England." In *Truth and Tales: Cultural Mobility and Medieval Media,* edited by Fiona Somerset and Nicholas Watson, 238–54. Columbus: The Ohio State University Press, 2015.

Van Horn, Jennifer. *The Power of Objects in Eighteenth-Century British America.* Chapel Hill: University of North Carolina Press, 2017.

Van Meter, David C. "The Ritualized Presentation of Weapons and the Ideology of Nobility in *Beowulf.*" *Journal of English and Germanic Philology* 95 (1996): 175–89.

Vasari, Giorgio. *Lives of the Painters, Sculptors, and Architects.* Translated by A. B. Hings. 4 vols. London: Dent, 1963.

———. *Lives of the Painters, Sculptors, and Architects.* Translated by Gaston du C. de Vere. 2 vols. New York: Modern Library, 1996.

Vaughan-Sterling, Judith. "The Anglo-Saxon *Metrical Charms*: Poetry as Ritual." *Journal of English and Germanic Philology* 82 (1983): 186–200.

Vergerio, Pier Paolo. *Epistolario di Pier Paolo Vergerio.* Edited by Leonard Smith. Fonti per la Storia d'Italia. Rome: Istituto Storico Italiano per il Medio Evo, 1934.

Vergil, Polydore. *Three Books of Polydore Vergil's English History, Comprising the Reigns of Henry VI, Edward IV, and Richard III.* Edited by Sir Henry Ellis. London: Camden Society, 1844.

Vernon, William Warren, and J. P. Lacaita, eds. *Benevenuti de Rambaldis de Imola Comentum super Dantis Aldigherij Comoediam.* 5 vols. Florence: G. Barbèra, 1887.

Waller, John G., and Lionel A. B. Waller. *A Series of Monumental Brasses from the Thirteenth to the Sixteenth Century.* London: J. B. Nichols and Sons, 1864.

Walsham, Alexandra. *The Reformation of the Landscape: Religion, Identity and Memory in Early Modern Britain and Ireland.* Oxford: Oxford University Press, 2011.

Walsingham, Thomas. *Gesta Abbatum Monasterii Sancti Albani.* Edited by Henry Thomas Riley. 3 vols. London: Longmans, 1867–69.

Wandhoff, Haiko. *Ekphrasis: Kunstbeschreibungen und virtuelle Räume in der Literatur des Mittelalters.* Trends in Medieval Philology 3. Berlin: de Gruyter, 2003.

Watson, Alan, trans. *The Digest of Justinian.* 4 vols. Rev. ed. Philadelphia: University of Pennsylvania Press, 1988.

Webb, Diana. *Pilgrimage in Medieval England.* London: Hambledon and London, 2000.

Webb, Ruth. *Ekphrasis, Imagination and Persuasion in Ancient Rhetorical Theory and Practice.* Farnham, UK: Ashgate, 2009.

Webster, Leslie. "Archaeology and *Beowulf.*" In *"Beowulf": An Edition,* edited by Bruce Mitchell and Fred C. Robinson, 183–94. Oxford: Blackwell, 1998.

———. "Encrypted Visions: Style and Sense in the Anglo-Saxon Minor Arts, A. D. 400–900." In *Anglo-Saxon Styles,* edited by Catherine E. Karkov and George Hardin Brown, 11–30. Albany: State University of New York Press, 2003.

———. "Ideal and Reality: Versions of Treasure in the Early Anglo-Saxon World." In *Treasure in the Medieval West,* edited by Elizabeth M. Tyler, 49–59. York: York University Press, 2000.

———. "Imagining Identities: The Case of the Staffordshire Hoard." In *Anglo-Saxon England and the Visual Imagination,* edited by John D. Niles, Stacy S. Klein, and Jonathan Wilcox, 25–48. Tempe: Arizona Center for Medieval and Renaissance Studies, 2016.

———. "Style: Influences, Chronology and Meaning." In *The Oxford Handbook of Anglo-Saxon Archaeology,* edited by Helena Hamerow, David A. Hinton, and Sally Crawford, 460–500. Oxford: Oxford University Press, 2011.

Weiss-Krejci, Estella. "Heart Burial in Medieval and Early Post-Medieval Central Europe." In *Body Parts and Bodies Whole,* edited by Katharina Rebay-Salisbury, Marie Louise Stig Sørensen, and Jessica Hughes, 119–34. Oxford: Oxbow, 2010.

Whatley, E. Gordon. "Constantine the Great, the Empress Helena, and the Relics of the True Cross." In *Medieval Hagiography: An Anthology,* edited by Thomas F. Head, 77–96. New York: Routledge, 2001.

———, "Heathens and Saints: *St. Erkenwald* in Its Legendary Context." *Speculum* 61 (1986): 330–63.

———, trans. and ed. *The Saint of London: The Life and Miracles of St. Erkenwald.* Binghamton, NY: Medieval and Renaissance Texts and Studies, 1989.

Whitaker, Muriel A. "The Chaucer Chest and the *Pardoner's Tale*: Didacticism in Narrative Art." *Chaucer Review* 34 (1999): 174–89.

White, John. *The Birth and Rebirth of Pictorial Space.* Cambridge, MA: Harvard University Press, 1987.

Whitehead, Christiania. *Castles of the Mind: A Study of Medieval Architectural Allegory.* Cardiff: University of Wales Press, 2003.

Whitelock, Dorothy. *From Bede to Alfred: Studies in Early Anglo-Saxon Literature and History.* London: Variorum Reprints, 1980.

———. "The Numismatic Interest of the Old English Version of the Legend of the Seven Sleepers." In *Anglo-Saxon Coins: Studies Presented to F. M. Stenton*, edited by R. H. M. Dolley, 188–94. London: Methuen, 1961. Reprinted in Dorothy Whitelock, *History, Law and Literature in 10th–11th Century England*, 188–94. London: Variorum, 1981.

Wilkinson, Paul. "Rare Seals Identify Significant Remains at St Albans Abbey." *Church Times*, December 15, 2017. Accessed June 2, 2020. https://www.churchtimes.co.uk/articles/2017/15-december/news/uk/rare-seals-identify-remains.

William of Malmesbury. *De gestis regum Anglorum libri quinque & Historiae novellae libri tres.* Edited by William Stubbs. 2 vols. Cambridge: Cambridge University Press, 2012.

Williams, Howard. "*Beowulf* and Archaeology: Megaliths Imagined and Encountered in Early Medieval Europe." In *The Lives of Prehistoric Monuments in Iron Age, Roman, and Medieval Europe*, edited by Marta Díaz-Guardamino, Leonardo García Sanjuán, and David Wheatley, 77–97. Oxford: Oxford University Press, 2015.

Withington, Robert. *English Pageantry: An Historical Outline.* 2 vols. Cambridge, MA: Harvard University Press, 1920.

Wood, Charles T. "Guenevere at Glastonbury? A Problem in Translation(s)." In *Glastonbury Abbey and the Arthurian Tradition*, edited by James P. Carley, 145–59. Cambridge: D. S. Brewer, 2001.

Wood, Christopher S. "The Perspective Treatise in Ruins: Lorenz Stoer, *Geometria et perspectiva*, 1567." In *The Treatise in Perspective: Published and Unpublished*, edited by Lyle Massey, 235–57. Washington, DC: National Gallery of Art, 2003.

Wordsworth, William. *Lines Composed a Few Miles above Tintern Abbey.* 1798.

Wright, Thomas. "On Antiquarian Excavations and Researches in the Middle Ages." *Archaelogica* 30 (1844): 438–48.

Yvernault, Martine. "The *House of Fame*: Unfamous Fame; La maison de papier, une entreprise de (dé)construction." In *L'articulation langue-littérature dans les textes médiévaux anglais*, edited by Collette Stévanovitch, 229–46. Collection GRENDEL 5. Nancy: Publications de l'AMAES, 2005.

Zöllner, Frank. *Leonardo da Vinci: The Complete Paintings and Drawings.* 2 vols. Cologne: Taschen, 2003.

CONTRIBUTORS

NEIL CARTLIDGE is Professor in the department of English Studies at the University of Durham. His books include *Medieval Marriage: Literary Approaches 1100–1300* (D. S. Brewer, 1997), *The Owl and the Nightingale: Text and Translation* (University of Exeter Press, 2001), and *The Works of Chardri* (Arizona Center for Medieval and Renaissance Studies, 2015). He has edited two collections of essays, *Boundaries in Medieval Romance* (D. S. Brewer, 2008) and *Heroes and Anti-Heroes in Medieval Romance* (D. S. Brewer, 2012), and is the author of over 50 journal articles and chapters.

ROBERTA FRANK, Marie Borroff Professor emerita at Yale University and University Professor emerita at the University of Toronto, has taught and written on Old English and Old Norse literature for a half century. She has just completed a book about the art of early Northern poetry.

LORI ANN GARNER is Associate Professor of English at Rhodes College in Memphis, Tennessee. She is the author of *Structuring Spaces: Oral Poetics and Architecture in Early Medieval England* (University of Notre Dame Press, 2011), as well as numerous articles exploring a range of Old and Middle English genres—including proverbs, histories, saints' lives, and healing remedies—within the dual contexts of oral tradition and literate culture.

JONATHAN GIL HARRIS is Professor of English and Founding Dean of Academic Affairs at Ashoka University in Haryana, India. He is the author of numerous books on early modern culture and globalization, including *Untimely Matter in the Time of Shakespeare* (University of Pennsylvania Press, 2008), *Shakespeare and Literary Theory*

(Oxford University Press, 2010), *Marvellous Repossessions: The Tempest, Globalization, and the Waking Dream of Paradise* (Ronsdale Press, 2012), the best-selling *The First Firangis: Remarkable Stories of Heroes, Healers, Charlatans, Courtesans & Other Foreigners Who Became Indian* (Aleph Books, 2015), and, most recently, *Masala Shakespeare: How a Firangi Writer Became Indian* (Aleph Books, 2018).

JAN-PEER HARTMANN is a fellow at the Collaborative Research Center "Episteme in Motion" at the Freie Universität Berlin. His articles on Old English poetry and early medieval Latin hagiography have appeared in *Leeds Studies in English* and *Medium Ævum*. He is in the process of publishing a monograph on early medieval English literature and archaeology.

JOHN HINES has taught at Cardiff University since 1983, firstly as lecturer and reader in English and subsequently as Professor of Archaeology. He publishes extensively on integrated approaches to cultural evidence and its transmission from late antiquity to modern times, especially across northern Europe.

DR. NAOMI HOWELL is Lecturer in Medieval Studies in the Department of English, University of Exeter. Her research explores the relationship between place, memory, and identity in the Middle Ages, particularly in the Anglo-Norman milieu. She is currently writing a book on tombs as sites of cultural encounter in medieval literature.

ANDREW HUI is Associate Professor of Humanities at Yale-NUS College, Singapore, and author of *Poetics of Ruins in Renaissance Literature* (Fordham University Press, 2017) and *A Theory of the Aphorism from Confucius to Twitter* (Princeton University Press, 2019).

ANDREW JAMES JOHNSTON is Chair of Medieval and Renaissance English Literature at the Freie Universität Berlin. His latest English-language monograph is *Performing the Middle Ages from "Beowulf" to "Othello"* (Brepols, 2008). His coedited collections include *The Medieval Motion Picture* (Palgrave Macmillan, 2014), *The Art of Vision: Ekphrasis in Medieval Literature and Culture* (The Ohio State University Press, 2015), and *Love, History and Emotion in Chaucer and Shakespeare* (Manchester University Press, 2016).

SARAH SALIH is Reader in English at King's College London. Her publications include *Versions of Virginity in Late Medieval England* (D. S. Brewer, 2001) and *Imagining the Pagan in Late Medieval England* (D. S. Brewer, 2019), and articles on various aspects of medieval textual and visual cultures. She is currently researching late medieval performance.

PHILIP SCHWYZER is Professor of Renaissance Literature at the University of Exeter. He is the author of studies including *Literature, Nationalism and Memory in Early Modern England and Wales* (Cambridge University Press, 2004), *Archaeologies of English Renaissance Literature* (Oxford University Press, 2007), and *Shakespeare and the Remains of Richard III* (Oxford University Press, 2013).

INDEX

Adam of Damerham, 81
Adam and Eve, 254
Adrian IV (pope), 161
Ælfric of Eynsham, 62
Aeneas, 54, 247–49, 251
Aeneid. See Virgil
Æthelred II "the Unready" (king), 131, 167–68
Æthelstan Ætheling, 131
Æthelthryth, Saint, 1n1, 35
Afghanistan, 14, 147, 170; Afghan box. See Roger de Norton
agency, 8, 10, 21–22, 24, 28, 30, 31–32, 34, 36, 154, 242, 253; actor, 4, 11, 21–22, 33–34, 36, 94; actor-network theory, 4–5, 21–22; agent, 5, 8, 17, 22, 28, 30, 35, 109, 118; assemblage, 4–5, 8
Agra, 202
Ajmer, 201n13, 203, 205, 207
Alban, Saint, 14, 149n8, 156, 160–63, 168, 169–70; shrine at St. Albans, 158–59, 161
Alberto degli Alberti, 211
Alcuin, 45n31, 186n31

Alexander the Great, 16, 165, 206, 207, 209
All the President's Men (movie), 43
Al-Mansur, Abu Ja'far Abdallah ibn Muhammad (Abbasid Caliph), 13, 103
Amphibalus, Saint, 149, 156n30, 160–61
anachrony (Nagel and Wood), 8–9, 11, 26–28, 37, 100
anachronism, 48, 108–9, 115
Anglo-Saxon Chronicle, 1
Anne, Saint, 26–27, 150; Cathedral in Apt, Provence, 150
Anthony, Saint, 178
antiquarianism, 3n5, 162n43, 173, 183, 198, 212
Antiquity, 3n5, 15, 27, 55, 194–95, 197–98, 200–201, 209–13, 216, 221, 223, 225, 227; Asian, 203; classical, 7; late antiquity, 28, 69, 79, 124, 164; Roman, 13, 107, 115
Apollo Belvedere, 223
Appadurai, Arjun, 4–5
archaeology, 1–17 (introduction), 21–22, 29, 42, 51–52, 56, 63, 73, 82, 88–89, 92, 95, 107, 120, 127, 162–63, 193–94, 200, 208–10, 240–41, 242n4, 243–44, 248, 254, 256–57;

285

as cultural practice, 3, 15, 21, 31, 34, 66, 73, 77, 92; as experience or perspective, 2, 4, 61–62, 66, 72–73, 77, 115, 194, 197; as heroic narrative, 22, 25, 32; as modern discipline, 3n5, 7–8, 21, 26, 55, 86, 92, 193–94, 208, 240, 241, 254; archaeologist, 6, 12, 22, 25, 41, 51, 56, 66, 73, 86, 88, 94, 193–94, 241–42; archaeological discovery, 31, 37, 78–81, 84–87, 90–94, 95, 97, 100, 104, 131, 145–48, 159, 160–63, 168–69, 170–71; early modern archaeology, 4, 27, 193; medieval archaeology, 4, 25, 31; archaeological narratives, 11, 22, 25, 82, 95, 98, 168; archaeological objects/artifacts, 1–3, 5–10, 12–13, 17, 39–40, 42–43, 45–49, 52, 55–56, 77, 105–8, 112–13, 115–18, 120, 122, 162, 170, 194, 244, 254–55; archaeological sites, 7; archaeological traces, 2, 7, 10–11. *See also* archaeo-theatrics; excavation/dig

archaeo-theatrics, 15, 193–95, 197–98, 200–203, 206–9

Ark of the Covenant, 22

Arnórr Þórðarson, 49

Arthur, King, 2, 11, 31–36, 78–95, 97–98, 100; cloven skull, 89, 93; future return, 33, 89; Glastonbury excavation, 11, 31, 78, 80–95; hasty burial, 87, 91; reburial, 90, 91; size of bones and skull, 33, 87–88, 91; tomb/grave, 31–34, 83, 87, 90; wax seal, 2

Arthurian literature, 2, 81

Ashoka (Buddhist Mauryan emperor), 204–5; edicts, 205; pillar, 203, 204 fig. 9.1, 205–6, 209

Auden, W. H., 46, 53

Auerbach, Erich, 14, 175–76, 178, 186

Augustine, Saint, 39, 229, 230 fig. 10.12; *The City of God*, 39n4

Augustine of Canterbury, 97

Augustus, Emperor, fossil collections, 39n4. *See also* Octavius

Avalon, 83, 89

Bacchus, 23

Baker, Peter S., 105

Barad, Karen, 6

barrow. *See* burial mound/barrow

Battle of Camlann, 83

Battle of Hydaspes, 207

Battle of Maldon (Old English poem), 121, 139

Bauer, Thomas, 105

Becket, Thomas. *See* Thomas Becket

Bede, *Historia ecclesiastica gentis anglorum*, 1n1, 35, 128, 144, 160n37, 162n43

Belting, Hans, 238

Benjamin, Walter, 96

Benvenuto Rambaldi da Imola, *Comentum super Dantis Aldighierij comœdiam*, 254

Beowulf, 3, 7, 9, 11, 13, 38–56 (chapter 2), 103–19 (chapter 5); 121, 123, 128, 143n95; Beowulf's barrow, 51, 54–55; *Brosinga mene/men Brísinga*, 46–47, 49, 50; dragon, 38, 43, 45, 47, 53, 128; dragon's lair/barrow, 7, 11, 38, 48, 51, 53–56, 108; Freawaru (Hrothgar's daughter), 45; Geatland, 43–44, 47, 53; giants' sword, 5, 10, 13, 39, 42, 52, 108–14, 116–18; Grendel, 5, 10, 108–9, 114, 143n95; Grendel's mother, 5, 109, 114, 117, 128n27; Heorot, 44, 49, 53, 54n59, 107–8; Hrothgar, 5, 39, 42–45, 52, 117, 143n95; Hygd, 43; Hygelac, 43–47, 87; Ingeld, 45; last survivor, 53; necklace/neck-torque, 42, 45–47, 50–51; underwater cave, 5, 10, 52, 116; Wealhtheow, 45, 47; Wiglaf, 11–12, 45–47, 53–54

Berchorius, Peter, 247n15

Biddick, Kathleen, 195n3

Bloomfield, Morton, 114

Bokenham. *See* Osbern Bokenham

Boleyn, Anne, 195

Book of the Duchess, The. *See* Chaucer

Botticelli, Sandro, *The Punishment of Korah*, 221, 222 fig. 10.7, 223

Bracciolini, Poggio, 214; *De varietate fortunae*, 214; *Opera omnia*, 215n11

Brísinga men. *See Beowulf*

British Museum, 13n35, 23n8, 103–4, 125 fig. 2, 126n19, 151n13, 151n14, 251

Browne, Thomas, *Hydriotaphia*, 54n60

Brussels Cross, 181n18

Burckhardt, Jacob, *The Civilization of the Renaissance in Italy*, 210

burial mound/barrow, 7, 24, 41–42; Bronze Age, 41; Neolithic, 41; Sutton Hoo Mound 1 (ship burial), 3, 41–42, 130

INDEX · 287

Cadouin, Monastery (Dordogne), 150
Cadwaladr (king), 98–100
Cædwalla of Wessex, King, 99n47
Caligula, Emperor, 165n51
Camden, William, 33, 162n43, 173n4
cameo, 146, 163–64, 165 fig. 7.5, 166–68
Canaletto, 236
Canterbury Tales. See Chaucer
Caron, Antoine, *Massacres of the Triumvirate*, 221, 222 fig. 10.8, 223
Carpaccio, Vittore: *The Dead Christ*, 219, 220 fig. 10.5; *Meditation on the Passion*, 216, 219 fig. 10.4
Carroll, Lewis, *Through the Looking-Glass, and What Alice Found There*, 43n28
Carruthers, Mary J., 55
Carter, Howard, 22
Cassiodorus, *Variae*, 54n60
Castiglione, Baldassare, 215, 239
Caxton, William, 1, 2n2, 33
Chardri, 61–62, 69–70, 72, 75–76; *The Life of St. Josaphaz*, 61, 71n29; *The Little Debate (Le petit plet)*, 61, 62n8; *La vie des set dormanz*, 12, 61–63, 65–76
Charles V (king), 164
Chartres Cameo (Jupiter Cameo), 164–65
Chaucer, Geoffrey, 17, 75, 77, 240, 244–45, 247, 249, 251, 253–57; *The Book of the Duchess*, 244, 255; *The Canterbury Tales*, 256; *The House of Fame*, 16, 244–57; "The Knight's Tale," 244; *The Legend of Good Women*, 244; "The Pardoner's Tale," 251; *The Parliament of Fowls*, 244; *The Romance of the Rose*, 244
Chertsey Abbey, Surrey, 251
Chessel Down, Isle of Wight, 42
Childeric I (king), tomb at Tournai, 80n6
Chi Rho, 166
Chomsky, Noam, 243
Christ, 23, 97, 150, 167, 169, 174, 176, 178–82, 184–86, 188–89, 216, 219, 220 fig. 10.5, 223, 225, 228
Christopher, Saint, 91
Chrysoloras, Manuel, 211
Claudian, *De raptu Proserpinae*, 252
Claudius, Emperor, 165n51

Clifford, James, 154n23
Cnut, King, 49
Cohen, Jeffrey Jerome, 34n45, 36, 41n20
coin, 12, 13, 15, 39, 58, 63–69, 72, 103–6, 118, 150, 151n13, 163, 166, 170
coinage, 62–63, 65–66, 104–5, 166
Coliseum. *See* Rome
Conrad, Sebastian, 105n4
Constantine I (emperor), 165–66, 169–70; Arch of, 221, 223
Constantinople, 58, 106
coronation processions/pageants, 15, 194–98, 200–201, 209
corpse, 10, 28, 36, 45, 47, 94, 214–15
Corpus Iuris Civilis, 70n26, 70n27
Coryate, Thomas, 15–16, 195, 201–3, 205–9; *Coryate's Crudities*, 201n14, 202; *Greetings from the Court of the Great Mughal*, 207n27
Cosmas and Damian, Saints, 30
Cousin, Jean, 231, *Enfants nus jouant dans des ruines*, 232 fig. 10.14
cross (Christian symbol), 32–33, 85, 186, 189; holy/'true' Cross, 15, 79, 174–75, 178, 180, 182, 185–90; religious object, 128, 152 fig. 7.2, 160, 174, 185–86. *See also* Brussels Cross; Ruthwell Cross
crucifixion, 180–81, 184–86, 188–89
Cupid, 244
Cuthbert, Saint, 151
Cynewulf, 183

Daedalus, 246, 253
D'Albon de Saint-André, Jacques, 223
Dante Alighieri, *Purgatorio*, 254
Daston, Lorraine, 6
Decius, Emperor, 12, 58–59, 65, 66n19, 67, 71–72
Deeds of the Abbots (Thomas Walsingham et al.). *See Gesta Abbatum*
Dekker, Thomas, 196
Delhi, 195, 201, 203–6, 208
Dempster, Thomas, 162n43
Deor (Old English poem), 107
Derrida, Jacques, 2, 55

Dido, 245, 251
dig. *See* excavation
dinar. *See* Offa
Dinshaw, Carolyn, 7
Diocletian, Emperor, 165, 216
Donne, John, 241
Dover Castle, 2
dragon. See *Beowulf*
dreams, 10, 28, 71, 79, 82, 84–85, 94, 100, 160–61, 180, 182, 187, 203, 207, 244–48, 251–52, 255, 257
Dream of the Rood (Old English poem), 179n17, 180–82, 186n31, 187–89
Dryden, John, 241
Duccio di Buoninsegna, *Rucellai Madonna*, 151
Duncan, Henry, 173n2, 177 fig. 8.1
Dunstan, Saint, 32; church, 196
Durham (England), 151

Edmund the Martyr, Saint, 80n6
Edward the Martyr, Saint, 24, 80n6
Edward the Confessor, Saint, 2, 24
Edward I (king), 24, 33, 91n26
Egil's Saga, 133n50
Eleanor of Castile, 157
Eliot, George, *Middlemarch: A Story of Provincial Life*, 51
Eliot, T. S., 241
Elizabeth I (queen), 195, 197, 200
Elizabethan, 48, 206
Englynion y Beddau (*Stanzas of the Grave*, Welsh poems), 82
Enlightenment, 78, 193, 242, 246
entanglement, 4–5, 12–14, 21, 51, 103, 105, 110, 112–13, 115–19, 154
Ephesus, 12, 58–59, 63, 66, 70, 73
Erkenwald, Saint, 10, 31, 34–37. See also *St. Erkenwald* (poem)
Ermanaric, King, 47
Estienne, Charles, *De dissectione partium corporis humani*, 215, 217 fig. 10.2
Eusebius, *Life of Constantine*, 166

excavation/dig, 3n5, 3n7, 8, 11, 15, 23–24, 26–28, 30–32, 34–35, 37, 41, 42n25, 60, 78, 80n6, 81n8, 82, 84–86, 89, 92–95, 100, 145–46, 157, 159, 160–63, 170–71, 193, 195, 209
Exodus (Old English poem), 121

Fabyan, Robert, *The New Chronicles of England and France*, 83, 84n13
fairy cup, 24
Färjestaden, Öland, 42
Felicity, Saint, 29
Felski, Rita, 27
Ferhatović, Denis, 4, 116
Feroz Shah Tughlaq (Mamluk sultan), 203; Feroz Shah Kotla, 203–5. See also Ashoka pillar
figura (Auerbach), 14–15, 175–76, 178, 185–90
Flood, 52, 109, 117
Flood, Finbarr Barry, 154–55
Florence, 151, 202, 227, 254
Foley, John Miles, 121n3, 122, 123n8, 141n88
Fontainebleau, 223
Foucault, Michel, 193
Foxe, John, 97
fragments: of archaeological objects, 1, 10, 41, 52, 117–18, 150, 152 fig. 7.2, 161, 172, 173n4, 213, 216, 225, 229, 237 fig. 10.17; of bodies, 30–31, of stories, 38
Francesco di Giorgio Martini, *Nativity*, 223, 224 fig. 10.9
Frank, Roberta, 3n7, 11–13, 38–56 (chapter 2), 42n25, 50n45, 53n55, 53n57, 54n58, 106
Freyja, 47, 50n45
Friedrich, Caspar David, 236
Fuseli, Henri (Johann Heinrich Füssli), *The Artist Moved by the Grandeur of Antique Fragments*, 237 fig. 10.17

Gaiman, Neil, *The Graveyard Book*, 53
Gawain, 2, 7
Geary, Patrick, 28n27
Gentile da Fabriano, *Adoration of the Magi*, 151
Geoffrey of Monmouth, 24n11, 31, 83, 98

INDEX • 289

Gerald of Wales, 11, 32, 81, 89, 93–94, 97–98, 100; *Liber de Principis Instructione*, 32n34, 33, 81, 83–85, 87, 89, 95; *Speculum Ecclesiae*, 32n33, 33n35, 33n39, 81, 84, 85, 88–90, 95

Gesta Abbatum Monasterii Sancti Albani (the *Deeds of the Abbots of St. Albans*, Thomas Walsingham et al.), 148, 158n32, 161n39, 161n41, 164, 167–68

Ginzburg, Carlo, 56n67

Giotto, 151n16

Giovanni de' Medici, 211

Glastonbury Abbey, 11, 31–34, 76, 78, 80–82, 84, 87, 89, 91–93, 97, 100, 161; excavation of King Arthur and Queen Guinevere, 11, 31–34, 78, 80–82, 84, 87, 89, 91–93, 97, 100; fire in 1184, 91; Magna Tabula, 76

Golden Legend, The (*Legenda aurea*, Jacobus de Voragine), 69, 160n36, 216

Gombrich, E. H., 227n17

Gough, Richard, 174n5

Gould, Stephen Jay, 51n50

Grabar, Oleg, 155n24

Grafton, Anthony, 214n10

grave, 15, 41, 82, 126, 130–31, 188; of Arthur and Guinevere, 31–33, 83, 87; of Cadwaladr, 98; of John of Wheathampstead, 162–63; of Richard III, 85n15, 88, 92–93; of Tamburlaine the Great, 203; of Yorick (*Hamlet*), 208–9; grave goods, 27, 80n6, 126, 130–31; grave-robbing, 54n61. *See also* barrow; tomb

Gregory I (pope), 214

Gregory of Tours, 69, 127n23

Grendel. See *Beowulf*

Grendel's mother. See *Beowulf*

Greyfriar's Research Team (University of Leicester), 81–83, 86, 88, 90, 92–95, 100; excavation of Richard III, 82–83; 92–95, 100. *See also* Leicester; Richard III

Grímur Jónsson Thorkelin, 41n16

Guinevere, Queen, 31, 33, 36, 85, 95

Gumbrecht, Hans Ulrich, 25–26, 37

Hadrian, Emperor, 69

hagiography, 1, 10, 36, 57, 60–61, 77, 80, 82, 91, 93, 243

Hamlet. See Shakespeare

Harris, Jonathan Gil, 3n5, 5, 15–16, 162n44, 193–209 (chapter 9)

Heaney, Seamus, 40n14, 54n62

heart-burial, 149

heart-case. See Roger de Norton

Heffernan, James A. W., 117n34

Henry II (king), 32, 84, 89

Heorot. See *Beowulf*

Herbarium, 123n9, 124, 125 fig. 6.1, 144

Herbert, George, 241

Hercules, 223

Hinds, Gareth, *Beowulf*, 52

Hines, John, 3, 16–17, 41n20, 130n36, 181n18, 187n34, 240–57 (chapter 11), 242n2, 243n5

historiography, 1, 4, 6, 11n32, 17, 105, 108, 118

Hodder, Ian, 5n13, 6

Holtorf, Cornelius, 22n4, 31

Homer, 117n34, 202, 252

House of Fame. See Chaucer

Hrabanus Maurus, 186n31

Hrothgar. See *Beowulf*

Humboldt Forum Berlin, 40n12

Humphrey, Duke of Gloucester, 162

Husband's Message, The (Old English poem), 183

Hygd. See *Beowulf*

Hygelac. See *Beowulf*

Icarus, 246

India, 15, 105, 155n26, 195, 201–7

Indiana Jones, 22

Indian epic, 204

Ingeld. See *Beowulf*

Ingham, Patricia Clare, 6

inscription: as manual practice, 249; in cave in Legend of the Seven Sleepers, 62, 72–75; in the context of burials, 27–28, 79; in Glastonbury, 84; on Ashoka pillar, 195, 204 fig. 9.1, 205–6; on buildings and structures generally, 198, 212, 214; on coins in Legend of the Seven Sleepers, 65; on Cuthbert's shroud, 151n15; on de Norton heart-case, 147, 170; on giant sword in *Beowulf,* 52, 109, 112, 116; on Ludgate and other London buildings, 198–201; on mounting for St. Albans cameo, 168; on Offa's coin, 12, 13n35, 103–6, 118, 151n13; on Ruthwell Cross, 15, 174, 178–85, 86n31, 188–89; on tomb in *Saint Erkenwald,* 35; on weapons, 126

Institutes of Gaius, 69

interlace, 13, 113–16

inventio, 1, 11, 14, 25, 28, 30–32, 60–61, 79–82, 84–86, 90–94, 97–98, 100, 159–63, 168; *inventio crucis,* 79

iPhone 5, 100

Ireland, 24

Isidore of Seville, *Etymologies,* 49, 50n42, 50n44

Jacob of Sarug, 69

Jacobus de Voragine, 216n14

Jahangir (Mughal emperor), 203

James I and VI (king of England and Scotland), coronation, 15, 194–95

Jerome, Saint, 213, 216, 219

Job, 216, 219

John, King of England, 98, 100, 157, 199; tomb at Worcester, 98

John, Saint (Evangelist), 129, 131, 134, 167, 178

John, Saint (of Patmos), *Book of Revelation,* 235, 236 fig. 10.16

John of Amundesham, *Annales monasterii S. Albani,* 148

John the Baptist, Saint, 167, 178, 219

John the hermit, 29–30

John Wheathampstead, 162–63

Jonson, Ben, 196

Joseph of Arimathea, 97

Josephus, Titus Flavius, 252

Journey Charm (Old English metrical charm), 122, 128–35, 141, 144

Judith (Old English poem), 121, 139–40

Jupiter (Jove), 164–65, 245, 252. *See also* Chartres cameo

Justinian I (emperor), *Digest,* 70

Kaadmau, 146, 164, 165 fig. 7.5, 166–68

kaleidoscope, 210

Kandahar, 205

Kelton, Arthur, 100; *Commendacyon of Welshmen,* 98–99

Kingsbury Jug, 163

Kinoshita, Sharon, 104n3

Klaeber, Frederick J., 42, 43n27

"Knight's Tale, The." *See* Chaucer

Kufic/pseudo-Kufic script, 12, 13n35, 14, 104n2, 147n4, 151, 153n19, 170

Lacnunga (Old English medical texts), 123–24, 127, 136, 144

Laȝamon, 83; *Brut,* 62

Lakoff, George, 52n51

Lancelot, 2

Langley, Philippa, 84–86, 90, 95–96, 100

Laocoön, 27

Laqueur, Thomas, 27

Latour, Bruno, 5, 21–22, 32

Leechbooks (Old English medical texts), 123n9, 124n11, 126–28, 144

Legend of Good Women, The. See Chaucer

Legend of the Seven Sleepers, 58–61, 77; Ælfric's version (*see* Ælfric); anonymous Old English version, 62–66, 68, 70, 73–76; Chardri's *Set Dormanz* (*see* Chardri); "vulgate" Latin version (L₁), 62, 64–65, 68, 71, 73–76

Legendys of Hooly Wummen. See Osbern Bokenham

Leicester, 78, 86–88, 91, 93, 96–97, 100; Bow Bridge, 83; car park, 11, 80, 84–86; church of the Greyfriars/excavation, 82–83; 92–95, 100; Richard III Visitor Centre, 90; university, 81, 86, 93

Leicester Cathedral, 91, 96; renovation and reordering, 91, 93

Leland, John, 97–98

Leonardo da Vinci, *Adoration of the Magi,* 225, 226 fig. 10.10/10.11, 227–28

Lepidus (Marcus Aemilius Lepidus, triumvir), 223

Lerer, Seth, 108, 189n36

Lessing, Gotthold Ephraim, 114

Leyerle, John, 113–14

Liber additamentorum. See Matthew Paris
Liber de Principis Instructione. See Gerald of Wales
Liber Monstrorum (Anglo-Latin collection), 87
Licinius, 165–66
Life of St. Margaret of Antioch. See Osbern Bokenham
"Life of St. Sebastian," (Jacobus de Voragine) 216
Loki, 50
Lollardy, 241
London, 10, 15, 31, 34–37, 42, 151n16, 194–202, 205; as New Troy or New Rome, 200; Fetter Lane, 42; Fleet Street, 196; Jewish district, 199–200; Museum of London, 251; St. Paul's Cathedral, 10, 31, 34, 36, 195–97; Tower of London, 195
London Stone, 23–24
Lorrain, Claude, 229
Loschi, Antonio, 214
Lucan, 252
Luck of Edenhall, 23–24
Lucretius, 214
Lud, King, 196–97, 200
Ludgate, 195–98, 200–202, 209
Luke, Saint (Evangelist), 129–30, 179n16
Lydgate, John, 160n36; *Troy Book*, 249
Lyly, John, *Alexander and Campaspe*, 207

Macaulay, Rose, 229
MacGregor, Neil, 40n12
Mahabharata (Sanskrit epic), 204
Malory, Thomas, *Morte Darthur*, 1–2, 33–34
Mandeville, John, 156; *The Book of Marvels and Travels*, 156; tomb, 158 fig. 7.4
Manilius, Marcus, 214
Mantegna, Andrea, *Martyrdom of St. Sebastian*, 216, 218 fig. 10.3
Margam Abbey's Chronicle, 33
Margaret of Antioch, Saint, 28–32, 35–36
Marin, Louis, 235
Mark, Saint (Evangelist), 129, 131, 179n16
Mark Antony (triumvir), 223

Marlowe, Christopher, *Tamburlaine the Great*, 15–16, 202–3, 205–6
Mars, 165, 252
Márquez, Gabriel García, *One Hundred Years of Solitude*, 39–40
Mary Magdalene, 178, 219
Matthew Paris (Matthæus Parisiensis), 14, 52, 146, 148, 156–58, 160, 161n41, 162n43, 164, 165 fig. 7.5, 167–68; *Chronica Majora*, 156, 158n32, 164; *Liber additamentorum*, 164, 165 fig. 7.5, 166–67; *Vie de St. Auban*, 14, 146, 148–49, 157, 160, 168, 169–70. See also *Gesta Abbatum*
Matthew, Saint (Evangelist), 129, 131, 135n64, 178n16, 225, 228n21
Maxims I (Old English poem), 134–35
medievalism, 95, 257
Mercia, 12, 103–5, 150
Merlin, 24
Mermaid Tavern, 201
Michelangelo, 223, 228
Milton, John, 241
Minnis, A. J., 244, 255–56
Minos of Crete, 246
Minotaur, 246
Mitchell, W. J. T., 114n30
Mohammed. See Muhammad
Montaigne, Michel de, 215
monuments, 75–76, 214, 223, 238, 249; at Bewcastle, 184n28; of antiquity, 210–11; of London, 195, 199; of St Albans Abbey, 148, 161; Roger de Norton's heart monument, 159; prehistoric, 7. See also Beowulf's barrow; monumental brasses; Ruthwell Cross/Monument
monumental brasses, 249; of Robert de Wyvill of Salisbury, 249, 250 fig. 11.1
monumentalization, 73, 214, 225
Mordred, 33
Moses, 200, 221, 223
mound. See burial mound/barrow
Mount Flask, 29
Muhammad, 13n35, 150–51
museum, 5, 16, 17, 22, 34, 52, 62, 252, 254–55, 257; museum theory/pedagogy, 17, 254–55

Nagel, Alexander, 8, 9, 26
Nativity scene, 216
Nature Goddess Silk, 151n15
Neidhart Fuchs, 251
New Historicism, 9
New Testament, 176
Niles, John D., 40–41, 113–14, 182–83, 188–89
Nine Herbs Charm (Old English metrical charm), 123
Nomé, François de (Monsù Desiderio), *Ruins with Augustine and the Child*, 229, 230 fig. 10.12
Nora, Pierre, 25–26, 35
Norton. *See* Roger de Norton

Octavius (Gaius Iulius Caesar Octavianus, later referred to as Augustus), 223
Offa of Mercia, King, 103, 160, 161; Offa's "dinar," 12–13, 104, 106, 118, 150–51
Old Testament, 118, 176, 221, 228
Olrik, Axel, 44n30
Olst, Netherlands, 42
Origenist controversy, 59
Osbern Bokenham, 24–25, 29, 31, 36; *Legendys of Hooly Wummen*, 29; *Life of St. Margaret of Antioch*, 28–29, 36; *Mappula Angliae*, 24–25
Otherness, 5, 57, 118, 157
Otter, Monika, 11n32, 28, 60–61, 79–80, 82, 160n35, 161n40
Overing, Gillian R., 39n3, 113n25
Ovid, 245, 252; *Metamorphoses*, 246
Owl and the Nightingale, The (Middle English poem), 62

Palazzo del Te (Mantua), 229, 230 fig. 10.13
palimpsest, 5, 7–8, 210, 243
Palladio, Andrea, 214
Pannini, Giovanni Paolo, 236
Panofsky, Erwin, 237n36, 238
Pantheon. *See* Rome
"Pardoner's Tale, The." *See* Chaucer
Parliament of Fowls, The. *See* Chaucer
parousia, 176, 187

Paul, Saint, 129–30; *Letter to the Ephesians*, 129–30; *First Letter to the Corinthians*, 186, 228
Paul, Saint (hermit), 178
Paz, James, 111, 116
Peacock Acquamanile, 155n24
Peacock Silk, 151
Pennant, Thomas, 172–73
performance, 85, 140, 187, 189n38, 194–98, 200–203, 205, 208–9, 256; performativity, 15–17, 187–88, 194–95, 198, 201, 203, 208–9, 243
Petrarch, 215
Pillar of Feroz Shah Kotla. *See* Feroz Shah Kotla
Piranesi, Giovanni Battista, 229, 236
Pliny the Elder, *Natural History*, 206
Polycletus, 254
polychrony, 5, 194n
Porus (king of India), 206–7
Poussin, Nicolas, 229, *Landscape with St. John of Patmos*, 235, 236 fig. 10.16
prehistory, 49
Prittlewell, 81n6
Procopius, *De Bello Gothico*, 39
Protestantism, 97–98, 159, 196, 200, 221, 223, 241
Psy, Gangnam Style, 100

Quintilian, 214

Rajasthan, 203
Raphael (Raffaello Sanzio da Urbino), 239
reenactment, 11, 60, 92–93, 95, 100
Reformation, 80n6, 97–98, 100, 157, 159, 196
relic, 2, 10–11, 15, 28–35, 37–38, 52, 55, 60–61, 71, 79–80, 81n9, 93, 150–51, 162, 209, 243, 254; relic theft, 28–29
reliquary, 2, 164, 174, 255
Renaissance, 16, 27, 49, 78, 97, 210–39 (chapter 10), 242–44, 257
Revelatio Sancti Stephani, 79, 84, 92
Richard I (king), 33, 90
Richard II (king), 37
Richard III (king), 8, 11, 78, 80–86, 88, 90–100; curved spine/"hunchback" 86,

87, 90–91; dispute over reburial, 92, 96; DNA, 86; grave, 85, 88, 92–93; hasty burial, 87–88, 91; holes in skull, 89, 92–93; "the King in the Car Park," 83, 85, 90; reburial, 96; tomb in Leicester Cathedral, 91

Richard III Society, 81, 86, 90, 96

Robert de Wyvill (bishop of Salisbury), 249, 250 fig. 11.1

Robert, Hubert, 236

Robertson, D. W., 26n19

Roger de Norton, 14, 145, 148, 156–58, 170; heart-case/Afghan box, 145, 146 fig. 7.1, 147–48, 150, 152–54, 156–57, 161, 168, 170

romance, 1, 244, 249, 251

Romance of the Rose, The. *See* Chaucer

Romano, Giulio, *Sala dei giganti*, 229, 230 fig. 10.13, 231

Roman (*as in* Roman Empire): antiquity, 1, 13, 107, 115; architecture, 23, 108; attire, 164, 196; burials, 163; carvings, 164; cities and settlements in Britain, 24, 160, 163; culture, 108, 118; Eastern Roman Empire, 70; engineering, 7; inscriptions, 184n26; law, 69–70; objects and monuments, 1, 35, 108, 126, 146, 163; occupation of Britain, 1; Roman civil war, 223; Roman Empire, 104, 108; ruins, 107–8, 116, 210–11; warfare, 1, 126, 144, 164

Rome (city), 13, 27, 62n8, 98–99, 104, 210–11, 213–16, 223, 235, 238; Coliseum, 220, 223; Pantheon, 211, 223; St. Peter's Basilica, 211

Rous, John, 83

ruin, 1, 7, 16, 108, 116, 207, 210–39 (chapter 10); of Feroz Shah Kotla, 203, 205; of Troy, 16, 202; of Verulamium, 160–61, 169; Roman, 107–9, 116, 118

Ruin, The (Old English poem), 183

runes, 35, 43, 110, 112n22, 174n6, 179, 181–84, 188–89

Ruthwell Cross/Monument, 172–74, 177 fig. 8.1, 178–90; poetic inscription, 15, 179–85, 187–90; runes, 15, 174, 179, 181–84, 188–89

Sæberht of Essex, King, 81n6

Salisbury, Earl of, 249

Saturn, 252

Saussure, Ferdinand de, 243

Schwyzer, Philip, 3, 4, 8, 10–11, 14, 78–100 (chapter 4), 160n35

Scott, George Gilbert, 145, 159

seal, 2, 10, 23, 73–75, 161; imprint of, 2

Sebastian, Saint, 216, 218 fig. 10.3

Sedgwick, Eve Kosofsky, 194n2

Semple, Sarah, 3n6, 7

Septimius Severus, triumphal arch, 223

Septizonium, 221

Serlio, Sebastiano, 16, 214, 229, 238, *Quinto libro d'architettura di Sebastiano Serlio Bolognese*, 212 fig. 10.1

Servatius, Saint, 150

Shaftesbury Abbey, 80n6

Shahada (Islamic Creed), 12, 13, 103

Shakespeare, William, 86, 90, 194–95; *Hamlet*, 15, 195, 208–9; Yorick, 208–9

Sherborne Castle, 249

Shippey, Tom, 114

shrine, 2, 15, 28, 29, 70, 76–77, 79–80, 150, 157n30, 158–61, 164, 255

Simmel, Georg, 235

Simpson, James, 9, 26, 31

Sir Gawain and the Green Knight, 7

Sistine Chapel, 221, 222 fig. 10.7

Sixtus V (pope), 221

Snartemo, Vest-Agder (Norway), 42

Spanish Armada, 196–97

Speculum ecclesiae. *See* Gerald of Wales

Speed, John, *The History of Great Britaine*, 83

Spivak, Gayatri Chakravorty, 2

spoliation, 1, 4, 116, 153, 160–61, 170, 211, 215

Staffordshire hoard, 41, 127n21

Statius, 252

St. Ann's Well, 26

St. Erkenwald, 10, 31, 34–37

Stoer, Lorenz, *Geometria et perspectiva*, 231, 234 fig. 10.15

Stonehenge, 24

Stow, John, *Survey of London*, 15, 194, 198–203, 209

St. Albans, 14, 145–48, 150, 153–54, 156–57, 158 fig. 7.4, 159–63, 165, 167–68, 170–71

St. Paul's Cathedral. *See* London

St. Peter's Basilica. *See* Rome

Surat, 203

Sutton Hoo. *See* burial mound/barrow

Swift, Jonathan, *Gulliver's Travels*, 39

tabula, 75, 76
Tamburlaine. *See* Marlowe, Christopher; Timur-e-Lang
teleology, 4, 17, 109n17, 154, 176, 238, 247
temporality, 4–12, 15, 21, 24, 26–27, 34, 37, 57, 60–61, 77, 95–97, 100, 115, 149, 153, 162n44, 163, 174, 176, 186, 188–89, 202, 206, 208, 239; entangled temporalities, 9, 115, 117; multiple temporalities, 7, 26, 35, 154, 170, 173; polychronic temporality, 5, 194. *See also* anachrony
theatrum historiae, 194, 198
Theodoric the Great (king of the Ostrogoths), 54n60
Theodosius II (emperor), 58, 71
Thomas Becket, Saint, 93, 160; shrine, 157
Þjóðólfr ór Hvini, 50
Thorkelin. *See* Grímur Jónsson Thorkelin
Thornbury, Emily V., 108
Timur-e-Lang (founder of the Timurid Empire), 202–3
Tolkien, J. R. R., 53, 109, 114n28, 117
tomb, 7n24, 34, 36–37, 54–55, 80–81, 148, 225; in *St. Erkenwald*, 10, 31, 35–36; of Alexander, 207n25; of Arthur, 32, 34, 83, 90 (*see also* Arthur, King); of Cadwaladr, 99; of Christ, 219; of John Mandeville, 156, 158; of King John, 98; of Richard III, 91 (*see also* Richard III); of Tutankhamun, 22
Topra, 203–4
Tower of London. *See* London
traces of the past, 10–12, 17, 34, 200
Trajan, Emperor, column, 223, 231
translatio (of relics), 28, 31, 33–34, 36, 79, 82, 90–91, 99–100, 148, 151, 161–63
treasure trove, 12, 58, 62–63, 66, 68–70
Treasure Act of 1996, 41
Troy, 16, 31, 35, 37, 200, 202, 247, 252
Trump, Donald J., 78n
typology, 135, 195n3, 209, 221

Uffizi Gallery, 151
Ulysses, 16, 202, 206
Urban VIII (pope), 211

Valerius Flaccus, 214
Van Dussen, Michael, 75–76
Vasari, Giorgio, 214, 229, 231; *Lives of the Artists*, 213–14, 231
Venantius Fortunatus, 186n31
Venus, 244–48, 251–55
Vercelli Book, 180
Vergerio, Pier Paolo, 211
Vergil, Polydore, *Three Books of Polydore Vergil's English History*, 83–84
Verulamium, 160–61, 163, 168, 169
Victoria and Albert Museum, 23–24, 153 fig. 7.3, 254
Vienna, 251
Virgil, 39, 54, 117, 252; *Aeneid*, 52, 54, 215, 245, 248, 251; *Georgics*, 39, 87
Virgin Mary, 145, 147, 148, 151, 158 fig. 7.4, 171, 174, 219
Vitruvius, 214

Wace, 83
Walsingham, Thomas, 158n. *See also Gesta Abbatum Monasterii Sancti Albani*
Walters Art Museum, 220
Wanderer, The (Old English poem), 134–35
Wealhtheow. *See Beowulf*
Westminster Abbey, 2, 195–97
Whitelock, Dorothy, 48, 66n19, 68–69
Wiglaf. *See Beowulf*
William of Malmesbury, 83
William of Newburgh, 52
William of St. Albans, *Passio Sancti Albani*, 168
Winchester, 2
Wið færstice (Old English metrical charm), 122, 135–44
Wood, Christopher S., 8–9, 26
Worcester Cathedral, 32, 98
Wordsworth, William, *Lines Composed a Few Miles Above Tintern Abbey*, 38
Wyvill. *See* Robert de Wyvill

York, Coppergate sword pommel, 23; Minster, 96
Yorick. *See* Shakespeare

INTERVENTIONS: NEW STUDIES IN MEDIEVAL CULTURE
ETHAN KNAPP, SERIES EDITOR

Interventions: New Studies in Medieval Culture publishes theoretically informed work in medieval literary and cultural studies. We are interested both in studies of medieval culture and in work on the continuing importance of medieval tropes and topics in contemporary intellectual life.

Material Remains: Reading the Past in Medieval and Early Modern British Literature
EDITED BY JAN-PEER HARTMANN AND ANDREW JAMES JOHNSTON

Translation Effects: Language, Time, and Community in Medieval England
MARY KATE HURLEY

Talk and Textual Production in Medieval England
MARISA LIBBON

Scripting the Nation: Court Poetry and the Authority of History in Late Medieval Scotland
KATHERINE H. TERRELL

Medieval Things: Agency, Materiality, and Narratives of Objects in Medieval German Literature and Beyond
BETTINA BILDHAUER

Death and the Pearl Maiden: Plague, Poetry, England
DAVID K. COLEY

Political Appetites: Food in Medieval English Romance
AARON HOSTETTER

Invention and Authorship in Medieval England
ROBERT R. EDWARDS

Challenging Communion: The Eucharist and Middle English Literature
JENNIFER GARRISON

Chaucer on Screen: Absence, Presence, and Adapting the Canterbury Tales
EDITED BY KATHLEEN COYNE KELLY AND TISON PUGH

Chaucer, Gower, and the Affect of Invention
STEELE NOWLIN

Fragments for a History of a Vanishing Humanism
EDITED BY MYRA SEAMAN AND EILEEN A. JOY

The Medieval Risk-Reward Society: Courts, Adventure, and Love in the European Middle Ages
WILL HASTY

The Politics of Ecology: Land, Life, and Law in Medieval Britain
EDITED BY RANDY P. SCHIFF AND JOSEPH TAYLOR

The Art of Vision: Ekphrasis in Medieval Literature and Culture
EDITED BY ANDREW JAMES JOHNSTON, ETHAN KNAPP, AND MARGITTA ROUSE

Desire in the Canterbury Tales
ELIZABETH SCALA

Imagining the Parish in Late Medieval England
ELLEN K. RENTZ

Truth and Tales: Cultural Mobility and Medieval Media
EDITED BY FIONA SOMERSET AND NICHOLAS WATSON

Eschatological Subjects: Divine and Literary Judgment in Fourteenth-Century French Poetry
J. M. MOREAU

Chaucer's (Anti-)Eroticisms and the Queer Middle Ages
    TISON PUGH
Trading Tongues: Merchants, Multilingualism, and Medieval Literature
    JONATHAN HSY
Translating Troy: Provincial Politics in Alliterative Romance
    ALEX MUELLER
Fictions of Evidence: Witnessing, Literature, and Community in the Late Middle Ages
    JAMIE K. TAYLOR
Answerable Style: The Idea of the Literary in Medieval England
    EDITED BY FRANK GRADY AND ANDREW GALLOWAY
Scribal Authorship and the Writing of History in Medieval England
    MATTHEW FISHER
Fashioning Change: The Trope of Clothing in High- and Late-Medieval England
    ANDREA DENNY-BROWN
Form and Reform: Reading across the Fifteenth Century
    EDITED BY SHANNON GAYK AND KATHLEEN TONRY
How to Make a Human: Animals and Violence in the Middle Ages
    KARL STEEL
Revivalist Fantasy: Alliterative Verse and Nationalist Literary History
    RANDY P. SCHIFF
Inventing Womanhood: Gender and Language in Later Middle English Writing
    TARA WILLIAMS
Body Against Soul: Gender and Sowlehele *in Middle English Allegory*
    MASHA RASKOLNIKOV

www.ingramcontent.com/pod-product-compliance
Lightning Source LLC
Chambersburg PA
CBHW030107010526
44116CB00005B/138